India: A Rising Middle Power

Other Titles in This Series

Westview Special Studies on South and Southeast Asia

India: A Rising Middle Power
edited by John W. Mellor

India, one of the largest and most broadly industrialized of the rising middle powers of the Third World, has increasing influence on the outcome of the major issues of global interdependency: nuclear proliferation, natural resources control, trade relations, and population growth. Yet, the Western world generally, and the United States in particular, remains ill equipped to understand and adapt to this rapidly changing global reality. The topics in this volume were chosen for their importance to understanding the basis of India's global role.

John W. Mellor, director of the International Food Policy Research Institute, was formerly chief economist with the U.S. Agency for International Development. Dr. Mellor has lived for several years in urban and rural areas of India.

Published in cooperation with The Asia Society

India: A Rising Middle Power

edited by John W. Mellor
Foreword by Phillips Talbot

Westview Press / Boulder, Colorado

Westview Special Studies on South and Southeast Asia

Published in 1979 in the United States of America by
   Westview Press, Inc.
   5500 Central Avenue
   Boulder, Colorado 80301
   Frederick A. Praeger, Publisher

Library of Congress Catalog Card Number: 79-50871
ISBN: 0-89158-298-3

Composition for this book was provided by the author.
Printed and bound in the United States of America.

Contents

Foreword

The current language of economic and social modernization does not easily fit the circumstances of India. India is indeed a developing country, yet it stands among the dozen top industrial nations of the world and has a growing post-industrial sector. Poverty, illiteracy and health deficiencies are certainly prevalent, yet few Western nations have larger pools of trained professional, scientific, technological and executive talents. Foreign economic assistance has undoubtedly made major contributions to India's planned development, but rarely at a rate of as much as five dollars a year per capita, and usually much less. Public participation in politics has been vigorous, but issues of productivity and distribution equity have not been resolved. India is a single political entity, but developmental problems and issues in India vary from state to state and from region to region as widely as they do across the whole range of Africa and Latin America, whose total populations do not match India's.

The fact is that India is India, made *sui generis* by its vast size, diversity and complexity. Efforts to fit India into broad theories of the development of pre-industrial countries have contributed to growing doubts about the pertinence of various development models that gained currency in the 1950s. Yet efforts to treat India without comparison to other pre-industrial or industrial nations have their own difficulties.

The Indian and Western specialists who came together for the conference which generated the papers included in this volume recognize these difficulties. From their diverse perspectives they seek to illuminate a broad spectrum of the components of India's modernizing growth: in domestic politics and international relations; in economic growth and trade; and in science and technology, including nuclear prospects and problems. As befits a conference in the United States these papers also address the changing perceptions of American social-economic-political relations with India and the virtues and pitfalls of proposals for a renewed American assistance program in India.

The portraits they paint are in some ways as diverse as the various realities of India itself. Yet they are unified in the quality of the authors' analytical skills, in their long and close experience in India, and in their shared conviction of the present and future importance of that second most populous of the world's nations.

The information, theses and arguments presented in this symposium are thought-provoking in themselves and will doubtless stimulate further discussion in both India and the United States. Toward that end, The Asia Society is pleased to facilitate this publication.

Phillips Talbot

Preface

This volume originated in the spring of 1976 when Arthur Gardiner, Jr., then Assistant Administrator for Asia of the Agency for International Development (AID), and I, then Chief Economist for the Agency, felt the need for re-examination of U.S. policy toward India and for analysis of the role renewed American foreign assistance to India could play in a context of improved Indo-American relations. We discussed whether or not the requisite paper could be written within the Agency. We quickly concluded that the issues were complex and were not likely to be dealt with adequately in an internally prepared document. It seemed equally unlikely that a single person outside the agency could be found to deal with an adequate number of issues which would have to range widely over a number of fields. We, therefore, called a meeting of half a dozen persons from the academic community for advice as to how the needed analysis could best be carried out. That meeting was held in the early fall of 1976.

In November of 1976, following the presidential election, I presumed that there would be an urgent need for an in-depth analysis of U.S.-Indian relations. In general, the new administration was likely to have a different set of policies toward the Third World, and especially toward the middle powers, such as India. Having drafted a paper delineating options for a major increase in foreign assistance earlier, it also became apparent to me that such an increase in foreign assistance to India was completely inconsistent with the United States policies and attitudes then prevalent toward India through the previous administration. A change in U.S. foreign policy toward India would, therefore, seem to be a prerequisite for any increase in assistance. Besides, India was not only important in its own right, but because of its size, absorptive capacity, and the political system was critical to any attempt to restore the overall level of United States foreign assistance to levels comparable to the other OECD (market economy, industrial) countries. Given the difficulty of the trade, commodity, and other options for improving United States-Third World relations, such restoration of foreign assistance levels would prove a key element in reducing the tension then characterizing those relations. Thus, it was with a great sense of urgency, in retrospect not fully justified by events, that I drew upon our fall discussions and arranged a set of papers on the key elements relevant to future U.S.-Indian relations. The drafts of those papers were ready by the spring of 1977.

For reasons of its own priorities as well as the disabilities of the bureaucracy in the several concerned departments of the government, it was apparent that the new Administration would not be able to move quickly on either a revitalized foreign assistance or an improved basis for its relations with the rising middle powers of the Third World. The earlier rapid pace for commissioning of the papers, therefore, became more leisurely. A meeting of the authors with a small number of officials from AID was held in June of 1977. A number of suggestions were made for a revision of the papers. It was also decided to hold a conference based on the papers with discussants providing alternative perspectives.

On that basis, AID contracted with the Asia Society to organize such a conference to arrange for the original papers to be rewritten and revised by the authors for presentation at the conference and for later publication in a volume. It was presumed that the Asia Society would bring the knowledge of India, a range of contacts in the scholarly community and a rigorous objectivity which would not only improve the output as background for United States policy, but would also facilitate development of the material in a manner of value to the scholarly community and the public at large. It was believed that the issues raised in these papers were of considerable importance to the American public and that making them widely available would stimulate the discussion which is so essential to development of intelligent policy in a democratic nation.

The conference was held at Seven Springs Farms, Mount Kisco, New York, September 22 to 24, 1977. The discussions were, to say the least, high spirited. Not only were there substantial differences amongst the authors of the various papers, but the discussants who had been chosen specifically to obtain different points of view did indeed perform that function. In addition, several persons from AID, from other agencies of the United States government, and from agencies outside the government participated in the discussions. The product was another round of major revisions in the various papers, this time in preparation for final publication. It is the outcome of that long process which is reflected in this volume.

The range of topics important in United States-Indian relations is so diverse that it was essential that a volume of this type draw upon the expertise of many different people. In doing so, it became apparent that one of the several costs of the substantial deterioration of U.S.-Indian relations over the last decade or so has been a sharp decline in the number of Americans who are highly knowledgeable of India. Thus, at a time when Indo-American relations are becoming increasingly important, the insights necessary for an effective policy are unusually scarce and becoming scarcer. Nevertheless, by stretching broadly it has been possible to deal with key issues relevant to Indo-American relations moderately, thoroughly, and perceptively.

I am grateful to Phillips Talbot, President of the Asia Society, for providing not only the hospitality of the Asia Society in organizing the conference, but also for his encouragement for the total project; for his intellectual stimulation, and for the very useful role which he played at the conference, including the summing up which was critical to the final product.

The Asia Society initially deputed Marshall Bouton to organize the effort. He was able to contribute substantially before he left in the summer of 1977 to join Ambassador Goheen as his Special Assistant in the American Embassy in New Delhi. He was replaced by **Philip** Oldenburg, who developed the conference, including arranging for the discussants, following up on changes in the papers and generally administering the effort. A number of people in AID were helpful in various stages of the project. I mentioned earlier Arthur Gardiner, Jr.'s, seminal role. Jack Sullivan, the present Assistant Administrator for Asia, was strongly encouraging and continually helpful. Eric Griffel, Jonathan Silverstone, John Erikson and Constantine Michalopoulos were also of considerable help in developing the project. Outside of AID James Voorhees served as research assistant on the project and Wayne Dexter and Philippus Willems rendered editing services. Final typing of the manuscript was done by Lucy McCoy. I am grateful for all of these efforts.

My own intellectual input bridges my time at Cornell University and nearly two years on deputation to AID. I must express my thanks particularly to the Board of Trustees of the International Food Policy Research Institute, where I now serve as Director, for allowing a modest portion of my time to put the finishing touches on this effort. The Institute, of course, is not responsible in any way for the views which are expressed here, and did no more than facilitate my participation in completing a job initiated in earlier capacities.

Washington, D.C.   John W. Mellor
October 1978

India and the United States

John W. Mellor and Philip Oldenburg

The United States and the several large Third World countries are now in the early stages of a major change in their relations. And compared to the traditional powers of Europe, or to Japan, the rising middle powers of the Third World have population and natural resource bases more nearly comparable to those of the United States and the Soviet Union. The rising political, economic, and military power and the large aggregate size of leading Third World states indicate they will eventually play a global role. This will require new modes of response by the United States as such issues as population growth, natural resource control, nuclear proliferation, and trade relations become increasingly important.

Americans have recognized China as a global force throughout the postwar period because of its historical association with the United States, its proximity to the Soviet Union, and its colossal size. In contrast the United States has found it difficult to accommodate the changing global circumstances of India, the largest, after China, and most broadly industrialized of the Third World countries. While India has become a middle power with respect to many issues of importance to the United States, the public image of poverty and incapacity continues to make it difficult for policy to change, even when the policy establishment recognizes the need. That need for policy change is urgent, and current negotiations should recognize not only the rapidity of change in the relationships of the two countries but also how these relationships will develop over the next decade or so.

The Reality of Size and Power

India now has the industrial base needed to mobilize its huge population as a world force. And as that base grows and political development proceeds, the massive population and large, diverse geography of the nation will count for India, as they do for other nations, in international negotiations.

At the beginning of the First Five Year Plan in 1950 India's population was twice that of the United States; in 1978 it was almost three times larger. On the basis of somewhat optimistic assumptions about economic development, India by the year 2000 will have a demographic pattern that will eventually stabilize its population at about 1.4 billion.[1] India's population will then be five times that of the United States and about twice that of the Soviet Union and the United States combined. India's population density relative to the area of cropland would still be less than that of present-day Germany and about one-third that of Japan. India's climate, soil, and water resources are conducive to much higher levels of cropping intensity than Germany's.

Population growth retards economic development and growth in national power as long as a country has low rates of capital accumulation and low levels of education. Once broadly participatory growth is well underway, however, high population densities and an underutilized labor force are conducive to high rates of economic growth and international power.

India's appalling poverty and lack of development-oriented institutions at the end of the colonial era should not be allowed to mislead as to the underlying resource base. The Gangetic plain, already supporting high population densities, is a highly productive agricultural resource that is responsive to modern high-yield agricultural technology. Only a small proportion of its potential has been exploited. India's hydroelectric and coal resources, although expensive to develop, are massive. Oil exploration is still in an early stage but off-shore potentials suggest eventual self-sufficiency at much higher than present levels of consumption. India's thorium reserves are large, and the nation has underway a long-term drive to develop a thorium-based breeder reactor technology. Geologic exploration has been delayed by Indian policy to create its own institutional capacity. Even so, known reserves of iron ore, which represent 10 percent of the world's total, and those of a wide range of other minerals suggest that India has the potential for a relatively independent economy. This is in sharp contrast with Western Europe.

India's human and natural resources of course represent a potential for growth rather than current reality. Even now, however, India ranks thirteenth in industrial output and its current gross national product of over $100 billion makes it the world's ninth largest economy. Except for the People's Republic of China, India has the most diversified industrial sector of the Third World. By the year 2000 India will be seventh in overall gross national product and eighth in industrial production, assuming that the nation achieves the high growth rate depicted in Chapter 4 and that rates in the presently industrialized nations continue at current levels.

A large, sophisticated, well-organized capacity for scientific and technological development is essential for a major power, not only for effective exploitation of its resources, which are always in substantial part unique, but also for attaining self-sufficiency in high-technology military potentials.

[1] Robert S. McNamara, *Address to the Massachusetts Institute of Technology* (Washington: World Bank, 1977), p. 11.

India's science and technology complex is immense. India is third among nations in the number of scientists and publications, though it ranks lower in quality. As indicated in Chapter 12, India's scientific and technological capacity ranks in the world's top 10, is comparable with that of Italy, and is growing relatively rapidly. The decision to join the nuclear club in May 1974 reflects only the tip of nuclear science capacity, let alone total science capacity.

India's high rank in science and technology has been achieved even though an exceedingly small proportion of the country's resources is devoted to this purpose. The tradition of elitism in education and long and continuing contact with the United States, Western Europe, and the Soviet Union have gradually built a relatively large capacity. Although it is difficult to make such comparisons, India may be ahead of China in scientific capacity despite the much larger size of the Chinese economy. Perhaps only Brazil among other Third World nations can soon play a substantial leadership role in science and technology.

Military development reflects growth of industry, science and technology, and the sheer size of India.[2] In 1947 the Indian armed forces totaled about 300,000 but had almost no high-level officers and only a skeletal navy and air force. Thirty years and four wars later, India has the world's third largest standing army (1.2 million persons), fifth largest air force, eighth largest navy. It has demonstrated the ability to acquire a strategic nuclear weapon and delivery system within a decade or so. Development of military production capacity is even more substantial: 41 major ordnance and defense establishments employing 225,000 workers produce such diverse items as small arms, field and anitaircraft recoilless guns, howitzers, mortars, support electronics items, antitank, antiaircraft, and naval missiles, armored tanks, personnel carriers: subsonic and supersonic planes, helicopters, antisubmarine frigates, fast patrol boats, and missile boats. Except for submarines and nuclear defense systems, this is comparable to China's capacity. India is attempting to phase out remaining dependence on foreign supply of weapons and weapons design by 1985, while continuing to expand the range of weapons, including domestically produced, intermediate range rockets. All of this has been accomplished by expenditure of a relatively moderate 3 percent of gross national product per annum.

India's size and elitist educational tradition has produced the most highly trained and experienced diplomatic negotiators among Third World nations. They deal skillfully with the many highly technical and complex legal issues of modern diplomacy, from law of the sea to nuclear controls. Despite differences in ap-

---

[2] The following are drawn largely from Onkar Marwah, "Military Power and Policy in India," in Onkar Marwah and Jonathan Pollack, eds., *Asia's Major Powers* (Boulder, Colorado: Westview Press, 1978).

proach, American and Indian negotiators, even in the past decade of strained relations, have frequently been able to work out acceptable compromise positions on Third World issues.

The American Image of India

The image of India in the United States, developed and reinforced by school textbooks, the press, and the academic literature, remains one of poverty and helplessness.

The Asia Society, in a review of some 300 school textbooks in use in 1974-75, found that the presentation on India was the most negative of all Asian countries treated.[3] According to a recent State Department analysis, American attitudes focused on disease, death, and illiteracy more than for any other country. Indians are believed to be unable to handle technology, even though the nation is one of the world's largest industrial powers.[4] Press coverage of India is dominated by "human interest" stories that emphasize starving people and "peculiar and unfathomable religious customs." The prevailing image is perhaps best represented by Daniel Moynihan's widely quoted question: "What does [India] export but communicable disease?"[5] From a former United States ambassador to India fully aware of her multibillion-dollar-a-year exports, which include more than $250 million of manufactured items to the United States, such a statement reflects a clear view of the perceptions in the galleries to which he was playing.

Why is there so deep a chasm between image and reality? First, such views support certain U.S. interests that have been pursued over the past decade or two. Second, they are based at least partly on India as it was in the colonial period and are thus dated. Third, India has an open society that lends itself to criticism and its documentation. Fourth, and perhaps most important, India has been a major recipient of foreign assistance, which has been viewed frequently as almsgiving rather than as a liberal pursuit of American self-interest. Fifth, India's perceived past proclivity to moralize has not helped to improve its image in the United States, which itself was a major moralizer and perhaps particularly resentful of moral pronouncements from poor, Third World countries.

For at least two decades, the United States sought to foster a balance of power between Pakistan and India in South Asia despite large differences in size. This reflected the effort to maintain Third World countries in a subsidiary position, even

[3] Asia Society, *Asia and American Textbooks* (New York: Asia Society, 1976).

[4] U.S. Department of State, Bureau of Educational and Cultural Affairs, *United States-Indian Educational and Cultural Relations* (1972).

[5] *Playboy*, March 1977, p. 78.

on Third World issues, by minimizing the importance of the more powerful. The Third World's positions on such issues as nonalignment, foreign assistance flows, rules governing operations of international financial institutions, and commodity agreements could be at least partly discredited by characterizing as inept their largest and most articulate exponent.

The United States also sought to justify low levels of foreign assistance by emphasizing the largest potential recipient's poor capacity to use assistance. This argument has been used to offset the special claim to western assistance that India might otherwise have as the "world's largest democracy." From the U.S. point of view, it has been especially important to argue for low aid to India in order to keep overall foreign assistance flows small with a high proportion of that small flow meeting short-run political demands. It is not surprising that an establishment-oriented American press runs a preponderance of stories consistent with these interests.

But U.S. policy in South Asia is changing. In the new policy context a quite different image of India is needed which recognizes its pre-eminent role as a South Asia regional power and as a growing middle power on the global scene. This is supported by the division of Pakistan, its continuing political instability, and the declining importance of small allies on the Soviet border. In addition, India's greatly accelerated trade performance and its entry into Western commercial capital markets are attracting increasing attention. Finally, the view that a country's political system does matter, as signalled by the Carter administration's initially clumsy expression of its concern for human rights, is gaining ground. India is one of the most advanced Third World countries in its democratic political development.

The new attitude toward India is part of a general change toward recognition of Third World regional powers: note the increasing attention to Brazil, Nigeria, Iran and Indonesia. The growing importance of global problems of population growth, natural resource supply, and energy conservation and development has turned Western attention towards the large Third World countries that have a major impact on such questions.

As the United States moves into an era of negotiation with India over highly complex issues, it will be important for the American public to recognize that India's national aspirations may at times conflict with U.S. policy, and that negotiations must deal with longer-term Indian interests as well as those of the United States. Already, press coverage of India reflects the new images needed to support those realities.

Americans are prone to judge India's economic performance on short-run progress in reducing extreme poverty. However, India has consistently given priority to long-run objectives, choosing large-scale capital goods industries over small-scale production of consumer goods for the poor, and evolutionary broadening of political representation rather than revolutionary transfer of power to the masses. Progress has been scant measured against the objective of short-term poverty alleviation, but very substantial in terms of longer-term objectives.

Economic development is a protracted process of creating institutions and training massive numbers of people to operate them. It is difficult to buy time in those processes. This has been a general problem in judging the effectiveness of foreign aid and in judging the economic progress of Third World countries. Indeed the very processes of building these institutions may often be seen by foreigners as a masochistic refusal to make use of readily available foreign capital, technology, personnel, and even institutions. The building of postcolonial India has moved on three interrelated fronts: the political system has been broadened immensely to encompass a majority of the population; the administrative structure now includes complex development as well as law and order functions; and the industrial sector has been diversified to produce both capital and consumer goods, many of them highly sophisticated.

India's political system was initially dominated by a small urban elite made up of the leadership of the nationalist movement and an elitist civil service. Both had ties to large industrial and commercial interests and to organized labor. That leadership was devoted to democratic forms, and a parliament was elected on the basis of adult franchise in 1951—52. An expanding proportion (from 46 percent to 61 percent) of the "world's largest electorate" has voted in national elections since then. At the state level, elected representatives wield impressive influence in directing benefits to their constituents and acting as channels of complaint and pressure within the bureaucracy. The system moved fairly rapidly to broaden its base of support, most notably by bringing the bulk of the peasantry into the system, but also by including small business and trading interests. The evolution of such a system from authoritarian colonial rule was accompanied by tension and uneven progress. As the political base expands to represent more and more complex interests, the addition of further interests may become more difficult. There have been times, including Mrs. Gandhi's major electoral triumphs of 1971 and 1972, when it appeared that the rural landless poor who make up most of the low-income 40 percent of the population, would organize into an effective interest group. But this has not occurred. Like their counterpart in the United States (in this case, the lower 10 percent in income distribution), they vote and affect the outcome of elections but are not an effective pressure group.

Development of a democratic pluralistic system is likely to be noted more for its tensions, instability, and failure to encompass the poor than for its ability to resolve complex disputes. In contrast, India has managed to solve major disputes on language policy and regional autonomy, problems originally exacerbated by the needs of the former colonial power. At the same time, religious, caste-based, and even Communist organizations have been brought into the largely peaceful democratic process. And the negative verdict of India's poor on the regime of "discipline" Mrs. Gandhi instituted in June 1975 was clear, despite the real economic benefits the regime had brought.

Building effective, dynamic institutions for economic development is always difficult. To do so while democratic institutions are growing magnifies the appearance of inefficiency because of the difficulty evolving bureaucracies and political mechanisms have in making development decisions. Those problems have often diverted attention from the general excellence of the Indian administrative structure as it evolved from a colonial force for law and order to a development force. If the Indian civil service had initially been what "developers" would like, India would already be a developed nation. If it had been less than it was, India might well have disintegrated. Indeed, there are those who claim that Vallabhbhai Patel's greatest contribution to a united India was not the skillful merging of the princely states for which he is properly credited, but his success in preserving India's civil service as an all-India cadre committed to national unity.

Accompanying the administrative and bureaucratic changes was the conversion of the Indian economy to a diversified industrial structure. This involved a shift toward steel and heavy machinery, with which India had little experience, and away from such traditional sectors as textiles. The result was slow growth in the short run, but a much more diverse base that provided greater flexibility for the long run. This approach could not measurably improve incomes for the lowest-income 40 percent, although they undoubtedly have shared somewhat in the lower death rates, increased education, and improved health. In theory at least, the base was being laid for their future participation in the political and economic life of the nation. The poor in India, like those during the Western industrial revolution, are paying most of the price of rising national power.

Except for the brief period of the emergency, India has had an open society with an active press and intellectual community. Indian political and economic affairs are subject to constant intensive criticism. Foreign critics find data for India more readily available than for China, Pakistan, and several other developing countries. Further, the colonial heritage provided a class of Western-educated people, many of whom continued to identify with the West. Many of this elite class feel alienated from the populist tendencies of democratic India, and they continue to provide highly critical information to uncritical foreigners. In addition, there is a constant flow of constructive criticism from internal sources. Intended as a means for improvement, this criticism can be used out of context to demonstrate incompetence.

Foreign aid has had a particularly unfortunate effect on the attitudes of a significant portion of the Western scholarly community. First, it encouraged them to judge and prescribe to India, and to advise Americans who provide aid. Second, it encouraged them to act as though they had ownership rights in India rather than guest privileges. In the case of China, quite aside from currying favor for visas, the American scholar tends to present a sympathetic interpretation to an American audience that wishes to understand.

India has confronted the immense problems of political, administrative, and economic change with an openness that enabled others to see all the tensions and difficulties. Many foreigners saw these difficulties in the context of a foreign aid program that they felt gave unlimited license to criticize. The result was a loss of perspective as to the progress being made and a tendency to underrate India's growing importance, thus creating a difficult environment for adjusting U.S. policy to the new realities.

United States Interest in India

For at least the past decade, the United States has assumed that it does not have significant foreign policy interests with respect to India. That attitude derives from the relatively low level of commercial trade between the two countries, the absence of strategic raw material imports from India, the low level of direct U.S. private investment in India, and the consistent unwillingness of India to enter into close political alliances in support of U.S. objectives. Neglect of India is consistent with a policy of strengthening weaker neighbors who will enter into close alliance with the United States. This policy has reduced India's ability to play an independent role in its own region.

The failure to see the importance of U.S. interests in India reflects out-of-date mercantilist as well as realpolitik views. It neglects the growing importance of global issues and the rise of new Third World middle powers with whom power must increasingly be shared. Such a view also reflects unwillingness to recognize America's incapacity to directly control events. Using power to manipulate events to serve U.S. interests within a system controlled substantially by others requires patience, a long-term perspective, and a thorough understanding of the interests and objectives of other parties. It is important that the United States begin to build that capacity, particularly in its dealings with the rising Third World countries.

The United States has four major interests with respect to India. Each involves consideration of India as a major force interacting with other powers. First are ideological issues, including choice of political system, humanitarian concerns, and civil rights. Second are interrelated global issues, including population growth, natural resource access, and environmental protection. Third is a set of commercial issues, including trade and capital flows. Fourth are issues directly related to preservation of power, including control of access to nuclear weaponry.

It is important that the United States define its interest in political systems in the Third World. Within a quarter of a century, Third World countries will have over three-quarters of the world's population, the United States only 3 percent. Nevertheless, the immense economy of the United States will still account for one quarter of the global gross national product and will continue to be a major political influence. This is not to suggest that the United States can define desired political systems and impose them on other countries. The world has moved beyond that stage. Rather, the United States must understand how its actions in military support, trade, commercial capital flows, and foreign assistance influence the balance of political forces within countries and their choice of economic and political system.

Through most of the postindependence period, India has been evolving a pluralistic democratic political system similar in many respects to that of the United States. Pluralism increases the potential for interaction at many levels between the societies of the two countries. The knowledge and the understanding arising from that interaction can assist resolution of conflict as it develops. Broad-based democratic systems also have common objectives that facilitate mutual understanding even if they cannot remove economic conflict. In contrast, the underlying ideological differences between the United States and the Soviet Union or the People's Republic of China constantly threaten breakdown in relations. Thus, the difficulties India and the United States have in reaching an understanding may arise more from unrealistic images and perceptions in the United States than from differences between their systems.

Cast against these long-run advantages to the United States of nurturing democratic government are short-run, narrow political and commercial interests that involve the acceptance of expediency, including corrupt means and the risk of trading away national integrity.

The United States has substantial humanitarian concern with respect to the Third World. Articulate and influential political groups and church organizations attach great weight to moral and humanitarian considerations in supporting U.S. foreign assistance. This applies particularly to India, which has over 60 percent of those in the Third World who are so poor as to be deficient in basic caloric intake. Furthermore, India has the trained personnel and institutional structure to effectively use such assistance. During 1962-74, however, average U.S. foreign assistance per capita for 28 countries exceeded the quantities recommended for India by John Lewis in Chapter 10, and 11 countries averaged at least three times more. But India received only half the recommended level.

Reducing poverty commands considerable attention in Indian politics. A major intellectual effort and a significant share of real resources are devoted to devising and experimenting with effective programs. Indian development policy has aimed explicitly at reducing poverty since the big push toward industrialization began in the mid-1950s. In the early years, relatively inexpensive (and unfortunately, ineffective) community development and cottage industry programs were developed to reduce poverty. In the early 1970s, India anticipated the "basic human needs " approach by formulating the Fifth Five Year Plan to emphasize production to meet the consumption needs of the poor. However, many interest groups were better organized than the poor. In addition, preservation of national integrity and independence often required a higher priority. Broad participation in development is, of course, consistent with and may even be necessary to national integration and expanded regional and global power. The dilemma faced by India has been its incapacity so far to achieve growth rapidly enough to both ameliorate poverty and meet other needs. The nation also has been unwilling to take the radical step of trying to eliminate poverty through redistribution as the People's Republic of China did. Inability to raise adequate resources for simultaneously procuring equitable growth and immediate reduction in poverty has placed great strains on India's evolving democratic institutions and processes. Foreign assistance could facilitate faster growth, reduce the risks of a more broadly participatory strategy, and help ameliorate poverty in the short run without revolutionary change.

Political systems and humanitarian concerns clearly interact with civil rights. The recent, halting American initiative on human rights reflects all of these issues. This initiative is still ill developed and confusing. For example, an overriding concern for food and shelter needs might imply a radical redistribution of assets and a change in the political system, which might subvert civil rights and democratic processes. The United States needs to articulate development and foreign assistance strategies that will encourage reduction of poverty while preserving democratic institutions and basic civil liberties. India is one of the few Third World countries with reasonable prospects for resolving these conflicts within a few decades.

Cultural and scientific exchanges offer additional opportunities for India and the United States to concurrently create a demand for improved relations. More than 100,000 Indians have come to the United States in the past 10 years. These immigrants, mostly in the professional classes, help create interest in, and support for, more positive relations between the two countries.

Population growth and the related issues of demand on natural resources and food supplies are increasingly influenced by India's development. Few global issues are as complex or as subject to rancorous differences as population growth. The issue is constantly at the forefront, obsessively so in U.S. policy vis-à-vis the Third World. The U.S. interest is often naively characterized either as charitable (saving the poor from the folly of their own procreation), or crassly self-protective (protecting itself from hordes of low-income people spilling across its borders). But the real self-interest is much more complex, though no less powerful.

It is commonly assumed that in the future Third World countries, some of which are very large and populous, will be generally industrialized, with modern bases of power. Of vital interest to the United States is that population growth in these countries will imply greatly increased demands on those global resources, including capital, technology, natural resources, and food, now more or less controlled by the United States. It also has implications for U.S. concern about the quality of the environment. All these implications taken together bring an air of crisis to the U.S. perception of population problems.

India has about a third of the population of the Third World and contributes a major portion of its growth. Historical observations make it clear that two conditions are important in reducing the rate of growth. First, population growth rates decline only in response to broad-based participation in development. Second, such a decline is reinforced by improved technology and knowledge of birth control. Rising incomes now have a larger, faster effect on birth rates than they did several decades ago. For example, Japan's crude birth rate fell faster than those of most Western nations: by 17 births per thousand in 36 years (1920-55), a rate of ½ per year. Taiwan's rate fell even faster, by 10 births in 8 years, about 1¼ per year.[6] The United States has an interest in influencing the incentives that affect the choice between more and less broadly participatory processes of growth, although it may also be concerned with other, potentially conflicting, objectives and it must certainly recognize Third World national integrity and independence. Thus U.S. concern with population growth in India can be manifested effectively only through assistance to stimulate income growth and to encourage broader participation in that growth.

A substantial part of the world food problem also lies with India. That nation will account for 20 percent of the total food deficit for the developing market economy countries in 1990, according to a study that projected past trends of production and conservatively defined future trends of consumption.[7] Whether that gap increases or decreases depends on India's choice of development strategy and its political and economic system. Aid flows, trade opportunities, and international political relations will influence that choice.

[6] James E. Kocher, *Rural Development, Income Distribution, and Fertility Decline* (New York: Population Council, 1973), pp. 64–65.

[7] International Food Policy Research Institute, *Food Needs of Developing Countries: Projections of Production and Consumption to 1990* (Washington: International Food Policy Research Institute, 1977) p. 22.

The United States faces complex crosscurrents with respect to trade with India. On the one hand, there is continuing concern that India will be able to pour more labor-intensive goods into the American economy than labor and industry can adjust to in the short run. On the other hand, as one of the largest and industrially most sophisticated low-income countries, India probably offers one of the largest potential markets for substantial U.S. exports of sophisticated capital goods and technology. In addition, a healthy, rapidly growing India may well be able to increase its effective demand for food faster than its farmers can increase output. This could result in substantial potentials for large commercial agricultural exports to India. Whether development occurs will depend very much on the pace and the pattern of Indian economic development. The U.S. interest in that process is clear.

India's large purchases already influence world prices of food, fertilizers, and other goods. As industrialization proceeds, India will compete for other scarce resources. India can offer Third World suppliers of scarce resources not only sophisticated technical goods at lower prices than Western competitors but also economic relations that are not tied to Western-based multinational corporations.

India has an important place in North-South negotiations on commodities and trade. India is a major seller on world markets of primary commodities ranging from iron ore to jute and its trade relationships are growing. Perhaps more important, India has substantial capacity for analysis of economic issues. In international negotiations, ability to develop and modify positions on the basis of good staff work is exceedingly important. India's educational traditions and size provide a large number of people trained for this task. Thus, India's influence in such negotiations probably will become increasingly important, though less strident than in the 1950s.

There are other areas in which the United States will have to take note of India's new military and political strength. India has been a leader of Indian Ocean littoral states that have opposed the superpowers' naval buildup in the region. Its ties to various countries of the Middle East have been reinforced by the small flood of Indian technical and skilled workers who have gone to work in Saudi Arabia and Iran. As the second Third World entrant into the nuclear club, India has strengthened its role by its potential for science and technology leadership. India's position is clearly crucial in determining the extent of nuclear proliferation. India also has a larger interest than most countries in the outcome of the law of the sea negotiations because of its long coastlines and its potential capacity to exploit seabed resources.

India's foreign policy has changed several times since independence. The 1950s era of leadership in the nonaligned nations collapsed with the defeat by China in 1962, the death of Nehru in 1964, and the economic and political weakness that followed. Another change occurred with the 1971 victory over Pakistan, the successes of the "green revolution," and the decision, probably made in 1971-72, to explode a nuclear device. More recently India has begun to reassert itself in the various Third World forums and has attempted to prevent increased military rivalry by the superpowers in the Indian Ocean. Unlike India's role in the 1950s, this revival of India's leadership in world politics (at the very least in the North-South dialogue) is based on real economic, military, and political strength. But also unlike the 1950s role, it has so far been remarkably low-key.

The United States thus faces a difficult trade-off in its relations with India. Reluctance to share power must be weighed against ideological, humanitarian, global, and commercial measures that would hasten India's rise to major power status. For the United States the choice would seem to be between influencing the course of Indian development while hastening its growth of power, and, as the alternative, attempting to delay the rise in power at the cost of losing influence on that process.

The way the United States perceives India will have a major effect on relations between the two countries. The United States may continue to view the relationship as basically charitable and provide largess to India to alleviate the massive poverty and human suffering. Such a view might win popular support in the United States, but it would make it considerably more difficult to resolve differences of opinion, since negotiations with India must be, at least in some respects, on a peer basis.

Political Evolution— Party Bureaucracy and Institutions

Myron Weiner

India's political development has been nearly unique among the developing nations. Except for a twenty-month interlude during the latter portion of Prime Minister Indira Gandhi's rule, India has been an open, competitive political system, with political parties contending for power within an electoral process. Human rights, especially freedom of the press and legal protection against political arrests, have been widely observed; virtually all major political groups, including those in opposition, view governmental authority as legitimate; participation in the political system at the local, district, state, and national levels has been remarkably widespread for a country with such a low level of literacy and urbanization; the power base of the governing elite has been fairly broad, encompassing both rural and urban interests; a dynamic balance has been established between various levels of governmental authority, especially between the state and central governments; the role of the military and the police in the political system has been small, and compared with most other political systems in the developing countries, authority has been relatively nonrepressive; and finally, the level of administrative capabilities, again compared with other developing countries, has been remarkably high.

In recent years the Indian political system has undergone major transformations. In the early 1970s there was an increasing centralization of political authority, culminating in the declaration of an internal national emergency by the government in June 1975. During the emergency many of the fundamental rights provided by the Constitution were suspended, and the government became increasingly authoritarian. In early 1977 the prime minister called a national parliamentary election, presumably with the intention of legitimizing the many institutional changes brought about during the emergency. However, the result was an overwhelming electoral defeat for the governing Congress party and for the prime minister herself, the election of a Janata party government, the termination of the emergency, and the restoration of the democratic process.

Over the past two decades foreign assistance presumably played some role in India's internal political developments. For one thing, the resources that came into India from outside were not inconsequential, and the kind of aid provided—

foreign exchange plus food assistance—facilitated a particular kind of economic development that tended to benefit some groups rather than others. For another thing, the United States and other Western donors *intended* to have some impact on the country's political development, if not directly, then at least by shaping the pattern of economic development. Western donors were eager to see India remain in the non-Communist (if nonaligned) camp, and expressed the hope that India's economic development would take place within a democratic political system. There were also other political and economic values that the donors, especially the United States, sought to maximize.

This attempt to assess the impact that foreign assistance *may* have had on India's *political* development has two components.

The first is to describe, analyze, and compare the fundamental values and goals of India's governing elites with those of the donors. A central theme of this analysis is that foreign assistance was, in the main, used by the regime for the pursuit of *its* goals and values rather than those of the donors, and that while certain values appeared to be the same, they were not always weighed in the same way. When the differences became apparent to both sides, the result was a deterioration in the donor-recipient relationship. By looking at both the convergence and divergence of value objectives between Western donors and Indian recipients, one may have a better understanding not only of the conflict that developed between donors and recipients over the economic policies within which Western aid was to be used, but also of why the political and economic effects of assistance were different from what Western donors often hoped for and expected.

The second component of the analysis considers foreign assistance as one kind of resource used by the Indian government to further its goals and to cope with its political and economic problems. While in some respects foreign assistance was simply an addition to the total resources available to government, in other respects it was a different kind of resource that made it possible for government to do some things it might not otherwise have done or, as we shall argue, that lessened the likelihood that government would do other things that it might have been under pressure to do in the absence of foreign assistance. This analysis needs to consider what difference particular *types* of assistance made, and how changes in the *level* of assistance may have affected the patterns of political development.

By assessing the particular role that external assistance, as distinct from other kinds of resources, played in India's political development, we may also obtain a more realistic understanding of what should or should not be expected of future international assistance to India. The remainder of this chapter deals with the evolution of India's political system, looking first at the conflicting values of the elite; then at the problems of maintaining political order and political power and the resources available to the regime for doing so from 1947 to the mid-sixties; then at the breakdown of the political process (first in the mid-sixties, then from the mid-sixties onward) and the parallel development of bureaucratic authority. The chapter ends with a brief account of the major institutional changes that have taken place since the declaration of an emergency in mid-1975 and since the elections of early 1977. Chapter 3 reviews the role of foreign assistance in India's internal political development, first looking at the problems of assessing the impact of assistance, then considering U.S. political objectives, and finally turning to the way foreign assistance was used as a political resource by the regime. A concluding section considers the implications of these findings for American assistance policy.

Conflicting Objectives of India's Governing Elites

Since 1947, when India achieved independence, her governing political elites have had seven explicit objectives. Though these objectives, or values, were to be sought at the same time, they were not all of equal importance. The leadership spoke as if these values could all go together simultaneously, but in fact they were often incompatible; that is, some of them could be maximized only at the expense of others. Moreover, within the governing elite there were considerable differences as to how these objectives should be weighed—which ones should be given priority, and which ones could be sacrificed, if necessary.

This list of objectives appears, in one guise or another, in India's Constitution (at least before it was recently amended), in her Five Year Plan documents, and in the election manifestos and resolutions of both the Congress party and the Janata party. They include:

1. Maintaining political order; that is, keeping the level of violence between religious, linguistic, caste, tribal, class, and political groups to a minimum, and avoiding any large-scale hostilities that would threaten the "integrity," to use a favorite word, of the country
2. Modernizing the economy through industrial development, borrowing and adapting technologies, developing agriculture, expanding education, and so on
3. Reducing inequalities among castes and regions, and between the upper "privileged" classes and the lower social strata
4. Preserving national security, particularly in relation to Pakistan and China, India's major adversaries, and, more generally, establishing an important place for India in the international political system
5. Creating a socialistic pattern of development that restricts but does not eliminate the role of private capital, expands the public sector, and emphasizes the role of public goods as distinct from private ownership and profit
6. Preserving fundamental human rights—including free speech, freedom from

arbitrary arrest, the rights of political participation and political organization, free religious expression—or, to use the words of the Constitution, a
"democratic, secular order"

7. Achieving self-reliance, that is, avoiding dependence upon other states for
resources for either development or security, and therefore using foreign
assistance for a short period for the purpose of achieving a state of self-
reliance.

A cynical view of these seven objectives would be that many of them were
mere rhetoric, intended to win support from diverse constituencies rather than to
guide action. An examination of actual policies, some would say, suggests that
equity objectives, for example, were little more than populist slogans used by the
government to win electoral support. If not, critics ask, what prevented the government from adopting land reforms after the 1971 and 1972 elections when the
position of the Congress party and of the prime minister were so secure in both
the central and state governments? And as for the commitment to democratic
values, in light of the declaration of an emergency in June 1975 by the prime
minister, and its support by virtually every Congress member of parliament and by
the Congress Working Committee and the Congress Parliamentary Board, could
one say that the commitment to human rights and democratic procedures by the
governing Congress party was very deep?

Others accept the claims of the governing elite at face value but conclude that
these objectives were incompatible, particularly, some would say, in light of the
resources available to the regime. Could India be self-reliant with respect to
foreign aid, John Lewis has asked, when it was committed to a program of industrial development that required massive capital infusions and foreign exchange
beyond what could be earned from the country's exports?[1]

Could the country effectively mobilize its resources for industrialization and
modernization, which seemed to require forced savings and postponement of
mass consumption, wrote Baldev Raj Nayar, while preserving a democratic or
"reconciliation" system?[2]

Could equity be achieved, asked John Mellor, when the government pursued
an elusive high-growth, capital-intensive strategy that neglected the development
of agriculture with its high potential for rural employment?[3]

[1] John P. Lewis, *Quiet Crisis in India: Economic Development and American Policy* (New
York: Doubleday and Co., 1964).

[2] Baldev Raj Nayar, *The Modernization Imperative and Indian Planning* (Delhi: Vikas
Publications, 1972).

[3] John W. Mellor, *The New Economics of Growth: A Strategy for India and the Developing World* (Ithaca, N.Y.: Cornell University Press, 1976).

Lawrence Veit asked, was the government's commitment to rapid industrialization, heavy industry, public sector enterprises, reliance upon import substitution rather than export promotion, restrictions upon foreign investment, and
reliance upon physical planning rather than the marketplace compatible with
either growth or equity objectives?[4]

Are large-scale political participation and the decentralization of political
power to the state governments compatible with national planning and national
integration, wondered Selig Harrison, or will they result in interstate tensions,
state-center antagonisms, and ultimately, secessionist movements and internal
disorder?[5]

And, wrote Jagdish Bhagwati and Padma Desai, were the socialist objectives
of distributive justice, equality, and the eradication of poverty compatible with a
development strategy that emphasized import substitution and sheltered markets,
and capital-intensive industrialization?[6]

In short, much of the writing on India by political scientists, economists, and
journalists during the past decades has emphasized the seeming contradictions of
these goals. Friends of India, themselves sympathetic to many, if not all, of these
goals, sought to prescribe strategies of development that would make as many of
these objectives as congruent as possible. One need only ready the first or last
chapters of books by Bhagwati and Desai, John Lewis, George Rosen, John
Mellor, Lawrence Veit, Francine Frankel, Rajni Kothari, and others to see such an
orientation.[7] Others, of a tougher bent of mind, emphasized the need to choose
among irreconcilable objectives, particularly the need to choose between political
and economic goals. Gunnar Myrdal, for example, without explicitly calling for an
end to democracy in India, stressed the inability of a "soft" state to take "hard"
decisions.[8] More bluntly, Baldev Raj Nayar wrote of the "cramping consequences

---

[4] Lawrence A. Veit, *India's Second Revolution: The Dimensions of Development* (New
York: McGraw-Hill Book Co., 1976).

[5] Selig Harrison, *India—The Most Dangerous Decades* (Princeton, N.J. : Princeton University Press, 1960).

[6] Jagdish N. Bhagwati and Padma Desai, *India: Planning for Industrialization* (London:
Oxford University Press, 1970).

[7] The books by Bhagwati and Desai, Lewis, Mellor, and Veit are cited above. Also see:
George Rosen, *Democracy and Economic Change in India* (Berkeley: University of California
Press, 1967); Francine Frankel, *India's Green Revolution: Economic Gains and Political Costs*
(Princeton, N.J.: Princeton University Press, 1971); and Rajni Kothari, *Politics in India*
(Boston: Little, Brown and Co., 1970).

[8] Gunnar Myrdal, *Asian Drama: An Inquiry into the Poverty of Nations* (New York,
Pantheon, 1968).

of a premature installation of a reconciliation system before a decisive break-through in respect to modernization and development."[9]

Many friends of India viewed foreign assistance as the most significant way that the Western democracies could provide the additional resources that might make possible India's pursuit of these varied, potentially conflicting, but in the main desirable, goals. "By all odds," wrote John Lewis, "the most distinctive feature of the Indian effort is its deep commitment to an orderly, peaceful procedure under which personal rights are respected—in short, to a constitutional procedure—of radical economic change." But, he went on to write, "the appetite for material improvement is now such in India . . . that the only government with any chance of adhering to constitutional procedures is one that is determined to achieve radical economic reform and expansion and that is capable of so doing."[10] Similar views were expressed by U.S. Ambassador Chester Bowles, by many members of Congress, and by most of the supporters of aid to India. The argument could be expressed in the form of a syllogism:

1. Constitutional procedures and democratic government can be maintained if there is a high rate of economic development.[11]
2. Economic development requires heavy inputs of new resources to accelerate the rate of investment.
3. Democratic regimes cannot survive if they have to extract too large a share of private income for investment in future development.
4. Additional inputs, therefore, need to come from outside.
5. Hence, there is a need for a high level of U.S. and other foreign assistance if India is to maintain its democratic institutions.

Some saw foreign aid as an instrument less for reconciling human rights with economic growth than for reconciling the objectives of growth and equity. John Mellor pointed to the role of foreign aid in resolving some of the contradictions inherent in the rural-led, employment-oriented strategy of growth that follows the earlier capital-intensive, import-substitution strategy. Foreign assistance, he

[9] Baldev Raj Nayar, "Political Mobilization in a Market Policy," in *Aspects of Political Mobilization in South Asia,* ed. Robert I. Crane (Syracuse, N.Y. : Maxwell School of Citizenship and Public Affairs, 1976), p. 147.

[10] Lewis, *Quiet Crisis in India,* p. 8.

[11] A number of social scientists took a very different view on the question of whether economic growth facilitated stable and democratic government. In a 1961 article, "Economic Development and Political Stability in India," *Dissent* 8 (1961), 2:172–79, Myron Weiner and Bert Hoselitz took issue with the theory that political stability could be achieved through economic growth. They argued that an ideology of "economism," which derived political institutions and processes from economics, appeared to form the basis of American programs for economic assistance.

argued, is essential in the transition period when export performance has not yet improved sufficiently to meet foreign exchange needs, and when international food aid is required to cope with weather-induced fluctuations in foodgrain production that "may weaken the will and the means to proceed with the new strategy."[12] A variant of this position is the argument put forward by John Lewis and by Ernest Stern of the World Bank, that a more humane society in India (though not necessarily a democratic one) is more likely if Western aid is used to assist India's growth *and* equity-oriented policies.

A third position, put forward in the mid-sixties, was that foreign aid could play a role in achieving *some* of the objectives of the Indian government by using aid as "performance conditioning." That is, aid could be used to influence the development strategy of the Indian government to hasten economic growth (a precondition, it is argued, to distributive justice) through the adoption of growth-oriented policies that rely not on physical controls but instead on such things as the market, investment in an unproductive public sector, and neglect of exports. In short, foreign assistance could be a form of leverage to press the government to make the hard choices between goals. What would be sacrificed, according to this approach to foreign assistance, are some of the objectives that Indians would describe as socialist. However, though the donor nations had some notions about priorities, so too did the Indian government, and it is to these that we now turn.

Maintenance of Political Order and of Political Power

Most of the senior leaders of the governing Congress party, believed that the seven proclaimed objectives could best be achieved if they themselves remained in power. More particularly, they argued, the maintenance of internal order and the preservation of national security, the most valued of these objectives, rested upon the continuance in power of the Congress party.

This assumption was never made explicit by the governing party, though the prime minister came close to asserting it after she declared an emergency. Congressmen widely shared the notion of what Rajni Kothari perceptively described as India's Congress party "system."[13] It was a system that welcomed, even thrived on, opposition, both within and outside the party. But it required that Congress remain in power. When Congress lost power in many states in 1967,

---

[12] Mellor, *The New Economics of Growth*, Chapter 9.

[13] Rajni Kothari, "The Congress 'System' in India," *Party Systems and Election Studies*, Occasional Papers of the Center for Developing Societies, No. 1 (Bombay, Allied Publishers, 1967), pp. 1–18; and W. H. Morris-Jones, "Parliament and Dominant Party: Indian Experience," *Parliamentary Affairs* 17 (Summer 1964), pp. 296–307.

the national leadership defined the political problem as one of restoring order by reestablishing Congress party control. The disorder that ensued in many of the non-Congress states after the 1967 elections confirmed the view that the Congress party was the ultimate guardian of both popular and orderly government. Many Congress leaders argued that in any event, whatever happened at the state level, political order throughout the country depended on the Congress party continuing in power at the national level, for the opposition parties were too disorganized to form a unified national government.

The governing Congress elites thus gave priority to three objectives: (1) maintaining their own position in power, (2) maintaining internal order, and (3) preserving and strengthening national security.

I am not suggesting that every policy adopted by the Indian government was intended to maximize one or more of these three objectives; I am only suggesting that whenever any of these objectives clashed with other objectives, these were given preference. Nor am I suggesting that each time government made a decision *intended* to maximize one of the essentially power-maintaining objectives, they necessarily succeeded. By starting with this assumption that there was a set of priorities and preferences in relation to other goals that were also preferred but were relatively lower on an ordinal scale, we can best understand many of the changes in policies and in political behavior over the past three decades, including the decisions related to the emergency. Moreover, more of India's political evolution can be explained when seen as a response to certain political objectives than when seen as a response to development and equity policies and objectives. At the same time it is essential to note that some of the political problems facing the leadership were in turn the consequences of economic policies that worsened the economic environment within which the government sought to maintain political order and to maintain power for itself.

Few governing elites within the newly independent countries have been confronted with the kinds of challenges to internal order encountered by India's postindependence government. The early years of independence saw massive exchange of populations between India and Pakistan, the slaughter of Muslims in India and Hindus in Pakistan, the assassination of Mahatma Gandhi by members of the Hindu right wing, violent conflict with Pakistan over Kashmir, and civil disturbances and the threat of further partitioning of India from Hyderabad. Yet within a few years both Hyderabad and Kashmir were brought under effective control by the Indian government, refugees from West Pakistan were largely resettled, Hindu-Muslim clashes within India were reduced to manageable proportions, and the exodus of Muslims was largely brought to an end.

The resources India's new governing leadership was able to bring to resolve these conflicts included a strong Congress party with local roots and wide support, and an administrative and military structure that few developing countries could match. The exodus of anti-Hindu Muslim political elites to Pakistan also proved to be an asset, for it left in India a moderate, nationalist Muslim leadership that could effectively cooperate with the Hindu nationalist leadership in a coalition committed to the restoration of communal harmony within the framework of a secular state. In postindependence India the Muslims, once the major adversaries of the nationalist leadership, became ardent supporters of the Congress government, both in the center and in the states.

But no sooner had the era of religious strife ended than India entered a period of linguistic strife in the 1950s. Again, accommodation proved workable. Violent outbursts in the Punjab, Bombay, Hyderabad, Mysore, and the Telugu-speaking areas of Madras ultimately led to a complex redrawing of political boundaries; and although the process of accommodation was often protracted and bitter, ultimately most of the outcomes were in accord with cultural and linguistic boundaries that satisfied regional sentiments. Where regional sentiment took a violent secessionist turn, as in Nagaland and Mizoram, it did so largely because the movement was supported with external arms. The closing of the borders, forceful action by the Indian military, and inducements in the form of regional autonomy combined to bring about a peaceful resolution within the Indian Union. In the northeast the Indian government appeared to have been more successful in coping with tribal dissent than the other states of South and Southeast Asia that have had similar difficulties with the rebellious tribes that dwell in the hill zones extending from northern Afghanistan through northern Pakistan, northern India, the hill tracts of Bangladesh, the northern regions of Burma, and further across Southeast Asia into Laos, Cambodia, and Vietnam.

In retrospect, four factors appear to have been particularly relevant to the success of the Indian government in managing religious, linguistic, and tribal conflict: one related to the peculiarities of India's social structure, a second to her political institutions and processes, a third to the organization and use of intelligence-gathering and coercive institutions, and a fourth to the strength of the Congress party.[14]

Since each state has its own peculiar ethnic configuration, conflicts within a state did not readily affect the other states. For this reason the Indian government was able to handle one conflict at a time without having to face the kind of massive national problem experienced by both Nigeria and Pakistan. The govern-

---

[14] This section draws substantially from the paper I prepared for the Rockefeller Commission on Critical Choices for Americans. See "Critical Choices for India and America," in *Southern Asia: The Politics of Poverty and Peace*, ed. Donald C. Hellman (Lexington, Massachusetts: D. C. Heath and Co., Lexington Books, 1976), pp. 19–78.

ment's handling of conflicts in Assam, for example, had little impact on Kerala or Andhra, and though the government did have to take precedent into account, it was often free to choose a politically appropriate solution for one region that was quite different from the solution chosen for another region. Thus, the government acceded to the demand for a separate state by the Sikhs in the Punjab, but rejected a similar demand by the Telangana region of Andhra.

Within the framework of a federal system the central government could also provide political autonomy to groups with territorial contiguity and political cohesion without jeopardizing the powers of the central government. The breakup of the Punjab, for example, did not threaten the central government; indeed it may well have strengthened support for the center by both the Sikh and Hindu Jat members of the armed forces who were eager to see a peaceful reconciliation within their home state.

The democratic system nurtured an attitude of responsiveness on the part of political leaders eager to find a solution that would least weaken their political hold. Both national and state leaders often dissipated demands by coopting leaders of ethnic communities through allocating seats in state assemblies and positions within cabinets to dissident tribals, Muslims, members of scheduled castes, and various linguistic minorities. Congress won the support of most of the country's minorities by satisfying their leaders' desires to share power, wealth, and status through representation in the state and national government.

Unwilling to rely exclusively upon reports from the state Congress parties, the Home Ministry strengthened its own intelligence-gathering network. The Home Ministry, with its responsibility for centrally run law-enforcement agencies, played a key role in the integration of the princely states in the Indian Union; in the management of the states reorganization controversy; in government's management of the tribal areas; in central government policy toward Kashmir; in intelligence and police work involved in counterinsurgency activities against the Communists in Hyderabad in the late forties and the Naxalites in the late sixties and early seventies.

In the mid-sixties, as we shall see later, when the capacity of the central government to politically manage conflicts within the states declined, the Home Ministry strengthened both its intelligence and police apparatus. The Central Reserve Police, the Home Guards, the Border Security Forces, and the Central Industrial Security Force all grew in size and importance. But in the fifties and early sixties there was less need for the central government to make use of its coercive instruments so long as the Congress party retained a strong popular local base.

In the 1950s, as I have argued elsewhere,[15] the Congress party built its strength

[15] Myron Weiner, *Party Building in a New Nation: The Indian National Congress* (Chicago: University of Chicago Press, 1967).

on the middle sectors in both rural and urban India. In rural constituencies, Congress strength rested largely on the peasant proprietors or agricultural classes; that is, the middle and upper castes who owned property in the countryside.

The support of this group rested initially on the steps taken by the Congress government to abolish India's landlord class. Preindependence agrarian India essentially had a four-class system: landlords, peasant proprietors, tenants, and landless laborers. The abolition of the *zamindari, jagirdari, watandari,* and other landlord systems after 1947 placed the states in a direct relationship with the peasant cultivators, who now owned their own land and paid taxes directly to the state governments. It is often overlooked in discussions of land reform in India that India did have an agrarian revolution—a peaceful one—of sorts. The peasants were the rural backbone of India's nationalist movement, while the landlord classes (including the princes, who were also landlords) tended to back the imperial power. The various landlord abolition acts passed by the state governments in the first decade of independence and the elimination of the powers of the princes by the central government substantially reduced the influence of classes potentially dangerous politically to the Congress governments and solidified the support of the rural peasantry for governments that gave them proprietary rights over their land.

The peasant proprietors subsequently became politically so well entrenched in the Congress party, in some of the opposition parties, and in the local administration that they successfully blocked the passage of legislation to impose ceilings on their landholdings (which would have redistributed land from the peasant proprietors to tenants and landless laborers), to collectivize land through compulsory cooperatives, and to impose an agricultural income tax.[16]

The Congress party was open to the rural elites who recognized that as Congress members and leaders they had considerable access to policymakers and to local and state bureaucrats. The capacity of Congress to provide suitable access to—and influence over—the distribution of patronage, the allocation of local development funds, and the administration of governmental regulations was a prime factor in the willingness of aspiring elites to seek power first within Congress. The very openness of Congress (which needed electoral support) turned most of these aspiring elites to the Congress party rather than to revolutionary channels, alienated politics, or the opposition.

---

[16] In this connection one set of statistics is particularly revealing. In 1950 the tax revenues of the Indian states totaled Rs 2.7 billion, of which Rs 1 billion was from direct taxes. Twenty years later, in 1970, direct taxes were Rs 5 billion but indirect taxes were Rs 18 billion. By 1975, even after the government launched its campaign for better income distribution, direct taxes had increased by one-half to Rs 7.8 billion, but indirect taxes had doubled to Rs 36.5 billion.

An important factor in the willingness of Congress party members to share power with aspiring elites was that the amount of power to be shared had been growing. The expansion of the functions of the state and national governments; the growth in the powers of village *panchayats;* the transfer of community development powers and finances from the state administration to elected village, *taluka,* and district bodies; the expansion in the number of party officeholders, and, in several states, the size of the cabinets—all these meant an expansion in the supply of power and offices to meet the growing demand.

In short, throughout the fifties and early sixties there existed ample resources for the political system to absorb those members of the middle sectors who aspired to political power. The system of *panchayati raj,* which extended local political control over large sections of the lower bureaucracy, was probably the most important institutional change facilitating this expansion of the political base. Thousands, perhaps tens of thousands, of new opportunities were created for local elites to gain more direct access to political power.

Panchayati raj strengthened the local Congress party organizations, for Congress generally proved to be more effective at winning the support of local elites than did the opposition parties. Congress control over the state governments provided a key inducement to local elites, who saw their affiliation to the local Congress as a means of extending influence into the state level administration.

In turn, the affiliation of local elites to Congress strengthened the Congress party organization within the states. At the state level, political leaders emerged with the skill to pull together the local elites in the Congress *taluka* and district Congress committees to ensure their own dominant position at the state level. The late fifties and early sixties thus became the era of state party "bosses," men who had learned the art of using the resources of the state administration to build a network of party supporters who, in turn, could win the support of a substantial portion of the rural electorate.

In some instances the state bosses were the heads of the Pradesh Congress Committees, but in most instances they soon became chief ministers of their states. Since there were often bitter contests for these positions, not all of the state leaders were able to retain power for long, but quite a few emerged from the local scramble with remarkably secure and durable power bases: Sukhadia in Rajasthan, Kairon in the Punjab, Sanjiva Reddi in Andhra, Kamaraj in Tamil Nadu, Atulya Ghosh in West Bengal, Patnaik in Orissa, and C. B. Gupta in Uttar Pradesh.

At the national level these men exercised power in the National Development Council (NDC), a body with considerable influence over the allocation of central resources for development. The National Development Council consisted of the prime minister as its chairman, the chief ministers of the states, and the members of the planning commission. Since the plan prepared by the planning commission was placed before the NDC for approval, it was here that the state governments were directly involved in the planning process.

The central government was constrained from making decisions that might affect the power base of the state chief ministers. Agricultural procurement and pricing policies, land reform legislation, the allocation of public sector investments, the allocation of federal funds for higher education, the allocation of industrial licenses and import licenses to local businessmen—all of these central decisions were invariably influenced by the chief ministers. The chief ministers recognized that their popular support rested upon their capacity to provide goods to a wide variety of social groups: price supports and protection against further land reform for the larger farmers; access to colleges and to employment in administration for the expanding middle class; and licenses and contracts for local entrepreneurs. If the lowest economic strata gained little, it was because they remained largely unorganized and tended to vote with the rural gentry, upon whom they depended for rural employment.

By the late fifties and early sixties, therefore, an important shift in political power had taken place in the Indian political system. As the older nationalist leaders who had brought the country to independence were disappearing from the political scene, power was devolving to state leaders. Moreover, the shift in power within the Congress party resulted in a shift in power within the governmental system itself from the center to the states. India's emerging federalism thus mirrored the federalism of the Congress party itself.

The selection of Lal Bahadur Shastri as Nehru's successor marked this shift in power. It was not simply the contrast between the two men: Nehru was an urbane, Western-educated national and international figure, while Shastri was Indian-educated, of rural origin, and still linked to the provinces. More indicative of the change was that the members of the Congress Working Committee who had chosen Shastri came out of the same social mold. They had secure political bases within their own states, and they saw Shastri as a man capable of taking their interests into account.

Breakdown of the Political Process: Development Since the Mid-Sixties

By the mid-sixties, and especially after the elections of 1967, the situation had sharply turned.[17] The Congress party was on an electoral slide. It had lost

[17] Congress was already beginning to decline in the early 1960s, which led Kamraj Nadar to propose a program by which the senior Congress leaders would return to the provinces to rebuild public support; but it was the 1967 elections that revealed how badly Congress had slipped in public support.

control of many of the state legislative assemblies, and in nearly half the states—including some of the largest—non-Congress coalition governments assumed power. Though Congress won a majority of the parliamentary seats, the victory was a precarious one, since defections (as there already had been in the states) might bring down the government. Although, the party lost support all over the country, the loss was particularly sharp in the urban areas. Congress lost a majority of the urban parliamentary constituencies, including the seats from New Delhi and most of Calcutta. Though no one party was emerging as a replacement for Congress, there were new, powerful regional opposition parties, some of which were split-offs from the parent Congress. The Jana Sangh also did well, particularly in towns and cities, suggesting that members of the urban middle classes were being pulled to the right in spite of the militancy of the Communists in Calcutta and in several other urban centers.

Moreover, the party bosses themselves did poorly in the elections. Many important state leaders were defeated. Most humiliating of all was the defeat of Kamaraj Nadar of Tamil Nadu, often described as Mrs. Gandhi's kingmaker, by a student leader.

The 1967 election was widely interpreted as the last one that Congress would win with a clear majority. It called attention to the way many structural features of the Indian political system seemed to depend upon a strong national Congress party in control of the states and the central government. If no party had a majority in parliament, would this place the president, until then a figurehead, in a position to influence the choice of prime minister and the makeup of a coalition government? If Congress governed the central government, but opposition parties controlled the states, how would this transform center-state relations? And, most fundamentally, did maintenance of internal order and preservation of a stable government depend upon a secure hold for the Congress party?

Why had the popular hold of the Congress party declined? A careful analysis prepared by Rajni Kothari and his colleagues at the Centre for the Study of Developing Societies demonstrated that the Congress vote had not declined substantially, but that non-Congress parties had "closed their ranks," and built effective electoral coalitions that had brought them seats in numbers more commensurate with their share of the votes. [18] Kothari also warned against projecting the decline in the Congress vote, noting that if the non-Congress governments did not function satisfactorily, and if the Congress leadership regrouped itself in

[18] Centre for the Study of Developing Societies, *Context of Electoral Change in India: General Elections 1967* (Bombay: Academic Books, 1969), p. 139. See especially the analysis of the organizational breakdown of the Congress party by Rajni Kothari, "Congress and Consensus," pp. 130–147, and "India's Political Transition," pp. 96–112.

several states, many who had voted against the Congress party in 1967 would return to the fold. Indeed, by-elections in the next few years suggested that Kothari was correct.

Nonetheless, one could point to elements that threatened to undermine the hold of the Congress party. Certainly, the performance of the economy in the two years prior to the election was disheartening for the government. Two years of drought and declining grain production made the country extraordinarily dependent upon the United States for food supplies. Moreover, with the country in the midst of an industrial recession, and short of foreign exchange as a result of the failure of the country's exports to keep pace with its imports, the free market value of the rupee had declined. And with a rise in prices came hoarding, black markets, and administrative corruption. Critics of the government's policies—outside as well as within India—argued that the capital-intensive industrial development strategy, the neglect of agriculture, a reliance upon import substitution, and the neglect of exports made the country dependent upon foreign aid and upon loans or grants of food. By 1966 a large portion of the countryside was supported by American food, and the black market for dollars soared as the real exchange value of the rupee plummeted. India's economic crisis was generated by a set of policies, not simply by the consequences of a weather-induced drought and declining grain production.

To a large extent this was the perception of the international aid community,[19] especially of economists in the U.S. government and in the World Bank. The Western donors urged the Indian government to change its development strategy: to place greater emphasis upon agricultural development, to further encourage the development of export industries, to liberalize import licensing procedures, and to rely more upon market mechanisms to allocate investment and to establish prices. As an initial but crucial step the donors urged the Indian government to devalue the Indian rupee; and to ease in the transition to the new strategy there were promises (later to be broken) of new loans and grants.

Politically, devaluation proved to be a near disaster. It was not simply that it was followed by a sharp rise in prices on the eve of the elections. More serious was the resentment toward the prime minister and close members of her "kitchen cabinet" by many state Congress party leaders. From their point of view the decision to devalue at the behest of foreign pressures in return for foreign aid was humiliating to nationalist sensibilities. For it emphasized the dependence of the government and of the economy upon foreign aid and the vulnerability of the

[19] For an account see David H. Denoon,"AID—High Politics, Technocracy or Farce?" (Ph.D. diss., Department of Political Science, Massachusetts Institute of Technology, June 1975), Chapter 3.

leadership to foreign influence in the formulation of domestic policies. It ultimately led state Congress leaders to raise the question of whether Mrs. Gandhi ought to continue as party leader and as prime minister.

Mrs. Gandhi might very well have been replaced by her critics within the Congress party shortly after the 1967 elections had not her most powerful critics themselves done badly in the elections. One by one, however, the defeated state leaders returned to parliament or to state assemblies through by-elections and began to reestablish their earlier positions.

The intra-party struggle that took place between 1967 and 1969, culminating in the split in the Congress party, has been sufficiently documented to permit its being excluded here.[20] Though the struggle was couched in ideological terms, most close observers agree that what was at stake was the power of the prime minister as opposed to that of the state chief ministers and party leaders, known collectively as the Syndicate. Ideological issues became weapons employed by the prime minister to win popular support and to pull away from the Syndicate those political leaders who had a left-of-center reputation. In this context, the prime minister's decision to nationalize banks, abolish privy purses, and end the privileges of former princes was not part of a broader campaign for social justice but rather was part of a struggle for power within the party. The prime minister's slogan of *garibi hatao* (remove poverty) was her answer to her opponent's cry of *Indira hatao* (remove Indira).

The most significant consequences of the split were that political power shifted (1) from a collective to an individual and personalized mode, and (2) from the states to the center. The patrimonial and centralized system that was to fully emerge after the declaration of an emergency in June 1975 had its origin in the split in the party and the changes within the party that soon followed.

The split in the Congress left the prime minister with a precarious hold in parliament. There were now two Congress parties. Mrs. Gandhi's Congress had the support of a majority of the Congress parliamentary delegation, but required the additional support of Communists and several independent M.P.'s to retain power. The Syndicate had the support of a majority of the state Congress party organizations, including many of the state chief ministers.

Between 1969, when the split occurred, and the elections of 1971, the prime minister set out to consolidate her position.

1. The central government assumed a more radical posture, emphasizing the government's commitment to a socialist strategy of development. A new licensing policy announced in early 1970 reversed the policy of decontrol

---

[20] For a succinct account see Robert L. Hardgrave, Jr., "The Congress in India: Crisis and Split," *Asian Survey* 10 (March 1970), pp. 256–262.

that had been set in motion after devaluation. A Monopolies and Restrictive Trade Practices Commission was created with power to restrict the expansion of larger firms so as to avoid a "concentration of economic power." The Managing Agency System was abolished by new legislation. And when the Supreme Court ruled that the government's decision to abolish the privy purses of the ex-princes was unconstitutional, the government issued an order "derecognizing" the princes.

2. The prime minister's image as a committed socialist was strengthened by the support of the Communist Party of India (CPI), and by pro-Communist elements within the Congress organized into a group known as the Congress Forum for Socialist Action (CFSA). Members of the CFSA were brought into key policymaking positions within the party and the government, where they pressed for Constitutional provisions to remove property as a fundamental right and for a restructuring and revitalization of the local Congress organizations so as to convert the party into an organization capable of bringing about the social transformation required by the party's socialist program. The alliance between the pro-Soviet Communists and the Congress was tested in the special midterm elections in Kerala in June 1970, the first statewide election after the split. With support from the pro-Gandhi left student movement, both the Congress and the CPI emerged with a substantial increase in the number of legislative assembly seats, with the Marxist Communists taking the greatest losses.

3. On the eve of national parliamentary elections, the prime minister took steps to consolidate central authority by assuming direct personal charge of the Home Affairs Ministry and by strengthening her own Cabinet Secretariat. She increased the size of the various central police units, the Home Guards, and the Central Industrial Security Force, all within the Home Ministry. Control over the Indian Administrative Service, the Intelligence Bureau, and the Central Bureau of Investigation were transferred to the Cabinet Secretariat from the Home Ministry. The Research and Analysis Wing (RAW) of the Cabinet Secretariat was expanded to carry out internal political surveillance.

4. Rather than rebuild the regular local party organization, the prime minister turned to the Youth Congress for grass roots organizational support, particularly in the urban areas. The Youth Congress was substantially reorganized. In Kerala and West Bengal, in particular, the youth groups proved to be effective at undermining the position of local Marxist organizations, often through the same strong-arm tactics that these organizations had themselves been using.

5. Elections were scheduled for early 1971 for the national parliament, but not for the state assemblies. This decoupling of state and national elections

proved to be a particularly effective way for the prime minister to emphasize the national dimensions of the election, and to maximize the benefits of her own personal campaign for popular support. The 1971 elections took on characteristics of a presidential context, with a campaign that emphasized Mrs. Gandhi's own role as a national leader, and as the symbol of a campaign to abolish poverty for rural India.

With the election of Mrs. Gandhi's Congress to an overwhelmingly dominant position in the national parliament—Congress won 350 seats as against 283 for the united Congress in 1967—the government continued to take steps toward the further centralization of authority.

Mrs. Gandhi's electoral triumph demonstrated her independence from the state party organizations and state political leaders, for her victory rested upon her own popular support. She was now in a position to consolidate her hold within the state party organizations and state governments. Through her domination of the Central Parliamentary Board of the Congress party, Mrs. Gandhi was able to control the allocation of seats to the Congress for the 1972 state assembly elections. Her national stature was further enhanced by India's defeat of Pakistan in the war over Bangladesh, which took place between the national parliamentary elections in early 1971 and the state assembly elections in 1972.

Most of the chief ministers who assumed power in the state after the Congress victories of 1972 were the personal choices of the prime minister. Even local Congress leaders who had supported Mrs. Gandhi in her intra-party struggle in 1969 were removed when they had a popular base of their own. The new chief ministers were completely dependent upon the prime minister for their positions. Several chief ministers who had dominated the state party machinery for decades were removed, replaced by younger leaders more personally loyal to the prime minister.[21]

In theory, this new centralization of power should have enabled the prime minister to carry out her promised reforms to eliminate poverty. In practice, this was not to be the case. Since the local Congress organization continued to be

---

[21] For a well-documented account of Mrs. Gandhi's successful efforts at centralizing the Congress party organization after the split, see Stanley Kochanek, "Mrs. Gandhi's Pyramid: the New Congress," in *Indira Gandhi's India: A Political System Reappraised,* ed. Henry Hart (Boulder, Colorado: Westview Press, 1976), pp. 93—124. Kochanek notes that between 1969, when the party split, and 1975, Congress had five presidents, each chosen by the prime minister and each, with the exception of Jagivan Ram, without an independent political base. He also describes the way in which the prime minister used her control over the Working Committee, the Parliamentary Board, and the Central Election Committee to intervene directly in the state parties to "prevent the emergence if independent power centers in the states." (p. 98). Kochanek's central thesis, with which I completely agree, is that Mrs. Gandhi sought to centralize what has historically and organizationally been a federal party structure.

manned by members of the local rural gentry, the state chief ministers were in no position to push through and implement any land reforms that would take land away from land-owning peasants. Moreover, since the chief ministers had not risen from within the party ranks but held power at the behest of the prime minister, they lacked the popular base to mobilize support for new policies. On the contrary, some chief ministers were particularly vulnerable to organized factional attacks from within the state organizations. The result was that the more centralized the party became, the more unstable were the state ministries. [22]

The combination of tight governmental controls over the private sector and factional conflicts within state party organizations proved to be a potent formula for large-scale political corruption. The various factions sought their share of "black money" from the business community to finance election campaigns.

In short, in spite of the overwhelming victory for the Congress party, and Mrs. Gandhi's personal electoral triumph, the party—and hence the country's political system—was in the midst of a growing crisis by 1973.

The prime minister had the power to control the chief ministers but the chief ministers, in the main, lacked the social base that would make it possible for them to govern effectively and to carry out any of the social reforms promised by the Congress party.

The pro-Communist sections of the Congress party were eager to build a cadre-based organization, and in several states they attempted to build a popular base in the urban areas. But these efforts were greeted with anxiety and hostility on the part of party regulars, who saw these efforts as an entering wedge for establishing Communist control over the party. An organized counterattack against the Communist-dominated Congress Forum for Socialist Action was led by a number of anti-Communists through a group known as the Nehru Forum. As a result of their efforts, in early 1973 both forums were dissolved by the Congress Parliamentary Board.

At the state level, however, clashes—some ideological, but mostly factional—continued between the chief ministers and their pro-Gandhi supporters on the one hand, and sections of the local party organizations on the other.

The political crises that erupted in several Indian states in 1973 were worsened by—but by no means determined by—the economic dislocations that affected the entire country that year. Indeed, the economic crisis—the effects of a rapid rise in the price of imported fertilizers, fuel, and food, all accompanying a decline in food production—was also worsened by the political crisis. In 1973 the central

---

[22] Between 1965 and 1973 twenty-two state governments were taken over by the central government through president's (i.e., central government) rule, compared with ten times during the previous sixteen years.

government nationalized the wholesale grain trade in spite of the private warnings of many members of the administration that the government lacked the machinery to do so. Presumably, one critical argument for nationalizing the grain trade was that it permitted the government to control the movement of food from surplus to deficit areas. Control over foodgrains was particularly important to the government for keeping food prices down in Uttar Pradesh, where elections were scheduled for early 1974. Allocations to other states were reportedly cut in order to move foodgrains to Uttar Pradesh.[23]

In both Gujarat and Bihar, the opposition parties, often with support from dissidents within Congress, launched attacks against the ministries. In Bihar, Congress was particularly vulnerable. It won only 32 percent of the votes in the 1972 elections, and had a bare majority of 52 percent of the legislative assembly seats. The party was divided, much of its leadership was corrupt, and the chief minister, even though he had been chosen by the prime minister, was overthrown by dissident elements within the party. But the new chief minister, though backed by the central government, was soon faced with popular agitation by students and teachers and, more broadly, by the urban middle class.

Two features of both the Bihar and Gujarat agitations call attention to changes in the Indian political system since the Congress party split of 1969. The first is that in both states agitation against state leadership was widely seen within the states, by the national government and by opposition groups throughout the country, as an attack against the center. Since both governments were dependent upon the center for their survival, the agitations were directed against the center rather than exclusively against the state governments. Moreover, in both states the opposition parties saw these campaigns as foreshadowing a national front of opposition parties in the forthcoming elections to parliament in early 1976. In short, the opposition parties envisaged the kind of effort—now perhaps on a larger scale—that had brought them to victory in many of the state elections in 1967 and to near victory in the national parliamentary elections that year.

A second feature of the movement in both states was the extent to which it had won the support of the urban middle class. Students, teachers, members of the lower civil service, even members of the state police, had turned out against state governments, which they held responsible for inflation, corruption, unemployment, and food shortages and which were beholden to the central government.

Whether the movements in Bihar and Gujarat, and the subsequent defeat of the Congress party in the Gujarat elections in June 1975, only a few weeks before the government declared a national emergency, foreshadowed a defeat for

[23] Dawn E. Jones and Rodney W. Jones, "Urban Upheaval in India: The 1974 Nav Nirman Riots in Gujarat," *Asian Survey* 16 (November 1976) 11:1012–1033.

Congress in the national parliamentary elections scheduled for early 1976 it is difficult to say. It should be noted, however, that even prior to the court decision that rendered the prime minister's election to her parliamentary seat invalid, books and articles appeared in India discussing the possibility that the Congress government would take authoritarian measures to avoid an electoral defeat. J. D. Sethi, a professor at the Delhi School of Economics, wrote in his *India in Crisis* in 1974 that "it might sound rash, particularly at this stage, but there are enough indications to show that corruption, violence, and populist policies and economics are driving this country toward some kind of authoritarianism."[24] N. A. Palkhivala, a prominent legal scholar and one-time member of the Indian Law Commission, wrote only months before the emergency was declared that the president could proclaim an emergency that would "suspend the fundamental rights guaranteed by Article 19."[25] Articles and books by well-respected journalists George Verghese, Kuldip Nayar,[26] and Ajit Bhattacharjea expressed concern at the disintegration of state governments, the rise of mass protest, and the possibility of an authoritarian response on the part of the central government.[27] And with prescience Sethi wrote, "In India no one has learnt how to give up power once he has acquired it. One should therefore not expect the Congress Party to give up power or see itself defeated at the polls."[28] "There is," he wrote, "already a nasty smell of authoritarianism in the atmosphere."[29]

Viewed retrospectively, the period from the mid-sixties to 1975 can be viewed as an era in which much of the social base of the Congress party eroded, with the result that the major political institutions and processes that had developed from independence onward became more fragile. The following three trends are notable:

[24] J. D. Sethi, *India in Crisis* (Delhi: Vikas Publishing House, 1975), p. 207.

[25] N. A. Palkhivala, *Our Constitution Defaced and Defiled* (New Delhi: Macmillan Company of India, 1974), p. 74.

[26] Kuldip Nayar, *India: The Critical Years* (Delhi: Vikas Publications, 1971) and Kuldip Nayar, *Between the Lines* (Delhi: Allied Publishers, 1969).

[27] The trend toward authoritarianism based not on an assessment of trends in Indian political development but upon an analysis of Mrs. Gandhi's personality can be found in Zareer Masani, *Indira Gandhi, A Biography* (London: Hamish Hamilton, 1975) and in an article by Nayantara Sahgal, "The Making of Mrs. Gandhi," *South Asian Review* (London) 8 (April 1975): 189—210.

[28] Sethi, *India in Crisis*, p. 207.

[29] Ibid., p. 205.

1. Both in its popular appeal and in its organizational strength the Congress party began to decline in 1962, then slipped precariously in the elections of 1967. The reorganized Congress briefly regained its popular following in the elections of 1971 and 1972, but failed to rebuild as an organization.

2. In the late sixties and early seventies the central government grew in relation to the states, but not because the center was more vigorously pursuing a program of encouraging economic growth or social justice, but because the Congress state leadership had grown more dependent upon the support of the center and less capable of developing its own sources of local power. The center grew at the cost of the stability of the state governments.

3. The legitimacy of governmental authority declined as indicated by a sharp increase from 1964 onward of both public and private violence. The number of riots rose sharply in 1964, then took another leap in 1967. There were similar increases in offenses against property and in crimes of violence. [30] Though for obvious reasons data are not available, the incidence of bureaucratic corruption—that is, the costs of doing business with government—appears to have increased, especially after 1972.

Underlying these trends was the decline in urban support for the Congress party.[31] In the 1952, 1957, and 1962 elections Congress won between 47 percent and 53 percent of the urban vote for state assembly seats (as against 43 percent to 45 percent of the rural vote), but by the 1967 elections a sizable portion of the urban electorate had defected from Congress. In the 1967 elections Congress declined to 38 percent of the urban vote, with the largest increases going to the right-wing Jana Sangh, especially in northern India. Congress won only 43 percent of the urban seats in 1967; it had won 67 percent in 1962.

The Congress debacle in 1967 led many Congress leaders to conclude that strong measures needed to be taken to meet the political threat from the right-wing parties: a more aggressive anti-Pakistan policy; a stronger military (perhaps including nuclear arms); more caution on land reform, cooperative farming, and other possibly threatening agrarian changes; and more attention to party work.

Mrs. Gandhi, however, concluded that the growth in Jana Sangh was more an expression of antiestablishment protests than of right-wing sentiments, and that a radicalization of the Congress program and image was needed to attract votes from the Jana Sangh. The policies she pursued after her break with the more con-

[30] Baldev Raj Nayar, *Violence and Crime in India* (Delhi: The Macmillan Company of India, 1975), p. 28. Nayar reports that the incidence of rioting was highest in the eastern region of India, in Tripura, Manipur, Assam, West Bengal, and Bihar (p. 81).

[31] Data on electoral patterns in urban India are from Myron Weiner and John Osgood Field, "India's Urban Constituencies," *Comparative Politics* 8 (January 1976) 2:183–222.

servative Congress leadership—the nationalization of banks, a proposal for a ceiling on urban property, attacks against the privileged princes—often appeared to be directed at urban constituencies. By 1969 Mrs. Gandhi had begun to capture the protest sentiment of urban Indians: lower-echelon civil servants, taxi drivers, university faculties, and students became her most enthusiastic supporters. Some of the largest crowds and demonstrations on her behalf were in New Delhi, hitherto a center of Jana Sangh strength.

Mrs. Gandhi's strategy of radicalizing the party in order to halt the drift of voters to right-wing parties proved effective. The new Congress swept the polls in the parliamentary elections in 1971, especially in urban areas, where Congress won thirty-three of the fifty-two urban parliamentary constituencies (as against eighteen in 1967) and captured all nine parliamentary urban constituencies previously won by Jana Sangh. The trend continued in the 1972 state assembly elections, when Congress won four out of every five urban seats.

Notwithstanding the Congress's comeback, however, the Communist vote in the urban constituencies in 1972 held firm, while urban support for Jana Sangh actually declined only marginally. It was the independent candidates and other political parties that had lost their support to Congress. The 1972 elections thus confirmed the trend toward the radicalization—and polarization—of urban India.

After 1972 Congress again began to lose urban support. Severe inflation in 1974 and 1975 (estimated at 30 percent annually) was accompanied, to quote from a resolution of the Congress Working Committee, by "organized strikes, go slow movements by government employees, railway employees and industrial employees . . . acts of sabotage paralyzing the railway and communication systems . . . student agitations and indiscipline"[32]—all urban-centered protest movements. Moreover, the urban press, both in English and in the regional languages, was becoming more sharply critical of the Congress governments; there was a disturbing mutiny of the police in the state of Uttar Pradesh; and major urban protest movements were underway in Bihar, and then in Gujarat, where Congress was defeated in the legislative assembly elections of mid-June 1975.

By 1974 the government was thus paying the political price for high inflation,[33] for a development strategy that had paid too little attention to increasing

[32] *Overseas Hindustan Times,* July 24, 1975.

[33] It would be unreasonable to "blame" the government of India for the high inflation rate, for inflation was clearly a worldwide phenomenon over which the government of India had only limited control. In fact, it is striking how committed the Indian government had been to keeping the inflation rate low for more than two decades, a recognition on their part of the need to keep the level of urban dissatisfaction to a minimum; indeed, the sudden disaffection of the urban classes, once in 1967, and again in 1974 when the inflation levels were high, also reflects the relatively low level of inflation during other years.

employment at a rate commensurate with the growth of the labor force, and for an educational strategy that had resulted in a rapid increase in the size of the urban middle class.

In 1970 there were already 3.2 million students registered in institutions of higher education in India, as against 895,000 in 1961 and 362,000 in 1950.[34] Growth in both unemployment and inflation led the urban middle class to a variety of protest movements: sons of the soil nativist movements in Bombay, Bangalore, Gauhati, and Hyderabad; the Jana Sangh (with its nationalist appeal); the revolutionary Naxalites (which attracted many educated urban youths). Some took part in various student and youth movements or engaged in factional struggles for power within Congress. In short, a central destabilizing political development in the mid-seventies was the rising discontent among the educated or partly educated urban middle classes, as well as among aspirants to middle class occupations.

Even the rural elite base of the Congress party was no longer so secure. Local rural elites remained anxious over threats by the central government that ceilings on landholdings would be imposed. And many local Congressmen of rural standing were disgruntled by the intervention of the central government in the choice of state leaders, which deprived them of influence at the state level. Moreover, one should keep in mind the growing links between the urban middle classes and the rural peasant proprietors whose sons and daughters had been entering secondary schools and colleges in an effort to join the urban middle class. The slow growth of urban employment thus seriously affected the mobility of India's rural gentry classes.

Nor had the prime minister succeeded in compensating for the losses of these middle sectors in urban and rural India by attracting support from the lower income groups. With two successive years of drought, a drop in foodgrain production, a rise in food prices, a growth in rural unemployment, a recession in the industrial sector, and increased retrenchment, there was hardly any improvement for either the urban or rural poor.[35]

----

[34] J. P. Naik, *Policy and Performance in India Education 1947–74* (New Delhi: Orient Longman, 1975), p. 95. The number of colleges increased from 695 in 1950 to 3,896 in 1971.

[35] Closely linked to the urban middle classes is what is often referred to as the "unorganized" or "informal" service sector of the urban economy—washermen, domestic servants, hawkers, peddlars, newspaper sellers, rickshaw pullers, and so on—who earn their income largely by providing services to the urban middle classes, and live in makeshift accommodations next to the urban middle class area they service. Since their income is heavily dependent upon the middle class, when middle class income declines in a period of inflation this low-income service sector is badly hit. Though this class is not organized into trade unions or organized associations, it is often drawn into the political arena by political parties seeking

As the popular base of the Congress declined, as its legitimacy weakened, as the central government proved less able to cope with instability at the state level through political means, the government turned to measures pursued by so many other governments in developing countries concerned with preserving internal political order by extending the elite's hold on political power. Even before the emergency was declared, as we have seen, steps were taken to strengthen the central government, to expand the central police, to enlarge the government's intelligence services, and to strengthen the police powers of the state through the passage of the Maintenance of Internal Security Act.[36] The stage was thus set for the emergency of June 1975.

Growth of the Bureaucratic State

Even before the emergency was declared, the power of the bureaucracy in India was substantial and growing. As the prime minister's trust of the Congress party elite declined after the 1967 elections, and as she shifted leftward, especially after 1969, her reliance upon left-leaning members of the civil service increased.[37] Among her most trusted advisors were P. N. Haksar, head of the prime minister's secretariat and later deputy chairman of the Planning Commission; and D.P. Dhar, one-time Ambassador to the Soviet Union and subsequently chairman of the Policy Planning Committee of the Ministry of External Affairs. Both were widely viewed as Marxists. By the early 1970s, Mrs. Gandhi's closest advisors within the civil service were reportedly critical of the role played by the country's politicians and bigger business interests and were seeking ways to curb both. They supported a variety of restrictive measures against portions of the private sector. New pro-

participants for public demonstrations and agitations. This group, which gave public support to Mrs. Gandhi in the 1969 split, was reported to have participated in the agitations against the prime minister and against the state Congress party leaders in Bihar and Gujarat in 1974 and 1975.

[36] Like its predecessor, the Preventive Detention Act, MISA was intended to be not punitive but preventive. MISA empowers central and state governments to detain persons if in the government's judgment the person is likely to act in a manner prejudicial to the defense of India, the security of the country, or the maintenance of public order. After the emergency was declared, an ordinance was issued that forbade the disclosure of the grounds for detention even before a court.

[37] An excellent account of these developments can be found in a book-length manuscript by Professor Francine Frankel, *India's Political Economy Since Independence* (Princeton: Princeton University Press, forthcoming), notably in Chapter 11 "Reprise: Class Accommodation or Class Struggle?" I appreciate the opportunity afforded to me by Professor Frankel for sharing this study in its manuscript version.

cedures were established that required larger business houses to obtain the approval of the Monopolies Committee and often the Economic Affairs Committee of the cabinet (and hence of the central bureaucracy and the prime minister) for new investments. The Constitution was amended to remove property from the list of Fundamental Rights. The grain trade was nationalized, as was the coal industry. On many of these issues there was support both from members of the prime minister's secretariat and from other close advisors within the central secretariat, and from the pro-left members of the CSFA group within Congress. Both groups also pushed for closer ties with the Soviet Union, especially in the areas of trade; the left in Congress for ideological reasons, and the bureaucracy because it was eager to find a ready international market for the underutilized capacity of the public sector.

We can only surmise that there were conflicts within the administration in the late sixties and early seventies when, as we noted earlier, power was shifted as the Central Bureau of Investigation, the Intelligence Bureau, and the All India Administrative Service were removed from the Ministry of Home Affairs and transferred to the Cabinet Secretariat. Much of this shifting took place in 1970 during a period of cabinet reshuffling and reorganization. It is striking that Mrs. Gandhi herself then took personal charge of the Ministry of Home Affairs at a time when the central police units were being expanded.

The growing importance of the bureaucracy in the seventies was a reversal of earlier trends. At the rural level the independent authority of the civil service had actually declined in the 1950s, and that of popularly elected local representatives and officials of the local Congress party had increased. The *panchayati raj* program, with its popularly elected local bodies at the village, *taluka,* and district level was a major effort to democratize (that is, to debureaucratize) the development process at the local level. The community development program, which provided a network of services to rural areas and encouraged rural participation in the development process, was one of India's earlier development programs and was widely regarded as an international model for other developing countries. However limited its effects may have been on facilitating agricultural growth—its critics say that it was not accompanied by a substantial investment in agricultural inputs—it did have an important impact on the division of power between the rural bureaucracy and elected rural officeholders.

In rural India, the political process partly displaced the bureaucratic process, but in the industrial sector the power of the bureaucracy expanded substantially. During the Second and Third Five Year Plans the public sector grew, and there was also an increase in governmental regulation over the private sector. The ideological left within Congress and a substantial section of the national level bureaucracy shared an interest in extending the role of the public sector and regulating the private sector, though their rationales were often quite different.

By 1966 some 9.4 million workers were employed in India's public sector as opposed to 6.8 million in the organized private sector; in 1975 there were 12.8 million workers in the public sector and the same 6.8 million in the private sector. In short, while employment in the private sector remained constant over the decade, public sector employment expanded by 4.2 percent a year, with the largest increases in mining (as a result of the nationalization of coal), manufacturing, trade and commerce, and public services. By 1975 some 66 percent of the labor force in the organized sector in India was employed by government, as against 58 percent some nine years earlier.

To the international aid community, however, especially to the U.S. Agency for International Development (AID) and the World Bank, the importance of the bureaucracy was the extent to which it regulated the economy—production, procurement, investment, distribution, pricing, and so on. Governmental controls— that is, controls by the bureaucracy—were the primary means by which Indian planners allocated resources in both the public and private sectors. Many of these controls originated during the Second World War when the British wanted to maintain an adequate supply of war materials. After independence the government passed the Industries Act, which gave the central government the power to license industries and issue import permits, and soon thereafter procedures were established for regulating production, procurement, distribution, and pricing in a variety of industries. As David Denoon explains the broad appeal of governmental control, the left sees it as Indian socialism, planning technicians and bureaucrats see it as a benefit to their careers, and bigger businessmen get a protected market and high profits in return for "contributions" to the Congress party.[38]

The interests of the bureaucracy in controls, and their ideological acceptance by the party, are important explanations, but a deeper cultural element should perhaps be added; one that involves the attitudes of government toward obtaining compliance from its citizens. Regimes seek compliance in three ways: (1) by appealing to values shared by the citizenry, (2) through the use of incentives, and (3) through various forms of coercion. Though all political systems rely in one degree or another upon all three methods, systems vary considerably in the extent to which they use each. The Indian government, like many regimes in developing countries (but less so than revolutionary regimes), makes extensive use of exhortations; that is, public appeals to what the government believes are shared values, such as secularism, nationalism, anticasteism, antiprovincialism, justice for the poor, and nonviolence. The use of the postemergency twenty-point program by the prime minister and the five-point program of Sanjay Gandhi are the most recent examples of attempts to achieve compliance by appeals to shared values.

[38] Denoon, "AID—High Politics, Technocracy or Farce?" p. 139.

Incentives play a smaller role in India than in the United States, where it is expected that people can be induced to behave in the common interest if suitably rewarded. In India controls, regulations, licensing, compulsory procurement, and compulsory savings are among a variety of coercive mechanisms used by the government to induce compliance with its objectives. Behind these controls rests the assumption that individuals should behave in expected ways because it is their duty to do so, and that individuals should not be rewarded for acting in the public interest. It is also presumed that individuals are more likely to comply with authority if they are required to do so than if they are rewarded for doing so.

Moreover, those who exercise authority tend to believe that their authority rests upon the capacity to command compliance, rather than on their ability to provide rewards for suitable behavior. Authority is conceived as command: it is exercised by demanding compliance, not by inducing people through rewards.[39] Reliance upon regulations and other forms of coercion is normal administrative behavior in India. Policies to cope with public problems are ordinarily defined in terms of coercive intervention. If there is too much inflation, then regulate prices; if there is too much hoarding, then arrest hoarders; if industry is spatially too concentrated, then regulate industrial locations; if there is too little food supply in some regions, then regulate grain distribution; if there are too many imports draining the country's foreign exchange, then require import permits.

The failure of regulations to induce appropriate behavior is generally interpreted not as a failure in policy but as a failure in implementation, suggesting that stronger measures should be adopted to carry out government policy. Moreover, since controls (especially during periods of scarcity) are justified by government on the grounds that in their absence people are likely to behave in antisocial ways, noncompliance and hence antisocial behavior tends to reinforce the argument. Thus, if price controls are accompanied by hoarding, or licensing is accompanied by corruption on the part of businessmen, the argument that businessmen are antisocial has been "verified." Paradoxically, then, the more regulations are violated, the more government is persuaded that additional controls are re-

---

[39] Stanley Heginbotham argues that bureaucratic authority in India is committed to orderly procedures rather than to goals. "Political, social, economic and religious thinking within the Hindu cultural tradition," he writes, "reflects a view of the community as an organic entity whose continued well-being is dependent on the carefully specified cooperative actions of its component parts. Maintenance of harmony and order in the community is the goal, but it is achievable only if its members are *restrained from pursuing their own self-interest*, since such pursuits are satisfied only through the loss of others of benefits due them. . . . The clear and authoritative definition of dues and rights, a strong sense of duty on the part of the citizenry, and powerful enforcement bodies are thus necessary components of an effective polity." (Stanley J. Heginbotham, "The Civil Service and the Emergency," in *Indira Gandhi's India: A Political System Reappraised*, ed. Henry Hart (Boulder, Colorado: Westview Press, 1976), p. 82.

quired.[40]

With the suspension during the emergency of many of the fundamental rights provisions of the Constitution, which had imposed some limits on the regulatory and coercive powers of the state, the government turned to coercive measures to induce compliance. Opponents of the regime were arrested, trade union strikes were prohibited, public meetings were banned, censorship was imposed on the press, and there was harassment by tax authorities. The most dramatic and widespread effort to use coercive measures to induce behavioral change was a variety of compulsory pressures for sterilization in much of northern India. The forceful removal of several hundred thousand low-income slum dwellers from squatter settlements in Delhi is still another example.

In some respects, however, during the emergency the bureaucracy reduced coercive regulations and replaced them with incentives, particularly in relation to the business community. There was an export incentive scheme that included such benefits as cash subsidies, import replenishment, and liberal export credit facilities; export licensing requirements were waived for many items, and imports were liberalized; the use of industrial licensing to affect sectoral distribution of production and investment was reduced; and decontrol of prices occurred in some items. However, it should be noted that these incentives and decontrol measures, all of which were intended to encourage expansion of industrial production and exports, had not been accompanied by a dismantling of the licensing and regulating agencies and procedures; the regulations and the government agencies remained intact. It is not surprising therefore that many businessmen in India, while welcoming the new economic policies, viewed these policy changes as strategic shifts and not the result of fundamental changes in governmental attitudes.

Institutional Changes During the Emergency

The most striking feature of the institutional changes that occurred during the emergency was the extent to which they represented a marked shift from developments that had taken place from 1947 through the mid-sixties, but were a continuation of many of the trends we have described for the period since 1965.

The earlier period was characterized by increased political participation; a strong Congress party organization; a decline in the power of the bureaucracy (especially in rural India); a balance of power between the states and the center, with a substantial growth in the authority of the state governments; an expansion of the power base of the governing leadership incorporating the middle sectors

[40] Albert Hirschman has diagnosed similar patterns in several countries of Latin America. See his "Political Economy of Import Substituting Industrialization in Latin America" in *A Bias for Hope: Essays on Development and Latin America* (New Haven: Yale University Press, 1971), Chapter 3.

in both rural and urban India; the evolution of a tradition of human rights, which facilitated the growth of a free press, political organizations, and interest associations; and a widespread belief in the legitimacy of governmental authority.

As we have seen, the trend in the decade before the declaration of an emergency was toward a decline (and then a fast rise) in the level of support for the Congress party, a decline in the strength of the Congress organization itself, a growth in parliamentary police and intelligence organizations, increased centralization of authority and a corresponding decline in the power of state governments, sporadic (but to the Congress government threatening) moves by opposition parties to consolidate their campaigns against the government, a decline in the legitimacy of governmental authority, and a general weakening of the capacity of the government to handle internal conflicts in a noncoercive fashion.

After the emergency was declared in June 1975 the government imposed restrictions on the press, arrested opponents of the government, suspended the open political process that had characterized India for twenty-eight years, and postponed national parliamentary elections. Amendments were made to the Constitution limiting the powers of the judiciary, increasing the powers of the central government, and strengthening the position of the prime minister. Amendments were used to make changes in order that the government might maintain its legitimate authority and continuity with the older institutional system; amendments helped emphasize that India continued to retain a democratic system (but not "Westminister forms"). However, these changes were not accepted by opponents of the government.

With the suspension of the electoral process and open politics, power shifted away from the Congress party and from the elected representatives in the states and central legislatures to the bureaucracy, which had primary responsibility for carrying out the policies set down by the prime minister. The Research and Analysis Wing of the prime minister's secretariat and other intelligence organizations of the central government provided the central government and the prime minister with the political information necessary to make critical political judgments—such as the center's decisions to establish president's rule in the states of Gujarat, Tamil Nadu, and Orissa. The various central police organizations were also important for dealing with the underground that began functioning after the emergency was declared. The powers of state and central politicians were curtailed (and many were imprisoned) but the position of local elites in rural areas remained untouched. Interest associations—chambers of commerce, trade unions, student associations—continued to operate, but under governmental controls that led some to characterize government policy toward these groups as an attempt to create a corporate state, following the Iberian model.

In an effort to create a popular base in a situation in which the Congress party itself appeared to have lost much of its following, the prime minister, or more precisely, her son, Sanjay Gandhi, sought to use the Youth Congress as an instrument for popular mobilization. Through its "liberalization" policies toward the private sector, the government shifted toward a growth policy intended not only to stimulate the economy but to win support for the regime from sections of the business community. The rhetoric of the government continued to be leftist, but its basic economic policies were what generally would be regarded as right leaning. This shift led to considerable tension between the government and its supporters on the left, particularly the Communist party of India, whose opposition to Sanjay Gandhi and the Youth Congress became a source of conflict in several states, notably Orissa and West Bengal.

A number of observers pointed to the "middle class" tone of the regime because of the primacy it gave to urban beautification, the sterilization of the high-fertility lower classes, the removal of urban slums, punctuality, discipline, and political order. This orientation was particularly explicit in the five-point program of the prime minister's son, Sanjay Gandhi, which included tree planting, family planning, and the end of the dowry system.

Finally, we should note the personal character of the regime during the emergency. A number of emergency ordinances, laws, and even constitutional amendments passed after the emergency were directed at protecting the personal position of the prime minister against court actions. In the press, in government pronouncements, and on party posters, it was the prime minister or her son who received constant attention. Sanjay Gandhi was provided with state facilities and was treated by state government officials as if he were a high government figure, though he held no position in the government. Proximity to either the prime minister or her son was widely understood in India to be a measure of political influence. There was a widespread sense, as in a patrimonial system, that the ruler treated administration as his (or her) personal affair while, in turn, officials treated their administrative responsibilities as an extension of their loyalty and duty to the ruler. "Kingly administration," wrote Max Weber about pre-Moghul India in terms that are not inappropriate for describing the primacy of the prime minister and the bureaucracy during the emergency, "became patrimonial and bureaucratic. On the one hand, it developed a regulated hierarchical order of officials with local and functional competence and appeals; on the other hand, however, administrative and court offices were kept separate and the jurisdictional spheres of a bewildering manifold of offices were fluid, indeterminate, irrational, and subject to chance influences."[41]

[41] Max Weber, *The Religion of India: The Sociology of Hinduism and Buddhism* (Glencoe, Illinois: Free Press, 1958), p. 67.

Elections and the End of the Emergency

` Prime Minister Gandhi, in a surprise announcement in mid-January 1977, declared that a national election to parliament would be held in mid-March. At the time many, apparently including Mrs. Gandhi, expected that the elections would legitimize her declaration of an emergency, demonstrate that the country supported her moves to institutionalize many features of the emergency, and provide her son, Sanjay, with an opportunity to establish his power within the Congress parliamentary delegation and thereby ensure his own eventual succession to the prime ministership. For a variety of reasons Mrs. Gandhi was confident of a victorious outcome. She assumed that opposition leaders, many of whom were released from jail only after her announcement of the elections, would be unable to forge a united front. She also assumed that many of the policies adopted during the emergency were popular; programs to allocate housing sites to Harijans, redistribute land to the landless, abolish bonded labor, end or at least reduce rural indebtedness, and provide alternative housing for urban squatters. And while each of these measures had its detractors, the government believed that, in the main, they were successful and popular. Sanjay Gandhi had been acclaimed by the chief ministers of states he had visited, large crowds appeared at his public meetings, press coverage of his five-point program was enthusiastic, and his Youth Congress was attracting, at least according to reports in the press, tens and even hundreds of thousands of followers. Sanjay's promise, and Mrs. Gandhi's hope, that the Youth Congress would emerge as a kind of alternative Congress built upon a popular base of energetic young people seemed within grasp.

All this, we know now, was fantasy. Like many authoritarian regimes, this one was unaware of how unpopular many of its policies and programs were, or indeed of how little popular support there was for the regime and for the emergency. This lack of effective feedback in itself might not have jeopardized the regime had it not made the extraordinary, if not unique, decision to test its popularity by holding an election. Other authoritarian regimes have held elections; none has held a genuinely honest one.

The election campaign has been described elsewhere.[42] Here we need only note that the elections brought an end to thirty years of Congress party rule, eleven years of government under the prime ministership of Indira Gandhi, twenty months of an emergency that set India on a course of authoritarian government and that brought to power, through peaceful means, a new national political

[42] See Myron Weiner, "The 1977 Parliamentary Elections in India," *Asian Survey* 17 (July 1977), 7:619–26; for a perceptive account of the impact of the emergency in a village in Maharashtra, see the excellent article by Lee I. Schlesinger, "The Emergency in an Indian Village," *Asian Survey* 17 (July 1977), 7:627–47.

party, the Janata party. The emergency was ended, and the new government proceeded to undo many of the institutional changes that had been introduced by Prime Minister Gandhi. The Research and Analysis Wing, the prime minister's internal intelligence apparatus, was stripped of its powers; the threats against freedom of the press and freedom of assembly were ended; steps were taken to end governmental control over the single news service created by Mrs. Gandhi's information ministry; the independence of the courts was reestablished. State elections were held in the north Indian states where the Congress party had been overwhelmingly defeated for the parliamentary elections. In Uttar Pradesh, Bihar, Madhya Pradesh, Rajasthan, Haryana, Himachal Pradesh, and the Punjab a Janata party government was elected; in West Bengal the Communist Party of India (Marxist) formed a new government, and in Tamil Nadu the All India Annadurai DMK took power. The new Janata government declared that the Janata party state governments could choose their own chief ministers without imposition from the center, and that in its domestic policies the government would give more attention to rural development and to programs that would maximize employment. Many of the economic liberalization measures adopted by Mrs. Gandhi were further extended, and the government announced that foreign investors would be allowed to function within India on the same basis as domestic investors. The new government also announced that it would seek a more balanced relationship with the great powers, a statement understood to mean that steps would be taken to improve relations with the United States and other Western powers. Among the early acts of the government were an exchange of correspondence between President Carter and Prime Minister Morarji Desai, and an announcement by the Indian prime minister that the government did not contemplate any new nuclear testing, that it did not intend to develop an arsenal of nuclear weapons, and that the new Indian Ambassador to the United States would be Nani A. Palkhivala, a prominent lawyer known for his commitment to human rights. In turn, the Carter administration welcomed the reestablishment of democratic procedures in India, announced that it would attempt to arrest the growing Soviet and American naval competition in the Indian Ocean, pressed the French government to halt the sale of a nuclear reprocessing plant to Pakistan, announced that it would not sell F-7 fighter aircraft to the Pakistani government, and informed the Indian government that it was prepared to resume the economic assistance program that the Nixon administration had terminated during the Indo-Pakistan clash over Bangladesh.

Assessing the Political Impact of Foreign Assistance

Myron Weiner

How should one assess the role played by foreign assistance in the evolution of India's political institutions since independence? Foreign aid agencies, in an effort to justify their programs, naturally point to all successes within the recipient country as the results of foreign assistance, or at least as a success to which foreign assistance substantially contributed. Hence, when food productivity in India increased during the period of the green revolution aid agencies took some credit for the improvement. So, too, have aid donors taken credit for growth in industrial production, stable prices, an increase in exports, improved income distribution, and so on.

Donors have somewhat more difficulty in taking credit for political developments, except to argue that the economic improvements have resulted in political benefits. Thus, stable prices and increased per capita income are pointed to as contributions to a country's political stability, to the maintenance of a non-Communist regime, or in the case of India, to the preservation (before 1975) of India's democratic order.

Donors will often argue that economic assistance should be provided in order to prevent certain economic, and therefore political, catastrophes. Hence, food should be provided during a period of scarcity to prevent widespread dissatisfaction that might lead to insurrectionary movements and political instability; or foreign aid is needed to provide foreign exchange to maintain imports so as to avoid severe inflation and a disaffected middle class. When economic assistance is provided, aid agencies argue (especially before congressional committees) that the assistance was effective because the predicted catastrophes were avoided. But, as with all counterfactual history, proof is impossible. The reverse argument is also used: had aid been larger, then certain undesirable economic and political developments might have been avoided. Had India received larger amounts of foreign assistance in 1973 and 1974 when the international price of India's primary imports—food, fertilizers, and oil—had risen, some have suggested, India might have been able to avoid the inflationary spiral and food shortages that intensified the political crisis leading to the declaration of an emergency in 1975. Again, this is untestable counterfactual history. Perhaps it is the domestic political process within which the donor makes decisions as to how much and what kind of aid should be provided that tends to generate a rhetoric of exaggerated claims and expectations.

How useful is it to assess the political effects of specific development projects funded by foreign aid? Baldev Raj Nayar attempted to do so by comparing the voting patterns in districts with community development and national extension programs with voting patterns in districts that lacked such programs—and found that support for Congress, which had grown in both areas, had increased more in constituencies without government-aided programs.[1] Warren Ilchman performed a similar study by looking at the voting patterns in constituencies containing a sample of forty-four foreign-assisted development projects.[2] He found that between 1957 and 1962 Congress lost slightly fewer parliamentary seats in constituencies with such projects, but for the state assembly elections Congress lost slightly more than in the country as a whole. There was no particular pattern of Communist wins and losses in these constituencies, nor was there any significant relationship between constituencies with projects supported by the Soviet Union and the electoral performance of the Communist party.

Studies of the electoral effects of government-aided projects say more about the political effects of development than about the impact of foreign assistance. To the extent that the aid recipient can transfer resources from one sector of the economy to another, does it matter which projects, which sector of the economy, or even which region received *foreign* assistance? The total performance of the Indian economy was so linked to the strategy pursued by the government, which in turn was facilitated by foreign assistance, that it is not very useful to explore the political effects of specific foreign-assisted projects. If we are to make any assessment of the impact foreign assistance had on India's internal political developments we should first start with a description and analysis of U.S. political objectives for its economic assistance programs, then examine how the aid actually meshed with the kind of political-economic strategy of development actually pursued by the Indian government.

The Objectives of American Aid to India

Hardly anyone would quarrel with the statement of Professor Hans Morgenthau that "of the seeming and real innovations which the modern age has introduced into the practice of foreign policy, none has proven more baffling to

[1] Baldev Raj Nayar, "Community Development Programme, Its Political Impact," *Economic Weekly* 12 (September 17, 1960), 1401–12.

[2] Warren F. Ilchman, "A Political Economy of Foreign Aid: The Case of India," *Asian Survey* 7 (October 1967), 10:667–88.

both understanding and action than foreign aid."[3] To whom should assistance be given, with what criteria, in what amounts, and in what form are questions closely bound to controversies concerning the objectives of foreign assistance.

On one side of the argument are those who take a wholly economic position. "The purpose of an international program of aid to underdeveloped countries," wrote P. N. Rosenstein-Rodan, "is to accelerate their economic development up to a point where a satisfactory rate of growth can be achieved on a self-sustaining basis."[4]

In the same vein, Senator Fulbright, speaking in 1966, when liberals still formed an important constituency for foreign assistance, proposed the conversion of foreign aid

> from an instrument of national foreign policy to an international program for the limited transfer of wealth from rich countries to poor countries in accordance with the same principle of community responsibility that in our own country underlies progressive taxation, social welfare programs, and the effective transfer of wealth from the rich States to the poor States through programs of Federal aid.[5]

On the other side of the argument are those who look upon foreign assistance as an instrument of foreign policy, to be used along with other instruments, for the achievement of American objectives. Milton Friedman, a critic of aid, noted that "foreign economic aid is widely regarded as a weapon in the ideological war in which the United States is now involved. Its assigned role is to help win over to our side those uncommitted nations that are also underdeveloped and poor."[6] A more specific expression of this view can be found in the 1964 AID presentation to Congress in support of assistance to India:

> India today is the major Free World power center between Japan and Western Europe. Strategically, it commands the Arabian Sea, the Indian Ocean and vital air and land routes between Europe and the Far East. Economically, it has the potential for becoming a strong industrial power. Ideologically, it is the largest exponent of democracy among the emerging countries and commands among those countries considerable influence in world councils. U.S. objectives in India are to: (a) assist India to remain independent; (b) maintain close associations with the Free World; and (c) improve India's defense capabilities to enable it to resist current and future pressures from Communist China.[7]

---

[3] Hans Morgenthau, "A Political Theory of Foreign Aid," *American Political Science Review* 56 (1962), 301.

[4] P.N. Rosenstein-Rodan, "Internal Aid for Underdeveloped Countries," in *Foreign Aid*, ed. Jagdish Bhagwati and Richard S. Eckaus (New York: Penguin Books, 1970), p. 81.

[5] Cited by T. Balogh, "Multilateral Versus Bilateral Aid," ibid., p. 205.

[6] Milton Friedman, "Foreign Economic Aid: Means and Objectives," ibid., p. 63.

[7] U.S. Agency for International Development, "1964 Congressional Presentation," p. 19.

There have been a variety of attempts to reconcile these two viewpoints, the most widely known and influential being the report to the Senate committee, "Objectives of the United States Economic Assistance Programs," by the M.I.T. Center for International Studies, subsequently developed by the authors, Max Millikan and Walt Rostow, into *A Proposal: Key to an Effective Foreign Policy.*[8] That report argued that foreign assistance would stimulate economic growth, that this would reduce the danger of international conflict since nationalist governments would turn their attention to internal development, and that it could "in say two or three decades, result in an overwhelming preponderance of societies with a successful record of solving their problems without resort to coercion or violence. The establishment of such a preponderance of stable, effective, and democratic societies gives the best promise of a favorable settlement of the cold war and of a peaceful, progressive environment."[9]

The distinctive feature of the Millikan-Rostow proposal was its emphasis on the *long-run* compatibility of the objectives of economic growth and U.S. security interests. They therefore rejected the argument of those who saw aid as fulfilling short-run objectives, that is, securing military allies for the United States or using aid to make regimes more stable, concluding that the U.S. government should employ wholly economic criteria in the allocation of assistance.

Any examination of which countries received economic assistance from the United States over the past twenty-five years and the fluctuations in bilateral assistance by country year by year quickly reveals the extent to which short-run U.S. policy objectives have been the dominant criteria. Nonetheless, the kind of arguments used by Millikan and Rostow were reflected in some aspects of the aid program, most notably in assistance to India.

Between 1956 and 1975 India received more than $10 billion in various types of assistance from the United States. About half of this assistance was foodgrains under PL 480. Apart from providing India with food, this program also loaned (and subsequently converted much of the loan into a grant) the rupees earned from the sale of grain back to the Indian government for development assistance. The remaining half was largely in the form of development loans.

Aid to India was not justified on short-term objectives since India was not an ally of the United States. India provided the United States with no military bases; nor was there, at least before 1962, any sense of a shared military threat. Nor was India a supporter of American policy in the Third World; indeed, not only were

[8] Max Millikan and W. W. Rostow, *A Proposal: Key to an Effective Foreign Policy* (New York: Harper & Row, 1957).

[9] G. Ohlin, "The Evolution of Foreign Aid," ibid., p. 28.

there genuine differences in perspective on international issues, but at times it almost seemed to American policymakers that the Indian government was perverse in its efforts to publicly express its opposition to the United States even when such expression was uncalled for, often at most unpropitious moments in U.S.-Indian relations. It was almost as if the aid relationship between the two countries necessitated a constant reassertion by the Indian government of its independence from the United States.

This is not to suggest that the United States was not guided by political considerations in its aid to India. The increase in development loans after 1962 was related to India's growing conflicts with China and the decline and eventual termination of aid were related to the U.S. rapprochement with China, and to U.S. disapproval of India's conflict with Pakistan over Bangladesh.

But within the political parameters that influenced the size of the aid program—indeed, whether there would be one at all—American political objectives for aid were couched in broad, long-range terms. The description and analysis of these objectives and values can be drawn entirely from the public record, in this case from AID congressional presentations between 1960 and 1976, from reviews of the India program by AID, and from papers prepared by the State Department for presentation to Congress on U.S. aid to India. These documents reveal six explicit political objectives or values:

1. A central objective was to help India maintain her *democratic* institutions. "The next few years," said a 1960 report, "will be crucial for India. Its leaders must prove that India can develop its economy under democratic institutions at a pace sufficient to satisfy at least the minimum aspirations of its 400 million people. If it cannot do so, circumstances may force it into totalitarianism drawing examples from the practices and progress of its Asia competitor, Communist China."[10] The 1961 report, in the same vein, said that "the basic United States policy objective with regard to India . . . is that India remain in the free world and demonstrate that an underdeveloped country can achieve a satisfactory rate of economic progress in a free society."[11]

2. *Self-reliance* for India was another objective that reflected American goals and values. AID documents emphasized that foreign aid was only a small part of India's total development effort and that India did her own planning and raised most of her own resources. "This arrangement," said one AID

[10] U.S. Agency for International Development, "1960 Congressional Presentation," p. 55.

[11] U.S. Agency for International Development, "1961 Congressional Presentation," p. 133.

document, "has placed the United States in the position of cooperating with India rather than having India cooperate with the United States. . . . Whatever programs are largely sponsored by the Americans are merely part of the total Indian program. . . . [In the case of India] the United States helps a nation which helps itself."[12]

3. *Self-help* on the part of the Indian population is a variant of this theme. American support for India's community development program and for its national extension scheme did not rest simply on the importance of these programs for economic growth. "The most important result [of these programs]," wrote John P. Ferris, then Chief of the Foreign Operations Administration for India, "is the intangible one of creating an atmosphere of determined self-help and hope for the future in rural India—where the verdict on India's democratic development efforts is most likely to be written. A new democratic spirit is sweeping the country." Participation in the development process at the local level was a value in itself, even if it did not increase agricultural productivity, he wrote. "Regardless of its apparent failure to stimulate in a major way food production, it [the community development program] has been a vast education in self-help and democracy, which is more than worth the total effort put into it."[13]

4. The strengthening of India's *private sector* appears in AID documents as an objective of U.S. policy. Ferris, describing the U.S. role in establishing an Industrial Credit and Investment Corporation of India in 1955, said that this institution had contributed to "progress toward faster capital accumulation of private industrial capital . . . [and this will] increase the flow of foreign investment into India."[14] The 1961 report, explaining an American decision to fund several new investment institutions in India, noted that "a major impediment to the establishment of new productive enterprises in India has been the difficulty of marshalling adequate domestic capital resources. . . . To fill this deficiency $113.2 million of the rupees generated by U.S. aid programs in India are being channeled into private investment."[15] This encouragement of the private sector is found in virtually all

[12] U.S. Agency for International Development, *A Review of Selected Indo-American Technical Assistance Programs* (1960), p. 4.

[13] John P. Ferris, "Some Lessons of the U.S.-India Foreign Aid Program," *Public Administration Review* 25 (Spring 1955), 2:91.

[14] Ibid., p. 95.

[15] U.S. Agency for International Development, "1961 Congressional Presentation," p. 57.

of the appropriation proposals made by AID before Congress. The 1961 list of objectives of U.S. technical cooperation with India spoke of the need "to provide facilities to encourage private industry and attract private foreign investments."[16]

Closely linked to the American attitude toward private development was the question of controls. "U.S. aid," said the 1968 report, "supports the reduced administrative control over the Indian economy and increased reliance on the market mechanism" but noted that "there remain . . . strong prejudices against a larger role for the private sector and against allowing the market to influence investment and resource allocation."[17]

Some of the reports described AID successes in promoting the role of the private sector in India. A 1966 report noted that "India has made some tentative steps in the direction of relaxing government controls on business. . . . Program assistance is valuable in helping the Indian government to assume the risks of these actions and in helping to finance the rising import demand of the private industrial sector."[18] A 1971 document noted that India had moved toward "mobilizing individual initiative and broadening competitive participation" by reducing "cumbersome administrative controls" and "increased reliance on market forces."[19]

5. Keeping India within the *free world* was another explicit political objective. According to AID's review of the India program:

> U.S. interests in the success of India's economic development rest on those factors which contribute to India's growing importance as a member of the Free World: its size, as the second most populous country of the world; its geographical position between the western and eastern segments of the Free World; its basic traditions of individualism, political liberty and functioning parliamentary democracy; its growing stature and leadership among the newly independent nations of the world; its importance as a source of necessary materials and as a market for western countries.[20]

[16] Ibid., p. 59.

[17] U.S. Agency for International Development, "Summary of Country Program: India, 1968," p. 39.

[18] U.S. Agency for International Development, "1971 Congressional Presentation," p. 40.

[19] U.S. Agency for International Development, "Summary of Country Program: India," 1971, p. 3.

[20] U.S. Agency for International Development, "Mutual Security Program, fiscal year 1960, summary prepared for Congressional presentation," p. 55.

After the war with China in October 1962, AID was more explicit about India's defense needs. The 1964 report cited as a goal the need to "improve India's defense capabilities to enable it to resist current and future pressures from Communist China."[21] This shift in emphasis presumably was a reflection of the defense appropriations the United States made to India in 1963. In 1965 the United States provided military assistance "in order to relieve pressure on India's balance of payments and to insure that the economic development program is not unduly affected by India's need to provide increased resources for defense."[22] AID also explicitly described economic assistance as a contribution to India's defense against Communist China: "Achievement of these objectives requires economic expansion sufficient to finance rising defense needs and maintain the confidence of the Indian people in the ability of their democratic system to improve their standard of living."[23]

6. *Equity* in income distribution, as an objective of U.S. assistance, does not appear as a rationale in any of these documents until 1971, when the annual report listed as a U.S. objective to "increase employment opportunities and per capita income, with emphasis on disadvantaged groups within the economy." The same report noted that the "Indian political debate is giving renewed attention to basic problems of poverty and social equity, particularly in rural areas."[24] With the passage of the Foreign Assistance Act of 1973 AID documents increasingly spoke of "plans to accord highest priority to programs designed to improve the living standards of the poorest majority of India's vast population."[25] This emphasis, however, appeared at a time when the United States was no longer providing India with new bilateral aid, though World Bank assistance had substantially increased: from an annual level of $150 million in fiscal year (FY) 1967 to $500 million in FY 1973.

[21] U.S. Agency for International Development, "1964 Congressional Presentation," p. 19.

[22] U.S. Agency for International Development, "1965 Congressional Presentation," p. 117.

[23] Ibid.

[24] U.S. Agency for International Development, "Summary of Country Program: India," 1971, p. 3.

[25] "AID Comments on the Separate View of the Honorable Clarence D. Long," p. 12. This memo is an extended reply to Congressman Long's criticism of India's economic performance presented before the House Appropriations Committee on March 10, 1975 in a report entitled "India—The Strange Case of Wasted Billions."

To a large extent these values and goals of American economic assistance represented a rationale for U.S. support for India rather than guidelines for specific economic activities. Some specific projects were funded because they strengthened the private sector (and some activities, like steel, were not funded because they were in the public sector), but the fact is that American economic assistance largely contributed to the growth of the public rather than private sector in India. Similarly, some specific military assistance was provided India to deal with her defense needs, but the amount of such assistance was small, and in any event after 1963 nonfood aid actually declined. Nor were the various internal political objectives—for example, maintaining Indian democracy—to be achieved through any specific features of the assistance program other than general efforts to improve the economy. Aid donors were not particularly concerned with the domestic political gains to the Indian government of foreign assistance; nor when aid donors subsequently tried to influence the direction of Indian development strategy in the mid-sixties were they particularly concerned with the political consequences of attempting to exercise influence. For the donors, political objectives provided a general rationale for aid, but the criteria for how aid should be used were primarily dictated by economic rather than political objectives.

Foreign Assistance as a Political Resource

Foreign aid is a different kind of resource, both politically and economically, from resources that are raised within a country. The amount and form of foreign aid resources are not, as is the case with taxes, under the control of the recipient. The behavior of the recipient, how the recipient proposes to use the resources, and whether the resources are effectively utilized, all affect the donor's decisions. The donor may also increase or reduce the amount of assistance for reasons that have nothing to do with the behavior of the recipient or with the effectiveness of aid, but that may be determined by the donor's own domestic political constituencies, or by international exigencies. No matter how generous the donor may be at any given time, aid can be reduced or even terminated. As a resource, therefore, aid is unreliable, and never without cost or risk to the recipient. No wonder, then, that recipients of foreign assistance are ambivalent.

For the Indian government, foreign assistance was just such an ambivalent resource. In the beginning foreign assistance made it possible for the Indian government to do what it wanted to do; but later, as we shall see, the problems foreign assistance created for the regime outweighed many of the benefits, to the point where it became a political liability rather than a political resource.

In considering how foreign assistance was used as a political resource, it is useful to consider first how much and in what form foreign aid came. India received $13 billion in net resource transfers between 1951—52 and 1969—70. In per capita terms the amount was small, and as a percentage of India's national income it was also small. But as John Mellor points out, in three respects foreign assistance was substantial: (1) as a proportion of capital formation, it averaged 16 percent per year during this period; (2) as a percentage of total central government expenditures it averaged 18 percent and in some years it made up more than a quarter of total central government expenditures; and (3) as a proportion of India's exports, it averaged 31 percent, and in the Second Five Year Plan it was as high as 36 percent; in the Third Five Year Plan, 39 percent.[26]

As Mellor and others have noted, the very substantial amounts of aid provided by donors to meet India's foreign exchange requirements made the capital-intensive strategy of the Second and Third Five Year plans possible. Mellor argues that aid donors "not only sympathized with the growth strategy, but in many cases may have actually promoted it."[27] The bulk of the aid, he noted, was explicitly earmarked for industrial development rather than agriculture precisely because the donors preferred projects with a large foreign exchange component.

Food aid totaled nearly $5 billion between 1955 and 1975, forming, according to Mellor, from half to three quarters or more of India's annual food imports during this period. Food aid served at least two purposes: it released foreign exchange for the purchase of capital goods, and it provided rupee earnings for the Indian government. Food aid thus not only made it unnecessary for the government to divert its limited foreign exchange from capital goods to food imports, it also reduced the pressure on the government to increase taxes to expand its rupee revenues. In this respect, foreign assistance was a substitute for other resources that were politically more difficult to raise.

Foreign assistance also constituted a kind of endorsement for India's development efforts and development strategy. The annual reports of the World Bank, the International Monetary Fund, the U.S. AID mission and other donors provided important political support. Whatever criticism might have come from India's right wing concerning the heavy emphasis on the development of the public sector, or upon strict government regulation of the private sector, was somewhat mitigated by the generally favorable reports from capitalist sources, especially during the first, second, and third plan periods.

Indeed, in the 1950s and early 1960s India's efforts were held up as a model in international circles: here was a country giving primary attention to internal

---

[26] John W. Mellor, *The New Economics of Growth: A Strategy for India and the Developing World* (Ithaca, New York: Cornell University Press, 1976), p. 220.

[27] Ibid., p. 224.

development rather than external aggrandizement; a government with a comprehensive plan to which Western donors could respond; well-defined, well-structured planning institutions, especially the Planning Commission, with which Western economists could interact and whose documents could be used for demonstrating the country's "absorptive capacity" for assistance; and various model programs, such as the Community Development Program, the National Extension Scheme, new public finance institutions, and agricultural research centers, all of which could provide examples for other developing countries looking for models.

Indians also became experts themselves, skilled not only in development planning, but in dealing with Western agencies and functioning in the complex milieu of international institutions, from the World Bank to the specialized agencies of the United Nations. While the Chinese withdrew (or were excluded) from these international agencies, the Indians moved into central positions. The result was a growing sense among India's intellectuals that their development efforts were globally important, that whatever the defects of specific programs and policies, India had a government that was widely esteemed. Moreover, the careers of individual Indians were also enhanced. Even radical intellectuals—who in other countries turned their energies into revolutionary channels—found a place if not within the Indian planning apparatus, then in the World Bank, the International Monetary Fund, or one of the many UN agencies concerned with development.

Foreign assistance also opened up for Indians a large number of opportunities for education abroad, for trips to international conferences, and for a broader range of contacts between educated Indians and the outside world. Prime Minister Nehru was particularly eager to expand Indian association with the rest of the world, not only with other countries in the West, but with the Soviet bloc and with the newly emerging countries of Asia and Africa. Access to the outside world was also a resource that could be controlled and distributed by government. In the fifties and sixties these various opportunities for trips and study abroad were only marginally controlled by the government of India; though everyone had to obtain a foreign exchange clearance for travel abroad, this was a control that was loosely exercised. But in the years shortly preceding and during the emergency the government passed tighter regulations that made it more difficult for Indian scholars, journalists, politicians, and officials to freely accept invitations for trips abroad without close governmental monitoring.

Even more difficult to measure—and therefore easy to ignore—was the impact of contacts between Indian academics, journalists, administrators, and politicians with Americans and West Europeans. Foreign assistance programs—and here one should include the contributions of American foundations as well as those of foreign governments—contributed to the growth of educational and research institutes and other intellectual centers that tended to generate international contacts. Perhaps it is not too far-fetched to suggest that the fact that many (though by no means all) Americans and West Europeans commended India for her democratic institutions may have played a role in generating pride among Indians about their political institutions. Western involvement in India and the contacts that Indians had with the West probably also tended to make Indians explain and justify their policies and their society to outsiders. Indians cared what the outside world thought[28] —to a far greater extent than, say, the leaders of Indonesia, China, Pakistan, or Nigeria, not to mention the smaller developing countries.

Whether this concern on the part of many educated Indians for the opinions of the outside world was an asset or a liability to the regime is a matter of some un-certainty. That India was held up to standards that it could not meet ("the soft state") may have increased the disaffection of many of India's middle classes; on the other hand, it suggested that they desired to continue the political system even when things were going wrong.

By the mid-sixties it became clear to many Indians and to the donors them-selves that there were features of the Indian development strategy that had led to a decline in the growth rate, and that Western assistance had made it possible for the Indian government to adopt economically unsuccessful policies. For one thing, the emphasis in the development program on heavy industry rather than on agriculture and the concern with import substitution rather than with exports was, at least in the short run, actually increasing India's dependence upon the West rather than leading to increasing self-reliance.

Food assistance provided by the United States under PL 480 and the expecta-tion on the part of Indian planners that if there were a substantial shortfall in agricultural production they could turn to the United States for assistance made it possible for India to pursue a development strategy that gave low priority to agriculture. Indeed, in the mid-seventies, when it became apparent that food was no longer available from the United States in large quantities so that India had to make up its deficits by purchasing foodgrain on the world market at high prices, the Indian government redirected its resources to stimulate agricultural

---

[28] Including the prime minister. The incessant criticism of Mrs. Gandhi during the emer-gency by the British, American, and West German media and by many public figures in the West may have been an element in Mrs. Gandhi's decision to call a national election. Though she denounced Western critics for failing to understand that the emergency was necessary, under Indian conditions, to provide the country with stability and discipline, her frequent interviews with Western reporters to explain and justify her position showed how sensitive she was to what they wrote. In her announcement that elections would be held, she pointedly said that elections would "uphold the fair name of India."

development. In short, U.S. food aid in the fifties and sixties may have been a disincentive to India's economic planners to support agriculture, even though the intent of the donors was to stimulate agricultural growth.

Moreover, the addition of substantial quantities of foodgrain into the Indian market, not only in years of severe shortages but in more normal years as well, tended to keep food prices down, and while this may have been advantageous to the urban population (and therefore politically beneficial to the government), it created a disincentive for farmers to buy the inputs necessary to accelerate agricultural growth. When food prices did rise in 1968 and 1969 Indian farmers invested more in fertilizers, new high-yielding-variety seeds, irrigation facilities, and other agricultural inputs. Might not there have been a rise in agricultural productivity earlier had prices for farmers been more favorable, as they most likely would have been had there been no PL 480?[29]

The availability of foreign exchange from Western donors similarly reduced incentives for developing export industries. The encouragement of import substitution probably raised the cost of India's industrial development, reduced the return on investment in the industrial sector, and discouraged investment in export industries—developments that led to a worsening balance of payments in the mid-sixties and growing dependence upon the West for additional aid to cover the cost of imports. Later, when foreign assistance failed to keep pace with the rising price of imported oil, fertilizers, and food, Indian planners changed their policies to encourage the growth of export industries. But in the interim India's share of world trade drastically declined. According to World Bank estimates, between 1950–51 and 1968–69 the average compound growth of exports in value terms was only 2 percent per annum. Since 1968–69 with growth in the export of sugar, engineering goods, and garments, exports have been increasing by 5 percent per annum. Nonetheless, India's share of world exports in 1973–74 was little more than half of a percent (0.55 percent) while in 1951–52 it was 2 percent.

While it would be unreasonable to attribute the inefficiencies of India's public sector to foreign assistance, the *size* of the public sector is undoubtedly partly the result of foreign assistance. Investment in the public sector was Rs 9.5 billion

---

[29] Baldev Raj Nayar, *The Modernization Imperative and Indian Planning* (Delhi: Vikas Publications, 1972) argues that the neglect of agriculture in the fifties when the share of resources allocated to agriculture declined from 15 percent of public sector outlays in the first plan to 11 percent in the second was deliberate, since the government chose to put its resources elsewhere. He argues that American aid policies actually encouraged India to be negligent in agriculture in order to dispose of its own agricultural surpluses. Moreover, writes Nayar, "by depressing local prices for agricultural products, the surplus resulted in blunting the incentives for farmers to grow more" (p. 183), a position widely shared by Indian and many Western economists.

in 1961; it was up to Rs 50.5 billion a little more than a decade later in 1972. For those who favored the development of the private sector in India through the use of foreign assistance, the growth of the public sector and the restrictions on the expansion of private enterprise demonstrated the inappropriateness of government to government assistance. Many critics also noted the poor performance of the public sector: the generally low return on investments, the high level of administrative inefficiency, and the substantially underutilized capacity of many public sector firms. In an effort to find markets for the underutilized capacity of the public sector (and for many of the inefficient sheltered private firms as well), the Indian government sought and obtained barter agreements with the Soviet bloc. "In external trade," wrote Asoka Mehta, one-time deputy chairman of the Planning Commission, "the more we lean on trade with the wholly planned economies, the greater becomes the danger of condoning inefficiency in our production. When that sheltered relationship ends, as it must, our industries will be ill-equipped to face the hazards of world markets."[30] These criticisms   suggest that the Western donors, without intending to do so, and in fact intending to do just the opposite, supported a policy of expanding an inefficient public sector and thereby caused an increase in India's trade with the Soviet bloc rather than with the economies of the West.

To each of these criticisms there are of course complex defenses, but that is beside the point. The point is that by the mid-sixties the Western donors became increasingly critical of India's development strategy and took measures to change that strategy, with the result that *Western criticism and Western efforts to exercise influence through aid became a liability to the regime.*

A close reexamination of India's economic strategy by the World Bank in 1966 led Western donors to press India to devalue the rupee as part of a larger shift in development strategy, which involved a shift to agriculture, a decline in emphasis on the capital goods sector, and a greater reliance upon the use of market mechanisms for allocating resources.[31] The donors shifted to a new policy of "performance conditioning" which implied, in effect, that future aid to India would be conditional upon an improvement in the performance of the Indian economy. The clash between the donors and the Indian government resulting from these criticisms had these political consequences:

1. The decision to devalue the rupee, as we indicated in our earlier analysis, was interpreted by many Indians as a response to Western pressures (as in-

[30] Asoka Mehta, *India Today* (New Delhi: S. Chand and Co., 1974), p. 63.

[31] For a more detailed analysis of the World Bank study (the so-called Bell Report), see David H. Denoon, "AID—High Politics, Technocracy or Farce?" (Ph.D. diss., Department of Political Science, Massachusetts Institute of Technology, June 1975), Chapter 3.

deed it was), implying that foreign assistance had created such a degree of dependence that foreign governments and institutions now had the power to determine India's domestic development strategies.

2. The devaluation itself, coming on the eve of the third general elections, came too close to the elections for the government to reap any of the long-term benefits; the immediate effect was a further increase in prices, with an attendant decline in urban support for the government.

3. The failure of the donors to increase their assistance after devaluation as promised earlier—a failure explained by the donors as the result of the un-willingness of the Indian government to follow through on its promises to remove controls, which in turn, the Indian government described as the con-sequence of the unwillingness of the donors to increase their aid, led to an embittering of relations between the United States, the World Bank, and the Indian government. While the United States increasingly emphasized the notion of performance conditioning, and in effect the legitimate right of the donor to supervise the economic policies of the recipients, the Indian government rejected such a role as intervention in their internal affairs, and pressed instead for automatic transfers of resources that precluded any such intervention.

The point is that by the late sixties, though the government of India was seek-ing additional assistance, and was bitter about the failure of the Western donors to increase their assistance, many in the government and within the governing party felt that foreign assistance had become a liability.

Foreign assistance can thus be viewed as a political resource in two related respects: (1) it provides additional financial resources, not tied to the tax struc-ture, which enable the government to invest in whatever it sees as economically (and politically) desirable; and (2) it generates support for (or opposition to) the regime itself. It was in this second respect that aid had faltered as a political re-source. Western criticism of India's development strategy, Western pressures (and successes) in influencing some features of that strategy, and the subsequent failure of the Western donors to compensate with increased assistance for the political losses that resulted—all served to make members of the government, the govern-ing party, and the opposition increasingly critical of foreign assistance. When American bilateral assistance ended at the time of India's war with Pakistan over Bangladesh, it simply confirmed the growing recognition by the Indian govern-ment that bilateral aid was inextricably tied to (1) U.S. assessments of India's economic policies and economic performance, and (2) U.S. assessments of its strategic objectives in the South Asia region, and it confirmed that American views on both had changed since the early sixties.

Implications for Policy

The Carter administration has indicated that it is prepared to resume economic assistance to India if the Indian government desires it. For President Carter the offer of aid represents an expression of the commitment he made in his inaugural address to support those countries that shared with the United States "an abiding respect for human rights." The resumption of aid to a country that was once the largest single recipient of American economic assistance would also create the possibility that the United States would expand its share of assistance to the Third World and would come closer to the contributions made by other industrial powers. The question is whether it is in India's interests to re-create a bilateral aid program.

The functions that aid performed in India's internal economic and political development in the 1960s are no longer as salient today. To recapitulate earlier points, aid proved then to be a political resource in the following ways:

1. It made it possible for the government to keep food prices down without heavy drains on foreign exchange, thereby strengthening the political position of the government in the urban sector.
2. It nourished the development of public sector industries, thereby providing opportunities for the growth of an industrial labor force and an urban middle class, and it assured the government of support from the bureaucracy and from those who leaned leftwards.
3. It made possible an import substitution policy that sheltered the private sector, thereby creating a close and dependent relationship between business and bureaucracy.
4. By facilitating the green revolution and, earlier, by expanding the country's irrigated areas, it strengthened the position of the peasant proprietor classes, who provided the government with electoral support from the poorer classes in the countryside subject to their influence or control.

The expansion of exports, the decline in food imports, and the growing volume of remittances from migrants abroad have all contributed to building a substantial foreign exchange surplus in recent years. At the same time several good harvests have created an agricultural surplus of an estimated seventeen million tons of food grain by early 1977. Aid, therefore, is no longer required either to meet the country's food deficit or to provide the foreign exchange for imports needed for a capital intensive industrial development program. "The primary function of aid today is . . . to make up for the insufficiency of domestic savings and provide budgetary support to the government," wrote an editorial writer in *Economic and Political Weekly*. "The forms of aid have changed accordingly, as can be seen from the IDA [International Development Association] loans for agricultural development or the loans to finance current maintenance imports. In that sense, aid has become more, not less, indispensable. Hence the anxiety to ensure that the accumulation of foreign exchange reserves does not jeopardize the prospects of fresh aid."[32]

Foreign assistance—now predominantly from the World Bank—makes it possible for the government to pursue development activities at current levels without having to substantially increase the rate of taxation. As is well known, the least-taxed sector in India, for reasons that are politically apparent, is the peasant proprietor class. In 1975–76, according to the annual report of India's Reserve Bank, collections from land revenue and agricultural income tax together constituted only 6.2 percent of tax receipts of the state governments.[33] The political risks of seeking additional resources from a social class whose support is so essential for the government clearly would be substantial.

The long-term need for resources is certainly likely to increase. In the 1980s India will be feeling the effects of the country's rapid population growth of the 1960s: an accelerated increase in the number of people entering the labor force, increased fragmentation of land holdings, an increase in the size of the agricultural labor force, more rapid urban growth. With these demographically induced changes will come increasing demand for food, growing pressure for urban and rural employment, and even greater strains on the education system. The need to accelerate the rate of investment, to expand economic growth through an expansion of agriculture, and to create more jobs will be even greater than now. How these objectives are achieved will depend upon the kinds of economic policies chosen by India's political leadership in the next few years. Whatever strategy is pursued, the need for resources will grow.

A new influx of resources from outside seems unlikely to come from any source other than the United States. A substantial increase in consortium assistance to India seems unlikely in the absence of American participation. Multilateral assistance to India has been growing in the past decade, but its growth too is highly dependent upon the share of the American contribution. Soviet assistance to India, even during the period of closer Indo-Soviet ties, was never very large, nor were the terms always very generous. The establishment of a bilateral aid program by the United States, no matter how small initially, might provide the instrument for substantial resource transfers as India's needs grow and American attitudes toward the developing countries—and India in particular—change. Moreover, the more American assistance to India is targeted toward assist-

[32] *Economic and Political Weekly* 11 (September 15, 1976), p. 1554.

[33] Ibid., p. 1556.

ing low income groups, the more politically palatable an aid program will be in the United States, especially for a Democratic administration.

How to augment India's resources to accelerate her rate of growth will be a major domestic issue within India and an issue for international agencies and governments committed to reducing the gap between the developed and developing countries. But there are innumerable problems in returning to the bilateral aid programs that existed in the 1950s and 1960s, problems that are at least as great on the Indian side as on the American side.

1. The first is that any bilateral aid program is bound to imply performance conditioning. AID, overseeing congressional committees, and the new media pay detailed attention to India's aid program, especially to India's efforts to assist the lowest income groups. A close scrutiny of India's aid program is bound to result in criticism, not only because of the normal fallibility of any government, but because critics of foreign aid programs—on both the American left and the American right—are bound to seek and find fault with the Indian government's program. The tenuous relationship that currently exists between New Delhi and Washington seems hardly likely to withstand the kind of criticism that would emerge from congressional hearings and media scrutiny.

2. Pressures would soon arise in the United States to use an assistance program as a form of leverage for influencing the domestic or foreign policies of the Indian government. A variety of American interest groups, including sections of the American bureaucracy, would seek to influence Indian policy on such matters as the development and regulation of nuclear power, family planning, the seabed treaty, arms transfers, and trade policies. Even if the administration succeeds in restraining such interests and does not itself seek to exercise leverage, the Indian government is bound to view bilateral aid as an element constraining India's capacity to bargain with the United States.

3. Suspicion of American intentions remains so deep in some Indian circles that the U.S. aid program would be subjected to the kind of scrutiny one ordinarily gives to a threatening power rather than to an assisting friend. Is the United States seeking to make India dependent in order to exercise influence? Is foreign aid a way of pushing the door open for American investors? A vehicle for disposing of American surplus commodities? An instrument for U.S. intelligence? And the cruelest cut of all may be the one with some semblance of truth: that bilateral aid is a way of avoiding politically and economically painful modifications in U.S. trade policy that

would provide Indian exporters with increased access to the American market.[34]

Now that the Indian political process is again open, there is likely to be at least as much criticism of the American assistance program in India as there will be of the Indian development in the United States. Again, the impact of such criticism on Indo-American relations is likely to be substantial.

4. A bilateral U.S. aid program would be politically divisive within India. While some of the Indian criticism of assistance will come from those who are hostile to the United States, much of it will also come from those who see an attack on foreign assistance as a way to undermine the government. The reestablishment of bilateral aid would be seen within India, and so argued by Congress and Communist opponents of the Janata party, as a step away from the policy of self-reliance. And within the governing Janata party—a party that is, after all, a coalition of diverse interests and ideologies—there would be considerable dissatisfaction with the reestablishment of bilateral assistance. Many of the Janata party leaders were themselves critics of Mrs. Gandhi's 1966 decision to devalue the rupee, and many who were members of Mrs. Gandhi's government recall with resentment President Johnson's "short-leash" policy; at a time when India's foreign exchange needs are minimal, they would find it hard to justify the reestablishment of bilateral assistance simply as a response to the need for more domestic resources. Bilateral American aid would thus create severe strains between those who want new resources to accelerate growth and equity programs and the nationalists who prefer self-reliance; and within the left between those who welcome resources for low-end poverty programs and those who have a deep suspicion of American intentions.

5. Many Indians fear that foreign aid could all too easily become a crutch. Foreign exchange through international resource transfers tends to relieve some of the pressure for seeking new export markets. Food assistance eases the pressure for an aggressive program for agricultural expansion. External resources for investment reduce the need for tax reform. Is it unreasonable to assume that a democratic leadership faced with multiple pressures would not view aid as a way of avoiding some politically unpleasant choices?

6. Finally, there is the issue of whether a Third World country with aspirations for global—if not great power—status can tolerate the kind of asymmetrical

---

[34] Multilateral aid is not widely viewed in India as contrary to the policy of self-reliance, presumably because multilateral aid imposes fewer constraints on India's bargaining capacity with individual countries, particularly with the United States.

relationship implied in a bilateral aid program. It is not surprising that neither India nor China has been able to sustain an enduring bilateral aid relationship with either of the two superpowers. In the quest for global status, neither of the two largest developing countries can afford to be dependent—or appear to be dependent—on one of the superpowers for development assistance.

The Indian government would, of course, welcome international aid transfers, but it will seek transfers that would deprive the donor of any control over how that assistance might be used or, if possible, even over the volume of the transfers. For this reason the Indian government is likely to prefer more generous trade arrangements, multilateral assistance, commodity agreements, debt rescheduling, academic and technical exchanges, an international seabed authority whose income would be independent of governmental decisions, and a variety of other international policies and programs from which India, along with other developing countries, might benefit. For those who wish to help India develop, these are instruments politically preferable to an American bilateral aid program.

Comment

Lloyd I. Rudolph

Perhaps the best way to begin comment on Myron Weiner's perceptive and comprehensive attack on bilateral aid is to agree with him. Multilateral aid should continue to be the principal vehicle for the U.S. aid relationship with India because it poses fewer political problems within and between the two countries than does bilateral aid. But is it necessary to forego bilateral aid to safeguard Indo-American relations from the dangers of political disruption and to support optimal economic policies in India? If bilateral aid was the occasion or cause for unnecessary misunderstanding and conflict in the past, must it be so in the future? One way to answer this question is to remark that it is possible to learn from and build on past experience.

The Changing Political Contexts

Since the events of the sixties, when aid accompanied doctrines and practices that alienated Indians and Americans from each other—performance condition, short tether, political pressure to shape up on the Vietnam War on the American side, an obstinate (some would say perverse) propensity to pass judgment, and a deep suspicion of aid as dependency-creating on the Indian side—actors and positions have changed sufficiently to restore dialogue based on the presumption of good will. There are new governments in the United States and India. The Carter and Desai governments' values and objectives and the personal rapport between the two heads of government are much closer than they were under Presidents Johnson and Nixon and Prime Minister Indira Gandhi. Both countries have been to the brink and back: India under the emergency's authoritarian rule, followed by the liberation of the March (and June) 1977 election; America under the threatening shadow of the Vietnam War and Watergate, followed in 1974 by the return to normalcy under the Ford administration and in 1976 by the successful anti-Washington, pro-people campaign of Jimmy Carter. What has been rejected and what has been affirmed in India and America have a large common denominator that has brought the two countries closer together. Authoritarian rule and the imperial presidency were rejected. Modest idealisms—Gandhian, Baptist humanitarian—are once again affirmed. A less aggressive American posture is reciprocated by a less defensive India posture. Jimmy Carter is given more to persuasion than to Johnsonian arm-twisting and Nixonian sabre-rattling. A less Fabian Morarji Desai can be more at ease with American welfare capitalism. A more powerful and less crisis-ridden India can better tolerate foreign dialogue.

The two men who became the symbols of this change have established contact and rapport with each other. Important as it is to avoid the mistakes of the past aid relationship between the U.S. government and the Indian government—and Myron Weiner's paper is eloquent in elaboration of these mistakes—it is even more important to inquire why and how the two countries and the men who lead them now perceive each other and the future.

Learning from the knowledge that past domestic political events provide is not the only experience that has transformed Indo-U.S. relations. Myron Weiner raises serious questions about the kind of economy India built with aid and about the performance of that economy. The assessment of aid and of the consequences that flowed from it must take into account recent changes in Indian economic performance and circumstances. Some of these changes arise from the longer-run effects of earlier investment strategies and policies, some from differing visions of what kind of economy and polity India means to be and become. But before I take issue with some of Myron Weiner's propositions about past economic policy and management and about India's macroeconomic objectives, I want to spell out in a bit more detail the recent convergence of values and interests between the U.S. government under the Carter administration and the Indian government under the Desai government.

Both governments have put a high priority on human rights and disarmament. However difficult it may be to decompose these general objectives and to make them operational in policy terms, the two governments agree that they should be on the agenda and given considerable weight in the inevitable conflict among other, often contradictory, objectives and interests. Disarmament in the Indian Ocean, or at least a freeze on present levels of force and facilities; a commitment by Desai not to pursue nuclear weapons; the elimination, in Morarji Desai's words, of destitution, are more specific even if not operational examples of the shared goals. The evaporation under Mrs. Gandhi's government in the last versions of the Five Year Plan of the commitment to zero aid already established that the Indian frame of mind in 1977 is different from what it was in 1972. The Janata government's view of a new balance in nonalignment, a view more benign in its estimate of American objectives, also suggests rapprochement, although if the Desai or Carter governments are tempted to "overbalance" the relationship, it could become a renewed source of domestic political difficulties on the Indian side. The U.S. Congress's divorce of military from economic aid in recent legislation establishes a salutary separation of developmental and strategic objectives. Aid to India, multilateral and consortium as well as strictly bilateral, takes on new meaning and possibilities in the framework of these shared goals and perceptions.

Longer-run objectives touching American and world security have brought the two governments closer and provide a context for a resumed aid relationship. These objectives, summarized in the phrase *redistribution with growth*, have been frequently articulated by the president of the World Bank and others. They have been designed to preempt not easily specified, but nonetheless likely, disorders and violence in world economic and political relations and require for their realization national and international intervention. India represents an exemplary possibility for approximating these objectives under conditions of freedom.

Post-Vietnam and post-Kissinger America exhibits a revived if chastened interest in democracy abroad. Even though the connections between economic conditions and political regimes, between aid and democracy, are ambiguous and hard to specify, some propositions are plausible. The internal mobilization of resources for growth and redistribution is a difficult task, given low, if increasing, propensities to save. Such mobilization may be easier in the short run under authoritarian regimes. Mrs. Gandhi's government was able, for example, to mobilize dearness (cost of living) allowances as compulsory savings at the expense of an industrial work force that has not experienced an advance in real wages for more than ten years, a program the Desai government did not feel in a position to continue. External transfers, including bilateral aid, clearly ease the political costs that equivalent internal mobilization would incur and are, in this sense, a subsidy to the more open political processes that official American opinion now seems to favor.

The reformulation of detente with the Soviet Union and the less romantic, more realistic approach to post-Mao China adopted by the Carter administration are visible signs that the globalism of Nixon-Kissinger foreign policy is being replaced by a world view that recognizes the strategic importance of "second tier" states for world security. India is also an exemplary second tier state. A rich poor nation and a dominant regional power, its economy is more independent, its political and economic reach and influence are as great, and its military self-sufficiency and capacity are more established than any other Third World and some First and Second World states. The Carter administration's attention to the role of second tier states in the conduct of its strategic and economic diplomacy places India, as a major power at the forefront of second tier states, in a crucial position. In addition then to the central position India occupies in the effort to promote world order through redistributionist intervention, it also occupies a leading position in an emergent strategic diplomacy that attends to how major powers and intraregional relations affect the prospects for peace.

The convergence of goals in the late seventies may not prove any more permanent than the divergence of goals in the late sixties. My point is merely that now and possibly for some years to come, the actors and positions coincide sufficiently to make bilateral aid a plausible instrument.

The Lessons of 1965–67

Myron Weiner quite rightly points out that American and Indian goals with respect to aid can and did diverge widely, with the result that aid became a reminder of differences and a cause of friction rather than a promoter of good relations. Divergence peaked in the extraordinary years 1965 to 1967, when the Bell report, embodying U.S. government as well as World Bank thinking, was used in an attempt to impose a revised economic strategy on a divided and extraordinarily vulnerable Indian government. The 1965–67 period has become paradigmatic not only for Myron Weiner, but also for a good many others in official and academic circles, as a reminder of the dangers that bilateral aid poses for Indo-American relations. Yet there are elements in the events of these years that will not be repeated or that policy can avoid. Lyndon Johnson's heavy-handed political insensitivity need not be a permanent condition in the conduct of American foreign policy. And there is little likelihood of there being another Vietnam War, which diverted American resources from more worthwhile domestic and foreign programs. The special natural disasters and political crises in India that characterized the 1965–67 period are not likely to recur either, although some may at lower levels of intensity and in less lethal combinations. Despite recent congressional efforts to deny assistance or arms to states that violate human rights and nuclear proliferation standards, performance conditioning, with its implications for untoward presidential intervention, has probably had its day too. Insensitivity to the consequences of American policies and pressure for domestic politics in India need not exist as they did under President Johnson, whose remarkable political instincts and skills unfortunately stopped at the water's edge.

I agree with Myron Weiner that the 1966 devaluation of the rupee was a turning point and that it epitomized performance conditioning, a euphemism for foreign intervention in Indian economic policy. But I differ in the interpretation of the events and lessons that accompanied and surrounded devaluation. I would emphasize more heavily than he the special congeries of circumstances surrounding devaluation, and the possibility of a happier outcome if U.S. government and World Bank objectives had been pursued with a better appreciation of the constraints and possibilities that characterized India's politics and economy.

Mrs. Gandhi's political leadership was at stake in the devaluation crisis. She and a small circle of close advisers (Ashok Mehta, C. Subramaniam, L. K. Jha) wanted to adopt most of the policies being recommended by the World Bank and circles in the U.S. government. Neither the U.S. government nor the World Bank properly realized that these congenial voices were a minority among Congress government and party leaders, and that they were extraordinarily vulnerable. Not least among the opponents was Kamaraj Nadar, president of the Congress party, who was moving toward ousting Mrs. Gandhi from the prime ministership. Mrs. Gandhi had only recently become prime minister, less because of her proven abilities and strength within the party than because she was the only means to block Morarji Desai's claims. The decision to devalue came early in her incumbency and in the midst of the aftermath of a less than successful war with Pakistan (September 1965); a very poor monsoon (1965–66), which caused the index of foodgrain production to fall 20 percent in one year, slowing the economy and fueling inflationary pressures; and several extraordinarily delicate and potentially explosive communal crises (Punjabi Suba and anti-cow-slaughter agitation). The devaluation came on the eve of several constraining and impending events, the fourth general election and the next monsoon, both of which could and did further weaken the Congress party and the economy.

The circumstances and timing of devaluation prepared an environment in which only the most skillful political and economic diplomacy could have turned aid to American and Indian advantage. As it happened, such diplomacy was conspicuously absent. The aid relationship went from sour to bitter to nonexistent, not so much because, as Weiner argues, a political resource *deus ex machina*-like became a domestic liability as because the outlook and actions of the Johnson and Nixon administrations, and to a lesser degree, the World Bank, made aid a liability. Agency as much as inevitability was at work: many of the reasons that led the Johnson and Nixon administrations to act in ways that made aid a liability were extraneous to U.S. interests with respect to India, and were gratuitously interventionist.[1]

The U.S. government's insistence that its share of the consortium's $900 million in nonproject aid included the so-called $100 million Humphrey loan, offered by the vice president in January, 1966, when he attended the funeral of Lal Bahadur Shastri, to finance the construction of fertilizer plants, hampered and delayed the World Bank's efforts to conclude negotiations on the $900 million aid package. The Indian government assumed that the $100 million Humphrey loan would be applied against the unallocated aid quota suspended in September, 1965 at the time of the Indo-Pakistan war and that, in any case, being a project

[1] For the larger framework and a more comprehensive justification of these judgments see Lloyd I. Rudolph and Susanne Hoeber Rudolph, *The Coordination of Complexity in South Asia*, Report of the Commission on the Organization of the Government for the Conduct of Foreign Policy, vol. 7, appendix V (Washington, D.C.: Government Printing Office, 1975).

loan, was not to be counted as part of the $900 million in nonproject aid. President Johnson's mounting and increasingly public campaign to decrease the U.S. government's aid burden by embarrassing and intimidating America's European allies into increasing theirs, also slowed the effort to make final the consortium's aid package. The World Bank was not able to announce its intention to supply nonproject consortium aid for six weeks after devaluation and the consortium was not able to meet in order to make the $900 million aid package official until November 7, 1966, six months after rupee devaluation. The difficulties the Indian economy encountered during this period, not least among them the uncertainty and timing of consortium aid, help to explain "the unwillingness of the Indian government to follow through on its promises of decontrols." As Mason and Asher suggest, it was the inability of World Bank president George Woods to sustain the timing and level of aid commitment made in connection with devaluation that greatly enhanced the intensity and effectiveness of the political attack on Indira Gandhi.[2]

Myron Weiner's summary (Chapter 3) of the conjunction of events surrounding rupee devaluation much simplifies both actions and motives among donors and recipients. It was not so much that the consortium donors—of whom the U.S. government was the principal, even the hegemonic, member—did not increase their aid that upset the triangular relationship among the U.S. government, Indian government and World Bank as it was that the World Bank, as the convener of the consortium, was unable, largely because the U.S. government failed to cooperate, to deliver on its commitments with respect to the timing, duration, and amount of aid that was to be made available when India devalued. The figures that Ashok Mehta, India's planning minister and Prime Minister Gandhi's emissary, took to Washington in April 1966 to discuss with World Bank president George Woods were $1.5 billion in immediate consortium aid, of which $1.1 billion was to be nonproject aid, and $1.5 billion in consortium aid for the subsequent four years of India's Fourth Five Year Plan. These expectations were not out of line with levels of consortium aid in the previous two years. They were countered by a World Bank proposal of $900 million, a figure that seemed to reflect feedback from the Johnson administration via World Bank monitoring of the National Advisory Council for International Monetary and Financial Policies (NAC),[3]

---

[2] The membership of the National Advisory Council for International Monetary and Financial Policies included representatives from State, Treasury, AID, and the Federal Reserve Bank. NAC coordinated and guided United States executive directors of various international banks.

[3] See Chester Bowles' account of the announcement by C. Subramanian in December, 1965. *Promises to Keep* (New York: Harper & Row, Harper Colophon, 1971), p. 559.

whose views reflected the president's growing irritation with India's attitude toward the Vietnam War and its poor economic performance. (Nonproject consortium disbursements were $428 million in 1966—67 and $689 million in 1967—68.) President Johnson was particularly interested in the agricultural sector and in India's becoming self-reliant with respect to food, but he was ill-informed about India's earlier efforts and announced programs directed to the same goal.[4] His almost exclusive focus on agricultural self-sufficiency tended to constrain the U.S. government's capacity to respond to India's other economic objectives and needs as expressed in its severe adverse balance of payments and, more important for the longer run, in fourth plan investment. Aid weariness, which began to mount in the mid-sixties, tended to focus on India, particularly on its capital intensive strategy and its socialist public sector. It was expressed in the Clay Committee report of 1963 that helped to scuttle the Kennedy-Galbraith proposal to fund a large public sector steel plant at Bokaro,[5] and in the increasingly severe cuts by Congress of aid budgets. This weariness, it should be noted, did not have a strong basis in poor economic performance. It coincided with years in which indicators of growth in India were still positive, and before the turndown in growth rates that occurred in the decade 1965—76.[6] The conjunction in 1965—66 of aid weariness and, perhaps most decisive, increased presidential attention to Vietnam, which displaced India in the budget year 1966—67 as the single largest recipient of foreign aid, lay behind the U.S. government's reluctance to commit its share ($350 million) to the consortium aid package that George Woods, as president of the World Bank, had agreed to provide when India devalued.[7] Neither the specific (antisocialist) aid weariness of the Clay Committee nor the Vietnam drain are elements of the climate in the late seventies.

The failure of the Indian government to remove controls adequately and in a timely fashion resulted from causes that went beyond the delay occasioned by the World Bank's difficulties in mobilizing consortium aid and beyond bureaucratic vested interest and partisan and ideological opposition to devaluation within and outside government. Food scarcity and the speculative hoarding of commodities

[4] Padma Desai, "The Bokaro Steel Plant: A Study of Soviet Economic Assistance," (Cambridge, Massachusetts: Center for International Studies, MIT, 1971), Mimeo, and J.K. Galbraith, *Ambassador's Journal* (Boston: Houghton Mifflin Co., 1969), p. 544.

[5] See Harinder Shourie, "The Devaluation of the Indian Rupee, 1966: A Decisional Analysis," (M.A. Thesis, Committee on International Relations, University of Chicago, 1977).

[6] Chester Bowles, *Promises to Keep*, p. 515.

[7] Baldev Raj Nayar, *The Modernization Imperative and Indian Planning* (Delhi: Vikas Publications, 1972), p. 483.

and goods that accompanied it exacerbated the inflationary effects of a *de facto* 58 percent devaluation, which drained goods into exports from domestic markets already depleted by an industrial recession and made imports more costly. It was during this period that Lyndon Johnson, in misguided efforts to gain, if not India's support, at least its silence with respect to the Vietnam War and to ensure that India would continue to keep the pressure on the effort for self-reliance, applied the short tether that disrupted India's already frantic effort to plan and administer the allocation of food. Also in this period, India, in the face of major disappointments and uncertainties, abandoned its efforts to formulate a fourth plan. This was the same year that Indira Gandhi, who had only recently become prime minister, was saved by the impending fourth general election from an effort by Congress party president Kamaraj Nadar to oust her from office on the issue of devaluation and misguided dependence. In that election, Congress support as measured in votes fell to its lowest level since independence. When Mrs. Gandhi consented on July 12 in Moscow to a joint Indo-Soviet statement that called for an end to U.S. bombing of North Vietnam and made vague references to the machinations of imperialistic powers she did so, like Lal Bahadur Shastri before her, not only out of a conviction that the U.S. war in Vietnam was misguided and a threat to world peace but also to protect herself from the storm of criticism, particularly from the left of her own party, that followed devaluation and the apparent inability of the World Bank to deliver on aid. The delay and subsequent shortfall in delivering the assistance that could have helped justify the devaluation decision played into the hands of critics who charged her with capitulation to American blandishments and pressure. The prime minister was caught in a whip-saw; her adherence to the Moscow communique "demolished much of the good will which had been created in Washington during her visit there"[8] but failed to assuage the wrath of Kamaraj Nadar, Krishna Menon, T. T. Krishnamachari, and a host of other critics.

The American lack of appreciation of the Indian government's internal economic and political situation in 1965—67, the special economic trauma of two consecutive severe monsoon failures, and the international environment created by Vietnam and the declining years of the cold war are all elements of a crisis that U.S. policy and political will could have confronted with more forethought. As in the case of the disastrous monsoons and the Vietnam War, this combination of events does not have a high probability of recurrence in the next five years.

---

[8] *Overseas Hindustan Times*, December 15, 1977, p. 4. India's exports increased 10.9 percent over the comparable six-month period for 1976—77 while world trade grew by 5.7 percent over the same period.

The Importance of Capital in a Mixed Development Strategy

Myron Weiner argues "that Western assistance had made it possible for the Indian government to adopt economically unsuccessful policies," (Chapter 3). These include excessive emphasis on the capital intensive public sector as well as on industry generally at the expense of agriculture.

This line of argument poses several problems. First, India's development strategy was based on investment mixes, not on an industrial rather than an agricultural emphasis. Agriculture was not neglected to the degree and for the length of time that Weiner implies. Second, the counterfactual exercise attempted below suggests that an initial heavily agricultural strategy would have had costs that have not been adequately attended to by its proponents, and would have created other sorts of problems in today's economic framework. Third, the capital-intensive public sector has not proved to be the white elephant that it appeared to be for some time in the late sixties; it has, in the mid-seventies, given the Indian economy strengths for which the Nehru government explicitly opted. Finally, the consequences of assistance were more positive if one accepts the preceding propositions.

Agriculture and industry were more balanced, and agriculture fared better than the Weiner account suggests. Table 1 compares percentage levels of investment in organized industry with those in agriculture-irrigation from the first through the fifth plan (1951–75). The modest shifts from agriculture to industry may be more a matter of lack of readiness in the first plan period for the necessary level of industrial investment than of downgrading of agriculture in the second plan. Special programs to stimulate agricultural production date from much earlier than the early seventies when the Weiner paper suggests they began. While we are not entitled to regard the extraordinary 1975–76 crop year as a sure indicator of the future, or as a guarantee against serious downswings, it can be taken as evidence of a trend indicating higher general levels of production.[9]

Second, let us pursue for a minute some counterfactual reflections that take seriously an alternative investment scenario on behalf of agriculture in the second and third plans. What if India had pursued an agricultural strategy, that is, if it had within broad limits become "monsoon proof" and able to feed a growing population? Following John Mellor's analysis and prescriptions, this strategy should have translated minimally into an agricultural growth rate averaging 3.5 percent per annum against a population growth rate that declined from 2.5 percent per annum, and production of consumer and wage goods for agricultural buyers rather than of capital goods.[10] It would have meant that in good monsoon years India could export agricultural products; not just its traditional agricultural exports of tea, jute, and sugar, but also foodgrains and commercial crops. It also

Table 1   Pattern of Plan Outlay in the Public Sector

(Millions of rupees)

	First Plan (1951–56) Actuals	Percent a/	Second Plan (1956–61) Actuals	Percent	Third Plan (1961–66) Actuals	Percent	Annual Plans (1966–69) Actuals	Percent	Fourth Plan (1969–74) Original Outlay	Percent	Anticipated	Percent	Fifth Plan (1974–79) Outlay	Percent	Annual Plans (1974–75) Outlay	Percent
Agriculture and Community Development	3,570	15	5,680	12	10,890	13	11,070	17	27,280	17	27,430	17	47,300	13	6,380	13
Major and Medium Irrigation; Flood Control	4,010	17	4,850	10	6,640	8	4,710	7	10,870	7	12,050	7	26,810	7	3,850	8
Power	2,600	11	4,270	9	12,520	15	12,130	19	24,480	15	28,800	18	61,900	17	7,670	16
Village and Small Industries	300	1	2,000	4	2,410	3	1,260	2	2,930	2	2,540	2	89,640	24	690	1
Organized Industry and Minerals	1,490	6	6,900	14	17,260	20	15,100	23	33,370	21	29,830	18	...	...	10,930	23

Transport and Communications	5,570	24	13,850	29	21,120	25	12,220	18	32,370	20	29,830	18	71,150	19	10,270	21
Social Services and Miscellaneous	6,020	26	10,440	22	14,930	17	9,760	15	27,720	17	31,530	19	75,700	20	8,650	18
Total	23,560		48,000		85,770		66,250		159,020		162,010		372,500		48,440	

Sources: Government of India: *Pocket Book of Economic Information, 1973–74*, pp. 294–95. John W. Mellor, *The New Economics of Growth: A Strategy for India and the Developing World* (Ithaca, N.Y.: Cornell University Press, 1976), Appendix Table 2, for first and second plan outlays.

a/ Percentages may not sum to 100 due to rounding.

b/ Includes buffer stocks: Rs. 1,400 million for 1968–69. As against the original plan provision of Rs. 2,550 million, the anticipated outlay on buffer stocks is expected to be Rs. 2,970 million.

c/ Aggregate of irrigation and power.

d/ Aggregate of organized and unorganized industrial sectors.

would have meant importing capital equipment and a large range of industrial middle range goods such as steel, purchases that would presumably be financed by primary product exports. In the time frame of 1975–77, when world commodity prices (including food prices) have been depressed, this strategy could have entailed high costs and led to greatly increased needs for external assistance.

On the other hand, the chosen emphasis has produced, under recent short-run conditions, a much more positive picture than Myron Weiner suggests. India's food surplus of more than 20 million tons in storage with a third good monsoon in prospect, its remarkable, indeed embarrassing, balance of payments surplus (now over $4 billion), buoyant exports and positive trade balances, and tax revenues as a percent of national income of 18.9 percent—all raise serious doubts at least for the present and the immediate future about whether the costs of India's development strategy were indeed as high as Myron Weiner suggests.

Third, from the perspective of the past three years it seems doubtful whether India's economy would be better placed today if U.S. aid had not been used to build the public sector, which Weiner depicts as a socialist white elephant whose care and feeding has kept India dependent on aid for food and foreign exchange and which has exacerbated rather than eased unemployment. This characterization, with the possible exception of the unemployment problem, does not square with India's present economic circumstances nor with the mixed investment strategy that may account for them. In the last few years, most public sector firms have produced up to, and sometimes above, rated capacity, supplied appreciable earnings to public savings, and contributed to a significant, if sometimes subsidized, component in improved export performance.

Most significant, the mixed strategy, including its capital-intensive component, is producing the kind of economy that the Indian political classes of the fifties explicitly chose, one that is relatively independent and capable of reproducing itself. The choices of the fifties gave considerable weight to autonomy with respect to investment goods, those of the sixties to military security.

Finally, Weiner attributes India's alleged failure to produce enough food not only to the strategy pursued by India's planners, but also to the availability of PL 480 food aid (Chapter 3). This view ignores the principal reason for Nehru's decision to use it. Nehru's decision to industrialize was a Soviet-style choice, but one that he thought could be pursued without Soviet-style repressive means to extract the surplus required. Like aid to alleviate balance of payment problems, PL 480 food aid helped make the strategy viable. It subsidized food for the urban consumer while industrial investment progressed.

Ironically, there are supporters of Nehru's industrial strategy who are critics of PL 480 food aid. They condemn it, not because it slowed or blocked the growth of agricultural production, but because it was a form of dependence imposed on India for the benefit of American agricultural producers whose surpluses had to be disposed of.[11]One cannot easily take this position if one accepts Nehru's choice of industrialization under conditions of freedom and democracy. Food aid proved to be an essential element in this combination. The fact that American agricultural producers also benefited merely established what is often the case in human affairs, that actors with differing interests or objectives can engage in exchange that is mutually beneficial.

Dependence and Aid

Finally, the Weiner paper argues that aid has increased Indian dependence: "The emphasis in the development program on heavy industry rather than on agriculture and the concern with import substitution rather than with exports was, at least in the short run, actually increasing self-reliance," (Chapter 3). There are some initial problems about the factual basis of this assertion. Up to the time of the oil price increases, when aid levels jumped substantially, levels of aid to India appear to have fluctuated or declined rather than described a rising curve. More particularly, the level of aid that may be ascribed to food deficits declined as often as it rose, depending on annual needs. There was no PL 480 food after 1971–72, and India has paid in recent years for its food. In 1972–73, just before the oil price hike, India achieved a favorable balance of payments. By 1975–76 and 1976–77, India's balance of payments was again positive, and its balance of trade was surplus in 1976–77 and the first six months of 1977–78.[12] These measures hardly indicate dependence.

But the passage raises some more fundamental problems about the meaning and existence of dependence. Dependence as this passage has used the term refers to a shortage of foreign exchange that induces a state to seek and rely on foreign aid donors to make up balance of payments deficits. Aid makes it possible to pay for imports of investment and industrial goods and, particularly important for Myron Weiner's case, for food. But India's own vision of what constitutes dependency, as well as a wider conception, would give a higher rank to the issues of trade relations, foreign investment, and the requirements of military security. And here the picture leads to different, even more positive conclusions. The chapters in this volume by Mellor and Ezekiel document a remarkable diversification both of trading partners for imports and exports and in the products bought and, more important, sold. These changes constitute a decline in dependence in the Hobsonian terms that have mattered to India for twenty-five years.

India also places a higher value than would many who are concerned about the Indian economy on the relatively low proportion of foreign investment to total investment and on the policies that ensure Indian control of economic policy, management, and the disposition of earnings. India has rather explicitly chosen not to emulate Brazil or South Korea, where foreign savings play a very large part in development strategy, and it has done so for political reasons. India was among the first nonaligned powers and remains one even after the passing of polarity. Because it eschews pacts and military alliances—although it has allowed itself some leaning—it has had to purchase the weapons and military equipment that it needs. Again, policy analysts may differ on the wisdom of these policies, but it is difficult to contest that they contribute to independence.

Finally, as Table 2 makes clear, India receives aid from a wide variety of sources, predominantly multilateral, but including states and groups of states in the First, Second, and Fourth Worlds that are characterized by a variety of ideological orientations and types of economies. Because the United States is the single largest contributor to the World Bank and other multilateral lending institutions, and because India is the single largest recipient of multilateral aid, the United States plays a larger, albeit more indirect, part in India's aid relations with the world than it does with respect to its trade, investment, or security relations.

Even so, it would be going too far to find in this constellation of aid relations grounds for arguing that India was dependent on the United States for aid. The Indian government and Indian policy intellectuals no longer talk or write about achieving zero aid, but this does not mean a return to the days when direct U.S. aid was a major, even the principal, source of public savings for planned investment.

Concluding Remark

Myron Weiner's depiction of bilateral aid to India has something in common with Marley's ghost. Marley's ghost, it will be remembered, terrified Scrooge by showing him the horrors of his past life. The ghost of bilateral aid similarly shows us the difficulties of past aid efforts, difficulties that are probably less horrendous than those of Scrooge's former life. Dickens used Marley's ghost to reform Scrooge. The chastened merchant resolved to get along with his fellow human beings, particularly his associates, family, and friends. Like Scrooge, the U.S. government has already learned from its past misadventures, and has turned increasingly to multilateral aid. But the political and economic calculations and performance conditioning invoked by the ghost of aid past are eliminated or reformulated; why cannot new-style bilateral aid survive too? The bilateral aid that Britain and Germany, for example, now use shares the positive features of multilateral aid—that is, long terms, nominal interest, untied loans that promote economic growth and equity—and also facilitates access and communication between their governments and the governments of the states that are its recipients.

Myron Weiner has rattled the ghost of old-style bilateral aid not to teach the U.S. government how to avoid its mistakes, but to lay it to rest. It seems equally plausible that the U.S. government should learn from the ghost of aid past how to use new-style bilateral aid to serve its own and India's purposes.

Table 2   External Assistance to India by Source

(Millions of rupees)

	Up to End of Third Plan	Percent	1967–68	Percent	1969–70	Percent	1971–72	Percent	1973–74	Percent	1974–75	Percent
IBRD and IDA	7,246	13	300	4	1,297	20	3,795	40	4,907	42	7,113	43
United States	29,305	51	4,487	62	2,222	35	1,672	17	229	2	1,402	8
Other Consortium Countries	13,934	24	2,204	31	2,757	43	4,162	43	5,456	48	5,669	34
Eastern European Countries and USSR	6,103	11	121	2	…	…	…	…	800	7	0	…
Others	529	1	76	1	67	1	23	…	214	2	2,528	15
of which: (OPEC)	…	…	…	…	…	…	…	…	…	…	(1,840)	(11)
(EEC)	…	…	…	…	…	…	…	…	…	…	(660)	(4)
Total	57,117	100	7,188	100	6,343	99	9,652	100	11,706	101	16,712	100

Source: Government of India, *Economic Survey, 1975–76*, pp. 111–13.

IV

The Indian Economy: Objectives, Performance and Prospects

John W. Mellor

The pace of Indian economic development in the postindependence period has been impressive, compared not only with its own colonial period, but also with other low-income countries. In many respects, growth has been similar to that of the People's Republic of China, which faces problems of similar complexity and diversity. A common failure to recognize the magnitude of India's accomplishment has led to misunderstanding of objectives, underestimation of the potential for future achievement, and lost opportunity to understand development processes in Third World countries.

In the last five decades of the colonial period, food grain production in British India increased only 0.1 percent per year.[1] Dependence on imports increased and per capita consumption declined.[2] During the First and Second Five Year Plans (1951 to 1961), the growth rate for foodgrain production shot up to 3.1 percent per year (2.8 percent on a weather-adjusted basis), while population grew at a 1.9 percent rate. By the late 1960s, the growth rate had accelerated to 3.3 percent as emphasis shifted from the land and labor regimes of a traditional society to modern techniques based on high-yielding varieties, improved practices, and inorganic fertilizer.[3]

Industrial growth has, of course, been even more rapid. India now ranks thirteenth in industrial output and is projected to move to eighth over the next two decades. India's steel and machinery industries also rank thirteenth, while the

---

[1] Blyn, George, *Agricultural Trends in India, 1891–1947: Output, Availability, and Productivity* (Philadelphia: University of Pennsylvania Press, 1966), p. 96.

[2] Ibid., pp. 334, 337; John W. Mellor, *The New Economics of Growth: A Strategy for India and the Developing World* (Ithaca, N.Y.: Cornell University Press, 1976).

[3] For a full discussion of the data and the causal forces, see: John W. Mellor, *The New Economics of Growth: A Strategy for India and the Developing World* (Ithaca, N.Y.: Cornell University Press, 1976), pp. 48–75, and John W. Mellor *et al, Developing Rural India: Plan and Practice* (Ithaca, N.Y.: Cornell University Press, 1968).

range of capital and consumer goods produced has broadened dramatically, offering unusual flexibility for future growth.

Most important, there has been a large increase in the capacity to train technical, scientific, and administrative personnel, as well as massive expansion of the institutional infrastructure essential to use these personnel effectively. India's university enrollment, only 0.3 million in 1951, reached 1.7 million in 1968, and is now over 4 million.[4]

The agriculture of Punjab, initially one of the more prosperous states in India, has grown more rapidly than that of Taiwan, which is noted for its effective use of agricultural growth to provide the foundation for that country's impressive postwar economic development.[5] Although the Punjab is one of India's smaller states, its population of 16 million is the same as Taiwan's. Punjab started with lower income and a more rural economy. Although the Punjab's overall rate of economic growth was slower than Taiwan's (for technical reasons agriculture is rarely able to grow as rapidly as a vigorous industrial sector), the lower initial stage of development makes the Punjab record all the more impressive. The southern state of Tamil Nadu, which is larger and has a more diverse resource base, also has had rapid growth, only moderately slower than Punjab. Thus, the record for those Indian states with favorable initial conditions compares favorably with that of similarly situated small countries.

China is the only comparably large and diverse country at a similar stage of development. India's political system does not allow the abrogation of property rights and radical redistribution of income, which offer the only means to immediately end poverty in a low-income country. Thus, the similarity of the growth records of the two countries suggests that so far the main trade-off between the two political systems has been broad income distribution and poverty alleviation on the one hand, and a more pluralistic, open society on the other.

India's foodgrain production trend has been some 30 percent faster than China's and has gradually accelerated over time. Industrial growth in the two countries has been suprisingly similar: 6.7 percent for China and 6.1 percent for India. China has boosted its large-scale heavy-industry sector (e.g., steel) considerably more rapidly than India, as would be expected of a centrally planned and organized nation. The overall growth rates have been within half a percent of each other, with the edge to India.[6]

---

[4] Government of India, Planning Commission, *Draft Fifth Five Year Plan,* vol. 2, p. 198.

[5] See: Punjab, Economic and Social Organization, *Statistical Abstract of Punjab, 1974,* and Economic Planning Council Republic of China, *Taiwan Statistical Data Book, 1975.*

[6] Comparisons with China are difficult because of a paucity of data and because China's

It is still early to determine whether India's more open and pluralistic approach to education and science provides a better base for future growth. The number of highly trained people has grown more rapidly in India than in China, especially in the 1960s and 1970s.[7] India also has a much larger number of foreign-trained technicians.

Given the impressive record of the Indian economy, the widespread criticism is surprising. The tendency can be explained in part by the large absolute inefficiencies in any growth process: as with engineering and biological processes, only a small fraction of the calculable development potential can be achieved.

Like the People's Republic of China and other countries with low incomes, India cannot yet match the growth rates of countries with more broadly based education and higher per capita income. Until the requisite base of trained people and higher income is built, growth will be slow even though the effort may be large. As that base is built, growth may accelerate, sometimes suddenly and unexpectedly, as it did in Taiwan and South Korea in the early 1960s.[8]

Disenchantment with Indian development also arises from conflicting objectives. Progress on any one objective is impeded by the effort required by others.

Failure to comprehend the extraordinarily low base from which India's development began is another source of disappointment. In 1950, average per capita income was $82 in 1973 dollars. The diets of more than 40 percent of the population had inadequate calories for an active life. Food production had for decades been growing at a much lower rate than population. Ninety percent of adults were illiterate and only 1 percent of the population were graduates of colleges and universities. 80 percent of the population resided in rural areas. In sum, India had an extraordinarily poor base from which to increase rates of saving and investment, train personnel, and develop the broad institutional base essential to high growth rates.

Annual foreign aid to India averaged only $1.50 per capita from 1951 to

accounting systems are quite different from those of other countries. Further, in China faster growing subsectors of industry are more fully reported than the whole sector. For a careful comparative analysis with detailed and correct adjustments of accounts and the basis for the preceding discussion, see Subramanian Swamy, *Economic Growth in China and India 1952–70: A Comparative Appraisal* (Chicago: University of Chicago Press, 1973), pp. 11, 45, and 63.

[7] See: India, Office of the Registrar General, *Census of India, 1972, Series 1 India.* Economic Characteristics of the Population (Selected Tables), pp. 76–79; and Leo A. Orleans, "China's Science and Technology" in *People's Republic of China: An Assessment of the Economy*, U.S. Congress, Joint Economic Committee, 1972.

[8] World Bank, *World Tables, 1976* (Baltimore: Johns Hopkins University Press, 1976).

1970.[9] However, the total of $14 billion for 1951 to 1974 appeared large in absolute terms, which led to inflated expectations.[10] When these failed to materialize, critics usually blamed administrative inefficiency and corruption. Pessimism about India's economic performance has been enhanced by the international political factors, discussed in Chapter 1 and which are associated with the decline in foreign assistance to India in the late 1960s. However, many of these factors are now changing, creating a favorable environment for reexamination of India's economic performance.

Finally the prolonged period of economic stagnation from 1965 to 1975 supported pessimism about Indian development. The reasons for the stagnation, the basis for changing the growth strategy, the prospects for the evolution of a new strategy and potentials for return to accelerated growth are discussed below, as are requisites for accelerated growth for the next two decades and the probabilities of such acceleration.

Strategy, Structure, and Objectives

The great debate over strategy for India's development occurred in the 1950s. It focused on P. C. Mahalanobis's grand design for the Second Five Year Plan. The debate concerned the primacy of large-scale heavy industry relative to agriculture and the effect of this strategy on the rate of economic growth. Side discussion dealt with the implications to the poor, timing of the benefits to them, and means of mitigating poverty until growth was achieved.

The alternative strategies differed greatly in their potential effect on what was to be produced and who was to produce it; on the role of the central government; on the distribution of national power between central, state, and local governments and among socioeconomic classes; and on India's independence in international affairs. The Mahalanobis strategy was chosen in effect primarily because of its potential contribution to national unification and global power.

The theory behind the Mahalanobis plan was elegantly simple, internally consistent, and particularly suitable to a large country presumed to have poor prospects for growth in agriculture and in exports.[11] Consistent with widely accepted economic theory, growth was seen as coming from an increased supply of capital

[9] John W. Mellor, *The New Economics of Growth*, p. 218.

[10] Ibid., p. 219.

[11] The most comprehensive statements of the intellectual foundations of the Second Plan are to found in P.C. Mahalanobis, "Some Observations on the Process of Growth in National Income," *Sankhya* 12 (September, 1953), 4:307–12, and idem, "The Approach of Operational Research to Planning in India," *Sankhya* 16 (December 1955), 1 and 2: 3–130.

goods. The faster the capital stock grew, the faster the economy's growth. Although labor was recognized as an important factor, high levels of underemployment were seen as confirmation that labor could be mobilized only if more capital were available.

In the Mahalanobis approach, growth was to be accelerated by allocating existing productive resources directly to the production of capital goods. The more resources so allocated, the faster productive capacity would grow and the greater would be the future capacity to produce consumer goods. It was recognized that poverty and welfare considerations would limit the proportion of the economy's resources that could initially be allocated to production of capital goods. However, the increase in output from the initial allocation of resources to capital goods would largely be saved and reinvested in more capital goods production. Over time, an increasing proportion of national output would be saved and invested, and the rate of growth would accelerate. This latter point was an important feature of the theory. Growth would accelerate rapidly *if* the resources invested in capital goods production were productively used.

In this theory, growth initially conflicts with both employment and income of the poor. Employment requires wage payments, which add to consumption and divert resources from producing capital goods. Similarly, investing scarce resources in agriculture, a consumer goods sector, detracts from investment in capital goods and hence from long-term growth. It is these latter characteristics that so limit this strategy's benefits to the poor in the short run.

Mahalanobis's concept was related to the economic growth theory developed for Western high-income countries by Roy Harrod and Evsey Domar, and by G. S. Feldman for the autarkical growth strategy of the Soviet Union.[12] These theories dominated Western economic thought as well as operation of national and international aid programs from the late 1950s into the 1970s.

Opponents of the Second Five Year Plan strategy emphasized its failure to mobilize labor, the inefficiencies of centralized administration, the inadequate efforts to develop private potentials to save and to manage, and the neglect of agriculture.[13] In particular, they emphasized that without vigorous growth in agri-

[12] A comparative analysis of the Mahalanobis, Harrod-Domar and dualistic models and a statement of the conditions necessary for an alternative model, providing a dynamic place for agriculture and employment, are given in Mellor, "Models of Economic Growth and Land-Augmenting Technological Change in Foodgrain Production," in *Agricultural Policy in Developing Countries*, ed. Nural Islam (London: Macmillan Co., 1974), pp. 3—30.

[13] See: C.N. Vakil and P.R. Brahmanand, *Planning for an Expanding Economy* (Bombay: Vora, 1956); B.R. Shenoy, *Indian Planning and Economic Development* (Bombay: Asia Publishing House, 1963); and Peter Thomas Bauer, *Indian Economic Policy and Development* (London: Allen and Unwin, 1961).

culture, a deficiency of wage goods, evidenced by rising prices of food, would impede and finally halt the growth process. There was a related concern for the short-run prospects for the poor.

Proponents of the heavy-industry strategy recognized that it would result in low employment and few resources allocated to agriculture. These needs were to be met by policies for agricultural and cottage-industry development parallel to but not an integral part of the strategy of growth. Labor was to be mobilized for these purposes. Its efficiency was to be increased through community development and other programs that relied chiefly on exhortation, rationalization, and organization. Critics argued that these measures were inefficient and would do little for the poor. The critics proved to be correct. Proponents of the Second Five Year Plan strategy also presumed that the government would be able to contain growth in demand, particularly from higher-income people. The opponents noted that the latter expectation was particularly unrealistic given the political objectives and conditions.

The relatively unsuccessful Indian strategy for meeting the needs of the poor in the 1950s is also similar to the development fashions of the 1970s. The current emphasis on appropriate technology, basic human needs and local participation is, in effect, an attempt to meet the employment and consumption needs of the poor without radical redistribution of assets and income and with little use of scarce foreign exchange and capital. In the Second Five Year Plan strategy those resources were to be left for large-scale industrial development; with the basic human needs strategy, the demand for foreign assistance is to be reduced.

The People's Republic of China also emphasized development of large-scale heavy industry.[14] Both nations attempted to contain the demand for resources in agriculture and for consumer goods generally. But in contrast to India, China was able to provide basic consumption needs for the lower-income people by a radical redistribution of assets and income. Thus India was more likely to be forced off its strategy if the promised rise in income was delayed.

Critics of the Second Five Year Plan were correct about the outcome and the reason for it. Large-scale heavy industry grew much more slowly than had been anticipated. Consequently, and consistent with the theory, savings and investment rates rose only slowly after the initial sharp rise in the 1950s. Agriculture performed in an undistinguished manner, employment grew only slowly, and the lot of the poor remained largely unimproved.

The predictability of these shortcomings emphasizes that political objectives determined the choice of development strategy and the relative sectoral emphases.

---

[14] Government of India, Ministry of Food and Agriculture, *Report of the Indian Delegation to China on Agricultural Planning and Techniques*, July–August 1956, pp. 40–41.

The Second Five Year Plan strategy helped meet two objectives particularly important to India's earlier leadership. It helped unify the nation through centralization of power and authority, and it built the economic structure essential to eventually achieving major power status. The chosen growth strategy alone could not meet a third objective of rapidly reducing poverty.

In the first decades of independence, the most crucial political objective was binding and annealing the nation. The seeds of division, nurtured during the colonial period, could well have grown rapidly. The effort, led by Sardar Patel, to bring the princely states into the Indian Union required major government attention at least through the merger of Hyderabad in 1949. As late as 1960 Selig Harrison could still write of the possible and even likely division of the Indian polity into separate countries.[15] For India's central leadership, preventing such division transcended all economic concerns that did not support that objective.

The Mahalanobis strategy was central planning at its ultimate. It attracted foreign assistance to the national government, which increased its ability to allocate resources without incurring the political debit that would have resulted from raising those resources domestically. The steel mills, heavy machinery, and large-scale dams gave a positive image to the strategy. Critics of the heavy-industry strategy correctly emphasized the inefficiencies of centralized planning, but they were criticizing what was perhaps most politically important for those times. Thus, K. Santhanam at the end of India's Second Five Year Plan wrote that "planning has superseded the Federation and our country is functioning almost like a unitary system in many respects,"[16] and Krishnaswami described the harmony of political centralization with the style of Indian planning:

> The combination of circumstances—the bias in favor of the Center, the extra-Constitutional influence exercised by the organization and functioning of the Congress Party, the setting up the Planning Commission and the enveloping process of planning—has tended to bring about a degree of centralization far beyond what was dreamt of even by the makers of the Constitution.[17]

The economic foundation of international power derives from the size of the military-industrial complex and its ability to absorb the loss of military industrial imports; the extent to which control of consumption and domestic production

---

[15] Selig Harrison, *India: The Most Dangerious Decades* (Princeton, N.J.: Princeton University Press, 1960).

[16] K. Santhanam, *Union-State Relations in India* (London: Asia Publishing House, 1960), p. 56.

[17] A. Krishnaswami, *The Indian Union and the States* (Oxford: Pergamon Press, 1964), p. 23.

can offset lost access to imported food; and the extent to which trade relationships minimize dependence on major powers and build dependence of lesser powers. Obviously, there are significant tradeoffs within these categories.

The Second Five Year Plan strategy to build a modern heavy-industry sector was intended to minimize Indian dependence on industrial imports. The planning model sought self-sufficiency for the products, a complex input-output matrix depicted as essential to the economy. Over time this industrial emphasis provided India with increasing staying power in case of loss of imports. This was clearly shown by India's increasingly dominant position after each of the three wars with Pakistan. By the 1970s India was substantially self-sufficient in most elements of ground warfare and was making progress on self-sufficiency for its navy.

Although industry was emphasized over agriculture, there was little increase in dependence on food imports as a result of the Second Five Year Plan strategy. Food imports continue to be influenced largely by weather: imports have been high in years of poor weather and low in good years. The strategy provided for relatively little increase in demand for food as employment and incomes of the poor would rise only slightly. A strategy that emphasized agriculture, food production, employment, and increased welfare of the poor, on the other hand, might well have resulted in a commitment to poverty abatement that would have raised effective demand even more than supply and required greater imports, particularly in poor crop years.

The trade implications of the Mahalanobis self-sufficiency strategy are complex. The planning models specified direct and indirect requirements of goods, which in turn determined industrial development and expansion needs. The strategy turned India away from the export to Western markets of consumer goods such as textiles, shoes and electronics. India's share of the textile exports of the less developed countries dropped from 38 percent in 1953 to 7 percent in 1970.[18] Concurrently, the strategy generated modest surpluses of a number of capital-intensive products, including steel, which were exported. In addition, the emphasis on capital goods production introduced India to a number of relatively labor-intensive products, such as machine tools, for which there were important export potentials. For example, exports of engineering goods expanded eightfold (in real terms) between 1960 and 1973.[19]

Failure to reduce poverty was the most striking deficiency of India's strategy. Nevertheless, socialist India has continued to pay lip service to reduction of

[18] John W. Mellor, *The New Economics of Growth,* p. 209.

[19] Reserve Bank of India, *RBI Bulletin,* September 1974, p. 1844.

income inequalities and elimination of extreme poverty. The First Five Year Plan stated:

> The central objective of planning in India at the present stage is to initiate a process of development which will raise living standards and open out to the people new opportunities for a richer and more varied life. Economic planning has to be viewed as an integral part of a wider process aiming not merely at the development of resources in a narrow technical sense, but at the development of human faculties and the building up of an institutional framework adequate to the needs and aspirations of the people.[20]

The Second Five Year Plan stated:

> The pattern of development and the structure of socioeconomic relations must be so planned that they result not only in appreciable increases in national income and employment, but also in greater equality in income and wealth. The benefits of economic development must accrue more and more to the relatively less privileged classes of society, and there should be progressive reduction of the concentrations of income, wealth and economic power.[21]

Similarly, the Third Five Year Plan sought "to establish greater equality of opportunity and bring about reduction in (social and economic) disparities." [22]

By the 1970s it was abundantly clear that these equity objectives were not being achieved. Indeed, the very nature of the plans and the associated strategy were inimical to the fulfillment of these goals. Three broad alternatives were available for dealing with poverty. The first, radical redistribution of assets and income as in the People's Republic of China, was rejected on political grounds. Indeed, one of the major purposes of early Western aid to India was to reduce the likelihood of India's making radical changes in its political system to meet the needs of the poor through redistribution.[23]

Second, India could have chosen a strategy of growth with more emphasis on agriculture and light industry and less on large-scale heavy industry. India now appears to be turning to this strategy. However, it would have been less effective in meeting the other objectives, particularly in the first decades of independence. In addition, as discussed below, it is doubtful whether the knowledge and institutional structure of the 1950s were adequate for success of the second strategy.

The third alternative, complementing the heavy-industry strategy with approaches to cottage industry and agriculture that used few resources, was

---

[20] Government of India, Planning Commission, *First Five Year Plan*, p. 7.

[21] Government of India, Planning Commission, *Second Five Year Plan*, p. 22.

[22] Government of India, Planning Commission, *Third Five Year Plan*, p. 48.

[23] See Weiner's discussion in Chapters II and III.

attempted to some extent under the Second Five Year Plan. It failed, essentially for underlying technical reasons, and consequent inefficient use of resources and high costs, that may have been difficult to understand at the time. Growth that was much slower than expected left little basis for improving welfare of the poor.

The failure to raise the incomes of the poor resulted in their continued alienation from the economic system. While the chosen strategy probably was effective in binding disparate geographic regions of the nation together it did not harmonize the interests of the different economic classes. This damaged India's image in Western countries which are not enamored of growing industrial power in Third World nations and tend to judge economic progress in the Third World largely in terms of poverty alleviation. The question for the future is whether India can formulate a development strategy that improves the lot of the poor and also adequately serves other national and international political needs.

The Initial Conditions

India's economy at independence was characterized by pervasive and intense poverty; an agricultural sector that accounted for half of gross national product, but whose food production had been stagnant for decades at extremely low levels of productivity; a heavy-industry sector that was small, but still larger than that of almost any other country recently freed from colonial rule; an export trade dominated by commodities with very poor growth prospects; a large transport system well designed for colonial control but lacking the feeder lines necessary for broad-based growth; and an administrative structure well designed for centralized rule, but staffed with personnel lacking the training, experience, and depth for broad-based development effort. For the long run, the pluses were the size of the country, its natural resource base, and the substantial numbers of highly trained intellectuals. Each of these advantages would at times appear to be a disadvantage.

India's per capita income in 1950, four years after independence, was approximately $82 in 1973 dollars.[24] That compared with $127 for the Philippines, $210 for Taiwan, $220 for Iran, and $309 for Brazil.[25]

The proportion of the population in absolute poverty—defined as those who receive fewer than the minimum calories needed for a normal level of energy—has not changed significantly. At present some 40 percent of the population, over

[24] U.S. Agency for International Development, Bureau for Program and Policy Coordination, *Gross National Product, Trends by Region and Country 1950–1974.*

[25] Ibid.

240 million people, are in this category.[26] The grinding poverty in India today that contributes so much to an image of impoverishment is neither worse nor better than it was at independence. That is not to say that the quality of life has remained unchanged. Infant mortality has declined from approximately 183 per thousand in 1951 to 140 in 1977; life expectancy has increased from 32 to 50 years; the literacy rate has increased from 17 to 30 percent; and the proportion of children ages 6 to 11 in primary school has nearly doubled.[27] These improvements may not have reached the poorest, but a much larger proportion of the population is receiving health and education benefits analogous to those that were received by only a small elite before independence.

India is notable, even by Asian standards, for the large proportion of its total population that is landless labor. They make up 20 to 30 percent of the population and are the core of the poverty problem.[28]

When the West industrialized, labor was released from agriculture gradually. The growing industrial sector was generally able to absorb that labor, the presence of which encouraged industrial expansion. On some occasions, however, labor was released too rapidly, creating problems of instability that inhibited the industrial growth rate. In the post-colonial period India has faced a particularly intractable problem in its vast initial levels of landless poor and a consequent incapacity to absorb them.

In India, colonialism contributed to law and order, civil tranquility, improved public health services, reduced death rates and increased population growth. Agricultural output on the highly productive alluvial soils of much of India was sufficient to support a much larger population than could be put productively to work on the land.[29] Concurrently, the colonial regime discouraged the growth and development of modern industry and flooded the Indian market with low-cost, attractive consumer goods which depressed indigenous industry. As a result, India's potential to absorb its own population in either traditional or modern industry was at best small. Under such circumstances, it was inevitable that fragmentation of land would occur and a rural landless class would grow rapidly.

[26] V. M. Dandekar and Nilakantha Rath, "Poverty in India," *Economic and Political Weekly* 6 (January 1971), 1:29–30.

[27] *Draft Fifth Five Year Plan*, vol. 2, p. 233.

[28] John W. Mellor, *The New Economics of Growth*, pp. 76–77, 297.

[29] John W. Mellor and Robert D. Stevens, "The Average and Marginal Product of Farm Labor in Underdeveloped Economics," *Journal of Farm Economics* (August, 1956), pp. 780–91.

The British administrative system of tax farming reinforced these tendencies. The consequent rapid growth of a difficult-to-absorb landless class may well have been the worst, most destabilizing legacy of colonialism.

These problems were further exacerbated by the increased elitism of education. The elitist Hindu Brahmanic and the Moslem Maktab traditions in education, which have deep roots in Indian history, were reinforced by British influence. The local, indigenous educational system reached only a select few. The British emphasis on the establishment of quality institutions, even at the primary level, actually reduced the number of children completing elementary school in 1901 and 1902 below that of previous decades in the 19th century.[30] This emphasis on high-quality education for a select few limited the spread of education among the landless and limited their potential for adjusting to nonagricultural employment.

The poverty and instability of the massive landless labor class provide much of the basis for pessimism about the prospects for development in India. They also raise basic questions about development strategy. Should India choose a relatively repressive system of government to keep these impoverished masses under control while developing a broad foundation of heavy industry that may eventually provide the basis for explosive growth in the consumer goods industries and the consequent rapid absorption of the landless poor? Or should there be a radical redistribution of assets, as in China, to provide the basic minimum for these masses, thereby alleviating discontent and facilitating development of a capital-intensive base of industrial growth? Or should India adopt, as Taiwan did, a much more rapid, employment-oriented pattern of development based on agriculture, light industry and foreign trade, so that these impoverished masses may be absorbed sufficiently rapidly to avoid political troubles? In these decisions, the political and economic realities of the huge landless class are dominant considerations. The third option is perhaps the most attractive, but it is also the most fraught with danger if it fails to satisfy the expectations it will raise. Because it is more trade based it also requires more cooperation from the rich nations and may lead to greater dependency. For the Western industrial nations, the question is whether the third choice is sufficiently preferable to merit their economic support.

At independence India's agriculture was particularly ill suited to supplying the food needs associated with a high-employment strategy. Colonial agriculture had emphasized export crops, but very low levels of productivity and a poor institutional infrastructure for food crops. The colonial pattern could have been reversed at independence by reorganization of agriculture along the lines in fact proposed but little implemented by many British commissions prior to independence.

[30] K.G. Saidiyan, J.P. Naik, and S. Abid Husain, *Compulsory Education in India* (Delhi: Universal Bank and Stationery Co., 1966), p. 23.

However, this would have required a massive commitment of resources not available at the time of independence; and there was no way that support services for agriculture could have been reorganized quickly enough to show significant results in those early years.

India's industrial situation at independence was peculiar. Agriculture was dominant but represented, in a sense, only a massive pool of poverty. On the other hand, India had a centuries-long tradition of manufacturing, trade, and enterpreneurship, even though this tradition was no doubt stunted during the colonial period. Given India's per capita income, the percentage of gross national product generated in the industrial sector was considerably higher than one would expect from the Kuznets relationship. And, most significantly, there was an initial heavy-industry structure. Thus, for 1950, the Kuznets relationship would predict 7.5 percent of gross national product from manufacturing; India's actual figure was 16 percent.[31] Given the tendency to equate modernization with industrialization, it is not surprising that India took a particular interest in building from its initial industrial base.

The more employment-oriented, agriculture-based, fast-growth strategies depend substantially on rapid expansion of exports. This is so because these strategies require large imports of goods produced from highly capital-intensive industries which are paid for by exports of relatively more labor-intensive goods. A country that attempts a high-employment, rural-oriented growth strategy with a foreign exchange base heavily loaded toward commodities that have poor export possibilities starts with a major strike against it.

In the early 1950s, tea made up 15 to 20 percent of India's small total of exports. Tea has inelastic demand. Another 20 to 25 percent of India's exports was jute, which was facing relatively inelastic demand and substantial competition from synthetic fibers. Textiles composed 15 percent of exports.[32] These were largely of grey goods, which also were under substantial competitive pressure.

The destination of India's exports also was not conducive to growth. In 1951, 27 percent of India's exports went to the United Kingdom, 19 percent to the United States, and 2 percent to Japan. Total imports of those three countries rose

---

[31] Simon Kuznets, *The Economic Growth of Nations* (Cambridge: Harvard University Press, 1971), Table 26, pp. 188—89.

[32] John W. Mellor, *The New Economics of Growth*, p. 209; Manmohan Singh, *India's Export Trends and the Prospects for Self-contained Growth* (Oxford: Clarendon Press, 1964), pp. 14—15.

at respectively 5.8 percent, 11.8 percent, and 12.0 percent in the 1960s.[33] Obviously Taiwan and Korea, which diversified from Japan to the United States, faced more buoyant markets than India.

In these circumstances, Indian economic planners assumed that it would be necessary for India to tightly limit its imports. This reinforced the argument for the autarkic strategy of the Second Five Year Plan. It was assumed that foreign assistance and the large monetary reserves built up during the Korean War period when commodity prices were high would pay for import needs in the short period before exports could be increased. Again, the critical error was underestimating the time required for closing that gap.

A final and important characteristic of the initial conditions of Indian economic growth was the administrative structure. It reflected the elitist educational system favored by the British colonial administration.[34] At the top were a few highly sophisticated, Western-educated and Western-oriented administrators who were proficient in the British style of generalist administration. There were two major drawbacks. First, with their proficiency in the British style, this group lacked the technical qualifications for administering a vigorous economic development push.[35] These were hardly the people one would choose to run a steel mill, an agricultural research system, an agricultural university, or a development program for small-scale industry. But because of the politics and the economics of the development strategy, these activities were largely handled in the public sector and thus were subject to the administrative cadre rather than the private or professional sector where the insights of the traditional Indian entrepreneur or professional could have been drawn upon.

Second, the administrative cadre had very weak support from the lower levels of the civil service. This lack of depth encouraged and perhaps even required decisions to be funneled to the top, resulting in inflexibility inimical to economic

[33] John W. Mellor and Uma Lele, "The Interaction of Growth Strategy, Agriculture and Foreign Trade—The Case of India," *Trade, Agriculture and Development*, ed. George S. Tolley and Peter A. Zadrozny (Cambridge, Massachusetts: Ballinger, 1975), p. 107; John W. Mellor, *The New Economics of Growth*, Appendix Table 14.

[34] Barve Memorial Lecture (New Delhi, March 6, 1968), quoted in Jagdish N. Bhagwati and Padma Desai, *India, Planning for Industrialization* (London: Oxford University Press, 1970), pp. 131–32.

[35] Ralph Braibanti, "Reflections on Bureaucratic Reform in India," in *Administration and Economic Reform in India*, eds. Ralph Braibanti and Joseph J. Spengler (Durham, N.C.: Duke University Press, 1963), p. 55; S.P. Jagota, "Training of Public Servants in India," ibid., pp. 77–78.

development. Similarly, there was relatively little formal education among the rural people who have to apply much of the development scheme.

Accelerating Growth—1947 to 1965

The period from 1947 to 1965 was one of steady development of the basis for growth. The period began in the turmoil of independence. It closed with Nehru's death in 1964, the end of the Third Five Year Plan, temporary cessation of five year plans in 1965, and the cataclysmic, worst of the century drought of 1965—67.

Lord Mountbatten described India as "a ship on fire with ammunition in the hold," in March 1947. During the next four years the government's attention was devoted almost exclusively to the dramatically difficult politics of nation building. By 1951, the beginning of the First Five Year Plan, India had conducted a general election (in 1951—52) with more than 160 million voters, of whom 80 percent were illiterate; had integrated a set of princely states whose divisive tendencies had long been encouraged by British rule; had written and adopted a constitution of some force and durability; had absorbed 8 million refugees; had overcome a period of Communist activity described by the government as "bordering on open revolt"; and had resolved the complex question of whether to remain in the British Commonwealth. Many of these problems, including the Kashmir issue and the continuing destabilizing effect of underemployed refugees in West Bengal, would condition economic planning for decades. In spite of these problems, the first Planning Commission was appointed by 1950, reported by 1951, and had a plan underway in 1952.

The First Five Year Plan (1951—56) was largely based on earlier thought and effort. Little intellectual basis existed for planning a nation as poor, as short of capital and institutional infrastructure, and as agrarian as India. Since the early nineteenth century, Western economists had been much more concerned with cyclical fluctuations than secular growth. W. Arthur Lewis's now classic paper on development of the labor surplus economy was not published until 1954. Development economics consisted mostly of a small literature on economic development of the Balkans.

The First Five Year Plan emphasized agriculture and included reforms to end exploitation by landlords and traders, provisions for educating the farmer, and large-scale irrigation investment.[36]

Steadily improving weather from 1952 to 1955 gave the impression of great agricultural success. This strengthened the Mahalanobis strategy for a major push toward industrialization in the Second Five Year Plan. That plan was attractive to

[36] John W. Mellor *et al., Developing Rural India*, pp. 33—35.

aid donors who further developed it. Moreover, it seemed sufficiently successful to warrant a refined version for the Third Five Year Plan, even though problems were becoming evident: the poor crop year of 1957–58 suggested a major weakness in the approach to agriculture and development of large-scale industry was taking longer than expected.

From 1950 to 1965, the gross national product grew at a rate of over 4 percent per annum (1.5 percent per capita), agricultural output at about 2.8 percent, and industrial output at about 7 percent.[37] It is notable that the other side of the coin of no improvement in real incomes of the lower 40 percent of the population is much faster growth for the rest. Thus the upper 60 percent, some 360 million people, averaged a 2.3 percent growth rate in per capita income. In all likelihood the distribution is such that a population equal to the sum of Germany and France have experienced in excess of a 5 percent average annual growth rate in their real income. Nevertheless the most important developments in this period were the structural changes within the various sectors, changes that profoundly affected the prospects for future growth.

The radically accelerated growth rate for foodgrains in the 1950s arose principally from traditional sources: growth in both irrigated and unirrigated areas and increasing use of labor accounted for some 90 percent of the increased production;[38] inorganic fertilizer and associated new technology accounted for less than 10 percent. Substantial land reforms probably played an important background role.

As important and desirable as were these traditional forces, they proved unable to sustain growth into the 1960s. While increased irrigation maintained or increased in importance, other traditional sources of growth, including expanded crop acreage, receded sharply. Fertilizer use increased rapidly, however, accounting for 38 percent of the production increase in the Second Five Year Plan (1955–60), and 59 percent in the Third (1960–65). However, the net effect of these divergent forces was a decline in the growth rate for foodgrain production from 2.8 percent in the 1950s to 2.0 percent in 1960–65 (in each case adjusted for weather fluctuations). The rapid growth rate in the modern elements was still on too low a base to carry the aggregate.

Despite the decline, the basis for eventual acceleration of growth was now laid and would be the only bright spot in the generally dismal next decade. There was gradual recognition that modern agriculture is based on new technology, requiring research institutions, fertilizer supplies, irrigation, and other inputs, all in a com-

[37] John W. Mellor, *The New Economics of Growth*, p. 8.

[38] Ibid., p. 31.

plex institutional structure. Such a structure was evolving in the late 1950s and the 1960s.

Industrial production which grew at a 6.2 percent annual rate in the 1950s accelerated to annual growth of over 9 percent in the mid 1960s. More dramatic, production shifted radically to heavy industry and the public sector. Between 1951 and 1963 the share of investment goods in industrial output rose from 6 percent to 21 percent of value added, while the share of consumer goods fell from 58 percent to 38 percent.[39] In 1955—65, 55 to 60 percent of added investment in the organized industrial sector took place in the public sector.[40] The industries emphasized were highly capital intensive. During 1951—65, of 19 major industry categories the four most capital intensive increased their share of total capital investment, value added in production, and employment; with one exception, the four industry groups with the lowest capital intensity decreased their share. All four of the least capital-intensive industries produced final consumer goods; none of the top four did.

In keeping with the plan theory, industrial employment grew at considerably less than half the rate that it would have if investment in the various parts of the industrial sector had expanded at the same rate.[41] In addition, efficiency of new investment in large-scale public sector enterprises was low due to the scale of expansion and inexperience. The savings rate rose from 5 percent in 1950—51 to 9 percent in 1960—61 and to 11 percent in 1965—66. But neither the rate nor the absolute level of savings rose as much as expected, due to the lack of net earnings in the large-scale public sector.

India's overall growth rate for exports was poor. From 1950—51 to 1960—61 traditional exports remained at $1.3 billion while nontraditional exports nearly doubled, but were still only $0.3 billion. Nontraditional exports continued to grow and by 1965 were large enough to increase total exports at a significantly faster pace. However, India's export growth rate of 3.6 percent per annum was far below the 6.8 percent rate for developing countries as a whole. India's nontraditional exports actually grew faster than those of developing countries as a group but this was offset by slower growth in the traditional categories. Even in textiles, India did poorly while developing countries as a whole showed growth of 11 percent per annum in the 1960s.

India's relatively slow growth in exports from 1955 to 1975 stems primarily from the capital-intensive growth strategy and secondarily from the bureaucratic

---

[39] Bhagwati and Desai, pp. 100—07.

[40] Ibid., p. 137.

[41] John W. Mellor, *The New Economics of Growth*, p. 115.

restraints which, at least initially, were a product of that strategy. As a result, India failed to make use of its many low-cost workers to produce labor-intensive commodities for export to high-wage countries and for sale in its large and growing domestic market.

An 18 percent rise in the capital intensity of exports from 1964 to 1969 reflected the increased capital intensity of production.[42] In four of eight industrial trade categories, the weighted average capital intensity of exports increased. There was also a tendency for the more capital-intensive industries to have the fastest growth in exports, although the weighted average increase in capital intensity of exports was somewhat less than that for the economy as a whole.[43]

Stagnation—1965 to 1975

By 1965 the Indian economy had broadened and greatly enlarged its industrial sector, diversified its trade by geographic area and by commodities, with emphasis on exports with higher growth potential, more than doubled its savings rate, and laid the basis for modernizing the agricultural sector. The time appeared ripe for a takeoff. Instead, the Indian economy lapsed into a decade of stagnation. Agriculture did indeed accelerate its growth rate to some 3.3 percent per annum from 1965 to 1972. But industrial growth averaged only 3 percent per annum from 1965 to 1975; the savings rate actually declined slightly, and exports continued their generally lackluster performance.

This disaster is explained by a set of growing contradictions in the economy, an extraordinary natural disaster, and sharp decline in foreign assistance.

An unprecedented 6 percent rate of growth in industrial employment from 1960 to 1965 boosted demand for food while the growth in agricultural production slowed to a 2.1 percent rate and growth in agricultural marketings declined to 2.2 percent.[44] Rapid growth in food aid permitted foodgrain supplies to the

---

[42] John W. Mellor and Uma Lele, in George S. Tolley and Peter A. Zadrozny, eds., *Trade, Agriculture and Development*, p. 108. See also the analysis of Ranganath Bharadwaj confirming a rise in the capital intensity of exports vis-à-vis import displacement in 1958–59 compared to 1953–54, in *Structural Basis of India's Foreign Trade*, University of Bombay Series in Monetary and International Economics, No. 6, (Bombay 1962).

[43] Bank correlation coefficients between capital intensity and export growth from 1964 and 1969 were statistically significant at the 90 percent level. See John W. Mellor and Uma Lele, in George S. Tolley and Peter A. Zadrozny, eds., *Trade, Agriculture and Development*, n. 34.

[44] Data in this section, unless noted otherwise, are from: John W. Mellor, *The New Economics of Growth*.

nonfarm sector to grow at 4.1 percent per annum. Nevertheless, domestic agricultural prices rose one third relative to the price of manufactures from 1960 to 1964. The economy had become extraordinarily vulnerable to a decline in food aid which would allow rising wage goods prices and rising wage costs to strangle industrial growth. Alternatively the pace of agricultural growth would have to greatly accelerate to be in balance with the pace of industrial growth.

The savings rate was vulnerable to a similar squeeze. Foreign assistance accounted for a substantial portion of investment, the bulk of which was directed to a public sector that was still incapable of generating its own savings. Private sector profits were being squeezed by rising wage costs, derived from rising food costs, relatively stagnant domestic demand and rising taxes. The political system would not allow a high rate of savings from public resources. Under such circumstances, a decline in foreign assistance was bound to reduce the investment rate substantially, at least until the public sector could be made more efficient and the private sector stimulated to raise its own capital.

The development strategy of the Second and Third Five Year Plans placed a heavy decisionmaking and management burden on a bureaucracy that as yet had little technical competence for this responsibility. During the Second Five Year Plan, problems of allocation were relatively simple. The bulk of public investment went to the steel industry, so the inadequacy of the planning models intended to guide the administrators was not apparent.

During the Third Five Year Plan, however, decisions became more complex as industries expanded, consumer incomes rose, and the government began to encourage exports. The difficulty of these decisions was beyond the capacity of the economic models to instruct and of the bureaucracy to manage.

The contradictions in the system seemed insuperable in the short run: either savings must be extracted from the economy in the face of slow growth in income; or a strategy must be adopted to push export and agricultural growth and obtain massive financial backing from foreign sources to tide the economy over the transition. In any case, favorable weather would be needed to relieve the aid burden. Instead the weather was disastrous and foreign assistance dropped drastically. The 1965—66 drought, the worst in recorded history, was followed by another bad year, in 1966—67. Foodgrain production declined 19 percent in the first year and recovered by only 2.6 percent in the second.

Industrial production, which grew 8.9 percent per annum from 1960 to 1964, advanced at only 3.4 percent per annum from 1964 to 1968. During the 1966—67 drought period, industrial output did not grow at all. It increased by 6.4 percent the following year, rose 7.0 percent the year after that, then dropped to a 3.8 percent annual rate from 1970 to 1973.

Domestic savings as a proportion of national income dropped from 11.1 percent in 1965—66 to 9.0 percent in 1966—67 and to 7.9 percent in 1967—68, but partially recovered in 1968–69. The incentive and the ability to save and invest were diminished by the plunge in industrial profits because of higher costs and lower demand, by the rapid fall in real government expenditure due to a reduction in foreign aid receipts and lowered budget deficits, and by the decline in household income.

The industrial recession struck particularly hard at the capital goods industries. The *Economic Times* Index showed capital goods output shrinking at a 5.1 percent rate from 1965 to 1970 after it had grown at a 28.8 percent rate from 1960 to 1965.[45] The reasons for the recession include the drought, the decline in foreign aid, and the related excess capacity relative to demand. The government's dwindling ability to finance capital expenditure produced a dramatic cutback. For example, by 1970 output of railroad equipment was down to slightly less than a third of its 1967 level. Meanwhile, a shortage of railcars inhibited the movement of grain from the Punjab, fertilizer from the ports, and coal from Bihar.[46]

The bright spot in the post-1964 period was the accelerated growth of agriculture. Because this growth was the product of modernization with greater use of purchased inputs and an income bias toward higher income rural people, marketing grew at a 4.5 percent rate, one-third faster than production. However, growth in food supplies was much *less* favorable to growth in the late 1960s than in the early part of the decade because rapidly declining food aid reduced the growth in foodgrain availability to 2.3 percent a year.

The depressing effect of the rapid reduction in foreign aid after the Third Five Year Plan is not surprising given the importance of foreign assistance and the political and economic difficulties of substituting other growth strategies. Net foreign resource inflow to India declined from $1.3 billion in 1965–66 to an outflow of $120 million in 1972–73, reflecting reduced gross aid, sharp increases in debt repayment, and increase in foreign exchange reserves. The latter probably was prompted by uncertainties accompanying the decline in aid. The average decline of $200 million a year was equivalent to more than 20 percent of the average annual increments to gross investment from 1960–61 to 1965–66.[47]

So great a decline in foreign assistance had three crippling effects on short-run growth. First, it directly reduced the funds and resources available for investment—equivalent, in this case, to a major portion of the expected increments to

[45] *Economic Times* II (August 8, 1971), 156:7.

[46] K.S. Gill, "Wheat Marketing Behavior in Punjab and Haryana: Post Harvest Period, 1968–69/1970–71," *Punjab Agricultural University Bulletin*, 1971.

[47] John W. Mellor, *The New Economics of Growth*, p. 219.

savings. Second, given the previous strategy and the role played by foreign assistance, it imposed a proportionately larger reduction on producers of capital goods in the public sector. The scale and capital intensity of those producers made them particularly ill suited to rapid adaptation. The third effect follows from the decline in investment, which had at least a partial multiplier-accelerator consequence of reducing demand, income, and therefore further investment. Such an effect was made more likely by the significant decline in national income that accompanied the great drought of 1965—67. Indeed, even without the multiplier-accelerator effect, a reasonable set of assumptions would lead one to expect a sharp drop in net investment after the record dry period. Investment would then rise gradually until the end of the decline in aid six years later, when investment would begin to grow again at the old pace. That would place the resumption of rapid growth in 1972. But another drought and the drastic increase in oil and grain prices would then have postponed recovery an additional year or two.[48]

The Future Potential

By the middle 1970s, the Indian economy had weathered the immense adjustments of the preceding decade and was ready for a new period of sustained accelerated growth. Most important, the decline in foreign assistance and the shock of the large oil price increase had been absorbed. Net foreign aid, both in real terms and as a percent of national income, had moved from near zero to almost half the 1965 level. Export performance was exceedingly good, thanks substantially to the thriving Middle Eastern market. In addition, remittances from Indians living overseas climbed to more than $2.0 billion annually, again substantially due to new Middle Eastern opportunities, and exceeded total foreign assistance. India was able to build foreign exchange reserves of some $5 billion, comparable in real terms to those of World War II and to the inflated Korean War level of the early 1950s. Grain reserves rose to more than twice the highest level of the 1960s, enabling India to follow a highly expansionary economic policy and still weather at least two bad crop years. Similarly, the foreign exchange reserves could provide several years protection if it became necessary to adjust to a decline in aid or a deteriorating export position, or to correct an excessively expansionary policy. Further, the International Monetary Fund is now much better equipped politically and institutionally than in the 1960s to facilitate adjustments in the growth processes of developing countries.

Thus, India's development objectives and potentials in the late 1970s were in tune with a new strategy that could promise more of both growth and equity than

---

[48] For the assumptions and calculations see: Ibid., p. 223.

the Mahalanobis program. The new strategy, which had been forming in the late 1960s, differed from the Second Five Year Plan in five respects. First, agriculture was its core. Second, industrial growth was to be stimulated substantially by growing demand for exports and domestic consumption, rather than solely by domestic investment. Third, small and medium-scale consumer goods industries played a much more important role, tapping new sources of capital and entrepreneurship. Fourth, export in earnings, and hence foreign exchange, grew considerably more rapidly than in the past. Fifth, planning was more concerned with breaking critical bottlenecks to growth through public investment than with achieving a precise, self-sufficient balance in output.

Success requires at least a 3.5 percent growth rate for foodgrains and a 6 percent rate for nonfoodgrains in the agricultural sector. Such agricultural growth could support on the order of a 10 percent growth rate in industrial production. These rates are consistent and individually only moderately faster than the best previously attained. They would produce an overall growth rate in excess of 6 percent which would rise gradually to 8 percent by the year 2000 as the faster-growing industrial sector gained a larger share of output. Those growth rates would permit immense poverty alleviation and still allow a Japan size population to experience growth in per capita income at a rate comparable to those of Japan in the 1960s.

Such a strategy is more feasible than in earlier periods because the much broader industrial base can respond more readily to demand incentives, and the basis for agricultural growth is greatly improved. Such a strategy is also more appropriate to current objectives and political needs than it would have been a decade or two ago. The objective of national integration is now well in hand and hardly needs the cohesive efforts of central planning. The technical, scientific, and production base for greater international influence is sufficiently developed to justify removing controls and opting for faster growth and greater efficiency, even if some portions of the economy succumb to competition. Finally, a more broadly participatory growth structure may be both more possible and more necessary now than a decade ago. In the last 25 years India has had little success in dealing with the poverty of the lowest 40 percent of the income distribution. This has proved costly to India's foreign image as well as risking national divisions along class lines. It may now be necessary to deal with the poverty problem more effectively if the domestic polity is to remain healthy.

The new strategy depends much more on the market to order the details of growth than the old strategy, but it requires major public support in key areas. It is especially attuned to the reality that governments are unable to take more than a few concurrent initiatives. The priorities of course change with time, but at present they are clearly the following:

1. Massive expansion of electric power generating and distributing capacity.
2. Accelerated growth in irrigation.
3. Major development of an integrated capacity to generate and promulgate new agricultural technology.

The need for massive investment and public attention to expand electric power availability is a distinguishing feature of the new growth strategy. A rural, employment-oriented strategy requires less power per unit of output or per job created than does the approach embodied in the Second Five Year Plan. Nevertheless, three factors require that a large portion of public sector investment be allocated to power.

First, the strategy relies heavily on private investment in both agriculture and industry. Unreliable power greatly reduces returns to irrigation and small industry, which would reduce growth-inducing investment.

Second, in the Second and Third Five Year Plans, because of heavy demands by both capital-intensive and electric power industries, limited public sector resources had to be allocated between them. It was tempting to save capital on the power side by excessively optimistic assumptions about capacity utilization and by underestimating consumption, particularly in the light industry and consumer sectors. As a result, recurrent power shortages caused underutilization of capacity in heavy industry, thus lowering investment incentive and capability. This problem was greatly exacerbated during the decade of stagnation when power-generating capacity grew by only 10 percent a year. Several years of massive investment will be required to rectify the past deficiency and power shortages will continue for some time as India attempts to accelerate growth with the new strategy.

Third, because private sector growth will require a large share of resources, the public sector will be more constrained than in earlier plans. India should allocate a large share of its public sector investment to areas relatively less appropriate to private investment. Such a policy would favor a substantial portion of public investment to the power area.

Accelerated output from agriculture will require expansion of the irrigated area at rates that surpass the highest rate achieved in the heyday of the green revolution in the late 1960s. Although, what is needed appears achievable, it must occur in areas not as well endowed institutionally as the Punjab where much of the earlier growth occurred. It will probably require more of the large-scale irrigation projects that came under so much criticism in the 1960s because of their time-consuming and difficult development. In addition rapid expansion of small-scale well irrigation will reinforce the demand for electric power as the most efficient means of pumping water.

Power and irrigation expansion are likely to require a large portion of the government's resource and implementation capacity. Consequently, investment in large-scale industry will be limited mainly to what these industries can supply from internal resources. That of course will be much more than in the past due to the larger base and greater efficiency.

The irrigation investment will not pay unless new high yielding varieties appropriate to each of a large set of conditions are developed. Therefore new agricultural technology, particularly to increase yields, is crucial to the new strategy. But it is so difficult to obtain that a major priority must be given to expansion and improvement of agricultural research. That will not entail a large financial cost but it does require difficult administrative decisions.

In the context of the basic priorities much needs to be done in the areas already receiving significant attention. For example: problems of growth and equity interact closely in rural development. About one-fourth of agricultural output occurs on farms not fully integrated into the credit, marketing, and information systems characteristic of modern agriculture. India's efforts in these areas have been impressive. For example, the Small and Marginal Farmers Programs have helped spread new technologies. But, because small farmers need much more attention per acre farmed than large farmers, the need for trained personnel and institutional development is immense. There will also have to be substantial investment in roads and other elements of rural infrastructure in order to reach vast rural areas and integrate them into the larger economy. That integration also requires further development of local organizations to raise resources and use them effectively.

In addition to the physical priorities just discussed, India must give priority to continued debureaucratization of the economy. While institutional development must be vigorously pursued in some areas, the new strategy relies heavily on private investment in others: agriculture, industry and exports. For vigor in these areas, licensing and regulations must continue to be reduced.

What are the chances that these developments will occur? There is reason for optimism in the fact that they have all been underway for several years and are explicit in the ruling Janata party's platform, but the opposing vested interests are strong. The alliance of big business and socialists for heavy expenditures on large-scale industry is well entrenched as is their quite differently based relish for competition-reducing regulation. The government bureaucracy tends to like neither the dismantling of old controls nor the technocracy implied in the new areas of public sector growth, and politicians always like the patronage opportunities provided by the bureaucracy. Nevertheless, the government seems committed in principle.[49]

---

[49] For example, see statements by the Finance Minister in June 1977, and in his most recent budget speech (*Financial Express*, New Delhi, March 1, 1978).

Perhaps the most serious potential obstacles to the new strategy are a hostile foreign attitude, particularly toward export and aid needs; and inclement weather and development lags that would lower gains in agricultural production. Accelerated growth in exports is crucial to the strategy, both to finance necessary imports and to expand employment. If export growth is poor, foreign aid becomes more important to expand domestic markets and to provide essential capital goods. India's Finance Ministries have always been conservative and a favorable foreign assistance environment would encourage the government to accept the risks of greater investment and expanded domestic demand. Finally, because India is still so poor there is little resilience to absorb delay in results or external shocks. A promising beginning can continue, or all too easily disintegrate under mutually reinforcing pressures of economic and political forces.

Economically, the strategy would fail if agricultural production did not maintain a growth rate of approximately 3.5 percent and if the industrial sector did not achieve the 10 percent rate necessary to bolster employment, effective demand and incentive prices for food. The agricultural growth rate would not be achieved if expansion of power, irrigation, and agricultural research were inadequate.

Various political developments could also cause the strategy to fail. Urban labor may press for a level of expenditure on urban welfare programs that would leave insufficient funds for investment needs in the large-scale industrial sector, including power generation. Larger farmers may prevent the flow of resources to small farmers. Bureaucratic interests may slow the dismantling of controls, favor other imports over fertilizer, and prevent reorganization of crucial elements of the institutional structure. Finally, gradually broadening the political system to include the poor majority may bring pressures for cheap food, welfare expenditure, and pseudo socialism that would impede development and probably do little for the poor.

Judging the future course of events is, of course, difficult. It is essential, after a decade of stagnation, to provide sustained increases in employment, food supplies, and other consumer goods soon. Thus, the government must have the courage to accept the high risks of following an expansionary policy. The bottleneck of inadequate power supplies is very real and getting worse; it cannot be broken for several years even with the greatest effort. In addition, the danger of a poor crop year is always present. Two more years like 1965–67 would cut production by 46 million tons—twice the present reserves. Even normally bad weather would wipe out existing reserves in two years. Policies to expand demand could easily raise consumption by 8 million tons in two years, an amount equal to recent annual additions to stocks. Given the added uncertainty of export markets and foreign aid flows, it is no wonder that Indian economic policy is conservative.

These uncertainties lend importance to the actions of Western industrial nations. Unfavorable assistance, trade, and food policies could reinforce a conservative turn toward the old strategy, which would be particularly destabilizing under current conditions. Or, such an environment might ensure such slow growth that the political stability becomes difficult to maintain in the context of an open system. Then the centralizing political tendency of the late 1960s can be expected to reappear, reinforcing a return to the old growth strategy.

Comment

T. N. Srinivasan

I am not in full agreement with Mellor's analysis of India's economic performance since independence or with his assessment of future prospects.

With some justification, he argues that the major contours of Indian development planning and, indeed, the development strategy, were outlined in the Second Five Year Plan by Professor Mahalanobis, and that some elements of this strategy continue to be pursued even to this day.

But Mellor fails to convince when he argues that the Mahalanobis strategy was dictated by the objectives of national unification, of big power status, and perhaps of poverty abatement in a longer run. He concludes that achieving such objectives necessitated a strategy which "was central planning at its ultimate." Perhaps the term "central planning" has a different meaning to Mellor. To most economists, central planning means allocations of resources and the enforcement of allocations through central directives or commands. The Indian system, even during the days when the Planning Commission had some prestige and power, could hardly be characterized as a system attempting central planning in the above sense. In any case, the development of a military-industrial complex associated with big power status does not require central planning as a necessary condition. Nor is it the case that national unification is promoted by central planning. Quite the contrary: inability to persuade the center to assign this industry or plant to this state or that, has, in fact, created tensions and divisions.

The Mahalanobis strategy has been criticized by some, praised by others, and in any case discussed *ad nauseam* in Indian literature. I do not wish to go into detail except to point out some fallacies in Mellor's critique. First, contrary to Mellor's statement, Mahalanobis's Second Five Year Plan had employment creation as one of its explicitly stated objectives. Furthermore, this was to be achieved through labor-intensive production of basic consumer goods, as well as through construction associated with the creation of public works and industrial capital. Second, Mellor repeats the often asserted neglect of agriculture in the Second Plan. I have never been persuaded that the only measure of emphasis or neglect of a sector is the proportion of total investment allocated to that sector in one plan as compared to the previous. It is trivial to point out that a lower propor-tion of a larger total can mean an increase in absolute terms. Nor am I persuaded that additional investment in agriculture directly would have yielded substantial returns in the 1950s, before the availability of new technology and food imports at concessional terms.

In my view, the most serious drawback of the Mahalanobis strategy was its neglect of foreign trade opportunities. This meant that domestic use and produc-tion patterns had to be nearly the same, so that opportunities to save resources by shifting production patterns to reflect dynamic comparative advantages were not exploited. It is true that trade with the Eastern bloc countries, as well as with some others, notably Egypt, increased under bilateral, almost barterlike, arrange-ments during the late 1950s. However, India exported mainly traditional com-modities to these countries and the changes in commodity composition of exports away from the traditional were to come much later. But I would not go as far as Mellor does and suggest that because export possibilities were poor, India attached less weight to relations with the Western industrial countries and more to those with the Eastern bloc. Indeed, as I said earlier, the commodity composition of exports was broadly similar on exports to West and East.

Mellor is right in suggesting that, at least in their pronouncements, Indian planners and politicians had poverty amelioration and reduction in inequalities as major objectives of planning long before the World Bank, the International Labor Organization, and assorted do-gooders discovered the bottom 40 percent, basic needs, and so on. Indeed, no one put this better than Prime Minister Nehru, who in introducing the Third Five Year Plan to Parliament in 1960 said:

> Again it is said that the national incomes over the First and Second Plans have gone up by 42 percent and per capita income by 20 percent. Now a legitimate query is made—where has this gone? To some extent, of course, you can see where it has gone. I sometimes do address a large gathering in the villages, and I can see that they are better fed and better clothed, they build brick houses and they are generally better off. Nevertheless, that does not apply to everybody in India.[1]

In fact, it is this disquiet about development performance in poverty abate-ment that led to the appointment, in 1960, of the Mahalanobis Committee on Distribution of Income and Levels of Living to study the trends in the distribution of income and wealth and, in particular, to ascertain the extent to which the operation of the economic system had resulted in concentration of wealth and means of production. Even more significant, in 1962 the Perspective Planning

---

[1] Government of India Planning Commission, *Report of the Committee on Distribution of Income and Levels of Living*, part 1, February 1964, p. 1.

Division of the Planning Commission, under the leadership of the late Pitambar Pant, prepared a pioneering paper entitled "Perspectives of Development—India 1960—61 to 1975—76, Implications of Planning for a Minimum Level of Living." This paper contains all the essentials of the so-called basic needs approach to development that is being embraced and propounded by aid donors and international agencies, as well as by performers in the development conference circuit. My point here is not to suggest that we achieved all we sought to achieve, but only to state that the failure does not lie in lack of awareness of the issues on the part of the planners. The tactical, as well as strategic, failures of Indian planning have been extensively documented, for example, in the important book of Bhagwati and Desai cited by Mellor.

Mellor also comments on India's economic image in the Western world. One should normally have no use for these images. After all, a particularly bad harvest in India triggers the triage notion in the Western press; a particularly bountiful harvest the next year yields a good press. But such a silly approach to letting short-term events determine the evaluation of long-term prospects is not, unfortunately, the exclusive preserve of newspaper columnists and may be shared by aid donors. The only way to combat it is, first, to improve India's performance and, second, to educate the natives in the West.

I agree substantially with Mellor's discussion of the Indian economy's initial conditions at independence and its progress until Nehru's death in 1964. He is being rather simplistic in posing three alternative development strategies, which can be summarily described as Stalinist, Maoist, and a namby-pamby mixture of idealism and naiveté that can be employment oriented or basic needs oriented. Mellor opts for the last. In my view, Indian planners had a far broader view of the economy and the polity, and they placed as much emphasis on pursuing the goals of economic development without infringing on individual liberties in a democratic political framework. I doubt very much whether they thought in terms of Mellor's alternatives. On the contrary, the virtues of the mixed economy as a politico-economic arrangement are mentioned in every plan. Further, while the critics, including myself, drew attention to the failures of the planners at least until 1966, a learning process was going on. By 1966 some of the excesses of bureaucratic management of the economy were becoming apparent, and a new vista of opportunities was opening up, as in agriculture, and perceived, as in foreign trade. The system was responding, as it did in the case of devaluation of the rupee in June 1966. But the process stalled and as yet has not regained its momentum. To this decade of stagnation, as Mellor describes it, which hardly a year ago was described by the powers that were as dynamic, I now turn.

I have elsewhere discussed the statistical details of the performance of the

Indian economy since 1966.[2] Mellor attributes this stagnation to: first, a set of contradictions in the economy, that is, deficiencies in the agricultural sector that resulted in paucity of food and other wage goods on the one hand, and lack of demand for the products and supply of savings to the industrial sector on the other, inconsistency between means of growth and its financing, and administrative failures; second, natural disasters in two successive bad harvests in 1966 and 1967; and third, major external shocks of reduced external assistance and the oil price hike.

It is true that the prices of food in particular and agricultural commodities in general, relative to those of nonagricultural commodities, moved in favor of agriculture in the sixties and later. Some calculations of Mrs. Thamarajakshi show a similar trend in income terms of trade between agricultural and nonagricultural sectors. Some analysts, particularly Professor S. Chakravarty, have pointed to this movement in terms of trade as the villain of the piece. But this is only part of the story. The major cause of stagnation, in my view, is the abrupt halt in the growth of real investment in the public sector after 1966, compared with more or less steady growth at an annual rate exceeding 10 percent prior to 1966. This was due to a decline in public savings, which, in turn, was perhaps caused by the massive reduction in budgetary support derived from aid, particularly food aid. (Incidentally, there is no evidence of any shift in the private household savings behavior.) Faced with a reduction in aid, the government applied the ax to investment, since public consumption, particularly defense and social service outlays, could hardly be cut. The reduction in public investment had its impact on the production and absorption of capital goods and related industries and brought on industrial stagnation. Further, with the devaluation and the later linking of the rupee with the sinking pound, exports and foreign exchange earnings went up, only to be accumulated in reserves, since import demand slackened with the industrial stagnation. Private investment did not completely offset the fall in public investment, both because the industrial licensing system continued to act as a constraint and because the recession was eroding profitability. The oil price hike came after eight years of this stagnation; it did not significantly add directly to further stagnation.

While the administrative failings pointed out by Mellor were there, I am not convinced that they were more serious in this period than earlier. Indeed, the government took steps toward liberalization of controls during this period, while the management of public sector units became more professional. But without an ex-

[2] T. N. Srinivasan and N. S. S. Narayana, "Economic Performance Since the Third Plan and Its Implications for Policy," *Economic and Political Weekly*, Annual Number (February 1977).

pansionary policy these had only marginal effect. I am not persuaded that the bureaucracy faltered because of an inadequate set of guidelines; first, because no such set can be drawn up for a complex economy under rapidly changing conditions, and second, because of the tendency of a bureaucracy to play it safe and avoid risk taking by rigidly adhering to guidelines even when circumstance warrants a violation. Indeed, the management of public sector enterprises by the bureaucracy reflected the same risk avoidance.

Let me now turn to the future potential of the Indian economy. I agree with Mellor that the potential for considerably faster growth than India has had in the past three decades is there, and that the realization of this potential depends mainly on agricultural performance, and then on export performance. It would be useful in discussing future prospects to distinguish between the near term, that is, the next two to three years, and the period beyond. As I said earlier, the stagnation of the last 10 years is due mainly to stagnation in public investment. To the extent that an expansionary policy was not being followed in the past for fear of exacerbating inflationary pressures, the present availability of ample food stocks and foreign exchange reserves should help overcome that fear. It is possible that the government's project preparation will continue to be so dismal that there will not be enough fully appraised worthwhile projects on which to spend public resources. I would hope this is not the case. If it is, then the first priority is to identify and appraise investment projects. At any rate, with the available food and foreign exchange stocks, it should be possible to boost the near-term growth and employment in the standard Keynesian fashion.

The near-term growth achieved will not be easy to sustain in the future, unless some policy changes are made. And Mellor is right in arguing for stepped-up investment in irrigation, particularly ground water development, as well as in agricultural research and extension. I would also emphasize the need for institutional changes, that is, land reform: not of the unrealistic variety that Calcutta intellectuals talk about at cocktail hour, but a less dramatic, nonetheless effective, type that Minhas has forcefully argued for in his work on poverty abatement. For some reason, Mellor does not refer to this problem at all. Whether the investment in irrigation would involve a huge investment in rural electrification, as Mellor claims, is an open issue. It is possible that diesel, or even biogas-operated pumps, may be a cheaper alternative.

The policy changes on the industrial front will involve removing a purposeless administrative shackle on investment and a less wooden approach to monopoly control, indigenization, and import liberalization. To the extent that the recent good export performance reflects domestic stagnation, any expansionary policy may cut into exports if nothing else is done. It is essential to eliminate all impediments to an aggressive export drive, such as the nonavailability of imported inputs and restrictions on import of designs and know-how.

The needs for other policy changes, such as putting greater resources on primary education, are well known. Given these policy changes and a stable external environment, there is no reason why India should not grow considerably faster than before.

V

A World Role:
The Dialectics of
Purpose and Power

Baldev Raj Nayar

What is India's role in the world today? What changes have occurred in the country's role over the period since independence? What changes in its role can one reasonably forecast for the near future? These are important questions about a major national actor in the international system. Of even greater significance are questions relating to the perceptions held by the leadership about the appropriate role for the country: What is the elite's perception of a desirable role for India in the world? What role does it perceive to be feasible in the present structure of world power? What is its posture toward the congruence or incongruence of the two perceptions? Such questions about nations in general have been of special interest to students of international politics and foreign decisionmakers alike and are, under the rubric of "elite images," a major preoccupation of researchers today.

The Framework for Analysis

The term *role* in international politics is simply a shorthand description of the scope and direction of a country's foreign policy. A country's role in the international system is not a random occurrence or a result of accident, but is basically a function of its position in the power hierarchy in the world. That the United States does have far-flung military bases around the world and Tanzania does not is a function not of American virtue but of its power. That a collection of thirteen colonies on the western shores of the Atlantic expanded across the North American continent and into the Pacific is a function not of legality or bargaining but of military power. Despite the doctrine of sovereign equality of nations, the international system is an oligarchy. Within that system one can broadly distinguish among foreign policy roles as between a subject and an object. To have a subject role in international politics is to be a part of the dominant power structure that makes, in competition or collusion, the vital decisions about the fate and destiny of the international system and of the nations within it. Possessors of such a role are also referred to as great powers. In the present epoch the full-fledged status of a subject of international politics is confined to nuclear powers with a subcontinental geographic size. To be an object in international politics, as against a subject, is to be at the receiving end of the decisions made by the great powers. As minor powers, countries with object status often have limited foreign policy autonomy. Their maneuverability in foreign policy is a function of the relations among the great powers, and their lot is often to adapt as best possible to the decisions of the subject powers. A third in-between category is that of an independent center of power, which does not have the leverage to influence the course of the international system as a whole, but which does possess enough capabilities to have, within a given configuration of power, a considerable degree of foreign policy autonomy and the capacity to resist the application of unwelcome decisions, especially in the realm of security. While subject nations have system-wide or global influence, independent centers of power are often dominant or preeminent in a certain region. They may therefore also be referred to as regional powers or as *middle powers*, signifying their status as lying in between subjects and objects. Middle powers often tend to erect on the foundations of their regional dominance or preeminence a claim to some role at the subject level.

The typology of subject, middle power, and object gives us a notion of the place of a country in the power hierarchy of the world as well as the scope of its foreign policy. Another dimension along which foreign policy roles may be distinguished is whether a country is *revisionist* or *status quo*, that is, whether it is dissatisfied or not with its present status in the international system. This distinction gives us an idea of the direction of foreign policy.

In an international system whose main characteristic is the absence of any legitimate central authority, all nations are confronted with a security dilemma that results in a Hobbesian struggle for power. Typically, a great power resists the emergence of new great powers, for to accommodate others to a similar role is to diminish one's own power, and to that extent lose some control over one's own national security and welfare. Rather the tendency is to extend one's power as far as possible, to exercise dominion over others, and to reduce middle powers to the status of objects. This has nothing to do with any particular ideology or the internal political structure of states. There is no "exceptionalism" here; the nature of the international system and the security dilemma inherent in it invariably pushes subject states in a quite deterministic fashion, in that direction. To be sure, governments are rarely monolithic, even in closed societies, but a dominant, overriding posture comes to prevail that corresponds to the power position of a country, with subordinate perspectives becoming relevant primarily in a time of crisis or change in the world power hierarchy. Questions about motivation or moral evaluation also may well be meaningless here; this is how great powers are impelled to behave, because of their position in the power hierarchy, even as they use ideology to mask their drive to power and domination.

On the other hand, for those middle powers that have the potential, entrance into the exclusive club of subjects is also a compelling goal. This is so not simply for status or prestige purposes, but for national survival and welfare, for middle powers are constantly confronted with the prospect of domination by the great powers. However, the contrary impulses of great powers and middle powers often set them on a collision course, and the graduation of a middle power to the status of great power is no journey along a smooth path but one whose story is usually written in blood and fire. At the same time rivalry and competition among the great powers may facilitate the emergence of some middle powers as subjects. Basically, however, middle powers act reactively and defensively; it is the great powers that have a prior and initiating role, and it is their policies that compel attention.

Great powers typically choose from among three policies toward middle powers and potential subject powers: containment, satellization, and accommodation. Containment is clearly a larger phenomenon than one simply restricted to Communism, which is only one specific application of it. The policy is patently directed at all independent centers of power, especially those with an ambition to play subject roles. As George Liska states: "Great powers can treat and have reason to treat individual middle powers as regional rivals, and be led to help still lesser states to contain them under the pretense of restraining, unilaterally or co-operatively, all Third World conflict."[1] The intent, of course, is to reduce the international influence of the middle power as a claimant to a subject role, to subordinate its foreign policy to the requirements of the great power or to raise the costs of its foreign policy autonomy, and to prevent its rise to the status of a subject power. Not surprisingly, containment may lead to expansionism; indeed, expansionism is the other side of containment. The key to the containment of middle powers is the creation of a balance of power in the region favorable to the great power. Such a regional balance may be implemented through a policy of alliances, either tacit, explicit, or both, whereby the great power in one way or another aligns its influence and power with that of some local or extraregional power to balance off the targeted middle power. This may be supplemented by the direct military presence of the great power in the form of bases in the region. The policy of containment does not exclude bargaining; quite the contrary, its purpose is to establish the parameters for what in other contexts has been called "bargaining from strength" or to secure leverage.

Under a policy of satellization great powers regard middle powers "as regional

---

[1] See George Liska, "The Third World: Regional Systems and Global Order," in Robert E. Osgood *et al.*, *Retreat From Empire?* (Baltimore: Johns Hopkins University Press, 1973), p. 226.

allies in context with other great powers and proceed to reinforce them competitively, possibly as a means to reapportionment by way of reclientization."[2] The central mechanism in this policy is the acquisition of an interventionist capability in the internal and external affairs of a target country to provide the great power with leverage over the country's foreign policy. Satellization operates through the creation of dependencies in other countries on the subject power. Its chief instruments are economic aid and military alliances, which are important for the penetration and dependence they make possible in crucial sectors of the targeted nation. Finally, there is the policy of accommodation under which great powers "proceed either unilaterally or jointly progressively to devolve regional responsibilities to apparently constructively disposed middle powers." A critical consideration for the superpowers here is whether the middle power is "loyalist" or "rebellious."[3]

There is no reason to attribute rigidity to this analytical framework describing the policies of containment, satellization, and accommodation. In the first place, these policies should be treated not as mutually exclusive categories but rather as central tendencies in the foreign policy posture of a great power, which may incorporate one or more such tendencies at any given time. Furthermore, there may be variations within each policy; for example, containment may or may not be accompanied by isolation. Again, implementation of any one of these policies can never be absolute, but requires sophistication and subtlety; containment of a middle power in one region, for example, may necessitate modifying or supplementing containment of another middle power elsewhere. Nor do such policies remain static or permanent; changes in the distribution of power and the pattern of alliances and adversary relationships in the international system result in changes in superpower policies toward middle powers. It is important to emphasize this last point, for the interactions between a superpower and a middle power are not simply dyadic; they do not occur in a vacuum, but are embedded in a wider international system. The policy mix thus changes in response to power shifts in the international system. Also, the notions of containment and satellization refer to policy goals, not achievements, for nations that are the targets of such policies are not always without recourse in their resistance to them. It is meaningless, therefore, to speculate in the abstract as to how one superpower could have additionally hurt a middle power but did not; such speculation is simply another manifestation of the arrogance of power.[4]

[2] Ibid.

[3] Ibid.

[4] William J. Barnds, "United States Policy Toward South Asia," *Pacific Community* (July 1977), p. 654.

India's Role Aspirations

How does India relate to this schema? Undoubtedly, the international role of a state is a function of its power capabilities. Not unexpectedly, however, a certain ambiguity characterizes India's role and status in the international system. One scholar raised the significant question: "Is she the last and least of the great Powers, or is she the first of the lesser Powers?"[5] India's foreign policy behavior has certainly fluctuated between that of a great power and that of a minor power. Objectively, if one did not dichotomize the world's powers India would seem to be a middle power. However, foreign policy behavior is often influenced not only by a country's objective status but also by its elite's perception of its desired role. In India's case such a perception is not an ideal hope but stems from an appreciation of the country's potential as a great power. Indeed, Indian foreign policy may be said to constantly confront the tension between the country's role aspiration based on its potential for a great power role in international politics and its present weakness in material and military capabilities. It may further be said to have as its central task the protection of this potential in the face of present weakness.

Given its size, population, strategic location, and historical past, India cannot but aspire to a great power role in international politics, however distant in the future. Even though reduced in size by the partition of the country in 1947, India is the seventh largest country in the world; with 1.3 million square miles, it is about two-thirds the size of Europe (excluding the Soviet Union). Its population of more than 600 million makes it the second most populous country in the world. Its population is larger than that of the two superpowers combined, larger than that of all the Americas put together, and roughly equivalent to that of all the permanent members of the Security Council minus China. Admittedly, large population does not necessarily add to national capabilities, and indeed may make for national weakness, but it is an element that makes it difficult for India to accept that nations with much smaller populations continue to hold a monopoly of power in the international system.

Continental size, economy and resource base, a conscious effort not dissimilar to China's to develop a heavy industry base and a sophisticated scientific underpinning has enabled India to produce its own medium tanks, supersonic jet aircraft, helicopters, naval frigates, and infantry equipment, and to arrange for a nuclear explosion, all with application of a small fraction of its gross national product.

Strategically, India lies astride the Indian Ocean, flanking the Persian Gulf and

[5] Peter Lyon, "The Foreign Policy of India," in *The Foreign Policies of the Powers*, ed. F. S. Northledge (New York: Praeger Publishers, 1968), p. 287.

the Straits of Malacca; it lies athwart the routes from West Asia to Southeast Asia and East Asia. Furthermore, India has been the seat of historic civilization; whatever its problems in terms of adjustment to the requirements of a modern era, it evokes memories of past greatness—episodic though that might have been—and of past epochs of creativity not only in philosophy and literature but also in science and mathematics. The fact that the last several hundred years saw India under alien rule only makes aspirations to the restoration of greatness all the more deeply felt.

From the perspective, then, of its size, population, strategic location, the past creativity of its people, and its abundant natural resource endowment, most Indians have seen their country as a potential great power. In international politics, India's reference point is consequently not Pakistan, but the great powers. Pakistan is only relevant as a "spoiler" of India's ambition, acting often as a proxy for the present great powers.

It is precisely India's perception of itself as a potential great power—however distant the prospect may seem—combined with the recognition of its present weakness that led to the policy of nonalignment in the first place. Scholars have elaborated many different aspects of nonalignment, but most fundamental among them was, of course, the intention to maintain India's foreign policy autonomy. Given the perception of India's potential, a satellite role was clearly unacceptable. As Nehru said, "What does joining a bloc mean? After all it can only mean one thing: give up your view about a particular question, adopt the other party's view on that question in order to please it and gain its favor."[6] The import of this message has not been lost on Nehru's successors either. In June 1976, External Affairs Minister Chavan emphatically declared: "Our size, our potential strength, our traditions and heritage do not allow us to become a client state."[7] Less than a year later, his successor Atal Bihari Vajpayee reiterated the new government's commitment to nonalignment, proclaiming it to be a product of "our freedom struggle" and a plank of all political parties in India, and holding that a big country like India could not follow any other policy and could not be a camp follower of any other country.[8] It was, indeed, the desire to be independent in making India's own decisions and not to be a satellite of others that led Nehru to reject the organization of a formal bloc of even the nonaligned nations. Nonalignment did not mean refusing alignment with one bloc or another on particular

[6] Jawaharlal Nehru, *Independence and After* (New York: John Day Company, 1950), p. 218.

[7] *Times of India*, June 17, 1967.

[8] *India News* (Ottawa) May 16, 1977.

decisions or policies; it meant only that the country retained the freedom to move from one bloc to the other—on the so-called basis of the merits of the case—as would benefit the national interests of the country. Nor did it mean that the country could not lean toward one side, only that it would retain the freedom to lean to the other side. In other words, India would maintain a balanced relationship with the major powers over the long haul, not at all times.

Underlying the policy of nonalignment, however, was a perception of a future great power role for India. Here Nehru was not only the exponent of nonalignment, but also the one who gave expression to such a role for India in the future. Indeed, he articulated his vision of such a role long before independence, though he often masked it in moral language. On one occasion, in 1939, Nehru wrote:

> A free India, with her vast resources, can be a great service to the world and to humanity. India will always make a difference to the world; fate has marked us for big things. When we fall, we fall low; when we rise, inevitably we play our part in the world drama.[9]

The partition of the country should have induced a greater awareness of some serious security and foreign policy consequences resulting from it, but Nehru gave expression to similar sentiments even after independence. He once stated:

> Leaving these three big countries, the United States of America, the Soviet Union and China, aside for the moment, look at the world. There are many advanced, highly cultured countries. But if you peep into the future and if nothing goes wrong, wars and like—the obvious fourth country in the world is India.[10]

Such a perception of a future role for India may seem ridiculous and the expressions about it a premature vaunt in the context of the country's poverty. But there is no reason why Indian leaders need to be apologetic about their conception of India in the future occupying a great power role in the international system. After all, there is no other basis than that of economic and military power to the role that the United States and the Soviet Union have in the international system today, and there is no philosophical or logical basis that a country of India's size and population should be denied a similar role if—and undoubtedly an important "if" it is—if it can add economic and military capabilities commensurate with its size and population. Certainly, Nehru's perception of India's world role in the future was contingent upon India's modernization. Skepticism about

---

[9] Dorothy Norman, ed., *Nehru: The First Sixty Years* 2 vols. (New York: John Day Company, 1965), 2: 649—50.

[10] Jawaharlal Nehru, *Indian Foreign Policy: Selected Speeches September 1946—April 1961* (Delhi: Publications Division, Ministry of Information and Broadcasting, Government of India, 1961), p. 305. For other statements, see Norman, *Nehru: The First Sixty Years*, 2: 453—60, 468, 501.

India's ability to modernize may well be justified in view of her difficulties since the mid-sixties, but there is no *a priori* reason to assume that to be a permanent condition.

To aim for great power status, however, casts India in a revisionist role, for the underlying assumption is not only that India should emerge as a great power, but also that the present structure of power monopoly in the world is unacceptable. This assumption is as firmly held by his successors as it was by Nehru. It has not been India's foreign policy style to proclaim this from housetops, but the domination of the white man over the colored races, of Europe over Asia, of the two superpowers over the rest of the world, was not acceptable to Nehru. Nor is it to his successors. As a consequence, there has been a strong streak of revisionism or rebelliousness in India's foreign policy posture. This became manifest, of course, at the very dawn of independence. At that time, while engaged in a titanic struggle against each other, both superpowers firmly agreed that the world was divided into two camps and two camps only, and there was no room for a third camp. China, too, was then in agreement with this position. One can even say there was unplanned collusion between the two superpowers in their monumental conflict, for only in that situation could they strengthen their hold over their satellites.

India played not only an innovative but a courageous role in international politics at this time. It refused to acknowledge the division of the world into two rigid camps, and refused to be stampeded into membership of either. Rather, it chose nonalignment, stuck to it through adversity, and made it respectable for scores of other new nations to follow the same course. Regardless of how the United States might assess nonalignment today, India was the target of its fury and bitterness during the 1950s on account of that policy. Likewise, when the two superpowers were in explicit collaboration over the Nuclear Non-Proliferation Treaty, India resisted both blandishments and threats, and stuck to its position that the treaty was discriminatory and refused to sign it. Still again, India exploded a nuclear device, certain that the superpowers would frown upon any such development and would be critical of it. In doing so, it demonstrated that a structure of power confined to the present nuclear powers was unacceptable to it. Earlier, India had defied the scorn of the United States in building an independent arms industry in India. Long before the nuclear explosion, India's own arms industry was a point of concern to and bitter attack by Congressman Otto Passman and others in his appropriations subcommittee. There could not be a discussion about India in his subcommittee without bringing in for scorn and criticism the subject of jet aircraft production in India.[11] Finally, in the early

---

[11] See, for example, U.S. Congress, House, Committee on Appropriations, *Foreign Assistance and Related Agencies Appropriations for 1969* Hearings, 90th Cong., 2nd Sess., 1968, pp. 763–64.

1970s, India was not dissuaded from the protection of its national interests over the Bangladesh crisis, despite opposition from both the United States and China.

In its revisionist role, India's task has been far more arduous than China's. Since World War II, as a country China has been part of the dominant international structure of power; its status has never been at issue, only the regime that ought to have legitimate claim to that status. Perhaps for this reason there is never any mention of China in plans for the control of nuclear proliferation. In contrast, India is truly the first new nation or excolonial and underdeveloped country to seek entrance into the dominant power structure. Moreover, it is, unlike China and Japan, truly the first "colored" nation to work for that change. It may well be that these same reasons mark India as a particular target for containment, for hostile criticism of its single underground nuclear explosion, and for pressure to adopt a policy of nuclear abstention while the present nuclear powers add with abandon to their nuclear arsenals and detonate innumerable nuclear explosions.

Despite the revisionist streak in its foreign policy posture, by no stretch of imagination could India be described as a full-fledged rebellious power. India's acts of revisionism pertain to vital security interests, not to the overthrow of the structure of power in the international system. The country's leadership is not revolutionary, only reformist. It has no messianic vision for the rest of the world, notwithstanding—or perhaps because of—its professions of peace. Its aspirations to, and ambitions for, a subject role in the international system are not matched by domestic efforts at social and economic reconstruction. Nor is its disaffection with the present international structure of power matched by either stridency of words or actions abroad. The contrast here with China has been quite striking: the Chinese leadership seized power through a protracted armed struggle; the Indian leadership waged essentially a nonviolent, even though a mass nationalist, struggle. India's orientation to the international system parallels that of a trade union negotiator and bargainer more than that of a revolutionary at the barricades. Through much of its diplomatic history, therefore, India has been moderate rather than extremist, pragmatic rather than adventurist, deliberate rather than hasty, restrained rather than provocative, pacifist rather than warlike.

But there has also been naiveté and ingenuousness. Thus Nehru pressed for peace among the superpowers, as if his words would carry more weight than the sure knowledge of the adversaries about mutual destruction; urged cooperation among the superpowers, as if rapprochement rather than rivalry would be more beneficial to the underdeveloped countries; and hoped for economic assistance from rich to poor countries, as if the developed world would really wish to create economic and military rivals. Here, notwithstanding his misguided adventurism, Sukarno's insights were keener. Eventually, history will impart the lessons of realpolitik to the Indians as well—though it would be an exaggeration to say that they were completely innocent of such instruction earlier, especially at the regional level.

But on one matter there has been strong continuity in the perception of India's leadership; the centrality of securing and safeguarding an independent center of power with foreign policy autonomy. Perhaps innocence was always a pose, a cover for weakness. Opposition on principle to power politics and balance of power policies—but only to those of the great powers—was perhaps meant only to exclude external powers from India's strategic environment and thus enhance her own security and maybe even assure a sphere of influence in South Asia. But could words alone secure such a goal? Or would India, like all other nations, have to match her desires with the required capabilities? History would show that India could not avoid the requirement of balance between goals and capabilities, and in that history, the United States, as the strongest superpower, would play a fundamental part.

A Clash of Roles:
The United States as Hegemonic Superpower

Given India's conception of her own role in the world, she was bound soon to encounter the power of the United States, which had emerged at the end of World War II as *the* superpower in an essentially unifocal international system organized around itself. In the management of the world, the United States has essentially behaved as any other great power, but it has continued to believe in its own exceptionalism, holding its actions to be inspired by motivations other than the self-interest and drive to domination characteristic of other nations. It is difficult to accurately assess motivations, and it is actions that constitute the proper frame of reference for investigation. Here, it is obvious that America's behavior has been consistent with that of other great powers. One does not have to go to revisionist historians to establish this point. The editor of *Foreign Affairs*, the voice of the American foreign policy establishment, recently stated:

> The United States, contrary to popular mythology, has never been an isolationist country. Almost as soon as we became a nation we became interventionist. The United States used its armed forces abroad 159 times between 1798 and 1945.... Even between World Wars I and II—said to be the heyday of isolationism—we engaged in 19 military actions outside the Western Hemisphere. Since World War II we have used military forces in Korea, Indochina, Lebanon, the Dominican Republic, and the Congo. What all this indicates is that since its inception the United States has been unafraid to exercise power in world affairs.[12]

[12] James Chace, "American Intervention," *New York Times*, September 13, 1976. See also Robert W. Tucker, *The Radical Left and American Foreign Policy* (Baltimore: Johns Hopkins University Press, 1971).

In relation to middle powers, the United States has pursued the twin policies of satellization and containment over most of the postwar period. There is an intimate relationship between these two policies. Where satellization was resisted, containment has been pursued, and in the name of containment of some middle powers the United States has pursued the satellization of others. In turn, successful containment persuaded some middle powers to cooperate with the United States; in other words, to become satellized.

It is a seriously mistaken view to restrict the notion of containment to what is only one specific application: the containment of Communism. The American policy of containment has had as its targets all independent centers of power. Liska argues in justification:

> As long as the United States could be basically inspired by the norms proper to a globally pre-eminent world power, single-handedly upholding order in the several regions, the American attitude to potential regional imperialists had to be dogmatically negative. Middle-power self-assertion beyond a definite readily discernible point threatened to inhibit or bar U.S. access to still lesser states in a region, while creating a problem for the credibility and appeal of American opposition to Communist-tinged expansionism.[13]

This claim to unrestricted access globally by the United States, also referred to as "open door,"[14] has usually translated itself into a claim for American domination in any given region, with the United States emerging as the security manager of the region and the sole determinant of developments in the region. Its purpose is precisely to be the dominant power of the region, though it often proclaims that it is merely trying to prevent the Soviet Union from becoming the dominant power.

Behind this universal open door policy in the postwar period has been a messianic complex born of the emergence of the United States as the preeminent, indeed the only, global power at the end of World War II, ushering in what many believed to be the American Century or Pax Americana. Drew Middleton points out how after World War II, the United States envisioned "an unprecedented expansion of power and influence on a global scale," one "greater in extent than any known to history," and he underlines "the supreme national confidence it promoted in the American people." He continues: "Americans were emboldened to believe that there were no policies they could not implement, no dangers they could not overcome." Not until the military failure in Vietnam was there disillusionment with such power among "those internationalists who believed in an

---

[13] George Liska, *States in Evolution: Changing Societies and Traditional Systems in World Politics* (Baltimore: Johns Hopkins University Press, 1973), p. 152.

[14] Tucker, *The Radical Left*, p. 66.

America destined to dominate Asia and the Pacific."[15] But until then, the sense of American omnipotence possessed most Americans. Dean Rusk gave expression to this feeling of power, saying, "When the United States applies pressure on something, anything, it gives."[16] As the hegemonic superpower, the United States aimed, then, to extend its influence, power, and domination across the entire globe, restricting the Soviet Union to its own region for a considerable period of time. One State Department policy planning chief acknowledged: "In the period following World War II, our preeminent power encouraged us to believe we could shape the globe according to American designs." As if nostalgic, he stated that this is no longer the case: "Today, as we approach our third century, we find—like most other nations in history—that we can neither escape from the world nor dominate it."[17] Similarly, in a statement that is half admission about the past and half denial about the present, Secretary of State Kissinger said: "We have rejected the old extremes of world policeman and isolation."[18]

However, the earlier impulse toward an imperial role for the United States is still an elemental part of the American approach to foreign policy. For example, this is obvious in many statements James R. Schlesinger made when he was Secretary of Defense. In various contexts, he talked about the notion that "historical necessity has thrust upon us" the responsibility to maintain the global military equilibrium. "The burden of responsibility," he argued, "has fallen on the United States, and there is nobody else to pick up the torch if the United States fails to carry it."[19] Again, he pressed for a strong defense establishment "for the United States as a basis for its continued leadership in the world."[20] In 1976, President Kennedy's inaugural address, President Carter stated in Great Britain: "We are determined in the United States to use our great economic and social and political and military strength so that we can never be successfully challenged by

[15] Drew Middleton, *Retreat from Victory* (New York: Hawthorn Books, 1973), pp. 45—6, 213.

[16] Marvin Kalb and Bernard Kalb, *Kissinger* (Boston: Little, Brown and Co., 1974), p. 65.

[17] Winston Lord, "America's Purposes in an Ambiguous Age," *Department of State Bulletin* no. 1845 (November 4, 1974): 617.

[18] Henry A. Kissinger, "Toward a Global Community," *Department of State Bulletin*, no. 1848 (November 25, 1974): 740—46.

[19] Cited in U.S. Congress, House, Committee on Foreign Affairs, *Proposed Expansion of U.S. Military Facilities in the Indian Ocean* Hearings, 93rd Cong., 2nd Sess., 1974, p. 94.

[20] U.S. Department of Defense *Annual Defense Department Report: FY1976 and FY1975*, mimeographed, pp. 1—7.

any competing philosophy." He added that "we have an eagerness to compete in an ideological way around the world."[22]

The claim to global leadership arises not in a vacuum but out of the realization, certainly rooted in reality, of the immense power of the United States. This has been true as much in recent years as it was in the immediate postwar period. In 1967, one State Department official, Zbigniew Brezinski, stated, "If we look at the last 20 years there has been a shift. . . to what is today a period of U.S. paramountcy. . . . The U.S. today is the only effective global military power in the world. . . . We are the only power with far-flung global economic investments, economic involvement and global trade, and there is no parallel to us in the role our science and technology plays throughout the world."[23] Several years later, Secretary of State Kissinger reiterated the theme: "We still are the strongest nation in the world. We still are, militarily, in a powerful position." Again, in words reminiscent of the celebration of Athens by Pericles, he stated, "With one-third of the output of the non-Communist world, the American economy is still the great engine of world prosperity. Our technology, our food, our resources, our managerial genius and financial expertise, our experience of leadership are unmatched." Further, "The United States still represents the single greatest concentration of economic wealth and power to be found on the planet."[24] And President Nixon would say, "When we sneeze others get pneumonia and that will continue to be the case unless the U.S. recedes from the use of power."[25]

The policy of containment, flowing out of the American perception of its role in the world, is of continuing relevance to the United States in the contemporary world. The central mechanism in the containment of middle powers has been the creation in any given region of a balance of power favorable to the United States. The concept of regional balances is central to American foreign policy, and as James Chace points out, it often demands American intervention "to prevent the balance from being upset."[26] In 1974, Defense Secretary

[21] *New York Times*, July 5, 1976.

[22] *New York Times*, May 7, 1977.

[23] *Department of State Bulletin*, "The Implications for Change in United States Foreign Policy," no. 1462 (July 3, 1967).

[24] "Question and Answer Session Held by Secretary Kissinger at St. Louis and Kansas City," Ibid., no. 1875 (June 2, 1975), pp. 726, 713, 719.

[25] Elmo R. Zumwalt, Jr., *On Watch: A Memoir* (New York: Quadrangle/The New York Times Co., 1976), p. 480.

[26] *New York Times*, September 13, 1976.

Schlesinger gave a revealing expression both of the rational for middle power containment and of its instruments. In testimony before the Senate Foreign Relations Committee, he stated that the military assistance program in the form of sales, credits, and grants was "a part of the overall security program of the United States," and went on to argue that "there are parts of the world in which the United States does not and will not have the manpower to intervene and, *in order to maintain a military balance in those parts of the world,* foreign military assistance plays a role which should be related to overall political and military strategy of the United States." The United States was not capable, Schlesinger pointed out, of maintaining adequate conventional forces "to protect its larger interests and to ensure stability in all potentially volatile areas of the world," and it was therefore "the principal purpose of security assistance—both the grant aid and the military sales programs" to meet these requirements. He noted that "in this way, we seek to *achieve regional stability* in crucial areas of the world without the need for direct intervention by American Forces." Finally, while summing up his argument, he referred to Asia: "Where we do not have the forces to help maintain a conventional balance—as is the case, for example, in the Middle East and in much of Asia—we must rely primarily on the security assistance program. It is a low-risk, low-cost alternative to direct American involvement in areas of great importance."[27]

Listening to Defense Secretary Schlesinger's statement, Senator Percy quickly grasped the underlying principle about "the necessity to establish *military balance* in critical areas of the world for the purpose of a general equilibrium in military power." He further raised a profound question: "Both you and Admiral Moorer speak of developing *regional balances.* Is it the basis of this theory to support one power in each region or to try to *maintain a parity in arms in each region?*" Schlesinger did not challenge the thrust of the question, nor did he dispute the notion of parity or building one power as a counterweight against another, but he stressed the subtlety with which policy had to be handled in this regard:

> I do not think we can give any straightforward formula for answering that question. . . .Now, in the Middle East, given the cross currents that exist there, it is not easy to provide a simple formula. I would not suggest to you for a moment that, where you have these cross currents, such a simple formula can be provided. It has to be done with intuition and feeling and I would say it also involves the appreciation that there are some risks in the judgments involved.[28]

[27] U.S. Congress, Senate, Committee on Foreign Relations, *Foreign Assistance Authorization,* Hearings, 93rd Cong., 2nd Sess., 1974, pp. 192, 194, 195, 198. Emphasis added.

[28] Ibid., pp. 233, 235. Emphasis added.

The idea of balance and equilibrium has certainly been equally fundamental to the thought structure and political posture of Henry Kissinger. As one congressional study maintains, "With respect to the Third World, Kissinger emphasized on numerous occasions the necessity of maintaining regional balances."[29] Before congressional committees, Kissinger argued that security assistance "often offers the only way to maintain the stability of regional power balances."[30] Other U.S. officials have also given expression to the policy of regional balances. In 1975, in response to one subcommittee chairman's query about "the general guiding principles that govern our conduct in the sale of arms," a senior Defense Department official replied: "Balance is one of them."[31]

It is remarkable how worldwide the American conception of its international role is. The United States endeavors to create and maintain regional balances everywhere, whether near home or tens of thousands of miles away. No other power in the world even approaches the United States in either the reach of its power or in its ambition. Realistically, the United States has been truly the only global power. It has also been the sole global policeman. Official spokesmen of a country do not like it characterized as a policeman even if it performs that role. If they acknowledge the role it is only in retrospect; interestingly, Defense Secretary Laird noted in 1972: "If Congress continues to fund security assistance at inadequate levels—protection of our national interests could be accomplished only by the expanded use of our own military resources and the reversal of the trend toward a reduced U.S. presence abroad; in other words, a return toward the role of 'world policeman' for the United States."[32]

It is of crucial importance in evaluating U.S. policy toward any specific middle power to understand the general American posture on regional military balances throughout the globe. Given the insistent and open expression at the highest levels of the U.S. decisionmaking machinery of the overall American design on the creation and maintenance of regional military balances, it is myopic to search for special written or oral evidence about American purposes in particular cases where

---

[29] U.S. Congress, House, Committee on International Relations, *The Soviet Union and the Third World*, 95th Cong., 1st Sess., 1977, p. 157.

[30] U.S. Congress, Senate, Committee on Foreign Relations, *International Security Assistance*, Hearings, 94th Cong., 2nd Sess., 1976. p. 5.

[31] Amos Jordan, in U.S. Congress, House, Committee on International Relations, *The Persian Gulf, 1975*, Hearings, 94th Cong., 1st Sess., 1975, pp. 88, 92, 93.

[32] Cited in U.S. Congress, House, Committee on Foreign Affairs, *Foreign Assistance Act of 1973*, Hearings, 92nd Cong., 2nd Sess., p. 330.

the United States endeavors to create or maintain a regional military balance. Rather one would need to demonstrate the existence of some special reasons precluding the application of the policy of regional balances to a specific country. And indeed, for India, the American policy of containment played a fundamental part in the learning process about international politics.

History as Instructor

India may have had long-range aspirations for a subject role in international politics, yet the irony is that for much of its history as an independent state it has had to struggle immensely: to resist the imposition on India of the straitjacket of object status by the contemporary great powers; to oppose being turned into a satellite of such powers; and to prevent being overwhelmed in wars with antagonists built up by the great powers. The fundamental basis for that experience has been the relative weakness of India's capabilities and the simultaneous assertion of independence from the great powers.

As the preeminent superpower, the United States itself has in the past been in the forefront of placing this straitjacket of object status on India, of attempting to turn it into a satellite, and of arming its adversaries to prevent it from establishing an independent center of power outside the American sphere of influence. But by their concentration on American benevolence, the mass media and government rhetoric have quite successfully masked the harsh strategic choices that the United States has continuously imposed on India through the policies of containment and satellization. Of course, the United States has not been the only great power to apply such policies to India, but it was the one to have initiated the process and to have persisted in that course the longest. India's experience with such policies of the great powers and its struggle to maintain its autonomy and integrity can be examined in three broad periods: the 1950s, the 1960s, and the 1970s.

In the first few years following independence in 1947, India was too preoccupied with domestic tasks to pay much attention to world affairs. Nonetheless, it had already formulated the basic postulate of its foreign policy—nonalignment. At the time, India was both suspicious and favorably inclined toward the United States. It was suspicious because India perceived the United States as the successor to the British imperial policy of divide and rule in South Asia; to India, U.S. policy on Kashmir and other local issues was evidence of this. Moreover, Nehru saw American anti-Communism as essentially an instrument facilitating the extension of U.S. power throughout the world. At the same time, India was favorably inclined toward the United States, because it was uncertain about the intentions of both the Soviet Union and China, while it simultaneously faced

Communist insurrection at home. Indeed, in the early part of the postwar period, India's relations were closer to the Western bloc, precisely because it was thought that the West would be a deterrent to any hostile Communist activity. This was the period when Communist propaganda branded Nehru and other Indian leaders as "lackeys and running dogs of imperialism."

While India had already articulated the doctrine of nonalignment, it was with the opening of the 1950s that it assumed an active role in international politics, and on the global level at that. With the Korean War, India began to play its international role with finesse, holding itself forth as a self-appointed messenger for peace and as a self-assured mediator between the two superpowers. Its concerns were diffuse goals such as peace and harmony in the world rather than concrete Indian interests. No doubt, India felt that a peaceful world was essential to its development and stability. But beyond that there was the influence of the Gandhian heritage of idealism and pacifism with which Indian leaders had grown in their nonviolent struggle for independence. This heritage gave a tone of self-righteous moralizing to Indian pronouncements, which grated the Americans, who themselves assumed the monopoly in international morality.

More significantly, India was attempting to play a subject role in international politics even though it did not possess all the attributes necessary for such a role. However, with the grave imbalance between the diplomatic influence India sought and the capabilities it possessed, its claim to a subject role could not but arouse resentment and hostility in those whose own power and influence would as a consequence be adversely affected. Meanwhile, India endeavored to overcome its power weakness by politically mobilizing other Asian and African nations and by assuming, for a time, the leadership of the nonaligned nations. India's success in this enterprise resulted from its ideology of nonalignment, since peaceful co-existence and anticolonialism had an immense appeal for large segments of the world's population.

On a whole range of world issues—Korea, China, Indochina, Southeast Asia, the Japanese peace treaty—India was now especially assertive in opposition to the United States. This assertiveness in the first half of the 1950s came at a time when the United States was the sole subject in the international system and was determined to remain so. Not surprisingly, U.S. policy at the time was to convert the entire globe into an American sphere of influence, applying containment not only to the Soviet bloc but to all independent centers of power; witness the American counterbalancing of Egypt through Iraq and assisting the rebellion in Indonesia. It is noteworthy that in congressional hearings in 1954, when Congressman Coudbert asked, "Fundamentally does not that mean that the United States is undertaking to maintain for an indefinite period of years American dominance in the Far East?" Assistant Secretary of State Robertson laconically answered,

"Yes, exactly."[33] Nehru protested at this presumption on the part of the United States, but it was in this frame of mind that American decisionmakers encountered Indian assertiveness in international politics.

As a result of its foreign policy posture, India came to be viewed by the United States not only as a continuous irritant but also as an inveterate claimant to an independent role in international politics. Dean Acheson was visibly incensed by Nehru's activities on the world scene; as a respected American scholar pointedly observes, "A permanent state of irritation is the best summary description of Acheson's attitude toward India."[34] John Foster Dulles characterized India's nonalignment not only as "an obsolete conception" but also as "an immoral and shortsighted conception."[35] Acheson did not publicly condemn India for her nonalignment, but Acheson's attitude was indistinguishable from Dulles's."[36] Nonalignment became anathema to most Americans, and Nehru was dubbed an "aide and ally" of Communism by American leaders like George Meany.[37]

India's policy was objectionable to the United States not only because it placed an obstacle in the way of American containment of the Soviet Union but also because it attempted to create an additional world force—a force based not on military capabilities but on a political mobilization of national elites in Asia and Africa. From the American perspective, India had arrogated to itself the privileges of a putative independent center of power, thus contracting the American sphere of influence. As a consequence, India's position became unacceptable to the United States. It is in this context that the United States launched a policy of military containment and neutralization of India through the military buildup of Pakistan. Interestingly, even though the U.S.-Pakistan military alliance became effective in 1954 under a Republican administration, the proposal itself was of a much earlier origin: "John Foster Dulles was then Secretary of State, but he was carrying out a policy that had been initiated by Acheson."[38] In those years, it

---

[33] Royal Institute of International Affairs, *Survey of International Affairs 1954* (London: Oxford University Press, 1957), p. 284.

[34] Gaddis Smith, *Dean Acheson* (New York: Cooper Square Publishers, 1972), p. 375; see also Dean Acheson, *Present at the Creation* (New York: W.W. Norton and Co., 1969), pp. 334–36, 416–20.

[35] Michael A. Guhin, *John Foster Dulles: A Statesman and His Times* (New York: Columbia University Press, 1972), p. 259.

[36] Smith, *Dean Acheson*, p. 378.

[37] *New York Times*, December 14, 1955, p. 1; see also Durga Das, *India From Curzon to Nehru & After* (London: Wm. Collins, Sons and Co., 1969), p. 297.

[38] Smith, *Dean Acheson*, p. 377.

was not only containment that the United States applied to India, but also diplomatic isolation; the United States made every effort to exclude India from any participation in negotiations or security arrangements concerning Southeast Asia in 1954, as it had done a year earlier in relation to Korea.[39]

In all this it should be underlined that India did not physically—it could not in any case—hurt any of America's vital security interests. All that it had attempted to do was to refuse to be intimidated into the American sphere of influence and become an American satellite in the conduct of its foreign policy. But the United States, with its assumption of a messianic global role for itself, found this intolerable. It is noteworthy that at the time the Pakistani arms deal was initiated, there was absolutely no Soviet presence—apart from the normal diplomatic missions—in the South Asian subcontinent, in either the economic or military field. If anything, the Soviet posture toward India was cool, distant, and somewhat hostile, in view of India's membership in the British Commonwealth, the country's close economic and cultural ties with the West, and its recent tough crackdown on the Communists. In fact it was the rigid insistence of the United States to go through with the arms agreement with Pakistan, brushing aside Indian objections, that was to create both the incentive and the opportunity for India and the USSR to draw closer together. And there can be no question about the decisive initiating role of American intervention in the subcontinent in making the USSR a relevant actor in the international politics of the region. For India, the military intervention on the part of the United States was a stunning defeat for its policy to exclude external powers from the subcontinent, and emphasized the enormous gap between India's role pretensions and its capabilities.

It is a gross error to view American military aid to Pakistan as directed at Communism rather than specifically at India, even though a great deal of obscurantism manifestly prevails on this point. It is equally a fundamental error to regard it—and other similar policies—as simply a mistake. Rather, it formed part of what is for a great power an understandable foreign policy posture. The American decision on arms transfers to Pakistan flowed quite naturally, logically, and consistently from the general, axiomatic principle of American foreign policy of creating regional balances—the concept prevailed then and is not a creation of the Nixon administration in the 1970s[40]—in view of the Indian attempt (unrealistic though it may have been) to act independently on the global scene.

---

[39] Anthony Eden, *Full Circle* (Boston: Houghton Mifflin Co., 1960), pp. 94—99; and D.R. SarDesai, *Indian Foreign Policy in Cambodia, Laos, and Vietnam 1947—1964* (Berkeley: University of California Press, 1968), pp. 36—46.

[40] Selig S. Harrison, "America, India, and Pakistan: A Chance for a Fresh Start," *Harper's* 233 (July 1966): 67.

There is decisive independent testimony on American intentions in relation to India specifically. In justifying its military aid to Pakistan, the United States followed a two-faced tactic; one justification for public consumption, another for private information. As Selig Harrison pointed out a long time ago:

> For the record John Foster Dulles defined the new military pact with Pakistan as part of the global collective-security pattern then being developed to meet an expected recurrence of conventional aggression by Communist ground forces throughout Asia. Off the record, Vice President Nixon defined the objectives of some elements in Washington more candidly in briefings with newsmen. Pakistan's readiness to enter into a military pact offered an opportunity, the Vice President felt, to build a counterforce to Nehru's neutralism in the Indian leader's backyard. [41]

As vice president, Nixon himself was also an important participant in the decision, which followed a moving speech he made before the National Security Council after a wide-ranging tour through Asia. In that speech, Nixon expressed his feeling that "Nehru was contemptuous of flattery and respectful of strength," and force-fully urged military aid to Pakistan "as a counterforce to the confirmed neutral-ism of Jawaharlal Nehru's India." [42] As his admiring biographer Ralph de Toledano, to whom Nixon opened his files, observed, Nixon was "convinced that India's neutralism was an outgrowth of the prime minister's belief that India could be a dominant force only if the rest of non-Communist Asia were weak and unarmed." [43]

With Dulles too it was India's foreign policy that was the crucial element. As Chester Bowles wrote, "Soon stories began to appear of behind-the-scenes maneuvering within the State Department and Pentagon for a review of the earlier negative decision. Of particular concern was the report that Secretary of State Dulles, exasperated by Nehru's refusal to sign the Japanese Peace Treaty that he (Dulles) had negotiated or to modify India's nonaligned foreign policies, was in favor of the proposed buildup of the Pakistan military." [44] The contain-ment of India thus followed the failure of American attempts to make Indian foreign policy correspond to American aims or, in other words, to turn India into a foreign policy satellite of the United States. Senator Fulbright quite aptly warned that the military pact with Pakistan was basically an anti-Nehru tactic

[41] Ibid.

[42] Ralph de Toledano, *Nixon* (New York: Henry Holt, 1956) p. 164.

[43] Ibid.

[44] Chester Bowles, *Promises to Keep: My Years in Public Life 1941–1969* (New York: Harper & Row, 1971), p. 478.

"designed to force his hand." [45] Nehru was thus correct in perceiving that American decisionmakers "imagine that an alliance between Pakistan and the U.S. would bring such overwhelming pressure on India as to compel her to change her policy of nonalignment." [46]

However, one does not have to rely simply on verbal testimony to discern the intentions of American decisionmakers. Equally important is the actual pattern of state behavior of the United States. For one thing, the weapons-mix of military aid provided to Pakistan left no doubt that it was directed at India. For another, the United States was not unaware that Pakistan's own target in the acquisition of American arms was India. The Indian Government brought all this to the attention of the United States, but to no avail. As Bowles stated:

> The Indian Government pointed out that the military equipment that we were giving to Pakistan had no relevance to our alleged military objectives. If the Pakistan Army were actually designed to become part of a United States-sponsored defense system to discourage a Soviet or Chinese military movement through the Himalayas or the Hindu Kush Mountains, it would be seeking equipment appropriate for fighting in the mountain areas. However, the equipment we supplied Pakistan—tanks, motorized artillery and the like—was suitable for use only on a relatively flat terrain, in other words, on the plains of North India. Moreover, from the outset, the Pakistan Government had itself made clear that it had no quarrel with either the U.S.S.R. or China and privately admitted that its military build-up was, in fact, directed against India. [47]

One should not underestimate the extent and strategic significance of American military aid provided to Pakistan. Within about a decade, from 1954 to 1965, the United States supplied Pakistan with sophisticated weaponry—technologically far superior to India's—at bargain-basement prices to the tune of $1.5 billion, and Pakistan concentrated its new armaments on the western borders of India. The U.S. aid was nothing but the creation of military parity between India and Pakistan. The result, or course, was to strengthen Pakistani intransigence in its disputes with India and eventually to embolden Pakistan to initiate military conflict with India in 1965.

Meanwhile, the formal pretense that the American alliance with Pakistan was strictly directed against Communism was also given up. In a secret *aide memoire* in 1963 the U.S. government pledged to Pakistan that the commitment to Pakistan "was not limited to Communist countries but indeed specifically

---

[45] Selig S. Harrison, "India, Pakistan and the U.S.—II," *New Republic* 141 (August 24, 1959): 21.

[46] Kuldip Nayar, *India After Nehru* (Delhi: Vikas Publications, 1975), p. 52.

[47] Bowles, *Promises to Keep*, p. 480.

included India." [48] The military buildup of Pakistan to neutralize India in a regional balance had become almost sacred, unaffected by changes in administration. The policy of regional balance directed against India continued unabated, at least into the mid-1970s. Publicly, its adoption was denied, but in 1971 Kissinger claimed legitimacy for it as a superior historical and moral principle in a conversation with Henry Brandon:

> The situation also brought out the political theorist in Kissinger, or so he later claimed. As a believer in the global policy of balance of power, he was determined to put theory into practice and to show that the United States stood by the weaker against the strong in the hope that this would prevent actual conflict. Kissinger, just after Christmas 1971, pointed out to me that in the Pakistani case the United States followed the British example; he drew my attention to a speech by Winston Churchill in 1936, which to him was the best exposition of the balance-of-power principle. In that speech Churchill said: "We always took the harder course, joined with the less strong power, made a combination among them, and thus defeated and frustrated the Continental military tyrant whoever he was, whatever the nation he led."[49]

Similar sentiments were apparently expressed by Kissinger to his admiring biographers.[50] Subsequently, U.S. officials acknowledged, even if only in private, the application of the policy of building up Pakistan to set off India's power, but only in reference to the past.[51] In 1977, the new American Ambassador to India, Robert Goheen, stated more openly:

> The events of the last decade have brought it about that whether you look at it in geographical terms, in military terms or in economic terms, India and Pakistan really aren't competitors any more. India is clear and away the preeminent nation in the subcontinent, so that game we played for many years of trying to balance one off against the other—that's a dead game. And that was a terrific cause of friction between India and ourselves.[52]

.

[48] G.W. Choudhury, *India, Pakistan, Bangladesh, and the Major Powers* (New York: Free Press, 1975), pp. 112—13.

[49] Henry Brandon, *The Retreat of American Power* (New York: Doubleday and Co., 1973), pp. 252—53.

[50] Kalb and Kalb, *Kissinger*, p. 258.

[51] See Baldev Raj Nayar, *American Geopolitics and India* (New Delhi: Manohar, 1976), pp. 70—71.

[52] William Borders, "Mr. Goheen in Delhi: On Both Sides, New Ideas," *New York Times,* October 2, 1977.

The United States had thus adopted a rather consistent strategy from the early 1950s onwards. To be sure, there were over time some modifications in the modalities of that strategy; undoubtedly there were other subsidiary perspectives within different administrations; and, of course, there were other policies that were beneficial to India. But containment became the encompassing principle in relation to India, disciplining other policies.

To sum up, the cumulative evidence—from the overall foreign policy posture of the United States, the declarations at the time, retrospective statements, philosophical analyses and actual American state behavior—leads overwhelmingly and compellingly to the conclusion that in the American military buildup of Pakistan, India was the specific target of the general American policy of containment aimed at independent centers of power. It is disturbing, however, that American analysts, rather than coming to terms with such evidence, tend to attribute the conclusions drawn from it to native psychology.[53]

The inauguration of the policy of arms transfers to Pakistan by the United States in 1954 should have been an instructive lesson in realpolitik to India. India did undertake measures—though only political and diplomatic rather than military—to counteract the American military alliance with Pakistan. However, India continued to emphasize the missionary-pacifist and mediatory aspects of its foreign policy. It moved politically closer to the USSR and China and in doing so demonstrated that, despite its rhetoric, balance of power policies were inescapable for it as they were for others. Even so, India's reaction to American containment was a measured and graduated one so that it did not move itself irretrievably "beyond the reach of America's competitive counter-bidding."[54]

As part of the growing political relationship between India and the USSR from the mid-1950s on, the USSR extended economic aid in a dramatic form—the building of a steel plant. The United States had already established a low-level technical assistance program, but now an economic rivalry started between the USSR and the United States in order "to win friends and influence people" in India as in the rest of the nonaligned world. American aid to India soon assumed massive aggregate proportions even though on a per capita basis the country was well down the list of aid recipients. Initially, the program was "viewed primarily as a slush fund to entice the reluctant to 'our side' in the bipolar struggle."[55] Dulles maintained before Congressional hearings that not to offer aid

[53] Barnds, "United States Policy," p. 650.

[54] Pran Chopra, *India's Second Liberation* (Delhi: Vikas Publications, 1973), pp. 9—10.

[55] Seyom Brown, *The Faces of Power* (New York: Columbia University Press, 1968), p. 101.

"would in effect involve writing off India."[56] Ambassador, later Senator, John Sherman Cooper thought it "essential to help India out in order to prevent Russia's muscling in any more."[57] Subsequently, however, greater sophistication developed in casting the aid program in developmental terms and masking its political goals. Eventually, the program would be terminated in 1971 for political reasons, just as it had been inaugurated for political purposes.

If being the target of the economic rivalry between the two superpowers was immensely ego-satisfying for the Indian elite at the time and equally materially beneficial, India's attempted shortcut to global status could only be a flash in the pan, given her weakness in capabilities. And so it was. Several factors caused the decline in India's global role and diplomatic activity in the second half of the 1950s. First, there had developed greater direct diplomatic contact between the United States and the USSR symbolized by the "spirit of Camp David." Second, as the number of newly independent states in Asia and Africa increased, with some of them radical, India's world role was bound to diminish. Third, the increased urgency of her economic problems following the foreign exchange crisis of 1957 resulted in a less conspicuous world role. Fourth, India's economic dependence tarnished the missionary aspect of its nonalignment, with the world perceiving it as simply an economic client of the great powers. Fifth, security questions closer to home began to assume critical importance, lessening the relevance of an activist role in the world. Pakistan's increasing military buildup was already a matter of concern to India, but the growing border dispute with China—which Nehru had kept secret from the Indian public since 1954—made manifest the priority of security over the pursuit of status. These security concerns also drew India closer to the United States as the decade of the 1950s was ending.

Slowly but surely the lessons of realpolitik were being driven home to India, especially the importance of balance between role and capabilities. The coup de grace to India's global role occurred in a military clash with China in 1962, in which it suffered severe, though territorially limited, reverses. India had obviously behaved irresponsibly as a major power, devoting to defense a mere 2 percent of its gross national product. The point is not that the Indians did not make errors or provide provocation, but that China could attack so massively with impunity precisely because the Indians were militarily so weak. More specifically, India was to blame for initially neglecting the security of its borders and then being unwilling to accept the consequences of this initial neglect. The neglect may well

---

[56] Guhin, *John Foster Dulles*, p. 255.

[57] C.L. Sulzberger, *The Last of the Giants* (New York: Macmillan Co., 1970), p. 242.

have been the result of a rational choice not to provoke China when India was so lacking in capabilities, but such a rational choice only postponed the final reckoning. Indeed, the Chinese attack was a preemptive strike just at the time when India turned to improving its military capabilities in the border region.

For India, the real message of the border conflict was that the country's role pretensions were inconsistent with its capabilities. In retrospect, the military reverses of 1962 were a blessing in disguise for India, for the military buildup that followed enabled it to prevent defeat at the hands of Pakistan, a defeat that would have had far graver consequences for the country's territorial integrity.

Since a weak defense had been the cause of India's predicament in 1962, it was to defense that India gave priority attention during the 1960s. A drastic retrenchment in its international role followed, as India moved away from such diffuse goals as world peace to such concrete interests as security and economic growth. Concomitant with the tacit renunciation of a world role there emerged an increased realism about diplomacy. Greater attention also began to be paid to regional neighbors.

Since India lacked the internal economic base to build arms capabilities, it resorted to borrowing these from the United States and the USSR. Here a marked shift in the international power configuration helped it in such borrowing. In the aftermath of the Cuban missile crisis, the United States and the USSR were launched on a mutual rapprochement, marking the acceptance of the USSR as a full-fledged subject in the international system. Together the two major powers developed a policy of joint containment of China, which they felt was a disturbing and destabilizing element in the world power equilibrium. Both now recognized in India an area of cooperation in this containment, with the United States providing food and economic aid and the USSR furnishing military assistance.

There is nothing wrong in borrowing capabilities, whether in economic aid or military equipment, but the Indians allowed themselves—despite their rhetoric about self-reliance—to slip into excessive dependence, with the United States acquiring an especially intrusive presence in India. With this dependence came a muted foreign policy role and an effective dismantlement of nonalignment. Everything was justified by appeal to nonalignment, but in effect there had come into being a bi-alignment with the United States and the USSR, which diminished India's role among the nonaligned countries. Meanwhile, noting American aid to India, Pakistan became somewhat alienated from the United States and moved closer to China, gaining as a result increased prestige in the Third World.

The new configuration of international politics became manifest in the 1965 war between India and Pakistan. Both the United States and the USSR adopted a hands-off policy, but China attempted to unnerve India by supporting Pakistan. Although the result of the war was basically a stalemate, the Indians nonetheless felt relieved to have frustrated Pakistan's designs on Kashmir. They considered this an achievement, given the tremendous military buildup of Pakistan with modern American weaponry over the previous decade. The aftermath of the war, though, saw an enhancement of Soviet influence in the subcontinent. Increasingly sucked into Vietnam, ostensibly to contain China, the United States seemed to concede, though only temporarily, to the USSR the role of preeminent foreign power in South Asia. An apparent division of labor seemed to emerge in the containment of China—the United States in Vietnam, the USSR in South Asia.

With American blessing the USSR played a mediatory role at Tashkent, and subsequently emerged as the "security manager" of the subcontinent. In this new role, the USSR adopted a somewhat more neutral policy between India and Pakistan in place of the earlier partisan support of India, and even started providing military supplies to Pakistan. India was angered by the opening of still another military pipeline to Pakistan, which was already receiving military supplies from the United States and China. But in view of its own dependence on the USSR plus the American refusal to help India with military equipment, India could do little about it.

The costs of dependence for Indian autonomy were also driven home by the experience with American aid. At a time of dire need for food, the United States kept the Indians on a short tether in order to have them relent on issues of foreign policy, especially on Vietnam. It has often been claimed by U.S. officials and others that President Johnson's actions of repeatedly delaying food shipments until the very last minute, were motivated by the urge to shake the Indians into new agricultural policies. But this is an erroneous claim, for the Indians had already adopted these policies. As a *New York Times* editorial noted: "If India were seriously delinquent in self-help measures, there might be an argument for a squeeze at a more propitious time. But an inter-agency memorandum in October 1966, a special task force in November and a Congressional visit in December have all indicated that India's program is generally satisfactory."[58] The intent, however, was entirely different, and on this point the man then American Ambassador to India ought to have the last word:

> Predictably, the U.S. Government's reaction, and particularly that of the President, was violent. Cables from Washington burned with comments about "those ungrateful Indians," and the shipments of wheat were further delayed. Our official logic in regard to India seemed to run as follows: India is poor, we are rich, and India must have our assistance. Therefore it follows that if India cannot support U.S. policy, it should at least refrain from criticizing it, or accept the consequences.

[58] Cited in Bowles, *Promises to Keep*, p. 530. See also the testimony of Congressman Dole ibid., pp. 529—40.

This spirit at its worst was reflected in the remark a high White House official once made to me as we discussed one of Mrs. Gandhi's requests for America to "stop the bombing." Mrs. Gandhi, I asserted, was only saying what U Thant and the Pope had said over and over again. "But," replied the official, "the Pope and U Thant don't need our wheat." 59

In this matter, India refused to bend, resisting the satellization of its foreign policy. The experience proved a source of such humiliation, however, that Prime Minister Gandhi reportedly determined never again to be put in such a plight. [60]

The United States was able to pressure India into a devaluation of the rupee in 1966, [61] and had engaged in considerable arm-twisting of India over the Kashmir issue following the India-China war in 1962. [62] It became apparent that, while ready to sustain India as part of a policy of containment directed against the USSR and China, the United States was opposed to helping it build an independent center of power. The United States had earlier directly refused India aid for building of the heavy industry sector. [63] Likewise, it refused both to supply India with supersonic jet fighters and heavy tanks, which it made available to Pakistan, and—more important—to help India set up its own defense industry to produce such sophisticated weaponry. [64] The United States was prepared to be India's military protector if India accepted the complementary role of American client and protectorate, but was not ready to help India obtain the means for becoming an independent center of power. In this respect, India found a greater community of interest with the USSR, which more readily provided military aid, primarily because of its own conflict with China.

The 1960s demonstrated the failure of India to keep external powers out of the subcontinent. The period marked a low point in Indian foreign policy performance, with the country virtually turned into an object of external powers; this was especially galling when contrasted to the global role played by India during the 1950s. Again, it underscored the hazards not only of excessive dependence but also of rigid foreign policy postures. In the late 1960s, realizing its lack

---

59 Ibid., p. 526.

60 Zareer Masani, *Indira Gandhi: A Biography* (London: Hamish Hamilton, 1975), p. 164.

61 Ibid., pp. 158—62.

62 Kuldip Nayar, *India After Nehru*, pp. 41, 58.

63 P.J. Eldridge, *The Politics of Foreign Aid in India* (London: George Weidenfeld and Nicolson, 1969), p. 53.

64 Bowles, *Promises to Keep*, pp. 439—40; Kuldip Nayar, *India: The Critical Years* (Delhi: Vikas Publications, 1971), p. 101.

of maneuverability, India sent signals to postcultural revolution China but with little response. Finally, the 1960s underscored the point that internal political weakness and instability seriously aggravated the problems of coping with the international system, and raised questions of whether India's political system was adequate to meet the simultaneous requirements of national security, political independence, and economic development.

As if India's plight was not bad enough by the late 1960s, it became even more serious as the 1970s opened. Though not directed at India specifically, a sharp change in American foreign policy posture suddenly confronted India with a threatening new strategic environment. As Nixon assumed the presidency, it was apparent that the U.S. role in the world was eroding while that of the Soviet Union was growing. Accordingly, in a classic balance of power move to preserve the U.S. position as the chief subject in international politics, the United States pushed forward a rapprochement with China as a third subject power, a China that had in the meantime become a significant nuclear power.

The decision to move toward rapprochement with China eliminated the rationale for American support for India as part of the policy of containment against China. In fact, the United States soon acknowledged China in its new subject role as having legitimate interests in South Asia, primarily in the containment of India through support of Pakistan. "We will do nothing to harm legitimate Soviet and Chinese interests in the area,"[65] Nixon said in his 1971 foreign policy report. In the pursuit of a more fruitful relationship with China, preventing possible economic or political weakening of India was no longer of concern to the United States. Apparently, India was now written off by the Nixon administration not merely because it was weak and a "bottomless pit," but also because of its refusal to subordinate its interests to those of the United States, and because of the growing intimacy between India and the USSR. This last was partly a direct consequence of American overtures to China.

Out of Nixon's strategy flowed the policy of offsetting India's close ties to the USSR with continuing American support of Pakistan, while the United States held additional leverage through its projected increased naval presence in the Indian Ocean. Soviet influence in India was now to be countered not so much by international competition within India using economic aid as by an even heavier reliance on the use of an external counterforce against India, partly through Pakistan, now supported not only by the United States but also, in tacit agreement, by China. Nixon's foreign policy report of 1971 gave pointed expression to this new thrust:

[65] U.S. President, *Public Papers of the Presidents of the United States* (Washington, D.C.: Office of the *Federal Register*, National Archives and Record Service, 1957–), Richard Nixon, 1971, p. 281.

> We will try to keep our activities in the area in balance with those of the other major powers concerned. The policy of the Soviet Union appears to be aimed at creating a compatible area of stability on its southern borders, and at countering Chinese Communist influence. The People's Republic of China, for its part, has made a major effort to build a strong relationship with Pakistan. We will do nothing to harm legitimate Soviet and Chinese interests in the area. We are equally clear, however, that no outside power has a claim to a predominant influence, and that each can serve its own interests and the interests of South Asia by conducting its activities in the region accordingly.[66]

The underlying implication for India was obvious: the only place the United States had for India in its grand design for the new international order was as an object, and an object of *all* the great powers at that. The prospect of such a continued role was, of course, unacceptable to India. But during the Bangladesh crisis the United States vividly demonstrated its determination that India had better learn to adapt itself to that fate.

India's initial response to the situation created by the military crackdown by Pakistan in East Bengal and the resulting influx of some ten million refugees was bewilderment, helplessness, and indecisiveness. India was especially staggered by the American warning that it should expect no assistance from the United States in the event of Chinese intervention.[67] Learning how unreliable external support was, India decided about this time to prepare for a nuclear test. Given the obvious bias of the Nixon administration, the apparent tacit alliance between the United States and China against India, the threat to India's political existence and national integration, and the prospect of the continued status as an object of all three superpowers, India finally decided to defy the United States in the Bangladesh crisis. Nixon and Kissinger for once met more than their strategic match in Indira Gandhi, who demonstrated that others could play the game of realpolitik as well. In a masterly balance of power move she lifted India out of its foreign policy *immobilisme*, entering into a treaty of friendship with the USSR to assure diplomatic protection in case of a war on the subcontinent. India's critics might well proclaim the treaty to be inconsistent with nonalignment; but nonalignment was supposed to serve India, not India serve nonalignment in some morality play. Indira Gandhi established the essential point that henceforth India's security objectives would rank foremost in her foreign policy.

When war erupted, India demonstrated that if outside powers are excluded from the subcontinent it is indeed the preeminent power in the region, despite its economic and military weakness. With the United States and China neutralized

---

[66] Ibid.

[67] Masani, *Indira Gandhi*, p. 238; Kuldip Nayar, *India*, p. 267, and *India After Nehru*, p. 187.

by the USSR, both diplomatically and militarily, India was able to inflict a severe military defeat on America's proxy, Pakistan, and to deal the Nixon adminstration perhaps its only serious diplomatic reverse. Most important, India averted her own economic and political collapse under the reeling burden of ten million refugees. In the process, India appeared to have created a new strategic environment and to stand forth as the preeminent power in the subcontinent. There was considerable substance to the achievement of this new role, but it was to some extent also a temporary illusion in the euphoric aftermath of a military victory. Time would show that the creation of Bangladesh did not resolve India's security or diplomatic situation—of course, nothing ever does—because the underlying basis for that remained the continuing weakness in India's power capabilities.

In the immediate aftermath of the Bangladesh crisis, India attempted to become the "system builder" of South Asia. It wished for the exclusion of the great powers from the diplomacy of the region, and toward that end precluded any Tashkent-type conference, insisting instead on a bilateral settlement with Pakistan. At Simla, India and Pakistan agreed to resolve their problems bilaterally and work toward a more cooperative era. With its new political realism, India made overtures to China and to the United States so that it could have diversified relationships with the great powers. But it was under no illusion that the United States and China would end their policy of containment in the near future. For its part, India wanted them to be aware that it would endeavor to maintain its preeminence in the subcontinent and its status as an independent center of power. The nuclear explosion was one indicator of India's determination in this regard.

VI

Regional Power in a Multipolar World

Baldev Raj Nayar

The war in South Asia in 1971 resulted in a major restructuring of power in the region, raising India to a position of preeminence in the subcontinent and consequently making it an important middle power. More critically, there had occurred by the beginning of the decade significant changes in the larger international environment.

During the late 1940s and the 1950s the international system was divided into two somewhat rigid power blocs organized around the two superpowers. More realistically, however, the world was essentially a unifocal system organized around the United States as the hegemonic superpower and the sole subject in that system, with the USSR basically contained and isolated within its own region. The 1960s saw a disintegration of the rigid blocs, with China splitting off from the Soviet bloc and France asserting its independence in relation to the United States. More important, after the Cuban missile crisis, the United States acknowledged the USSR as a second subject in the international system in recognition of its nuclear capabilities. With the 1970s a further diffusion of power has occurred within the international system, with greater power accretion in several centers around the world. As part of this diffusion, the middle powers have acquired a greater political importance than before.

In 1972, Undersecretary of State John N. Irwin described the elements of continuity and change in the global power configuration when he stated, "The United States and the Soviet Union are likely to continue to be the only countries with worldwide strategic and conventional capabilities, but this fact should be of decreased importance as local powers become more significant in particular regions."[1] With the greater diffusion of power, the middle powers have come to possess a greater capacity for asserting local preeminence and the ability to destabilize their regions, thus affecting the relationship between the superpowers. Earlier, when the United States was the sole hegemonic superpower, it could build local powers against regional middle powers that asserted their indepen-

---

[1] Department of State, *Press Release*, no. 153, mimeographed, June 23, 1972, p. 4.

dence; with the wider diffusion of power in a more plural world it is no longer an easy policy to execute worldwide. The local power position of middle powers has driven up the costs of intervention and regional balancing. Consequently, there is an incentive for some American accommodation toward middle powers.

Meanwhile, the notion of power itself has undergone differentiation, resulting in greater complexity in an international system largely in a state of transition. Earlier, military and economic power basically coincided under the hegemony of the two superpowers, but by the 1970s military and economic power had become differentiated, with the result that in place of the previous single power structure there have now come to operate two power hierarchies in the world: one military-political and the other economic.[2] It is a tribute to American power that despite its relative decline over time the United States is at the apex of both hierarchies.

There is then first the military-political structure in which power is concentrated in a triangle encompassing the United States, the USSR and China. In this structure, Europe and Japan matter little, being dependent on the United States for their security. Despite the triangular politics, however, the real contenders are the United States and the USSR, the genuinely global powers, with China not yet in the same league. But between the two superpowers there is both competition and collusion. In the competitive relationship, the United States continues to follow a policy of containment toward the USSR. Detente does not supplant, but only supplements, containment. As Kissinger maintained. "The very concept of 'detente' has always been applicable only to an adversary relationship."[3] Indeed, the Nixon-Kissinger strategy was "to evolve detente into a new form of containment of the Soviet Union—or, better still, self-containment on the part of the Russians."[4] In the superpower competition, the middle powers are significant, for they are preeminent in their regions and thus are related to the central balance of power. As a consequence, neither superpower would be eager to alienate a middle power in normal circumstances for fear of driving it into the arms of the other.

Notwithstanding the superpower competition, there is also collusion (or cooperation) on the international scene between the United States and the USSR, stemming, as Brzezinski put it, from "the strategic relationship which places each of us in a position to destroy the other" and from "a certain sense of parity in the

---

[2] Ralf Dahrendorf, "International Power: A European Perspective," *Foreign Affairs 56* (October 1977): 72—88.

[3] *New York Times*, June 26, 1976.

[4] Leslie H. Gelb, "The Kissinger Legacy," *New York Times Magazine*, October 31, 1976, 14.

relationship derived from the fact that we're both global powers."[5] In this col-
lusive aspect of their relationship, the United States and the USSR do not wish to
see their dominance in the international system affected by the addition of any
new members to the nuclear club. There is unconcealed pressure on middle
powers by both superpowers to adhere to the Nuclear Non-Proliferation Treaty,
which is nothing but the contemporary incarnation of containment.

In addition to the military-power hierarchy, there is the economic structure in
which the dominant partners are the United States, Europe, and Japan, but in
which the USSR and China do not figure at all. Although much of the economic
power of the world is concentrated in this trilateral structure, this power has been
under attack from much of the Third World under the "new international
economic order" movement. The radicalism, vociferousness, and tenacity with
which the Third World, with Soviet and Chinese support, has pressed its demands
has created a deep impression on the United States as the leader of the First
World. However, there is no corresponding sentiment for any substantial concessions apart from "conscience cleaning" by way of a modest, but strategically
motivated, foreign aid program. Meaningful concessions, in any case, are a
function of leverage, and the Third World does not have much of that. But in
order to mute Third World protest the United States may adopt a policy of
selective cooptation or accommodation. Significantly, in 1975, just before joining
the government, a senior scholar at the Council on Foreign Relations stated:

> A third factor facilitating accommodation is the very small number of repre-
> sentatives that have to be co-opted into senior decisionmaking roles in the
> management structure of the international economy. In Africa, only Nigeria.
> In Latin America, Brazil and Venezuela, perhaps Mexico. In the Middle East,
> Saudi Arabia and Iran. And in Asia, India, Indonesia.[6]

Interestingly, President Carter's travel plans in 1977 included every one of these
countries of the Third World except for "uncertain" Mexico and Indonesia, which
President Ford visited in 1975.

The 1970s have thus been a period in which there is (1) a dominant political
structure characterized by competition and collusion between the two superpowers, and (2) a dominant economic structure, characterized by conflict
between the Third World and the First World, but in which selective cooptation is
a viable policy. It is in this international environment that India emerged in 1971
as a significant middle power.

[5] *New York Times*, October 19, 1977.

[6] Tom J. Farer, "The United States and the Third World: A Basis for Accommodation,"
Foreign Affairs 54 (October 1975): 93.

Contemporary Role and Posture

The overwhelming lesson that the international system—more accurately, the great powers—has taught India over the period since independence is the priority of realpolitik in international politics. As a result, India has based its foreign policy in the 1970s on a sound and realistic assessment of its capabilities, both in the roles it claims and those it eschews. India has not lost sight of its long-term aspirations based on a perception of the country's potential, but its expectations have been more narrowly defined in terms of present capabilities. Its capabilities now seem to dictate its role expectations. Here, there is for India cause for both confidence and restraint.

India's major strength lies in its defensive capabilities. First and foremost, the country's large area provides it considerable defense in depth in South Asia. Second, as the second most populous country in the world India has considerable reserves of manpower to draw on for defense. Third, despite its economic dependency, India has a rather autarkic continental-sized economy, a considerable modern industrial base, and the basic resources to draw upon, if necessary, for survival. Fourth, India has an army a million-strong and a considerable air force. Fifth, India has a large independent arms industry, providing it with considerable self-reliance in weapons acquisition. By virtue thus of its population and area, its economic and industrial structure, its large armed forces, and its genuine nationalism, India is quite strong in defensive capabilities. And in the context of South Asia, India is without doubt the preeminent power. It is the overall nature of India's defensive capabilities that explains the assessment of U.S. officials, often expressed in private, that the United States does not have much leverage against India. Such an assessment is clearly an exaggeration. Nonetheless, its defensive capabilities give India enough self-confidence to resist the imposition of the role of object on it, to build its own independent center of power, and to have the ambition to be the system-builder for the region.

On the other hand, India's offensive capabilities are weak or nonexistent. It has no strategic weapons and, even if a positive decision were made now, it would not have them for a long time to come. [7] Its armed forces are equipped for conventional warfare oriented toward the defense of its borders, and these forces are spread out on two long frontiers. Furthermore, India does not have any economic surplus or free-floating resources to "win friends or influence people"; nor does it have any clout as a trade monopoly. Rather it is itself dependent on outside powers; besides, it has been faced with intermittent economic crises at home. The lack of offensive military capabilities, economic dependency, and continued

---

[7] For an excellent study, see Ashok Kapoor, *India's Nuclear Option: Atomic Diplomacy and Decision Making* (New York: Praeger Publishers, 1976).

economic crises thus severely limit the assertion or projection of Indian power and influence not only outside the region but also within it.

India's current foreign policy posture would seem to flow out of an appreciation of the nature of its capabilities. No longer does India make any claim to a global role, since a global role is basically a function of strategic capabilities or superior economic muscle. Neither is there any eagerness to play a mediatory role, which in any case is not available; on the contrary, India must worry about collusion among the great powers. Nor does India wish to project power or influence in neighboring regions. Its long-standing refusal to project power based on ideological opposition to military alliances and power politics has now been fortified by a realistic appreciation of its own capabilities.

As part of India's global retrenchment there has occurred a downgrading of the United Nations and the group of nonaligned nations as arenas for achieving political-diplomatic objectives. This development has taken place because India lost influence, and because these arenas have themselves been either useless or adverse to India's political-diplomatic interests, as was evident from the actions of the United Nations and the nonaligned countries on Kashmir and Bangladesh. India nonetheless continues to swear by nonalignment and ritually attends the meetings of the nonaligned nations, but does not work ostentatiously for any leadership role or expect any concrete benefits in terms of its own national interests. Notwithstanding the depreciation of the United Nations and the nonaligned group in the political-security realm, India has been an active participant in the efforts of nonaligned and Third World countries to air economic grievances directed against the developed world. This is the common denominator among the underdeveloped countries, and the grievances are felt strongly enough to induce some unity among them in demands for a new international economic order. On the other hand, their lack of leverage does not provide much ground for optimism. Meanwhile, as part of the new realism, India has been giving priority to its economic relations with other countries, sidestepping political disagreements.

Though there has been downgrading of a global role in India's foreign policy posture, the South Asia region has assumed critical importance. The 1971 war resulted in India's achieving a preeminent power position in South Asia, but this position had been implicit at independence. It was the subsequent American and Chinese intervention that had neutralized it, and India's victory in 1971 merely restored the subcontinent to its original state. However, this preeminent power position itself impels outside great powers to counterbalance Indian power, for the lack of an effective regional balance against it would result in the loss of power and influence on the part of the great powers in the region. It was precisely this calculation rather than personal pique on the part of Nixon and Kissinger that was behind the presidential wrath against India, the tilt in favor of Pakistan, and the nuclear gunboat diplomacy in the Bay of Bengal during the 1971 crisis in South Asia.

On the other hand, India has learned from experience that the foreign policy costs of foreign intervention are severe, and there is a clear determination on its part to limit this intervention and preserve the present power configuration even if it involves violence. At the same time, India's capability deficiencies place limits on its policies in this regard. Certainly it has the capacity to destabilize neighbor states within the region, but it does not have the free-floating economic resources to serve as a pole of attraction for them. For the same reason, its neighbors must invite intervention from outside. For them India is powerful enough to be feared but not powerful enough to be respected. Bangladesh's alienation from India in 1975 is testimony to this point of deficiency in Indian capabilities.

The achievement of political preeminence by India in South Asia as a result of the restructuring of power in 1971 could not be without an impact on India's posture toward the major powers. However, it is important to comprehend the nature of the earlier posture, and the rationale for it, in order to appreciate adequately India's subsequent attempts to reshape it. The guiding principle in India's foreign policy posture since 1947 has been independence. Beyond that, without compromising its own territorial integrity, its fundamental values have been peaceful coexistence and mutual cooperation. India's diplomatic posture has been accommodative and conciliatory toward both her neighbors and the great powers. Even under provocation from its neighbors India has acted with moderation and restraint. But it has insisted that its neighbors not become proxies for external powers. Basically, however, India has been a status quo, not a revisionist, power, both ideologically and territorially. Noteworthy in this connection is its immediate withdrawal of troops from Bangladesh, its prompt return of captured territory to Pakistan, and its eagerness for reconciliation in South Asia after the 1971 war. Even when disagreements could not be resolved, India attempted to widen the spheres of cooperation in the areas of economic and cultural exchange. Indeed, one can say that given India's general posture, its relations with another country are more a function of the other country's attitude.

All this is not to suggest any special Indian talent for altruism, because India is not a self-abnegating state any more than others are, though it has at times given up something of value (as in the island dispute with Sri Lanka) in the interests of larger cooperation. India's posture may be partly a function of its capabilities, which are entirely defensive in nature; partly a continuation of the Nehru theme of peaceful coexistence; and partly a spillover from its internal political approach, which, given its great diversity, emphasizes compromise and pragmatism. Regardless, in a world torn by so much conflict it is striking that India's role in maintaining peace and stability has not been adequately appreciated. It has always been the hope at the highest levels of the government in India that the United States would eventually recognize and provide due recognition and accommodation to the Indian role in stability and constructive cooperation. Beyond that, as a pluralist society and a predominantly capitalistic economy, India has had a special reason to cultivate good relations with the United States.

However, given the history of containment aimed at India by both the United States and China, India had to cultivate reactively a close relationship with the USSR. It is noteworthy that since independence India has often found the United States opposing it, hurting India's immediate vital interests in the process. The partisan attitude of the United States on the Kashmir issue was the first occasion; subsequently, it was on the issues of arms to Pakistan, of Goa, and still later of Bangladesh. On each of these issues, which were of vital security interest for India, and which could be only of peripheral relevance to the security interests of the United States, the United States did not merely render diplomatic and strategic support to India's antagonists, but actively led diplomatic moves aimed at India. On Bangladesh particularly, when war broke out in 1971 the United States condemned India, pilloried it in the United Nations, and brought forward resolutions that would have rendered India's position hopeless. Ironically, faced with such American antagonism on issues of strategic importance to itself, India had to rely on the USSR to neutralize the military threat from the American naval task force sent against it in the Bay of Bengal. In the early 1970s the United States repeatedly demanded that India have balanced relationships with the major powers. However, it remained oblivious to the fact that it was the initial lack of balance in American policy toward India and Pakistan that paved the way for the initial Indo-Soviet understanding and that it was American persistence in that policy that sustained that understanding.

The USSR's drastically different attitude toward India was apparent not only on strategic issues but also on the Indian ambition to build an independent center of power in the subcontinent. Soviet assistance was forthcoming in the establishment of steel mills, heavy industry, and a local arms industry: precisely those matters where the United States refused to provide assistance. A noteworthy aspect of the relationship between India and the USSR has been the asymmetry in exchanged favors. The Soviets stood by India several times in its moments of peril, and provided technological and industrial assistance unavailable elsewhere. Yet curiously, the level of Indian reciprocity was insignificant. It is hard to identify any concrete benefits provided by India as *quid pro quo*. Obviously, the Soviets have acted out of self-interest, as do other nations, but their foreign policy posture over more than two decades has been supportive of India's interests.

Ironically, India's relationship with the USSR seemed to threaten its domestic autonomy the least. Though the diplomatic and security relationship between India and the USSR has been intimate, that relationship has had a curious lack of impact on India domestically.[8] Linguistic and cultural barriers have limited Soviet domestic impact. India is far more susceptible to Western penetration and the consequent erosion of domestic autonomy. More important, India remained a jealous guardian of its independence. American officals too recognized from time to time that India pursued an independent foreign policy, but such recognition seemed to have little impact on the American posture toward India. In 1969 the deputy AID administrator exclaimed, "India is a fiercely independent country," and added, "They are sensitive even about the appearance of taking direction from any of the major powers."[9] Similarly, in 1973 Assistant Secretary of State Sisco declared that "India is independent and intends to remain independent. I think this is a forecast that one can make with a good deal of assurance."[10] The influence of the USSR on India, in this context of Indian independence, derived most fundamentally from the Soviet policy of working with India rather than against India, unlike the policy that the United States has often adopted. In other words, the USSR largely pursued a policy of accommodation toward India rather than one of containment. The Indians were not so naive as to think that the USSR was altruistic in adopting such a policy; as Indira Gandhi explained to C. L. Sulzberger soon after the Bangladesh war, "Countries help one another because they need one another."[11] And undoubtedly things could change in the future, but the Indians could not fail to take note of the consistent support, with minor exceptions, that the USSR gave to Indian interests over such a long period.

Regardless of the Soviet support of Indian interests, India continued to yearn for a lessening of dependence on the USSR, a dependence that had developed as a reaction to American policy. For India seems to be most comfortable with a rough equivalence in its relations with the superpowers. Equidistance is its natural starting point, and this is subsequently modified in response to actions of other states. The opportunity to diversify India's relationships arose after the Bangladesh war: India reworked the power structure in South Asia in the teeth

[8] Stephen Clarkson, "Low Impact of Soviet Writing and Aid on Indian Thinking and Policy," *Survey* 20 (Winter 1974): 1–23.

[9] U.S. Congress, House, Committee on Foreign Affairs, *Foreign Assistance Act of 1969* Hearings, 91st Cong., 1st Sess., 1969, p. 756.

[10] U.S. Congress, House, Committee on Foreign Affairs, *United States Interests in and Policies Toward South Asia* Hearings, 93rd Cong., 1st Sess., 1973, p. 20.

[11] *New York Times,* February 17, 1972, p. 15.

of opposition of the United States and China, but with the crucial support of the USSR. Soon thereafter Indira Gandhi told C.L. Sulzberger that "one of our faults is that we are unable to display gratitude in any tangible sense for anything."[12] India then eagerly asserted its independence by insisting on negotiating directly and bilaterally with Pakistan rather than under Soviet auspices as at Tashkent after the 1965 war. Subsequently, the Indians expressed a desire for friendship with the United States; Prime Minister Gandhi stated, "We have always had the greatest admiration for the United States," and added, "I would welcome efforts to make a new start."[13] Foreign Minister Swaran Singh declared, "We have much in common with that great country and its people. We cherish the common values of an abiding nature such as our belief in democracy and a democratic life."[14] Later, the Indians demonstrated their independence from the USSR by their nuclear explosion in 1974, which was no less unacceptable to the USSR than it was to the United States. Still later, in 1976, in a swift foreign policy move India initiated the normalization of relations with China; this move could not but have upset the USSR. Simultaneously, India worked for a rapprochement with the United States.[15] Despite this attempt at diversification of its relationships India was anxious to maintain its friendship with the USSR. This was especially necessary because the results of the attempted diversification did not rest with India alone; they depended crucially on the posture of the other parties as well.

The American Posture under Nixon and Ford

The story of America's intervention in the subcontinent and its defeat in 1971 has been described in an earlier chapter. Here, the intention is to analyze the American posture toward India in its new role as the preeminent power in the subcontinent, first during the Nixon-Ford regime and then under the Carter Administration. The Carter policy represents somewhat of a departure but also builds on changes already made in the earlier administration's posture following India's accession to preeminence in the region. Analytically, the Nixon-Ford policy in the wake of the Bangladesh war proceeded on a double track, combining symbolic accommodation with actual containment.

Prior to the 1971 war the United States had seen no role for India as a regional

---

[12] Ibid.

[13] Ibid.

[14] New York Times, December 1, 1972, p. 1.

[15] See Baldev Raj Nayar, "India and the Superpowers: Continuity or Deviation?" Economic and Political Weekly 12 (July 23, 1977): 1185—89.

power. It viewed India as an object rather than as a regional power of any consequence. This was a correct assumption since India, despite its large size, had
been effectively neutralized by Pakistan, which had been built up militarily and
diplomatically by the United States and later also by China. Consequently, there
could have been no question of a policy of accommodation or devolution. However, as a real rearrangement of power took place in the subcontinent in 1971
and as India insisted on the recognition of the "new realities" as a precondition
for normalization of relations, the United States moved hesitantly toward an
acknowledgment of India's new status.

The first intimation of this came in an address on June 8, 1972 by Undersecretary John N. Irwin, who spoke of the new significance of regional powers in
their regions, and importantly added, "India already seems able to play a decisive
role in South Asia."[16] Subsequently, in his 1972 foreign policy report, President
Nixon incorporated a generous reference to India with his remarks about "great
nations like our two nations" and expressed a willingness for "a serious
dialogue."[17] In the 1973 foreign policy report Nixon declared, "The United
States respects India as a major country. We are prepared to treat India in
accordance with its new stature and responsibilities."[18] Other U.S. spokesmen
promised nonintervention in the subcontinent's affairs and support for the "Simla
process." Assistant Secretary of State Atherton stated in September 1974, "We
are determined to play a role which complements rather than impedes the natural
dynamics of the region itself."[19] Beyond that, the United States moved to
remove an important irritant in the relations between the two countries by
liquidating two-thirds of its accumulated rupee holdings in India acquired in
return for wheat shipments. A landmark in the normalization of relations and in
the symbolic accommodation with India was the visit of Secretary of State
Kissinger to India in 1974. Kissinger then endorsed nonalignment and the Simla
process, but more significantly stated: "The size and position of India give it a

[16] "The Future International and Political Environment: Growing Interdependence and
Complexity," *Department of State Bulletin* no. 1723 (July 3, 1972): 18.

[17] U.S. President, *Public Papers of the Presidents of the United States* (Washington, D.C.:
Office of the *Federal Register*, National Archives and Records Service, 1957–), Richard
Nixon, 1972, p. 303.

[18] Ibid., 1973, p. 457.

[19] U.S. Congress, House, Committee on Foreign Affairs, *South Asia, 1974* Hearings, 93rd
Cong., 2nd Sess., 1974, p. 7.

special role of leadership in South Asia and in world affairs."[20]

Regardless of the expression of such sentiments, this policy of apparent accommodation remained only symbolic. As a competent American observer stated, the Kissinger visit was significant for smoothing down "the rough spots remaining from the Nixon administration's tilt toward Pakistan." More important, he added: "But there was little substance behind his gestures"[21] While the American posture during the Nixon-Ford regime in its accommodative aspect was thus symbolic, it was quite concrete in its containment aspect.

A careful examination of American state behavior and rhetoric in the 1970s during the Nixon-Ford regime, especially as they bear on South Asia and its strategic environs, leads to the following two conclusions, essentially variations on a continuing American policy of containment of India:

1. In the 1970s the United States has conceived the area of appropriate containment for India no longer as restricted to South Asia but rather as a wider one so that *interregional* balances are utilized rather than merely intraregional balances. In other words, American balance of power policies are no longer intelligible in terms merely of South Asia, with India and Pakistan as the chief actors, but rather in a redefined and expanded area of operation of the balance of power policy aimed at the containment of India. Thus, not just Pakistan has been relevant to the containment of India; so have the Pakistan-Iran alliance on the western flank of India, and the Pakistan-China alliance on the northern frontiers of India. Worth noting here is the enormous flood of arms to Iran and their leakage to Pakistan[22] as well as the resumption of direct American arms shipments to Pakistan. Thus, in contrast to the earlier technique of a regional balance between India and Pakistan, the new mechanisms have been interregional balances supported by the United States, with Pakistan embedded in the extraregional alliances aimed at the containment of India.

2. The containment of India in the 1970s is no longer a burden single-handedly assumed by the United States, but has been rather a function of *a concert of powers* in which the United States is the most powerful and leading actor. In contrast to the earlier situation where the American policy of containment operated primarily as a U.S.-Pakistan alliance, the policy has

---

[20] "Toward a Global Community," *Department of State Bulletin* no. 1848 (November 25, 1974): 740–46.

[21] Lewis M. Simons, *Washington Post*, December 15, 1974, p. A-14.

[22] Marcus F. Franda, "America and Pakistan: The View From India," *Fieldstaff Reports* 19, no. 3 (1975): 8.

more recently been implemented through a larger concert of powers including the United States, China, Pakistan, and Iran.

Critical to the evolution of the "containment in concert" was the international
diplomacy of 1971; and especially the war that year. As one American scholar
emphasized:

> The Nixon Administration, despite public statements voicing only mild concern,
> clearly perceived the dangerous implications of the new situation on the sub
> continent for the United States. President Nixon responded by assisting in the
> defense buildup of pro-Western states in the region. Although from the begin
> ning the Administration's general policy was to supply arms and not men to
> those countries wishing to improve their defenses, after the Indo-Pakistani
> conflict the volume of arms sales to Western-linked countries in the Indian
> Ocean are swelled noticeably . . . . The United States also moved to strengthen
> her own position in the region by attempting to establish a naval facility on the
> tiny island of Diego Garcia.[23]

A more substantive consideration of the preceding analysis requires that attention
be given to four major points: (1) American perception of the United States as
security manager of the region; (2) Sino-U.S. convergence of interests in South
Asia; (3) Iran as surrogate balancer for South Asia; (4) intensification of American
military presence in the Indian Ocean.

The United States

There has been an enormous contradiction in the American posture between
the symbolic acknowledgment that India is the region's preeminent power and the
assumption by the United States that it is the region's actual dominant power and
its security manager. It might not have been the State Department's intention to
proclaim this role as security manager, but the declaration of its spokesman in
1975, at the time of the lifting of the arms embargo, made the assumption of the
role by the United States quite manifest:

> In weighing any individual export requests, we will take into account a number
> of factors, including the high importance we attach to continued progress
> toward India-Pakistan normalization, the effect of any particular sale on the
> outlook for regional peace and stability, the relationship between U.S. sales and
> those of other external arms suppliers, and of course, the relationship of the
> request to legitimate defense requirements and the level of armaments in the
> region.[24]

---

[23] Richard C. Thornton, "South Asia: Imbalance on the Subcontinent," *ORBIS* 19 (1975):
869–70.

[24] "Secretary Kissinger's News Conference of February 25," *Department of State Bulletin*
no. 1864 (March 17, 1975): 322.

This statement was subsequently repeated more than once before Congress. But in addition to seeing itself in this role of security manager, the United States held itself as the protector of Pakistan, and warned India to be on good behavior in South Asia, while maintaining that the United States would be the judge of such behavior and also the agent to counter it.

In his 1972 foreign policy report, President Nixon put India on notice: "Of interest to us also will be the posture that South Asia's most powerful country now adopts toward its neighbors." Describing Pakistan as "a close friend," he stressed that "our concern for the well-being and security of the people of Pakistan does not end with the end of a crisis."[25] More explicitly, in 1973 Assistant Secretary of State Sisco cautioned that "obviously we would regard any new threat to Pakistan's integrity as disruptive to the progress toward peace and stability in South Asia" and again warned of American concern at any policy "which in fact would constitute a new threat to Pakistan."[26] Repeated official U.S. declarations followed about "strong U.S. support for Pakistan's independence and territorial integrity . . . as a guiding principle of American foreign policy."[27] References to Pakistan as an "ally" also became more fulsome and frequent. The term *ally* arose from the Agreement of Cooperation of 1959, under which the United States is committed to protect the territorial integrity and sovereignty of Pakistan and to "take such appropriate action including the use of armed forces as may be mutually agreed upon."[28] That agreement was technically directed at international Communism but in the changed context of Sino-U.S. relations, and especially in view of the 1963 U.S. *aide memoire*, its continued operation can be seen as directed only against India. Indeed, at the time of the lifting of the arms embargo in 1975, U.S. officials told newspersons privately that they had given no assurance to India on the use of American weapons by Pakistan and had thus avoided providing India with any future propaganda tool.[29] For his part, Foreign Minister Chavan was moved to ask who this American

[25] U.S. President, *Public Papers of the Presidents of the United States,* Richard Nixon, 1972, p. 302.

[26] U.S. Congress, House, Committee on Foreign Affairs, *United States Interests In and Policies Toward South Asia* Hearings, 93rd Cong., 1st Sess., 1973, pp. 21–24.

[27] See *Department of State Bulletin* no. 1790 (October 15, 1973): 486; no. 1862 (March 3, 1975); 271; and no. 1941 (September 6, 1976: 318.

[28] U.S., Department of State, *United States Treaties and Other International Agreements.* vol. 10, pt. 1 "Pakistan: Cooperation," March 5, 1959.

[29] *Times of India,* March 13, 1975.

alliance with Pakistan was directed against.[30] It is important to remember this lack of balance in American relationships with the South Asian powers in light of American complaints about the lack of balance in India's relationships with the major powers.

In a more generalized posture there were in President Nixon's 1973 foreign policy report several warnings to India about its future behavior. The president stated: "India's policy toward its neighbors on the subcontinent and other countries in nearby parts of Asia is now an important determinant of regional stability, which is of interest to us." At another point, the President said, "Every major power—now including India, with its new power in the region—has a basic responsibility toward the international system to exercise its power with restraint." In no uncertain terms, the President sought to educate the Indians about the facts of relative power as between India and the United States:

> United States policies globally and regionally will support the independence of South Asian nations. Within the region, we shall encourage accommodation and help to promote conditions of security and stability. We see no reason why we cannot have bilateral ties with each country in South Asia consistent with its own aspirations and ours, and not directed against any other nation. We shall gear our relations with other major powers outside the region to encourage policies of restraint and noninterference. This is our responsibility as a great power, and should be theirs.[31]

This theme was repeated by Kissinger on his visit to New Delhi in 1974.[32]

The manner in which the United States has sought to establish itself as the protector of Pakistan in South Asia and the way it has laid down the conditions for Indian behavior make the United States—not India—the preeminent power in the subcontinent. In this role, the United States has also assumed for itself the responsibility to judge whether or not there is a threat to stability in South Asia, whether or not there is a strategic balance in the subcontinent, whether or not American actions disturb the strategic balance in the area, and whether or not any specific country has a credible deterrent. It provides great comfort for a super-power to believe that it provides protection to a weaker party, but it is well to remember Wilcox's conclusion that "most India-Pakistan interstate conflict since

---

[30] *Times of India*, March 11, 1975.

[31] U.S. President, *Public Papers of the Presidents of the United States*, Richard Nixon, 1973, p. 460.

[32] "Toward a Global Community," *Department of State Bulletin* no. 1848 (November 25, 1974): 740–46.

1947 has been generated by Pakistan. The weak party in this situation is also the revisionist power."[33] Also noteworthy is the assessment by Barnds: "The most striking feature of Pakistan's foreign policy was its extremely ambitious goals . . . seeking to gain security through strength rather than accommodation . . . ."[34] It is in this context that one should read Foreign Minister Chavan's allegation that fear of India was "planted" in Pakistan.[35] Nor should it be forgotten that, in in Indian eyes, Great Britain, then the world superpower, colonized India during the eighteenth and nineteenth centuries precisely through the device of so-called protective alliances.

Sino-U.S. Convergence of Interests

That there has been a tacit alliance between Pakistan and China directed against India has been obvious since the early 1960s. The wars of 1965 and 1971 in South Asia demonstrated how the two countries were united in their posture towards India. But more important, the 1971 war also showed that the United States and China had a common perspective on the subcontinent, obviously not by accident but as part of the larger design involving the United States and China. Indeed, as the foreign policy sage of the United States, Cyrus Sulzberger, observed, "In South Asia the U.S.A. and China recently found themselves virtually co-belligerents when they backed Pakistan . . . " and added that "in South Asia both China and the United States, working with rare harmony made bluff maneuvers against India's land and sea frontiers."[36]

As part of the containment of the USSR, there had already come into being, in the words of columnist Joseph Alsop, "the partial and informal Chinese-American alliance."[37] The common perspective between China and the United States was later given official expression specifically in relation to South Asia.

---

[33] Wayne A. Wilcox, in *Conflict in World Politics,* ed. Steven L. Spiegel and Kenneth N. Waltz (Cambridge, Mass: Winthrop Publishers, 1971), pp. 257–58.

[34] William J. Barnds, *India, Pakistan, and the Great Powers* (New York: Praeger Publishers, 1972), p. 71.

[35] *Times of India,* March 11, 1975.

[36] *New York Times,* February 2, 1972, p. 39.

[37] Joseph Alsop, "Thoughts Out of China," *New York Times Magazine,* March 11, 1973, p. 101.

Note the following exchange in 1974 between Assistant Secretary of State Atherton and Lee Hamilton:

> Mr. HAMILTON. Would you say that the United States and China both view South Asia in a similar perspective from a strategic point of view as against the Soviets? That is, we want to contain Soviet power in that area? . . . .
> Mr. ATHERTON. Our perspective is.
> Mr. HAMILTON. China wants to curtail Soviet power in that area, so do we.
> Mr. ATHERTON. And the Soviets want tc contain Chinese power.
> Mr. HAMILTON. And we want to contain Soviet power in that area of the world.
> Mr. ATHERTON. I think that is fair to say, yes.
> Mr. HAMILTON. So in that area we do view it similarly.
> Mr. ATHERTON. We do have a certain common view in that respect 38

This trend of thought was expressed more sharply by William Barnds:

> A working relationship with China is more important than any American interest in the subcontinent; some would argue that this requires the United States to keep in step with Chinese hostility toward India by parallel support of Pakistan.39

The explanation for this realpolitik basis for an adversary posture toward India is, of course, the central role played by the containment of the USSR in American foreign policy. Former Defense Secretary Schlesinger has stated, "The strength of China is valuable to us. Despite those continuing differences, *we do have certain common interests that both nations can pursue by parallel action.*"[40] In official briefings, Secretary of State Kissinger often referred to "Communist China being the best NATO ally we have."[41] And President Carter declared in reference to China: "We recognize *our parallel strategic interests* in maintaining stability in Asia."[42] To that end, apparently, the United States let France and Great Britain bypass allied control mechanisms in sales of strategic items to China,

[38] U.S. Congress, House Committee on Foreign Affairs, *South Asia, 1974*, p. 34.

[39] U.S. Congress, House, Committee on Foreign Affairs, *United States Interests In and Policies Toward South Asia*, Hearings 93rd Cong., 1st sess., 1973, pp. 133-34.

[40] James Schlesinger, *U.S. News & World Report* 81 (October 18, 1976): 40—42. Emphasis added.

[41] Elmo R. Zumwalt, Jr., *On Watch: A Memoir* (New York: Quadrangle, The New York Times Co., 1976), p. 484.

[42] *New York Times*, March 18, 1977, p. A-10. Emphasis added.

and eventually, in a crucial move, the United States itself decided to sell American defense-related technology to China.[43]

Seemingly, the Chinese have reciprocated with support for American foreign policy objectives. In 1974, the State Department's director of the Bureau of PoliticoMilitary Affairs, Seymour Weiss, asserted in relation to the establishment of a permanent American naval base in Diego Garcia, "The People's Republic of China applauded our involvement in the area." When the House subcommittee chairman asked, "Did I understand you to say the Chinese favored the decision?" Weiss emphatically answered, "Yes, sir, that is my understanding."[44] More generally, in 1977, Foreign Minister Huang Hua assured Secretary of State Vance, "In the present international situation our two countries face questions of common concern and have quite a few points in common."[45]

China is not the only element in the American calculus about the subcontinent, however. For more than two decades now the United States, Iran, and Pakistan have been members of CENTO, an alliance system brought into being at the initiative of the United States, which in the end decided to be only a de facto member. With the inauguration of the Nixon administration, the United States became engaged in building up Iran as a "loyalist" regional power. Toward this end, the United States has made gigantic arms transfers to Iran in the 1970s. U.S. officials acknowledge that these arms sales are not just commercial transactions, but are geared to American interests. Undersecretary of State Joseph J. Sisco expressed it as follows: "First of all, in my judgment, you cannot put these arms sales in terms of their interest alone. I think it serves a mutual interest in terms of security of the area. When I say 'mutual,' I mean the interests of the United States as well as their own. That would be the first point I would make to you."[46] One of the chief interests of the United States in providing and selling such arms is, of course, the creation of regional balances.

The massive arms transfers that have taken place in recent years obviously add immeasurably to Iran's military capabilities, and theoretically make it possible for Iran to assert an independent foreign policy role in the region, a quite legitimate aspiration for Iran, as for other nations. It is perhaps for that reason

[43] *New York Times*, April 25, 1976, and *New York Times*, September 11, 1977.

[44] U.S. Congress, House, Committee on Foreign Affairs, *Proposed Expansion of U.S. Military Facilities in the Indian Ocean* Hearings, 93rd Cong., Sess., 1974, pp. 45–46.

[45] *Peking Review*, September 2, 1977, p. 7.

[46] U.S. Congress, House Committee on International Relations, *The Persian Gulf, 1975* Hearings, 94th Cong., 1st Sess., 1975, p. 29.

and because of Iran's inherent economic strength that India has eagerly sought to reach an accommodation with Iran. However, Iran's dependence on the United States for both military hardware and personnel leaves no doubt that Iran must function within the parameters of American security interests. Strong testimony to this effect is provided by a thorough study done for the U.S. Senate. The study emphasizes how "the Iranian forces are, in many instances, integrated into the U.S. logistics and support system . . . . While Iran has greater freedom to choose the weapons it buys, its freedom to operate that equipment is, in the last resort, dependent upon the good graces of the U.S. Government." Further, as a result of this dependence, "most Iranian decisions regarding a major and sustained use of military power must inevitably take into account attitudes of the United States." Nor is this all; it is not just the involvement of American arms inventories that is essential, but also the involvement of American personnel in the actual operation of the sophisticated equipment.[47] In summary, Iran's severe dependence on American arms and American personnel underlines the basic point that it is likely to function in accord with American security interests. For this reason, some have seen Iran in a "Trojan horse" role on behalf of the United States.[48]

The gigantic arms transfers to Iran by the United States may be aimed at several powers in terms of regional balance. But it is quite clear that India is also a target of such balancing. Several important considerations bear on this point. First, the United States is a military ally of both Iran and Pakistan, and there is furthermore a political and military understanding over South Asia between Iran and Pakistan both as formal members of an alliance and otherwise. In 1973, an American expert on the area and former State Department official referred to the fact that "Iran is a good friend of Pakistan and accepts Pakistan's enemy, India, as Iran's enemy as well." He further explained that "a possibility that is too real, especially if the Sino-Soviet conflict intensifies, is of a China-Pakistan-Iran-United States alliance opposed to a Soviet-Indian-Arab alliance."[49]

Second, it should be noted that India is as important in Iran's strategic calculations and that it is a target in the military buildup of Iran in which the United States is so heavily involved. As authoritative defense analyst Drew Middleton commented, "Behind these immediate concerns there is an evident fear of the

---

[47] U.S. Congress, Senate, Committee on Foreign Relations, *U.S. Military Sales to Iran*, A Staff Report, July 1976, pp. vii, 50, 51, 52.

[48] Dev Murarka, *Montreal Star*, September 7, 1976.

[49] Testimony by Richard W. Cottam, in U.S. Congress, House, Committee on Foreign Affairs, *New Perspectives on the Persian Gulf* Hearings, 93rd Cong., 1st Sess., 1973, pp. 116–17.

effect on Iran of political dissolution in the area. Concern over Pakistan's survival in another war with India has lessened but has remained an element in long-range strategic thinking." Again, he pointed out, " Finally there is the recurrent fear, never long hidden, that India might some day enter a dissolving Pakistan to back rebellious Baluchi tribesmen near the Iranian frontier."[50]

At an official level, there is testimony from the Senate study about Iran's strategic calculations. The study stated that "the possibility of conflict in the East involving Iran, Afghanistan, Pakistan and India is probably more serious than all other contingencies" except insurgency and threat to oil. "Iran is especially concerned about the centrifugal tendencies within the Baluchistan regions of Southeast Iran and Pakistan. A new conflict between Pakistan and India, perhaps prompted by separatist tendencies in Baluchistan, could result in Iranian support for Pakistan since the Shah has stated that Iran would regard any attempt by India or another power to further dismember Pakistan as a threat to its own security." Furthermore, the study noted, "Iranian officials expressed concern about indirect, as well as direct, Soviet threats .in the future through the latter's ties with neighboring India, Afghanistan, and Iraq." Accordingly, Iran "has developed close military ties with Pakistan" and "there is evidence of incipient military competition between Iran/Pakistan, on the one hand, and India on the other." The study further listed India among Iran's "high intensity" future security threats.[51]

It is not only in the aggregate buildup of military capabilities that this competition is manifest but also in the location of bases and facilities. As the Senate study stressed, "The best empirical indicators of Iran's increased perception of the potential threat from the East, and the possibility of Iranian-Pakistani-Indian hostility, are the new basing programs that the Iranian armed forces have initiated in the central and southeastern sectors of the country." The new basing arrangements, including the huge triservice complex at Chah Bahar, are "a reflection of a change in threat perception from the north and west towards the south and east."[52] In addition, it should be emphasized tht Iran is being equipped by the United States with offensive and strike weapons systems, including the most advanced and potent equipment. As a consequence they have been a source of concern to India. In 1976, Prime Minister Indira Gandhi criticized such arms transfers: We know that a great deal of arms are being accumulated in our

---

[50] *New York Times,* July 14, 1975.

[51] U.S. Congress, Senate, *U.S. Military Sales to Iran,* pp. xi, 11, 15.

[52] U.S. Congress, Senate, *U.S. Military Sales to Iran,* pp. 11, 15.

neighborhood. So that [external] threat remains."[53] Later, she again expressed concern at the "accumulation of arms in this region," and warned that these posed a very serious danger for India.[54] The Senate study also pointed out that as a result of the Iranian buildup "India is beginning to worry more about the possibility of maritime conflict in the Indian Ocean."[55]

Third, the timing of the decision on massive arms transfers to Iran is noteworthy. If balance is the aim of U.S. arms transfers, it is intriguing that the decision in May 1972 by President Nixon to provide Iran, in the words of the Senate study, "virtually any weapons system it wanted," followed within six months of India's rise to power preeminence in South Asia. This "sweeping" decision, which was "unprecedented for a non-industrial country," was "based upon broad geostrategic and political considerations rather than exacting calculations about the balance of power in the Persian Gulf."[56] It should be emphasized that the presidential decision long preceded the October war of 1973 and the associated oil crisis.

Fourth, there is specific acknowledgment on the part of U.S. officials about the relationship to India of the Iranian arms buildup, which has been so eagerly fostered by the United States. In 1973 Tad Szulc pointed out that one American rationalization advanced for the arms sales was that "the Shah needs the arsenal in part because of his concern over the situation in the Indian sub-continent," and underlined the fact that "little noticed in this whole situation is that a virtual alliance has been built among Iran, Pakistan, Saudi Arabia, Kuwait, Abu Dhabi and Oman with quiet U.S. blessing."[57] The Senate study cited earlier emphasized that "U.S. officials share many of Iran's defense concerns." More specifically, in relation to Iran's various threat perceptions centered on India, Afghanistan and Iraq, "U.S. officials are also concerned about many of these threats to Iran; in particular, U.S. officials stress the importance of stability in the region . . . ."[58]

The linkage between India and the arms buildup in Iran, and thus between India and U.S. arms transfers to Iran, was emphasized by Undersecretary of State

---

[53] *Times of India,* June 26, 1976.

[54] *Times of India,* December 24, 1976.

[55] U.S. Senate, *U.S. Military Sales to Iran,* p. 11.

[56] Ibid., pp. 5, 41, 43.

[57] Tad Szulc, "Oil and Arms," *New Republic,* June 23, 1973, in U.S. Congress, House, Committee on Foreign Affairs, *New Perspectives on the Persian Gulf,* p. 213.

[58] U.S. Congress, Senate, *U.S. Military Sales to Iran,* pp. 38, vii, 49, xi.

Sisco in 1975: "With respect to the Indian Ocean . . . Iran sees a close arms relationship between the Soviet Union and India. If you look at this in geopolitical terms, I think you can see why Saudi Arabia or Iran desires substantial arms."[59] A year later, Deputy Secretary of Defense Robert Ellsworth stated, "The Iranians are also fearful of Soviet support of some of their neighbors, especially Iraq, Afghanistan, and India."[60] At the same time, Secretary of State Kissinger declared that "if you look at the stabilizing role that Iran has played in both Middle East *and South Asia* policy, we have found it to be in the national interest of the United States and the interest of regional stability to cooperate with Iran" through arms transfers.[61] Obviously, a stabilizing role by an outside power in South Asia that requires massive arms transfers from the United States is merely another description of the role of a surrogate balancer or surrogate policeman on behalf of the United States. Little wonder then that "in India's eyes, American objectives are much wider and include—apart from building up an anti-Soviet bulwark . . . —a considered policy to build up a counterpoise to India, now that Pakistan can no longer play this role."[62]

Intensification of U.S. Military Presence

The seriousness of India's strategic situation has been aggravated by the accelerated buildup in the direct physical American military presence in the strategic environment of South Asia. Apart from the earlier American naval base in Bahrain, the increased patrolling in the Indian Ocean following the 1971 crisis, and the periodic Midlink naval exercises of Central Treaty Organization (CENTO) powers in the Indian Ocean—hosted by Pakistan in 1974—the United States has been vastly expanding its naval base in Diego Garcia, which Senator Symington has termed "a major strategic base."[63]

Considerable obscurantism has prevailed over the aims of the American naval buildup at Diego Garcia. As the preeminent superpower the United States must

[59] U.S. Congress, House, *The Persian Gulf, 1975*, p. 27

[60] U.S. Congress, Senate, Committee on Foreign Relations, *U.S. Arms Sales Policy* Hearings, 94th Cong., 2nd Sess., 1976, p. 17.

[61] "News Conference by Secretary Kissinger and Minister Ansary," *Department of State Bulletin* no. 1941 (September 6, 1976): 314. Emphasis added.

[62] *The Guardian*, July 9, 1973, cited in G. W. Choudhury, *India, Pakistan, Bangladesh, and the Major Powers* (New York: Free Press, 1975), p. 223.

[63] U.S. Congress, Senate, Committee on Armed Services, *Disapprove Construction Projects on the Island of Diego Garcia* Hearings, 94th Cong., 1st Sess., 1975, p. 2.

undoubtedly be concerned with questions of naval balance in relation to the USSR and also with assuring oil supplies. But Diego Garcia long predates the Russian entrance into the Indian Ocean; the United States secured base rights as far back as 1960. The reasons for the Diego Garcia naval base are in the final analysis related to the American perception of U.S. power and its design to acquire a stronger interventionist capability in order to exert American influence and control over the littoral countries in the Indian Ocean area. American spokesmen have readily acknowledged such aims. In 1974, J. Owen Zurhellen, Jr., deputy director of the U.S. Arms Control and Disarmament Agency, stated:

> So our initial reason for deploying naval ships into the Indian Ocean was not because the Soviet Navy was there or was coming in; it was more in the direction, I feel, that we have interests in that area and these interests require us to be able, when the situation demands, to have our ships there.[64]

In a similar vein, Admiral Elmo Russell Zumwalt, Jr., Chief of Naval Operations, commented:

> As I pointed out earlier, while Soviet activity adds to the rationale for Diego Garcia, that rationale would exist independently of anything the Soviets are doing. We have very important interests in the area.[65]

In a further development of the rationale for Diego Garcia, Zurhellen declared, "Many of these are countries with whom we have close relations . . . in the general question of the exercise of our share of leadership in world affairs. We certainly have strong interests in many, if not almost all, of the countries of the Indian Ocean."[66] Admiral Zumwalt was even more explicit: "I think we have as a vital national interest the preservation of regimes which are friendly to the United States through encouraging them by our presence. The absence of U.S. forces there, I think, makes it likelier that they would succumb or be replaced by regimes less friendly in nature."[67]

Nor should it be assumed that the Diego Garcia base is entirely unrelated to India. Apparently India's defiance of the United States in the 1971 Bangladesh

[64] Ibid., p. 5.

[65] U.S. Congress, Senate, Committee on Foreign Relations, *Briefings on Diego Garcia* Hearings, 93rd Cong., 2nd sess., 1974, p. 7.

[66] U.S. Congress, House, *Proposed Expansion*, p. 7.

[67] Ibid., p. 152.

war had an impact on U.S. defense planning, for Zumwalt argued:

> Consequently, we believe the experience of last fall and of 1971 provided a
> rather blunt warning that if we are to have an effective, reliable and economic
> capability to deploy naval forces in times of crisis, we must provide ourselves
> with a minimal support facility in the area. Without it, we would soon find that
> we had stripped ourselves of the potential for bringing to bear in the Indian
> Ocean that part of our military forces which would be most effective and hence,
> most credible: our naval power.[68]

Indeed, the Diego Garcia base should be seen as directed at India partly as an
element in the American assumption of the role of security manager in the region.
As General Brown stated in 1975, "First, we have friends in the area who look to
us for some support, principally Iran and Pakistan with whom we participate in
the CENTO organization." Partly for that reason, he felt:

> A moderate U.S. air and naval presence provides a counter to adventurism from
> any source. Those who would be our adversaries must not question either our
> resolve or our capability to ensure that our interests are served. [69]

Overall, a consideration of the American posture toward South Asia; of the
nature of U.S. ties to Pakistan, China, and Iran; and of the American naval buildup In the Indian Ocean leaves little doubt that the containment of India has been
a function, in the 1970s, of a concert of powers and interregional balances. As
the American scholar Fred Greene maintained, the continued American posture
toward the Indian subcontinent was but "the balance of power doctrine against a
state that means no harm to us, merely to maintain a balance abroad."[70] It may
well be that the same concert of powers has other purposes as well, but that does
not mitigate the fact that India is part of the strategic calculations of the coalition;
nor does it diminish the reality of containment by the same coalition. Furthermore, the containment by this concert of powers through a virtual encirclement
confronts India with security problems from all directions. Perhaps South Asia is
not of much strategic interest for the United States, but, significantly, a small
input of American effort has an enormous impact on the power configuration
in the region. Furthermore, the cumulative effect of military buildup over the
years in the region is not undone by refusal to supply some items to U.S. allies or
by last-minute suspension of arms deliveries in the event of war.

---

[68] U.S. Congress, Senate, *Briefings on Diego Garcia*, p. 4.

[69] U.S. Congress, Senate, *Disapprove Construction Projects*, pp. 22—23.

[70] Cited in Pran Chopra, *India's Second Liberation* (New Delhi: Vikas Publications, 1973),
p. 13.

As a consequence, there has been considerable alarm in India because of the arms transfers to Iran and Pakistan and because of the buildup in America's own interventionist capabilities in the Indian Ocean. Indian concern at the accelerated U.S. naval buildup in the Indian Ocean was expressed by Prime Minister Indira Gandhi in 1975 when she stated that in the past India had been subjected to aggression from the north, but now it would also have to be prepared along its coastline.[71] In 1976, she warned the nation against "the latent external danger," and underlined the reasons for the containment of India: "Nobody even takes notice if a small country becomes strong. But India is so big that some powers feel that it should not become strong also." She further pointed out that these powers kept up a propaganda barrage against India, making "some of our neighbors rather apprehensive about us."[72]

The accelerated buildup of American capabilities and massive transfers of American arms have not been without their impact on strategic perceptions. One American observer, writing from New Delhi in 1975, stated that "it is not encouraging to report that Indian nationalist sentiment and American policy goals in South Asia seem to be on a collision course that appears built into the fabric of the post-Bangladesh and post-oil crisis world."[73] The same year, with a senior Pentagon official remarked in private, "If India wants to be the one power dominant in that area we are on a collision course," and warned that "it is terribly important for the Indian policy maker to decide what would be the ideal relationship with the U.S. in terms of our role in the area."[74]

New Management, New Directions?

If in 1975 observers could see India and the United States on a collision course, the second half of 1977 saw a glow of cordiality envelop Indo-U.S. relations, overshadowing even some points of serious potential conflict. It would be a mistake, though, to attribute this newfound cordiality to the accession to high office of Morarji Desai in India and Jimmy Carter in the United States, for the new trend had been generated in 1976, and the later cordiality represented, to a considerable degree, a cresting of that earlier trend.[75] But the changes in administration did emphasize the earlier shift.

[71] *New York Times*, April 17, 1975.

[72] *Times of India*, December 12, 1976.

[73] Franda, "America and Pakistan," p. 9.

[74] Interview in Washington, D.C., no. 79-e.

[75] Nayar, "India and the Superpowers."

In India, Desai proclaimed his government's adherence to a more "genuine" version of nonalignment. For its part, the Carter administration seemed to move further than the Nixon-Ford regime in acknowledging, without the earlier qualifications about American responsibilities in the region, India's preeminent position in South Asia. Deputy Secretary of State Warren M. Christopher proclaimed during a trip to India that the United States would henceforth "look to India as the leader of South Asia."[76] Later, new American Ambassador Robert Goheen declared, "India is clear and away the preeminent nation in the sub-continent".[77] Consistent with these declarations but contrary to past practice (though no doubt influenced in his decision by the military takeover in Pakistan), President Carter made India the only country in the subcontinent that was included in his itinerary. Meanwhile, some cooling took place in India's relationship with the USSR. Surveying his administration's first nine months in office, Carter mentioned with satisfaction that India once had "a strong alignment with the Soviet Union" but that now "the situation has reversed."[78] However, India was keen to see that any foreign policy changes it made were not at the cost of the substance of its relationship with the USSR.

Notwithstanding the new American posture of accommodation, it would be a serious error to view accommodation as entirely replacing the earlier structure of containment. Great powers do not, and should not be expected to, behave in that simple a fashion in relation to other major powers. Just as detente with the USSR does not replace containment but is an addition to it, accommodation toward India does not supplant containment, but only supplements it. With some modifications, the earlier structure of containment stands, perhaps assuming a more subterranean form, but still remaining intact. Also, the policy of containment itself does not remain static but assumes different incarnations.

Indeed, the surface cordiality between the Desai and Carter administrations masked a very fundamental conflict between India and the United States over the nuclear issue. In putting enormous pressure on India to surrender sovereignty over all her nuclear installations and submit them to international inspection, the United States used the leverage that derived from the dependence of the Tarapur nuclear power plant on American supplies of enriched uranium. The issue itself was not new; the Ford administration had already begun to tighten the screws on India by holding up uranium shipments. Fundamental to this new version of the short tether treatment has been the question of time, with the

---

[76] *New York Times*, August 19, 1977.

[77] *New York Times*, October 2, 1977.

[78] *New York Times*, October 23, 1977.

United States endeavoring to exploit its leverage before its "virtual monopoly as a fuel supplier comes to an end."[79]

With the inauguration of the Carter administration, the U.S. position toughened even further. What is remarkable in this posture, however, is the double standard that the United States employs. The United States makes the minutest calculations about the slightest shifts in the arms balance insofar as it affects her own security, and develops without any moral compunctions ever more complex destructive weapons systems, such as the neutron bomb and the cruise missile. At the same time, American statesmen repeatedly state their determination to remain number one. President Carter proclaimed in a secret directive that "the U.S. will not accept a posture of strategic inferiority,"[80] and Defense Secretary Brown declared that "we will not be outgunned."[81] Furthermore, the United States holds that any shift in power in favor of the USSR spells political disaster for itself and its allies; witness the statement by the President's national security advisor, Zbigniew Brzezinski, in October 1977:

> However, the perception by others or by oneself of someone else having quote unquote strategic superiority *can* influence political behavior. It can induce some countries to act in a fashion that sometimes has been described in 'Finlandization.' And it can induce self-imposed restraint on the party that feels weaker and, last but not least, it can induce the party that feels it enjoys strategic superiority to act politically in a more assertive fashion.[82]

The United States now proclaims its readiness to use nuclear weapons, if necessary, and—in tones reminiscent of Chinese declarations in the 1950s—plays down the consequences of a nuclear war. To quote Brzezinski once more:

> If we used all our nuclear weapons and the Russians used all of their nuclear weapons, about 10 percent of humanity would be killed. Now this is a disaster beyond the range of human comprehension. It's a disaster which is not morally justifiable in whatever fashion. But descriptively and analytically, it's not the end of humanity. It's not the destruction of humanity.[83]

It should not be forgotten that the United States has not only been the only power that has actually used nuclear weapons but that it has also several times

---

[79] Leslie H. Gelb, *New York Times*, August 24, 1976.

[80] *New York Times*, August 26, 1977.

[81] *New York Times*, September 16, 1977.

[82] "One Man's Eye on the World," *The Times* (London), October 10, 1977.

[83] Ibid.

threatened their use to coerce its opponents, as in Korea, the Taiwan Straits, and Indochina.

While the United States expresses grave concern about "Finlandization" for itself and its allies, there is no such acknowledgment for other powers that wish to remain independent and do not want to be under American protection. Likewise, while the United States plays down the consequences of its engaging in a nuclear war, it raises the specter of disaster over the acquisition of nuclear capabilities by others and seeks to keep them disarmed in terms of nuclear capabilities. But what is really being sought here is the perpetuation of the nuclear hegemony of the superpowers. Imagine the presumption implicit in the effort to impose nuclear disarmament on India, which is larger in population, albeit far poorer, than the United States and the USSR combined, while the superpowers daily perfect and augment their own nuclear arsenals. This disarmament effort really raises profound questions for India. If nonalignment is really genuine it must be backed by an adequate defense, which in the contemporary world means acquisition of nuclear capabilities. Nuclear abstention can only mean that you are really not nonaligned, because in the ultimate analysis you are dependent on someone else for protection. And to that extent, neither are you independent: you are effectively "Finlandized." Given the continued thrust for independence in Indian foreign policy such a prospect will not be acceptable in the long run, even if India reluctantly adjusts to its present weakness.

What emerges conclusively from the posture of the Carter administration is that it forthrightly acknowledges India to be the preeminent power *in* South Asia—a recognition of what India has already accomplished against American opposition—but simultaneously requires that South Asia remain a regional "ghetto" without influence in, or relevance to, the larger international system. Further, it requires India to renounce all ambition to play a role in the future evolution of that system. This is nothing but containment in a new form, and if accepted by India, it will become institutionalized into self-containment. Meanwhile, for the United States, if an atmosphere of cordiality between India and the United States helps that end, so much the better. It was a long struggle for India to resist one type of containment justified in the name of anticommunism and regional balances; now India will have to confront another type of containment in the name of world order. To be sure, the United States has some leverage to make India accept such an iniquitous arrangement, but it should not be surprised when Indian nationalism eventually revolts against it. "Thus *pax Americana* and Indian nationalism are once again at odds with each other," in the words of a knowledgeable commentator.[84]

[84] Girilal Jain, "President Carter's Visit," *Times of India*, September 28, 1977.

But India is not entirely helpless in this encounter. Indeed, its position is stronger than ever before, for "America is no longer the great aid-giver it was and India's need for assistance is no longer as desperate as it was in the sixties."[85] At least for the present, India is not dependent on the United States for either food or foreign exchange, thanks to the legacy of the previous Indian government. Furthermore, although there is no doubt that there is collusion between the United States and the USSR on the nuclear issue, India could, as a country of some significance, still exploit the competitive aspect of the superpower relationship. In sum, the issue as posed by Myron Weiner in 1976 retains its central relevance: "It remains to be seen whether the United States develops an adversary relationship with India driving it still further into the Soviet arena, or is responsive to India's quest for a larger role in regional and international politics."[86] This, indeed, is the critical issue; all else is subordinate.

Futurology And All That

What kind of prognosis can be made about the future role and posture of India? To evaluate foreign policy performance is hazardous enough, but to prognosticate is even more dangerous. Political alignments can persist for a long time and then change with bewildering speed. Sudden leadership changes can set nations on new and different courses. Recognizing the capriciousness implicit in the future, what projection can one make? Basically, India's role and posture would depend on developments in regard to two major variables: (1) India's capabilities, and (2) the international environment.

In terms of capabilities, India is likely to remain a united political entity. Of course its manifold diversity often raises the specter of disintegration, and India's adversaries have, in part, based their posture toward it on the assumed certainty of that possibility materializing. However, over the past thirty years India has experienced challenges, internal as well as external, of such severity that if disintegration were a potential it most probably would have occurred already. India's integration is partly a function of its established nationalism and its elite's policy of accommodation and reconciliation; it is also a function of its very diversity. Paradoxically, diversity is a threat to unity when there are only one or a few sharp divisions, not when there is an abundance of cleavages crosscutting each other. Any single group in India is such a small percentage of the total

---

[85] Ibid.

[86] Myron Weiner, "Critical Choices for India and America," in *Southern Asia: The Politics of Poverty & Peace*, ed. Donald C. Hellman (Lexington, Mass.: D. C. Heath and Co., Lexington Books, 1976), p. 78.

population that any secessionist threat can be easily managed. India's unity is thus no mere historical artifact; it is structurally based.

In the ultimate analysis, capabilities are a function of economic development. Here it is not simply a question of India's being a poor country but of its having to push forward vigorously to complete its modernization. By its very nature this is a long, drawn-out struggle marked by severe crises, which provide a temptation for external powers to intervene, either directly or through proxies. India's "stalemated modernization" of the 1960s would lead one to expect a considerable period ahead of political uncertainty and, possibly, experimentation. Meanwhile, India will have to expand its naval and air capabilities substantially; at least commensurate with the threats to its security, even if not enough to make it a relevant pole in the Asian balance of power. Even with such expansion, however, India will for several decades to come be concerned primarily with its own security rather than with projection of power abroad.

What of changes in the international environment and their impact on India's role and posture? Given that India has little capacity to change the international environment, it will necessarily have to adapt itself to changes originating with the interactions among the great powers. Over the next decade, Japan and Europe are likely to move in tandem with the United States because of their economic and military dependence. Unless India develops its nuclear option in some irreversible fashion it will not be a subject power in the Asian balance of power, though it will continue to be a relevant factor in it. Consequently, the relevant subject powers in terms of the Asian balance of power will be the United States, the USSR, and China. And there would seem to be five basic possibilities of alignments among these three great powers:[87]

1. A Sino-U.S. understanding on the containment of the USSR as the encompassing posture even as the United States works out, because of the dangers of nuclear war, arms control agreements with the USSR. This would essentially represent a continuity of the present pattern, with some modification caused by either deepening or lessening of that understanding. The United States and China are not likely to find India a partner in this joint containment of the USSR, given the Indo-Soviet friendship over a period of more than two decades. Within this pattern India might have to confront intervention by external powers in the subcontinent because of crises in either Bangladesh or Pakistan, which could even result in a redrawn political map of South Asia. India would have to exert itself strenuously to maintain its preeminence in the region. Also, India would be increasingly concerned

[87] See also Alastair Buchan, *Power and Equilibrium in the 1970's* (New York: Praeger Publishers, 1973).

at rivalry or challenge in the Indian Ocean from Iran, backed by the United States, China, or both.

2. A Sino-Soviet understanding against the United States. This would represent a restoration of the pattern of the 1950s, but it is not likely, given the depth of hostility over the last two decades between these two states. If it does develop, India might find itself under too much pressure from the United States to join in containment of the Sino-Soviet bloc. However, India would prove uncooperative in this regard, for it would not wish to alienate both its giant neighbors with the United States situated thousands of miles away. A Sino-Soviet understanding might reduce India's leverage with the USSR, but it might also to some extent ease India's own anxieties in relation to China's intentions. And, of course, India has had some experience in cultivating friendly relations with both powers as strong allies. It is also unlikely that the USSR will reach an understanding with China at the cost of India: it has had consistently friendly relations with India for more than two decades, whereas its relations with China have fluctuated wildly.

3. A U.S.-Soviet understanding aginst China. This would constitute a return to the pattern of the 1960s. India could then draw resources from both the USSR and the United States, but at the expense of its own freedom of maneuver. This pattern is perhaps unlikely to develop, because each partner will fear that the other may work out a rapprochement with China behind its back.

4. An equidistant relationship among the three superpowers. This is likely to develop as China acquires a second-strike nuclear capability and creates the necessity for detente between the USSR and China. This would most probably make India cultivate equidistant relations with China and the United States, while simultaneously endeavoring to protect its close relationship with the USSR. It would do the latter for reasons of insurance against unforeseen developments, and also because the United States has not acquired an image of reliability or consistency.

5. A joint U.S.-Sino-Soviet understanding about the power structure of the world. This would cause the most anxiety for India. It is in the possibility of such an understanding apart from any independent aspirations of India's own, that there lies the elemental push for India to develop, sustain, and fortify an independent center of power; and, for the present, to keep all options open to that end.

Summary and Conclusions

In the quarter-century after independence, India acquired greater maturity and realism in the management of its strategic environment, but with considerable pain and sacrifice. The greater maturity and realism in its foreign policy enabled India in 1971 to reclaim its position of political preeminence in South Asia, which has been eroded as a result of the policy of containment pursued by both the United States and China. Since then, India's foreign policy posture has been based on a realistic assessment of its capabilities, which are basically defensive rather than offensive. It has largely eschewed a global role, but on the other hand has developed a strong visceral commitment to protecting its regional preeminence.

India's foreign policy has undergone many significant changes since independence, even though India has continued to proclaim the same ideology of nonalignment. But there is one consistent thread throughout its history as an independent nation: its determination to maintain its foreign policy autonomy and not to accept foreign policy subordination to any other country. Outside that, India's general posture toward other nations since 1971, as before, has been one of moderation and cooperation.

Historically, as a result of the clash of roles between the United States as the hegemonic superpower and India as a middle power, India in the 1950s confronted a policy of containment by the United States, a policy imposed through the mechanism of creating an intraregional balance within South Asia between India and Pakistan. In the 1960s a similar policy of containment toward India was adopted by China as well. In both situations, India reacted by developing a closer relationship with the USSR. In the end, in 1971, the policy of containment through creating and maintaining an intraregional balance between India and Pakistan proved a failure. India's achievement of regional preeminence in that year was, of course, accomplished against opposition by the United States and China, but with the aid of the USSR. Notwithstanding, India soon thereafter endeavored to demonstrate its independence from the USSR by attempting to diversify its relationships with the other major powers. As a result, there was an improvement in the relations with these major powers, but meanwhile India had to take into account the strategic constraints placed by them on its security and freedom of maneuver.

The encompassing strategic reality for India in the 1970s has been a continued encounter with the policy of containment, managed now through a concert of powers comprising the United States, China, Pakistan, and Iran, and operated through the mechanism of interregional balances rather than the mere intraregional balance created before. Sufficient and compelling evidence has been presented on this aspect of India's strategic situation. As a consequence of its strategic predicament, India has attempted to safeguard its close relationship with the USSR. Notwithstanding that, with its vision of itself as an independent center of power, self-reliance to the farthest extent possible is a compelling lodestar for India. Here both the founder of its foreign policy and its historical experience have been profound instructors.

Not long ago Nehru opposed power politics and balance of power policies. In so doing, he placed himself against a universal and inevitable pattern in international politics. India, by its own foreign policy behavior in recent years has demonstrated that participation in power politics and balance of power policies is unavoidable. Nehru himself was not always immune from such considerations, though he kept this aspect in low key. But he surely can be faulted, whatever his motivation, for leading the country from its proper comprehension of the dynamics of international relations through his exaggerated emphasis on anti-power themes. If Nehru was wrong in this respect, he was certainly right in stressing that self-reliance was ultimately the best assurance for defense. Both world and Indian experience in the postwar period demonstrate the essential correctness of his position that in the final analysis a nation's defense consists of what it can provide for itself. The American betrayal of South Vietnam and of the Kurds, the manner in which the Soviets and the Chinese looked the other way in their consuming interest to cultivate better relations with the United States while the Americans bombed and blockaded their ally North Vietnam, the American warning to India in 1971 not to expect any help in case of Chinese intervention, the American resort to nuclear gunboat diplomacy against India later that year, the change in the Russian posture toward India in the late 1960s as the USSR acquired preeminent influence in South Asia—all these are testimony to the accuracy of Nehru's observation that a country must provide for its own defense and security.

But it is no ordinary defense and security that India has to provide, because many countries in the world have the potential—however distant—of eventually making an impact on the power structure of the world. Such a position certainly makes India a special target for actions that would weaken it, or keep it weak, by those powers whose own status would be adversely affected by Indian ascendancy. At the same time, that position casts a special obligation on India to provide not only for defense, but also for deterrence. Most intellectually aware Indians today fervently favor that course. They are not persuaded by those who, as a mask for the perpetuation of their own hegemony, seek to make India defenseless by its renunciation of deterrent capabilities; nor are they humored into believing that India has some special moral or spiritual contribution to make by remaining defenseless. Even if some Indian leaders with little experience of the harsh power realities of the world proclaim a renewed faith in Gandhism, such professions are of a disembodied nature, for they are no longer integral to the Indian experience as they were in the years immediately after independence. Besides, larger forces are at work propelling India in the direction of acquiring deterrent capabilities. In addition to the country's established nationalism, there is a built-in technological determinism toward acquiring deterrent capabilities once nuclear reactors are installed for peaceful purposes. Most important, the rest of the world does not place much trust in Indian declarations about peaceful uses of nuclear technology. Other nations will behave toward India as if it were already launched on the course of acquiring deterrent capabilities, and therefore persuade it to move in that direction. Deterrence is an insurance policy, which of course demands its appropriate cost. [88] Failure to acquire deterrent capabilities would make India's survival a hostage to foreign powers; it would also court failure in the endeavor to achieve India's long-held aspiration to be an independent center of power. In short, nuclear abstinence would make India's survival a hostage to foreign powers; it would court failure in the endeavor to achieve India's long-held aspiration to be an independent center of power. In short, nuclear abstinence would surely lead to "Finlandization."

In the struggle of a long-suppressed people to carve out a role in international politics commensurate with its size and importance, the Indian nation is symbolic of a larger historical process toward a wider distribution of power in the international system in place of the enduring hegemony of European and European-derived states over the colored populations of the world. This hegemony was itself generated by the diffusion of the greatest achievement of European civilization: industrialization and modernization. Once generated, industrialization and modernization have a certain irreversibility, although they may proceed not in a unilinear fashion, but by fits and starts. In turn, modernization and industrialization restructure the power configurations of the world by way of their impact on economic and military capabilities. As a consequence, they will undoubtedly diminish the power position of the presently dominant states. This is bound to occur, as has already been demonstrated by the diffusion of power in the international system in the postwar period. The question is whether the process is to be accomplished in cooperation or in conflict.

[88] On the theme, see K. Subrahmanyam, *Defense and Development* (Calcutta: Minerva Associates, 1973).

Comment

William J. Barnds

Professor Nayar's chapter raises a great many interesting points, ranging over the nature of world politics, the development of Indian foreign policy, and the American role in the world and its policies toward India. A brief commentary such as this can only touch on certain central issues, principally those involving Indian and American foreign policy.

U.S.-Indo relations have fluctuated dramatically over the past thirty years, and this has in recent years led many students of international relations to examine them in some detail in an attempt to explain the cause of such rapid—and often unpredicted—shifts. Other observers have been less impressed by the fluctuations than by the inability of the two countries to work out a mutually satisfactory relationship, and this had led them to search for an underlying—and enduring—foreign policy goal or motivation on the part of one or both countries.

Professor Nayar's analysis clearly places him in the second group. He does not ignore the fluctuations, but attributes them to temporarily changing circumstances inside one or the other country, or in world politics generally, rather than to shifts in basic goals. For the Indian elite this basic goal has been for India to retain its national autonomy in decisionmaking as an essential step toward an eventual move from potential to actual great power status. For the United States this goal has been to prevent the emergence of other great powers, since this would diminish its own power and security.

If this represented an iron law of international politics in general, and thus an imperative for U.S. policy toward India, there would be little point in spending time appraising U.S.-Indo relations or discussing the appropriate U.S. policy toward India. The United States would be impelled to behave in a manner designed to prevent Indian power from increasing. Fortunately, for nations in general—and for the jobs of historians and political scientists in particular—no such iron law prevails. The evidence contradicts such an argument, and Professor Nayar contradicts himself. He states that "great powers typically choose from among three policies toward middle powers and potential subject powers: containment, satellization, and accommodation." If a great power can accommodate a middle power, it clearly is not "impelled" to oppose it. Moreover, in the postwar period, U.S. policy toward Western Europe and Japan was one of accommodation. Indeed, it did more than accommodate them; it devoted considerable energy and resources to strengthening them, not only economically, but militarily as well. Similarly, as Professor Nayar later points out, "the Soviet Union has largely pursued a policy of accommodation in relation to India rather than one of containment."

One other general comment is appropriate to this point. This has to do with the categorization of great power policies toward middle powers—containment, satellization, and accommodation—that Professor Nayar quotes from George Liska and uses throughout his chapter. A certain amount of conceptualization often provides specific insights into the policies pursued. But there is a danger that to be accurate such conceptions will have to be at such a high level of abstraction as to be of limited utility. There is an even greater danger that once adopted they will lead the analyst to try to force the complex facts of political life into his conceptual scheme in an attempt to bring order to the messy world of international affairs.

A major element in Indian foreign policy is, as Professor Nayar points out, the Indian elite's belief that their country is a potential great power. The elite recognizes that such potential can only be realized over a considerable period of time, since it requires the industrialization and modernization of a country which, while abundantly equipped with many natural resources, has a very low level of per capita production. The need for modernization, combined with the relatively poor domestic performance during large parts of the period from 1965 to 1975, was one of the reasons the emergency was initially so widely accepted in 1975. However, authoritarianism also creates problems of its own. An authoritarian government probably would find it more difficult to follow a policy of accommodation and reconciliation in dealing with the country's diversity. In addition, an authoritarian government in India is likely to be controlled by those presently having power, and these people—who have been the principal beneficiaries of India's economic growth since independence—are unlikely to impose upon themselves the sacrifices necessary for faster progress. (The record during the emergency is an example, though a brief one, of this matter.) This does not mean that India will necessarily progress rapidly now that democracy has returned, but only that authoritarianism is not necessarily a promising solution to India's enormously difficult task of modernization.

Turning again to Indian foreign policy, I find myself in substantial agreement with most of what Professor Nayar has said on the subject. His comments on India's impressive defensive strength, together with its lack of power to project abroad, are essential to keep in mind. However, rather than elaborate these areas of agreement, let me briefly mention two specific points of disagreement which are important not only in themselves but because of their connection with U.S.-Indo relations. The first of these concerns India's policies toward its South Asian neighbors. Professor Nayar states that these have been "accommodative and conciliatory" and that India has acted with "moderation and restraint." He also characterizes India's goal in South Asia as one of achieving preeminence. Would not hegemony be a more accurate description, especially since he states (Chapter 5) that one of the failures of Indian foreign policy was its failure to exclude external powers from South Asia? In effect, New Delhi wants virtual veto power over the nature of relations between other South Asian states and the great powers. One can argue that the great powers—including the United States—should make the acceptance of India's vision of its role the central element of their policies toward the area, but this would represent acceptance of India's drive for hegemony rather than for preeminence.

India's drive for hegemony does not mean that it has wanted to see its neighbors disintegrate, much less to make them part of India. (Sikkim is untypical in too many ways to prove that India is expansionist.) But Indians have been rather insensitive to the fears their neighbors have had of India and have made little effort to understand these fears and to try to dispel them. Convinced that they have been conciliatory, they do not understand why others do not recognize this— much as Americans often feel bewildered when what they consider their good intentions go unrecognized.

The second point of disagreement concerns India's security position and dilemmas, which are often exaggerated. Can the acquisition of Goa conceivably be considered a "vital security interest for India?" India certainly has security problems, but New Delhi's tendency to overstate its security problems—for a variety of reasons, ranging from misperceptions to careful calculations—has been one reason that most Americans have found it difficult to think of India as a great power, even a potential one. (Professor Nayar is correct, of course, in stating that the predominant American image of India has been that of a poverty-stricken country needing help, and the differences between Indian and American images of India have been a major problem in their relations.)

The argument that the United States was impelled to oppose India has been discussed and discarded earlier as an adequate explanation for American policy toward India. But if the United States did not have to oppose India's effort to great power status, it could have worked to contain Indian power by supporting its enemies, as it long ago did regarding the People's Republic of China. Moreover, even if this was not the aim of or the motivation behind American policy, the United States could have taken actions for other reasons that increased India's burdens and limited its power. India's reaction would have been to some extent dependent upon its interpretation of the motivations behind American policy, and an assessment of the future possibilities for U.S.-Indo relations will depend to some extent upon the interpretation that comes to be accepted.

Professor Nayar argues that American actions toward the subcontinent were primarily directed toward checking India. In fact, they were taken primarily for other reasons, but they had the effect—during certain periods—of increasing India's security problems, though not as much as many Indians think they did. One noted Indian scholar, Bhabani Sen Gupta, has commented on this:

> The military pact of the United States with Pakistan . . . did not intolerably increase the defense burden of India . . . U.S. military transfers to Pakistan were rather limited, and strict rationing of spare parts restricted the fighting ability of Pakistan to not more than 30 days . . . . The defense budget of India remained relatively low through this period (the 1950s), consuming less than 2 percent of the GNP.[1]

At the same time, I agree with Professor Nayar that while U.S.-Indo relations probably will improve in the near future—and that Indian policy had begun to shift under Mrs. Gandhi—there are distinct limitations to the extent of improvements likely to occur. (Our reasoning on this contains differences as well as similarities, but the broad conclusions we reach are close together.) Indeed, a moderate but steady and sustained improvement in relations is more likely to yield positive results over the long term than a dramatic upsurge in enthusiasm and expectations, which in turn brings out feelings of disappointment, frustration, and betrayal when problems occur.

Before discussing the future at greater length, it would be useful to analyze past American policy toward South Asia, which is the subject of much of Professor Nayar's analysis. In doing this, it is important to make explicit two points that involve world politics and U.S. foreign policy generally before discussing their relevance to policy toward India. The first of these concerns the way foreign policy is made and executed, particularly in the United States. While Professor Nayar states that he recognizes that the U.S. government is not a monolith, he generally treats it as very close to one. In so doing, he underestimates the many elements and compromises that are involved in policymaking and execution. Different interest groups within the country often argue for different policies. Different people in the senior levels of an administration and Congress have different conceptions of the appropriate policies toward particular issues or areas. And one need not uncritically accept the "bureaucratic politics" model to see that it has some relevance to policymaking. This does not mean that all is confusion or

---

[1] Bhabani Sen Gupta, *Soviet Asian Relations in the 1970s and Beyond* (New York: Praeger Publishers, 1976), pp. 138–179.

near chaos. The President tries to pick subordinates whose views are such that they can work together—and with him—even though they differ on some issues. And while there are strong elements of continuity as administrations change, different leaders do have different views and sometimes shift directions. Under these circumstances, policy decisions contain large elements of compromise and adjustments to domestic views and pressures, as well as an attempt to formulate a clear and coherent policy designed to further a particular conception of the national interest. Thus most policies tend to be multicausal rather than unicausal, and an analysis that tries to fit actions into the second pattern often distorts the complexity of the realities involved.

The second point has to do with the nature of relations within states in the international system. The use of the term *satellization* throughout Professor Nayar's paper tends to muddy rather than clarify the matter. This is partly because the common political use of the term in recent decades has been to describe the relationship of the Eastern European states to the Soviet Union, which insisted that they follow the Soviet lead in terms of their domestic life, as well as their foreign policy, with only minor deviation permitted until quite recently. Despite its many faults, the United States hardly insisted that its allies be satellites in this sense.

More important, the great power-satellite (or subject-object) categorization oversimplifies, and thus distorts, the nature of the relationships between states in the modern world. Relationships of consequence between states basically involve a continuous process of bargaining as each seeks to influence the actions of the other in ways favorable to itself. In many cases the advantage in this bargaining clearly lies with one party, but for a variety of reasons—including the ability of the weaker party to play stronger powers off against each other—the influence of the stronger party in the alliance (whether formal or implicit) rarely amounts to the kind of control implied in the term satellization. According to Professor Nayar's framework of analysis, Pakistan would seem to have been satellized by the United States, but one would be hard put to find the American officials who felt they controlled Pakistan's foreign policy. The United States was unsuccessful in preventing Pakistan from moving closer to China in the early 1960s. Nor has anyone, to my knowledge, charged that the United States instigated Pakistan's actions in Kashmir that led to the 1965 war with India. Thus, there is generally a condition of mutual, though unequal, dependency between countries which gives each some leverage over the other.

If we are to discuss the reasons behind U.S. policy toward South Asia we are forced to deal with the question of motivations, which are difficult to define with precision. A country's actions as well as the words of its leaders have to be taken into account, and the matter of selection and weighting of evidence is extremely important. Just as it is very difficult to prove a particular motivation, so it is difficult to prove that no such motivation existed. Most Indians regard the United States as having been consistently anti-Indian on the Kashmir issue. Most Pakistanis regard Americans as having been unwilling to use the leverage that they claimed U.S. aid to India gave America to pressure India to reach a settlement. Most Americans would interpret the evidence as indicating that United States policy was an evenhanded attempt to aid the parties to reach a settlement.

Professor Nayar states that, "it is a gross error to view American military aid to Pakistan as directed at Communism rather than specifically at India, even though a great deal of obscurantism manifestly prevails on this point. It is equally a fundamental error to regard it—and other similar policies—as simply a mistake," (Chapter 5). He then cites a remark by Vice President Nixon about aid to Pakistan as a "counterforce" to Nehru's neutralism, and concludes that the American decision was obviously directed at India. He also cites the type of arms given Pakistan as indicating that the alliance was directed against India.

These arguments are weak and unconvincing. The United States clearly did not want nonalignment or neutralism to spread throughout the Third World and thus prevent it from extending its policy of containing Communism by building security pacts around the Communist bloc, but the policy goals were primarily concerned with containing Soviet and Chinese power. The U.S. government knew that its relations with India would suffer, and delayed the pact for this reason. But building the alliance network had a higher priority than maintaining good relations with India, so the United States went ahead with the pact. Pakistan, which could link the Middle East and Southeast Asia, was regarded as too important to exclude, especially since there were a limited number of countries willing to join the system. Selig Harrison and others who have studied the formation of the U.S.-Pakistani alliance provide considerable evidence on these matters. Once the alliance was formed, several factors operated to sustain it. One was the specific benefits it brought to the United States, such as airfields for U-2 flights and intelligence collection facilities. Second, once an alliance—especially a multilateral one—has been established, the domestic and international political costs of abandoning it are high, unless an extremely strong argument can be made for doing so. The third is the bargaining process I referred to earlier. A nation that acquires an ally has to meet some of its requirements to preserve the alliance. Thus, U.S. involvement in programs with Pakistan created trouble in Indo-U.S. relations not because the United States wanted to keep India down but because it wanted to keep Pakistan as an ally.

Indeed, few people who have charged the United States with having deliberately worked to prevent India's emergence as a great power appear to have considered what the United States could have done over the years if it had really wanted to keep India weak: it could have provided bombers, not only fighter aircraft, to Pakistan; it could have stepped up its military supplies to Pakistan during the 1965 Indo-Pakistani war rather than putting an arms embargo on shipments to South Asia, a move that damaged Pakistan far more than India; it could have taken a pro-Pakistan position on the Kashmir dispute; it could—if there had been a Sino-American axis—have recognized Chinese border claims along the Sino-Indian frontier. It is also interesting to note how little attention is given to the virtual halt of U.S. arms supplies to Pakistan since 1965.

What about the U.S. policy of seeking to maintain some sort of regional balance in various parts of the world? How should this be interpreted? There are, it seems to me, two possible views concerning the motivations behind such a policy—quite apart from questions concerning its general wisdom and the skill with which it is carried out. The first view is that it is designed to check the power of the larger regional power by building up other countries in the region. The second is that it is designed to provide a sense of security to the smaller powers who fear their larger neighbors in the region. Even if the effect of the second is the same as the first, as far as the potential regional hegemonist is concerned, the purpose is different.

Since we are dealing with elusive matters involving motivation, the selection and weighting of evidence, and so on, two other points are worth mentioning. There is a quite understandable but generally overlooked psychological dimension to the argument that U.S. policy was designed to keep India down. This charge has been difficult for Americans to take seriously, not only because of the aid they have extended to India, but because they have, by and large, thought it represented a gross inflation of India's importance in the world, at least in any policy-relevant time sphere. Yet it provides a measure of psychological satisfaction to Indians, not only because it provides a simple framework within which to interpret a complex world, but because it is easier for a large and proud nation to think of itself as the direct object of great power hostility than to think that it figures much more modestly in the calculation of others. Such ethnocentrism is not confined to any one nation, and all must guard against it. Otherwise, one can come to see a Sino-American-Pakistani-Iranian concert of powers designed to contain India, although it may be conceded that it has other purposes as well.

Not having served in government in recent years, I find it difficult to be confident of the precise intentions of American leaders during the 1970s. However, it is worthwhile to point out that during the ten years from 1956 to 1966 that I worked on South Asian affairs I never heard anyone discuss U.S. policy goals in terms of preventing India from developing economically or from becoming a major power. Nor have I, upon questioning others involved in these matters, found anyone who had heard such a goal set forth. Given the American inability to keep anything secret for long, there would surely be an abundance of evidence of such a policy goal if it had, in fact, existed.

I find it interesting that the idea that American policy was designed to check India's emergence arose after the 1971 upheaval. Indians quite naturally wanted the United States to condemn the Yahya Khan regime's brutalities and halt all assistance to it. They scarcely noted that the United States greatly curtailed its assistance to Pakistan during the civil war, while it would have done just the opposite if it had really wanted to damage India. While the United States should have remained neutral, as did Britain and France once war broke out, its votes in the United Nations were in line with those of an overwhelming majority of the members. U.S. policy on this issue, as in the case of Goa, can be better understood as the result of a concern for world order and of not wanting to see international disputes settled by force than as the result of an anti-Indian bias. (The fact that the United States is not wholly consistent on this is obvious, and is evidence that every nation finds it easier to condemn the faults of others than to see and prevent its own failings.) Some Americans have interpreted the sending of the naval task force into the Bay of Bengal—probably the critical action influencing Indian perceptions—as designed to warn India not to move against West Pakistan or to show China that the United States did not let its friends down. These may well have been factors in Nixon's decision, although I suspect that a complete answer remains dependent upon a psychological analysis of his tortured mind. This raises an interesting question concerning the impact of individuals on national policy. If Hubert Humphrey had secured the few extra votes he needed to win the presidency in 1968, would U.S. policy in the 1971 South Asian crisis have followed the course it did?

As stated earlier, Professor Nayar correctly traces the Indian shift toward a search for a better relationship with the United States to 1976, when Mrs. Gandhi was still in power, although he emphasizes that the relationship has become warmer since President Carter and Prime Minister Desai took office in 1977. Yet, he warns against expecting too much in the way of improved relations, especially since these two governments will not be in power indefinitely. He also recognizes that while Indo-Soviet relations have cooled as a result of many factors, any Indian government will take pains to avoid needlessly antagonizing—much less alienating—the Soviet Union. However, this need not be a serious problem in U.S.-Indo relations unless U.S.-Soviet relations become substantially worse and New Delhi moves much closer to Moscow. Without such developments, the United States government is unlikely to be seriously concerned about Indo-Soviet relations.

Nonetheless, there are several issues that could trouble U.S.-Indo relations even if one discounts the existence of a Sino-American-Pakistani-Iranian axis directed against India. First, and most fundamentally, as Professor Nayar states, the United States must decide if it is willing to accept India as a potential major power substantively, as well as symbolically. This may happen, but, for two reasons, it is by no means certain. First, very few Americans think of India as a potential major power, at least within what they regard as a policy-relevant time frame. What is possible is that senior U.S. officials may continue to think of India as the key South Asian power, and this alone would lead to improved relations. A second and related reason is that the United States is not likely to accord India a veto power over its relations with India's neighbors, especially if Iran is included in this category, or over its activities in the Indian Ocean. The United States probably will be aware of and more sensitive to India's concerns regarding these issues, which will improve matters. But the United States is unlikely to decide all of them on the basis of how its decisions will affect U.S.-Indo relations.

Other factors that are likely to trouble U.S.-Indo relations grow out of the great differences and distance between the two nations, which often put them on opposite sides of international issues. Questions involving the international economic order, the Arab-Israeli conflict, nuclear proliferation, and perhaps Southern Africa are examples, although India is hardly in the radical camp on most such issues. Nor should we expect the irritability factor to disappear, for the tendency of both countries to moralize was not limited to John Foster Dulles and Jawaharlal Nehru and thus did not disappear when they passed from the scene. Finally, the past unhappy history of U.S.-Indo relations has left scars on both sides which will disappear slowly at best. Most Indians feel they have been innocently wronged by the United States, although not all of them believe American policies were consciously designed to hurt India. Most Americans feel that they have been generous to India, but that American resources were ineffectively utilized and created resentment rather than appreciation.

Yet it would be a mistake to conclude that these problems will prevent further improvement of U.S.-Indo relations. Rather, they will serve to limit the extent of such an improvement. This is no cause for gloom, for a large part of the U.S.-Indo relationship is carried out by private or autonomous bodies, especially in the United States. As long as official U.S.-Indo relations are reasonably good—and firmly anchored—the private relationship can carry a large part of the load.

VII

Enlisting Post-1974 India to the Cause of Nonproliferation

George H. Quester

India, by its decision to detonate a nuclear explosive, created a troublesome situation for the world. Without that Indian detonation of May 1974 there would be much more optimism about the avoidance of nuclear proliferation, the further spread of nuclear weapons into the arsenal of additional countries.

The detonation threatens to trigger a wide range of aftereffects. The Indian move and the response of nuclear-supplier states such as the United States may seem to pose questions and set angering precedents for economically under-developed states around the world. Distant states such as Brazil or Argentina may see India's peaceful nuclear explosive detonation as paving the way for them to make similar moves. A neighbor of India's, such as Pakistan, may now feel greater concern for its military security, and may feel driven to seek nuclear weapons of its own.

Without the Indian detonation, therefore, there might indeed have been brighter prospects that possession of nuclear weapons could be contained to the five nations that have had them since 1964; the United States, the USSR, Britain, France, and China. Yet without that detonation there might also have been continued smugness and complacency in this regard, and far less anxiety about controlling nuclear weapons for the future. If nothing else, the Indian detonation thus altered a large community that might otherwise have seen the proliferation problem as solved.

Why is nuclear proliferation seen as something so bad that the Indian detonation was so generally denounced, and that we should now be focusing on how best to keep the Indian precedent from being repeated? [1]

Proliferation is sometimes thought bad simply because it may increase the likelihood of wars. While the presence of nuclear weapons may deter attack in a few situations, it can suggest preemptive strikes in others where two crude and

---

[1] For more extended discussions of the likely bad consequences of continued nuclear proliferation, see William Epstein, *The Last Chance* (New York: Free Press, 1976).

seemingly vulnerable nuclear weapons forces confront each other in ways that seem to favor taking the first strike.

Even if reasonable men disagree on the impact the spread of nuclear weapons will have on the likelihood of wars. such proliferation is more generally bad because it may increase the costs of wars. Whatever the causes of any war outbreak, between Israel and the Arabs, between the two Koreas, between India and Pakistan, or between Argentina and Brazil, far more damage will be done and far more people will be killed if that war brings nuclear weapons into use.

What can now be done to reduce the damage the Indian explosion has caused? Is there any way to get the political, psychological, or technological situation back to what it was before 1974? Is there some mix of measures that can generate a patchwork of new firebreaks against further proliferation, since the Indian move amounts to a leap across what had been thought of as a clear line?

India Is No Different

The United States explicitly entertains no notions of getting the USSR, China, France, or Britain to leave the nuclear weapons club. The Nuclear Non-proliferation Treaty (NPT) of 1968 indeed specifically allows these five countries to retain such weapons with any other states, and it requires all other states to renounce such explosives.[2] Why not then explictly tolerate India's entry into the nuclear weapons club as the sixth member, and hold the line there?

There are a number of difficulties with such an easygoing and open acceptance of India as the sixth. First, as noted, the 1968 NPT specifically makes no provision for tolerance of India or any other state as an additional nuclear weapons state. The manner in which the NPT was drafted thus seemed to some to amount to a challenge by the United States and the USSR to India in particular; a challenge that India unfortunately elected to call. Some will thus sense that the Indian detonation, if not responded to, will put into doubt the superpowers' resolve and responses vis-à-vis any other state crossing the line.

Even if there were not an obvious inconsistency between the wording of the NPT and India's behavior, many people around the world would have raised a second, more general, issue of fairness. What is so special about India? If India can get away with acquiring nuclear weapons why should anyone else be denied such weapons?

A third objection would come simply because of the apparent cynicism of India's labelling the nuclear explosive a peaceful device, instead of openly

[2] A detailed discussion of the Nuclear Nonproliferation Treaty (NPT) can be found in Stockholm International Peace Research Institution, *The Near-Nuclear Countries and the NPT* (New York: Humanities Press, 1972).

admitting that it was truly a bomb. If the "peaceful nuclear explosions" label can be abused in a situation where no serious application of such explosions is in sight, and if India is allowed to get away with such an obfuscation, will this not induce a more general cynicism and ludicrousness about all attempts to be serious about arms control? [3]

It is thus true that driving India out of the nuclear explosives club would be the approach most logically consistent with the framework of the Non-proliferation Treaty. It would tidy up what has become untidy, and would serve as a lesson to all other aspiring sixth nuclear powers. India would have to sign and ratify the NPT, promising not to acquire nuclear explosives. India would do the world a service by destroying any further nuclear warheads it has assembled and abstaining from any further detonations, by submitting to International Atomic Energy Agency (IAEA) inspection of all of its peaceful nuclear facilities—even those indigenously built—and by accounting for all of the plutonium and uranium circulated through its system to date. To achieve this, the United States and other nuclear suppliers might agree to hold back all further nuclear aid, or perhaps even economic aid, of all kinds until India acceded to the NPT and submitted to international controls.

A push for full NPT adherence or some other form of total acceptance of IAEA safeguards may indeed make sense for a number of the nuclear proliferation-prone situations around the world. Perhaps it is altogether appropriate (and was achieved) for West Germany and Japan, the two states in historical memory that might have roused the most direct nightmares when they reached for nuclear weapons.

India Is Different

Yet an important part of deciding whether to strive for full submission to the international inspection of the IAEA will now depend on the extent of the likely resistance: that is, on whether there are any good prospects for NPT adherence or an equivalent legal commitment. A continuing theme of the argument here will be that great damage can be done by fighting a losing battle to win what cannot be won. If one seeks but fails to find, one form of barrier to proliferation, one may in the process lose an alternative barrier and so do a great disservice to the cause.

India is indeed very different from most of these other nations cited, in several important ways. First of all, India has already made the irretractable move of

---

[3] A skeptical analysis of purported (PNE) projects can be found in Franklin A. Long "Peaceful Nuclear Explosions," *Bulletin of the Atomic Scientists* 32 (October 1976), 8:18—28.

detonating a nuclear explosive. Right or wrong, the world views an actual detonation as the irreversible step, for we have never seen any nation withdraw from this club once it has exploded its way into it.

It is indeed somewhat paradoxical that India is generally rated as a nuclear weapons state even though it may have only another warhead or two ready for use, while the world does not yet tend to place Israel in this category even though Israel may have 30 to 40 warheads ready for use.[4] If Israel were to sign and ratify the NPT and to open its entire landscape to inspection, it might thus yet establish a convincing image that it had stayed out of the nuclear weapons club; the whole world might see it that way, and Israel's neighbors might live in a manner consistent with seeing that way. It is far harder to visualize India's neighbors or the rest of the world quickly seeing an Indian renunciation of weapons as some sort of convincing withdrawal from the club.

More important, in part because of this *fait accompli*, the Indian public has adjusted itself very positively to the idea of possessing nuclear weapons. Where signature of the NPT may be accepted grudgingly in some other nations, and with relative equanimity and indifference in many, in India it would now encounter genuine popular hostility.

The evolution of the Nuclear Nonproliferation Treaty and of the more general awareness of the nuclear proliferation issue is quite interesting for the different paths into which the world's public opinion has wandered. A forecaster ten years ago might have had difficulty sorting out the publics of all the would-be "nth" countries, and would have had to guess that many of them would resist submission to the treaty and might come to demand the bomb. Yet very few of such states developed attitudes comparable to India's. Pro-bomb sentiment in India became strong by the time of the 1968 NPT debate, and stayed strong. By comparison, no such sentiment developed in Italy, Germany, Australia, or Japan. What had been pro-bomb sentiment in Sweden in 1960 had become very anti-bomb in 1970.

Brazil may be a counterexample, a country where public attitudes seem to lean toward peaceful nuclear explosives as they did in India.[5] Yet the difficulty with the Brazilian case is that opinion has all along had to be sampled in an atmosphere of military dictatorship, which all too often produces ringing endorsements of

---

[4] For fuller discussions of the Israeli proliferation problem, see Fuad Jabber, *Israel and Nuclear Weapons: Present Option and Future Strategies* (London: Chatto and Windus, 1971).

[5] Good analyses of Brazilian possibilities are to be found in William W. Lowrance, "Nuclear Futures for Sale: To Brazil from West Germany, 1975," *International Security* I (Fall 1976), 2: 147–166.

whatever the government's position is thought to be. The Indian opinion polls, by contrast, were taken before Mrs. Gandhi chose to declare her emergency.[6] (The Brazilian case is also different, happily, in that the state bureaucracy is more divided about the wisdom of a nuclear detonation than the bureaucracy was in India.)

Public involvement with the bomb in India might, of course, have seemed not to matter so much during Mrs. Gandhi's emergency. The detonation of the 1974 device indeed came suspiciously close to Mrs. Gandhi's difficulties with the railroad strike, and at least had the immediate impact of forcing the strike leaders to give in in face of the wave of public euphoria about the detonation. Yet the euphoria did not last, and Mrs. Gandhi's political opposition renewed their offensive within the year, stampeding her into proclaiming the emergency.

A few observers might thus have seen some blessing in the emergency, if it had then allowed the government to ignore the pro-bomb sentiment among the Indian public. If Mrs. Gandhi had decided to avoid elections in the future she would at least have put behind her the temptation to detonate additional nuclear explosives at strategic moments just before such elections. The alleged freedom to act developed in a dictatorial government might even have freed her to sign international agreements renouncing nuclear explosives, if she so chose.

Yet it would have been a mistake to exaggerate Mrs. Gandhi's freedom to ignore popular sentiment during the emergency, or to underrate the popularity of the nuclear program. (It may be a similar mistake to assume that the new regime succeeding her will have a great deal of freedom here.) Even autocratic regimes have to husband their bank accounts of popular support, lest the powers of dictatorship be overtaxed. Mrs. Gandhi apparently chose to use up much of this bank account in pushing a politically unpopular birth control program, with disastrous results. For her to have responded to outside world sentiment by renouncing nuclear explosives might have amounted to a comparable political disaster.

Much of what has just been said about some irreducible needs to be concerned about public opinion applies all the more to the opinions of the governmental bureaucracy. Neither Mrs. Gandhi nor her successors can ignore the fact that this bureaucracy has indeed come to identify itself with the nuclear program and with the explosives it produced; what was hailed as a great accomplishment of the

---

[6] For citations on Indian public opinion on nuclear weapons, see Robert M. Lawrence and Joel Larus, eds., *Nuclear Proliferation: Phase II* (Lawrence, Kansas: University Press of Kansas, 1974), p. 128. For information in Brazilian public opinion polls on the same question, see H. Jon Rosenbaum and Glenn Cooper, "Brazil and the Nuclear Proliferation Treaty, *International Affairs* 46 (January 1970),1:74—90.

Indian Government's scientific establishment cannot so easily be renounced afterward. Many of the rank and file of the bureaucracy and of the scientific establishment have made public commitments to the wisdom of India's nuclear projects, including the explosives program; very few have ever made a strong commitment in the opposite direction. India is indeed importantly different from other "nth" nations in this respect; in most of the other worrisome countries one can identify pro-bomb and anti-bomb factions within the bureaucracy, but the anti-bomb faction in India lost most of its strength and manpower as long as ten years ago.

The Indian nuclear program has by and large made sense for the civilian economy. This might not have turned out to be true if the OPEC states had not raised so enormously the price of oil as a competing energy source. But with the rise in energy prices the nuclear electric power production envisaged for India turns out to be cost-effective. As things stand, therefore, very little of the expense has to be charged to an explicit lust for nuclear explosives; the costs of India's Peaceful Nuclear Explosive (PNE) detonation might be close to the Indian Atomic Energy Commission's (AEC) estimates of some $400,000, making it indeed a very low cost spinoff from the nonexplosives portion of the program.[7]

India may hope to be an exporter as well as an effective user of nuclear technology in the future. The odds are stacked against India, however, in that the world's nuclear industry will always have an appetite for the very newest, most cost-effective reactors, and India is unlikely to be able to compete with the major suppliers here. The Indian move to nuclear industry, and particularly the attention-getting detonation of an explosive, undoubtedly has some impact in raising the world's image of Indian science. Yet the impact in 1974 was not what it would have been in 1964; the world has become a little more jaded about how much of a technical or military or political accomplishment it is to have detonated a prototype atomic bomb. One happy lesson from the Indian move, from an anti-proliferation standpoint, is that Brazilian and other observers might now conclude that there is less prestige than before in such an explosives program.

Even if other "nth" countries are still making up their minds about nuclear explosives, however, the decision threatens to remain relatively sealed for India itself, for all the reasons cited. The new government in New Delhi is not likely to feel much leeway, or want much leeway, on those nuclear decisions made by its predecessor that bother the outside world.

The decision to acquire practical experience in bomb assembly is now inherently irreversible. The decision to maintain a large nuclear establishment will

---

[7] For official estimates on the actual costs of the Indian explosion, see *Nature* 750 (July 5, 1974): 8.

not be cancelled, and indeed the outside world is not asking for a cancellation. The major decision of the Congress years was, however, that international inspection under IAEA safeguards would not be accepted on a blanket or full-scope basis over all Indian nuclear facilities, but that it would be allowed only on specified facilities purchased from abroad. It is this last gap in IAEA coverage that allowed the first Indian detonation, and that generates most fears of further weapons production. This gap is crucial to the American arms control interest, but Prime Minister Desai's government may be no more willing than its predecessor to surrender it.

The coalition of factions that defeated and succeeded Mrs. Gandhi was united mostly by its opposition to the emergency. The coalition includes such explicitly pro-bomb groups as the Jana Sangh, from which the Janata Foreign Minister Mr. Vajpayee is drawn, and it can hardly be counted upon to want to forswear all nuclear explosives in the future. Prime Minister Morarji Desai did give a press interview within several days after the election disavowing any desire for nuclear weapons (essentially the same disavowal that was part of the posture of the preceding administration), and hinting that peaceful nuclear explosives might not be tested if they were not needed. But in the same interview he also questioned Western criticism of the Indian nuclear program, implying that the "peaceful nuclear explosives" label should have been accepted at face value.[8] This may reflect confused or mixed feelings on his part about nuclear explosives; just as plausibly, it may reflect his awareness of the strong pro-nuclear explosives feeling of important parts of the Indian public at large.

While the January 1978 visit of President Carter to New Delhi generally served to reinforce the warming of Indo-American relations after the defeat of Mrs. Gandhi, an unfortunate positioning of a reporter's tape recorder revealed Carter's annoyance at failing to persuade Prime Minister Desai to accept full-scope safeguards or the NPT, with the specter of a "cold and very blunt" American note to follow at a later time.[9]

Direct Pressure Will Not Succeed

To restate an earlier argument, it may be that the most logical support for the NPT position in the Indian case would be to press for New Delhi's surrender of all nuclear explosives now in hand, and for submission henceforth to the obligations and inspections of that treaty. One could imagine some dire circumstances, for example three years of famine in a row, that might make India so

[8] *New York Times*, March 25, 1977, p. 6.

[9] *New York Times*, January 3, 1978, p. 1.

desperately beholden to outside assistance that it would let itself be bludgeoned into making this concession. But one can also imagine many kinds of situations where such outside world pressure for Indian adherence to the NPT system would simply produce a rebuff from New Delhi, which would be worse than nothing at all. Even the possibility of pressuring India to adhere might strike sympathetic Third World outsiders in entirely the wrong way, as a kind of rich country arrogance that would make further nuclear proliferation an all the more appropriate response.

In short, Indian acceptance of the status proposed by the 1968 NPT is unlikely for the short run and middle term, and we may have to live with this along with our principal task of enlisting post-1974 India for the avoidance of further nuclear proliferation.

Could one imagine setting the stage a little later for a more voluntary Indian withdrawal from the nuclear weapons club? Is this altogether unthinkable, even twenty years from now, in light of all that has been said above?

Perhaps not. There is no reason why the outside world should not maintain a continuous posture of soft sell here, never pressing India hard to renounce nuclear weapons, but leaving it clear that such a renunciation will always be welcome. One could perhaps imagine such a withdrawal coming more easily if it were coupled with a parallel withdrawal by one of the charter members of the club, most plausibly Great Britain. The continuing discussion with India might thus be phrased in terms of "what if you could take Britain (or some other state) out of the club with you?" This would, of course, still be bedeviled by the problem of how one makes one's withdrawal from nuclear weapons status entirely credible.

Much could happen over twenty years or so. One of the hopeful trends in general for the halting of nuclear proliferation, as mentioned, is that the overall glamour and sense of importance of nuclear weapons capabilities seems to be in decline. If nuclear weapons are not used in anger between now and the year 2000, and if the stability of boundaries by then seems far less visibly linked to nuclear weapons, much may become possible, even an uncoerced Indian abandonment of nuclear weapons. But this is all more likely by means of low key, subtle, and patient approaches in the absence of an environment of confrontation.

Our originally stated difficulties with accepting India as a *de facto* sixth nuclear weapons state may thus be less serious, especially if we have no other choice.

To be sure, there is the argument: if India can get away with it, why not everyone else? Yet that same argument applies also to the five charter members allowed to possess nuclear weapons under the NPT, and was indeed much used by Indians, in part to pave their way into the nuclear club. It may indeed seem unfair or illogical for anyone to possess nuclear weapons when others must renounce them, but this has never been a world ruled by fairness or abstract logic. To assume that nations all around the globe will demand weapons just because India got them is no more realistic than to assume that they would have done so because China and France had gotten them, or the United States and the USSR.

The questioning of superpower resolve also has been painted too abstractly in the initial discussion. Many nations around the world have good reason to assume that Moscow and Washington will react in a stronger and more coordinated way against any other aspiring nuclear weapons state than they did against India. India is in a real sense a special case, and special cases do not establish particularly relevant precedents. India was unusual because of its large population, and because it was the object of competing American and Russian courtship. India was also unusually poor, so that "punishing" the country could truly hurt or starve a great number of its people.

Other nations are indeed watching to see how the Indian precedent is handled, but this does not mean that they simply will feel free to make their own nuclear weapons if India is not severely punished and forced to undo its move. Many such nations will instead see India as a special case that proves nothing about Soviet and American resolve to halt proliferation; unless the two superpowers decide to make it a test of their resolve and then prove themselves lacking. Getting India to give up its bombs may thus be impossible, and a failure at the attempt might undermine the general effort at stopping further proliferation.

If all the world, the Russians, French, and West Germans included, can be persuaded not to sell nuclear facilities and nuclear fuel except where full-scope safeguards are implemented, then India might indeed be pressured into becoming a *de facto* adherent to the NPT. If an extended American push for such blanket safeguards were undertaken instead mainly to reflect the attitudes of the U.S. Congress and President Carter's election campaign, then it would face risks of failure and the possibility that more would have been lost than gained in the effort.

A fully logical look at the Indian case and the NPT does of course suggest that an inconsistency exists if the United States and the USSR do not do all they can to force India to commit itself to the treaty. Yet issues of precedent in politics often are in the eyes of the beholder. If the entire world, American commentators included, insists on regarding the Indian example as proof of a lack of superpower will, it may turn out to be so, as a self-confirming proposition. On the other hand, a world response of forgetting the Indian example or of failing to see such a clear logical connection to other potential cases could be much more happily self-confirming.

Finally, there is the particularly blatant Indian use of the peaceful nuclear explosion (PNE) label for what amounts to a weapons program. Is this really such a disservice to the worldwide cause of arms control, making a travesty of what some had proposed as a serious civilian-military distinction? It may instead have been a service, in various ways.

There are many arms control experts who all along doubted that such a distinction could ever be made meaningful, fearing that it would sooner or later be abused or, even innocently, become dangerously ambiguous. The Indians may thus have done us the favor of showing these dangers to the world very early. Few Americans now really believe in the commercial advantages of PNE, while most worry about the loophole such projects might offer to a weapons-minded state. The Indian detonation may turn out to have speeded the termination of PNE projects in other countries.

At the very least, Indian's peaceful detonation induced a general vigilance in the American Congress and public about nuclear proliferation, a vigilance far in excess of what had gone on before. Much of the tightening in contracts in the nuclear field by the United States and by other advanced supplier states comes in direct response to the loopholes in the Canadian-Indian contract, and to what passed through those loopholes.

Similarities and Differences

To make India less of a prod to further nuclear proliferation, the task for the United States is thus to watch carefully for aspects in which India is similar to other nations and for aspects in which it is different. Where India is similar to other nations, the task will be to manage the issues in ways that do not seem to pose frightening or immoral precedents for the outside world. Where India is unique and different, the goal for the antiproliferation effort should be precisely to point out that uniqueness to get the outside world to avoid badly drawn analogies.

Where are the similarities? India is poor and greatly in need of economic development. It desperately needs additional sources of energy, all the more so because of the increase in the price of oil. India will thus capture a great deal of sympathy around the world if it seems to be the object of brutal treatment by the industrially developed world or of cavalier analysis by experts on arms control.

Where issues of economic growth are concerned, it would be a mistake for the United States to seem callous about Indian welfare; to seem to be putting selfish arms control considerations ahead of the well-being of an economically deprived state. The United States should thus at all times be in the visible position of treating economic development plans seriously; of offering India fair access to the nuclear and nonnuclear technology, that can be of real benefit to its people, the technology that a generous nation would normally offer.

This does not mean that the United States should offer or subsidize nuclear technology whose cost-effectivess is very much in doubt. It may take decades to decide how truly cost-effective nuclear power production will be when considerations of ecology, safety, and physical security are taken into account. It does mean, however, that the United States should not let itself be seen as prematurely killing off or downgrading power production. If Sweden or France or Japan were first to conclude independently that the net cost of much nuclear power was greater than the gain, this message might reach India and other states soon enough, and would be all the more credible than if a finding were first proclaimed in Washington.[10]

Offering fair access to nuclear technology similarly does not mean that the United States must offer unsafeguarded facilities that can be directly assigned to military uses. Rather, the offer would have to match what is being offered to other states: safeguards over what the United States sells now.

While the United States originally declared that none of its technical assistance whatsoever had been used in the 1974 Indian detonation, the possibility was subsequently raised that United States heavy water had been used in the natural-uranium reactor that produced the plutonium for the Indian bomb.[11] It may indeed be very difficult to tell whether India used American heavy water or heavy water produced indigenously, given the inherent mixing of materials in a complicated nuclear system.

The broader criticism of American policy held that it made no difference whether specifically American heavy water was used for Indian nuclear explosives, because offering such materials for even assuredly peaceful nonexplosive products would free up Indian materials for the more military program. In effect, this argument says that the United States should not be in the position of lowering or eliminating the opportunity cost to India of making nuclear explosives. The counterclaim is that "India would go ahead anyhow to make explosives using her own heavy water." But to do so the Indian government would then at least have to impose a substantial cost on its peaceful economic development if the outside assistance were not available. The same argument could be made, of course, against the 1976 Soviet decision to sell heavy water to India.[12] The Soviet sale will apparently be accompanied by the strictest safeguards to assure that these

---

[10] A good overview of the cost-effectiveness of nuclear power and other energy sources can be found in Spurgeon Keeney, ed. *Nuclear Power: Issues and Choices* (Cambridge, Mass.: Ballinger Publishing Co., 1977).

[11] *New York Times*, August 9, 1976, p. 1.

[12] *New York Times*, December 9, 1976, p. 7.

particular materials are not used for explosives, but the sale may nonetheless allow the Indian regime to feel freer to use its own indigenously produced—and unsafeguarded—materials for weapons.

Such an argument about opportunity costs is undoubtedly correct, but there are a number of difficulties with applying it to India. First, it will strike many nations as an altogether new assertion of authority by the nuclear supplier states, and hence will take some time to capture legitimacy. It is one thing for a nuclear-supplier state to insist on the nonexplosives use of whatever property it supplies; this is only consistent with traditional notions of property rights. It is another thing for a supplier state to use its position to seem to dictate how all other pieces of nuclear property are used.

Over the next five years, the application of such a policy on all new sales may win a great deal of acceptance among the industrialized nonnuclear weapons states and even in the underdeveloped world. But the Indian case has unfortunately raised the issue early, before all the preparatory work has been done.

Second, of course, India has already detonated its bomb and is in a perhaps irreversibly different category from other states to which this "don't lower the opportunity cost" argument might be applied. As noted, it is far easier to stop bomb status from ever being conferred than to erase it afterward.

Third, the argument necessarily smacks of a certain amount of economic brutality. One could indeed argue that every single bit of foreign trade and assistance should be held back, lest it make it easier for India or another potential nuclear weapons state to fulfill its military ambitions. Even if limited to cutoffs of nuclear assistance, it in effect amounts to holding all civilian economic development hostage for good behavior on the proliferation front. Because India is so poor, however, this will be a much harder lever to push here than in other states to be dealt with over the coming years.

Some of the same practical needs for a double standard will arise with regard to the tightening up and renegotiation of various nuclear cooperation contracts the United States and other suppliers have signed over the years. Many contracts were far too vague in specifying that supplies were not to be used for explosives. India's use of Canada's assistance for its peaceful nuclear explosive exploited precisely such an ambiguity or loophole in their bilateral nuclear assistance agreement.

It may make perfect sense to force such a renegotiation in many cases, even when the local country will protest that this amounts to a high-handed failure by the United States of another donor to abide by its original word. Yet it will take a little time to set the right mood to have all such contracts renegotiated, and that time is long past in the Indian case. If the problem consists of getting countries like Spain and Argentina to accept tightened arrangements, it would be better to leave the Indian case out of the picture than to try to include it.

Since the Indian nuclear explosive has been labelled a "peaceful nuclear explosive" (PNE), what the existing nuclear weapons states do in the PNE field may have some impact on subsequent Indian policy. As with the generation of electricity using nuclear power, it might be well for the United States and the USSR to be aboveboard and deliberate here.

If such peaceful explosions begin to look genuinely promising, based perhaps on the calculations of less partisan observers, it would again be a mistake for the superpowers to act in a way that could be seen as putting arms control ahead of economic progress. Rather, some early moves should be made to create genuinely reliable international standards for any nation that needed to conduct a nuclear explosion; for India, Brazil, or anyone else.

On the other hand, this will not mean subsidizing such explosives if the evidence suggests that they will never be cost-effective, given their radioactive fallout. In both the superpowers, there have been signs of a pro-PNE lobby that has been riding this possibility as if it were a hobbyhorse. If such projects on balance came to look impracticable, Moscow and Washington could exert some subtle and acceptable pressure on New Delhi by clamping down on such lobbies and by signing a meaningful ban on the testing of all nuclear explosives, closing once and for all any loophole exception for allegedly peaceful projects.

It should be possible, therefore, for the United States and the Soviet Union and other technologically-equipped states to hem in any nation that claims it has an unsatiated need for peaceful explosions. If usable peaceful explosions are inherently impossible the reason for avoiding them will be obvious. If they are possible they will be carried through, perhaps under IAEA management.

Since India used some other plutonium to make an explosive, there is naturally concern about the accumulation of plutonium from the American-supplied enriched-uranium reactors at Tarapur, which might similarly be used for weapons. The United States secured inspection of this material by the IAEA in its original contract, and also the right to buy back the plutonium and return it to the United States. One must note, however, that the United States showed no eagerness to buy back this plutonium prior to the Indian detonation, and that the Indian government has displayed no clear resistance to having it bought back. Discussions around the world of what is to be done with such plutonium will generally be plagued with bickering about who is to pay the extra costs of moving such materials from country to country, about what the fair price for a buy-back is to be, and about whether reprocessing of the plutonium will make commercial sense. The Indian case will be no exception in this regard. Except in cases where such plutonium will be used for weapons, or when it can be exploited again in the future as reactor fuel, it amounts to a dangerous toxic material posing storage problems. The world is not full of communities anxious to become the location of a plutonium dump, and mixed feelings about the material will continue.

One can thus argue out the exact policies that the United States should follow with regard to the further supply of reactors, or to enriched uranium fuel, or to the buy-back of plutonium. Whatever the specific policies, however, the policy proposal here is that the United States act to minimize publicity about the nuclear tensions between the supplier states and India.

Rather than a period of ongoing litigation with India on nuclear matters, one might instead hope for a period of nonnews about India on the nuclear front, with few accusations about Indian duplicity or Western weakness. The plutonium in India would be repurchased or left in place depending on the balance of considerations. All future sales of nuclear material would be under full and tightly written IAEA safeguards. A quiet message would be delivered that all economic assistance, nuclear and conventional, would be more rapidly forthcoming and more easily delivered if India would forego or minimize further detonations.

If there is indeed a concrete Indian concession that the United States and the USSR should be striving for, it might come precisely in a continuation of what seems to have been deliberately or inadvertently delivered in the past two years: that India keep to a minimum the number of further nuclear detonations it conducts. This is not the same as asking India for openly announced assurances that it is foregoing such detonations; assurances that New Delhi may well be unwilling to deliver. It asks, rather, that India tacitly, with no policy pronouncement, simply contribute to an atmosphere of nuclear quiet.

Participants in discussions of economic aid for India might respond very pessimistically in this regard, noting that virtually every planning session since 1974 has seen much discussion of India's *de facto* nuclear weapon, in an almost morbid fascination with the topic.

Yet the question here, as always, is: "Compared to what?" Specialists on economic aid may see themselves and their colleagues as having become fixated on a weapons discussion, but this may simply reflect the novelty for AID experts of being forced to tune in on a new topic. By contrast, most experts on arms control might find it surprising how little attention and discussion the Indian bomb has drawn compared with the Chinese bomb in 1964 or even the French bomb in 1960. India most probably reached for nuclear explosives in hopes of duplicating the harvest of prestige that Peking seemed to reap in 1964, but the world has not delivered such a harvest. Some nations have conveyed a real resentment to New Delhi of its nuclear step; others have shown a feigned or real indifference.

There is a limit, therefore, to how convincingly we can diminish the precedent of the Indian action, but the limit is not as tight as we might have anticipated. With careful and subtle policy we can get most or perhaps all of the world to be unaffected by the Indian precedent. We may even be able to enlist India in erasing the precedent.

There are some serious proliferation problems in the world that have nothing to do with India's choice: Israel, South Africa, Taiwan, and perhaps South Korea. But there are a few tangible dominoes related to the Indian case.

Brazil and Argentina

Very understandable concerns have been expressed, especially since the Indian detonation, about various agreements for nuclear cooperation that have been signed between India and Brazil, and between India and Argentina. Since both Brazil and Argentina have shown interest in nuclear explosives options and, like India, have refused to sign the Nonproliferation Treaty, the question could obviously be raised as to whether India intended to assist further nuclear proliferation around the world.

A pessimist would point to the statements Indian spokesmen had issued during the 1967-1968 discussions of the NPT and in the months leading up to the detonation: statements defending the right of all nations to make independent and autonomous decisions on whether or not to acquire nuclear weapons or nuclear explosives.

Yet such statements, like all abstract and general statements on the proliferation question, should be viewed first and foremost as posturing and propaganda intended to defend India against world opinion pressures for the NPT. Similarly, the various nuclear cooperation agreements should be seen as having been links in the alliance of Brazil and India and Argentina against pressure for treaty signature. All this hardly suggests that India is in favor of, or even ambivalent about, further nuclear detonations by other countries of that 1968 alliance.

The professionals of the Indian foreign ministry are clearly too intelligent to be unaware that they can lose more than they gain if Brazil and other states get nuclear arsenals of their own. The Indian position is remarkably analogous to that of China, and indeed to that of each of the previous members of the club. Communist Chinese statements before the Chinese detonation regularly professed to believe that nuclear proliferation was generally desirable, that all nations had the right to nuclear weapons, and that all socialist nations should have them.[13]

---

[13] A useful discussion of Chinese statements on nuclear proliferation can be found in Ralph Clough *et al.*, *The United States, China, and Arms Control* (Washington: Brookings Institution, 1975).

After the Chinese detonation, however, such statements ceased to emanate from Peking.

Close reading of the Argentinian and Brazilian contracts with India similarly suggests that no exchange of information on nuclear explosives is going to occur, since classified matters are specifically excluded and all information on nuclear explosives in India is classified.[14] One would hope that there will be no bureaucratic inertia now in India that could cause public statements appropriate to 1968 to continue to get issued in 1978. It is sometimes difficult to get all one's Ambassadors and public spokesmen clued in to the change in the objective strategic situation. Yet the objective situation for India is reasonably clear. It is not in New Delhi's interest to induce further nuclear proliferation in far away places anymore than it would be sensible to encourage it among India's immediate neighbors.

Persons advocating a tough policy toward India after 1974 must thus remind themselves that India has a powerful carrot or stick to wield in return, namely the practical knowledge it has accumulated on bomb design. A central goal of enlisting India to the containment of proliferation will thus simply and obviously be that India not share its knowledge, for it surely could be of value in speeding any hopeful seventh power on its way. All the indications, as noted, are that India indeed intends to hold this information closely, as China has held it. An outside-world policy that drove New Delhi to desperation, however, might put an Indian government into the mood to swap nuclear information to anyone offering something in exchange.

Of course one should not be so blind as to deny that India has already done some damage in setting the stage for a Brazilian move into the nuclear explosives field. Both states made a great deal of the peaceful nuclear explosives argument, despite the fact that the world saw this as a simple euphemism for a bomb program. Both nations have been widely seen as desiring prestige and the role of a regionally dominant power.

Part of the nonproliferation task vis-a-vis India will thus be, as noted, to get New Delhi to stop comparing itself to Brazil, to stop behaving as if its natural flow of cooperation should be with other would-be possessors of nuclear weapons. Another part of the task will be for the United States and other opponents of nuclear proliferation themselves to stop comparing India and Brazil. The less we make the Indian precedent seem to apply to Brazil the better. As noted, there are some similarities. Yet there are also important differences.

Brazil has achieved a great deal of economic growth in recent years, depending

---

[14] On the Indian agreements with Brazil and Argentina, see *Science* 188 (May 30, 1975), 4191:911–919.

heavily on continuing inputs of American technology. The military regime governing Brazil has little claim to popularity aside from this economic growth. While some members of this ruling elite will want the bomb for the prestige it offers, others will remain quite chary of any move that might lead the United States to hold back nuclear and other technical assistance, or even to slow it down, thus jeopardizing the regime's sole basis for popular support.[15]

Even if the German-Brazilian contract for reactors and uranium enrichment facilities is executed smoothly, it does not therefore mean that Brazil will directly move to make nuclear explosives, or that this option was even a primary part of the intention stimulating the project. Brazil has an urgent need for the electricity available from water power at remote locations. There is no more efficient way to transmit this electricity to the industrial centers where it is needed than by using it to enrich uranium which is then used to fuel nuclear reactors at urban centers to produce additional electricity.

The German deal indeed demonstrates that Brazil has other suppliers to turn to besides the United States. Yet the closing of ranks of the nuclear suppliers, including West Germany, since 1974 shows that the Brazilian leadership will have to think twice before it chooses to alienate the entire Western industrialized world by any nuclear detonation.

Because Brazil is more involved than India in continued commercial interchange with the United States and its partners it is more easily pressured on both investment and trade fronts. And, because Brazil is better off than India, it is paradoxically a little more vulnerable to the West's economic pressures.

One important topic to which the United States might address itself in the next five years is some sort of Indian adherence to the Latin American Nuclear-Free Zone. The Treaty of Tlatelolco establishing this zone has attached to it a Protocol II calling for signature by all states possessing nuclear weapons.[16] Obviously the treaty, as written originally, envisaged that this would simply mean the United States, the USSR, Britain, France, and China. When the Indian nuclear detonation was conducted the question immediately arose whether the Tlatelolco Treaty would now also have to require Indian adherence to Protocol II as a prerequisite to its being binding.

---

[15] H. Jon Rosenbaum, "Brazil's Nuclear Aspiration," in *Nuclear Proliferation and the Near-Nuclear Countries*, ed. Onkar Marwah and Ann Schulz (Cambridge, Mass.: Ballinger Publishing Co., 1975), pp. 255–277.

[16] A full analysis of the Latin American Nuclear Free Zone Treaty can be found in John R. Redick, "Regional Nuclear Arms Control in Latin American," *International Organization* 28 (Spring 1975), 2:415–445.

A number of Latin American states have signed and ratified the Latin American Treaty while waiving the requirement that states possessing nuclear weapons adhere to this Protocol. Argentina has signed but not ratified. Most significant, Brazil signed and ratified the treaty, but is not yet bound because it did not waive the requirement for nuclear power adherence to the Protocols, perhaps assuming that Brazil could therefore escape being legally bound by the treaty. It is interesting, therefore, to explore the remaining legal moves required to tidy up the prerequisites to Brazil's being legally bound. Cuba and Argentina (and some smaller Latin American states) would have to accede to the treaty itself. Among the nuclear powers, the Soviet Union must yet accept Protocol II, and the United States and France must give up their objections to Protocol I. Finally, India might have to sign and ratify Protocol II, since the OPANAL Secretary General has indeed given his opinion that this might be legally necessary.

Assuming that India indeed does not want to contribute to the further spread of nuclear weapons, the possibility is at least worth exploring that such an Indian commitment to Protocol II could be achieved over time. Protocol II basically pledges nuclear weapons states to forego the use of nuclear weapons, or the threat of nuclear weapons, against any part of the zone—a pledge fully consistent with the various public statements of Indian foreign policy.

The Indian treaty adherence sought here might be delivered very casually, perhaps prefaced by a New Delhi statement that India still did not consider itself a nuclear weapons state, but that it respected the strong feelings of those Latin American states that had stated their inability to see a clear line between peaceful and military nuclear explosives. The model for such Indian action might be found in the Chinese adherence to the Latin American Treaty. Having earlier stated it could never adhere, Peking delivered its adherence after the personal pleas of President Echeverria of Mexico.

In legal terms, such an Indian move might make it harder for Brazil to move for a bomb of its own. It is unduly pessimistic to believe that nations are not at all inhibited by the international treaty commitments they feel themselves to have gotten into. In terms of political capital, moreover, such an Indian statement might further be useful in getting people to stop brooding about the Indian bomb or about the dominoes of further proliferation.

Pakistan and Asia

A necessary condition for getting India to keep quiet about its nuclear activities is that there be a relative lack of tension in the Asian frontier zones. One is tempted to predict such a lack of tension, since there have been fewer incidents between China and India than anyone would have predicted in 1962. Yet much of this unfortunately depends on the future evolution of Chinese foreign policy after the death of Mao, including considerations of Sino-Soviet relations and Chinese perceptions of Indo-Soviet relations. The possibilities for Sino-Indo relations range from improvement (which would reduce speculation about India's nuclear military potential to a minimum) to, at worst, a major border crisis with conventional and nuclear games of chicken along the frontier.

American foreign policy throughout will thus have to be one of balance and moderation, above all avoiding the appearance of playing off one state against another, and steering all toward essentially nonmilitary solutions. This is the best the United States can do in the way of extracting a contribution to the antiproliferation campaign. It may also be the best for the other arenas of foreign policy.

India might have spurred Pakistan to reach for nuclear weapons even if no Indian explosive had been detonated. Because of the memory of the old Indian Empire, or of the extent of British India, there has been a continually visible irredentism toward East and West Pakistan in the Indian political spectrum. The problem is obviously aggravated by the continuing disagreements about political legitimacy of Kashmir. It has also been made worse by the tendencies toward fragmentation in Pakistan, illustrated so dramatically in the brutal attempt at repression in East Pakistan that led to Indian intervention and the independence of Bangladesh.

The worst fears, not only of a Pakistani regime, but of many ordinary citizens, have thus been that India might at some point be carried forward by irredentism to reunite the British territories of 1947. This has often enough been the dream put forward by right-wing Hindu spokesmen in New Delhi, as expressed by the Jana Sangh party; it may not really be such an alien dream for many Indians.

The Indian detonation might have been enough to make Pakistan look for nuclear weapons options. Yet, paradoxically, New Delhi's nuclear decision may be accompanied by a fuller Indian resignation, at last, to Pakistani independence, even without Pakistan getting its own bombs in the meantime.

India got its nuclear explosives by clever use of spinoffs from what in many ways was sensible and justifiable as a peaceful nuclear electricity program. Yet if India can benefit from electricity-producing reactors, so can Pakistan. Even the reprocessing of plutonium from such reactors may make economic sense while at the same time creating a volume of weapons-grade fissionable material. (Eyebrows have thus been raised, and serious American objections expressed, about Pakistani plans to purchase a plutonium-reprocessing plant from France.) The paradox is thus that India's bomb subtly reminded one and all that Pakistan could have the bomb too. It might also be a reminder that any Indian enthusiasm for an incorporation of Pakistan into nonsectarian India is the one thing most likely to drive Pakistan to seek the ultimate nuclear veto on this.

Mrs. Gandhi's declaration of the emergency moved expressions of public opinion in India, and this for a time put a stop to the right-wing calls for the recovery of Pakistan. One does not know whether they will resume now in the aftermath of the emergency. In any event, the task of the American government will still fall within the same general outline: to steer political leaders in India toward full coexistence with Pakistan while discouraging Pakistan from trying to insure this by means of the nuclear short-cut.

The Indian government has at least been legally recognizing the existence of Pakistan, and not trying to press a pariah status on Pakistan in the manner in which the Arabs press Israel, or North Korea presses Seoul, or mainland China presses Taiwan. If Pakistan needs to have its national existence reasssured, there is less left to do; the task set for U.S. foreign policy in reassuring Pakistan's national existence is minor compared with the task of reassuring the existence of the threatened near-nuclear regimes just mentioned.

In addition to citing the demands of the U.S. Congress, spokesmen for the Carter administration's policies on full-scope safeguards for India also cite apprehensions about Pakistani intentions if India is not pulled back into a non-weapons status. Yet this explanation raises a number of questions. Will Pakistan indeed be sufficiently reasurred if India submits, given the fact that inherent doubts will be left about whether all Indian bomb potential has been locked up, and given the demonstrated Indian competence at bomb assembly? The goal, of course, is to get Pakistan to give up plans to purchase a plutonium reprocessing plant from France, but the assurance of a linkage here may be difficult to find.

One could of course go at the Pakistani nuclear threat from the other direction by seeking to persuade France to cancel the sale of the reprocessing plant (as may now have occurred), but persuading Paris to do this may require that Washington go along more with the French on other issues. The French government has opposed the requirement of full-scope safeguards, for example, and American persistence on this issue vis-à-vis India might thus have the opposite of the desired effect with regard to the Pakistani nuclear project.

What then would be concrete suggestions for U.S. policy here? The United States may have to be willing to sell Pakistan conventional arms in order to head off the acquisition of nuclear arms. Again, if there is no aid to cut off, there may be no levers for an antiproliferation policy. At the same time, the United States should continue to try to persuade France and other nuclear suppliers not to make Pakistan's nuclear weapons program possible.

The United States clearly must seek to restrain Pakistan from attacking India, and India from attacking Pakistan. A plausible ally here can be Iran, which apparently has warned India to put aside dreams of absorbing Pakistan and has offered to help India economically as long as this condition is met. The Shah of Iran has also proposed a nuclear-free zone arrangement for the Middle East area, clearly including Pakistan.[17] If the message from Teheran is, "We'll go nuclear if you do, but we won't if you don't," this may be of considerable help in striking the balance the United States desires.

There are many disadvantages for the world in the "peaceful" euphemism that India has adopted for its nuclear explosives. It seems so blatantly hypocritical that it suggests cynicism is generally appropriate on pronouncements on nuclear arms control. It seems to open an avenue whereby other states could reach for weapons under the cover of the same euphemism. It casts perhaps undeserved aspersions on what might have been serious pursuits of peaceful nuclear explosions at other locations around the world.

Yet there is at least one compensation for the costs of the PNE euphemism here. The Indian statements, if they mean anything, amount to a no-first-use declaration with regard to India's nuclear weapons. To say that the explosives are not weapons is, at the very least, to avoid threatening to use them against any state lacking such explosives, or against any nuclear weapons state that has not used its weapons. In effect, this makes India the second nuclear weapons state to adopt a declaratory no-first-use logically the equivalent of what China has declared more explicitly.

If years and years pass without India ever brandishing its new destructive potential, without India ever discussing scenarios in which its nuclear explosives would be used in warfare, a new interesting path would have been paved for the world. This is hardly as much of a contribution to nonproliferation as would have been made if India had never detonated a warhead in the first place, or if India were now to renounce all such explosives and submit to inspection. Yet it would be a contribution hardly to be sneezed at, and it is a goal worth pursuing in the interactions of United States-Indian diplomacy. The less India and the world say about its nuclear explosives, the better. If nothing is said officially about the ease of the transition to military uses, this is altogether desirable.

Some Conclusions

It is difficult finally to come to any conclusion but that the Indian nuclear detonation indeed has done a monumental disservice to the cause of world nuclear arms control, and that the damage can be stopped or limited only by a combination of clever policy and good luck.

---

[17] For an insightful analysis of the Iranian case, see Anne Hessing Cahn, "Determinants of the Nuclear Option: The Case of Iran," in *Nuclear Proliferation and the Near-Nuclear Countries,* ed. Marwah and Schulz, pp. 185–209.

Yet it is not easy to do controlled experiments in social science, or to answer the "what might have been" questions with any certainty. When speculating as to the true impact of India's detonation we should at least consider the possibility that some service was done in alerting the publics of many countries around the world to the real risk of further proliferation and in galvanizing them into more political action. If India had not detonated its bomb, would the world have been as suspicious of the German-Brazilian deal? Would the nuclear-suppliers conferences have gotten rolling as effectively? Would the French government have abandoned its excessively formalistic opposition to the Nonproliferation Treaty in favor of the more practical policies it is following now?

In either event, whether the Indian detonation was a curse or a blessing, the problem will remain of how to make the best of the situation; lamenting what is unrecoverable is very dangerous if it leads us to try for what is impossible.

The cause of halting further nuclear proliferation around the world would surely be easier if India did not exist. Yet it does exist, a less-developed state that insisted on acquiring nuclear weapons even when the tide in much of the rest of the world, developed and underdeveloped, was flowing in the opposite direction. That India exists, however, does not rule out the possibility that it can be ignored. If Iran and Italy and Brazil and Australia and Japan ignore the Indian precedent, much of the damage to the antiproliferation effort will have been undone. If the United States, the Soviet Union, and other states concerned about proliferation make it easier to ignore India, this may yet happen.

Comment

Onkar Marwah

Reactions to the Indian nuclear explosion have varied between two extremes. Some wish to punish India to make of it an example for other nuclear aspirants. A second group of analysts suggests that the Indian nuclear *fait accompli* be accepted while arms control efforts be directed at dissuading others from following the Indian path. Professor Quester's paper is a change from the preceding types of commentaries. He explores what action is possible with respect to India, and what can be done in relation to other states down the line. To that extent, he avoids the hortatory and condemnatory stances that have marked a substantial section of the nonproliferation literature but have provided little in the way of practical solutions to resolve the problem. Professor Quester's position is essentially as follows:

> India's nuclear explosion revived a dormant issue. The problem for U.S. policymakers is whether India should be allowed to get away easily with its truancy, or be treated as a special case on the premise that its situation is different from other potential proliferators.

> The fact is that India has already done what needed to be prevented. The impact of the nuclear explosion cannot be rescinded. There is wide domestic support for Indian nuclear activities so that direct pressure on the country will not succeed. What can now be attempted is the creation of conditions which lead to a voluntary Indian renunciation of nuclear weapons. To encourage such behavior on the part of the Indians, their country should be tuned out of arms controls discussions. Meanwhile, U.S. policy should indirectly seek to reinforce the conditions for a self-willed Indian abjuration of nuclear weapons.

> The cases of countries such as Brazil and Argentina are different. They are not anywhere near India's stage of nuclear competency. They are, therefore, more open to influence by nuclear technology supplier nations. India should be persuaded not to release its own sensitive nuclear technology to these and other nuclear aspirants.

> The effect of the Indian nuclear explosion should be minimized in other ways. For instance, India should be asked to adhere to the Latin American Nuclear-Free Zone Treaty. Pakistani fear of India should be assuaged and a possible nuclear venture by them aborted through compensatory measures such as the provision of more conventional arms.

I agree with the general thrust of Professor Quester's assessment that India be ignored and its visibility be reduced in the matter of current nonproliferation efforts. Indeed, nothing else can be done. India is the state least open to involuntary nuclear policy changes through sanctions envisaged by the U.S. administration or through application by the London nuclear technology supplier's group.

Consider the facts. India's civilian nuclear establishment is among the sixth or seventh largest and most diversified in the world. Among non-Communist Third World states, it is the oldest and the largest. As with other Indian endeavors, it is highly autarkic in function and capability. Beginning with the construction, without foreign help, of Asia's (outside of the USSR) first nuclear reactor in 1956, India had acquired the following major facilities by 1977:[1]

1. About a half dozen nuclear research reactors, all but one built without foreign participation.
2. Three 500-megawatt nuclear power stations and two more at different stages of construction or design.
3. The ability to design and construct from equipment manufactured indigenously one 500-megawatt nuclear power station every second year—the only country in the Third World with such a capability.
4. The competency to fabricate all sensitive nuclear instrumentation, fueling assemblies, special alloys and materials, heavy water, fissile plutonium and thorium from its own processes and plants, and according to speculation, thermonuclear fissile substances.
5. Asia's largest and first indigenously constructed variable-energy cyclotron.
6. A major nuclear research and engineering establishment outside Bombay employing approximately 10,000 technical and scientific personnel.
7. A second major nuclear research and engineering establishment nearing completion at Kalpakkam in south India, on the lines and scale of the Bombay establishment, for specialized research in thorium-fueled breeder reactor technology.
8. A cadre of about 30,000 trained nuclear research personnel included in the nationwide nuclear safety-badge service.
9. An integrated public-private sector industrial units organization to back the nuclear autarky drive, in all stages from the mining of ores to the commissioning of nuclear power plants.

---

[1] For details, see Government of India, Department of Atomic Energy: *Annual Report (s)*; Government of India, Atomic Energy Commission: *Atomic Energy and Space Research: A Profile for the Decade 1970–80;* Atomic Energy Commission, 1970: *Nuclear India* (Bombay: Bhabha Atomic Energy Center), *passim.* See also, Onkar Marwah, "India's Nuclear and Space Programs: Intent and Policy," *International Security,* 2(2) (Fall 1977), 96–121.

10. Five heavy water plants under construction, whose output would make India entirely self-sufficient in that material.

11. Two plutonium separation plants, the first handling 30 tons of irradiated fuel rods, the second able to process ten times as much as the first plant. (A third plant is also envisaged.)

12. Numerous other nuclear activities and support facilities: isotope production, cladding materials, mines, medicine, seismic arrays, fissile U-223 extraction processes, fusion and uranium-enrichment research, and so on.

India's nuclear program is so comprehensive and general in purpose that, in technical terms, it could support a weapons project and civilian needs simultaneously. In effect, and in the context of the preceding competencies, India's nuclear explosion of 18 May 1974 amounted to a major political decision but a relatively modest technical event.

Beyond the high level of autarky in nuclear matters, India—at this writing—possesses grain reserves of twenty million tons and foreign exchange holdings of five billion dollars.[2] Capable of producing 95 percent of all its requirements of heavy and electrical machinery, the country's industrial output is the thirteenth largest in the world. With the world's third biggest stock of technical and skilled manpower, India also has acquired a relatively independent scientific community.[3] Finally, its armament industry is the largest in the Third World, after China's, in value, volume, diversity of production, and R&D effort.[4] So, unless any of the preceding conditions change drastically for the worse, the usual means of exerting influence on any Indian policies, including nuclear policies will not be available to more powerful or affluent states.

Current U.S. policy to dampen nuclear proliferation appears to be pursued along six lines of effort. The first seeks to reinforce the safeguards system and plug loopholes so as to minimize the danger of nuclear fuel being diverted or stolen to make bombs. The second attempt is to build upon policy restraints; for example, to follow up on plans to ban nuclear explosions. The third step is to

---

[2] The outlook for 1978 is a record foodgrain production of over 125 million tonnes, along with a foreign exchange accumulation of 5 to 6 billion dollars. See, *India Today* (New Delhi) November 1–15, 1977, pp. 64–66; and January 16–31, 1978, p. 67.

[3] See UNESCO, *National Science Policy and Organization of Scientific Research in India.* (Paris: UNESCO, 1972), Tables 5–15, pp. 115–121. India's national stock of skilled and technical manpower figured at 1.2 million in 1970, and increases by 150% every ten years.

[4] For details, see Onkar Marwah, "Military Power and Policy in India," in Onkar Marwah and Jonathan Pollack, eds., *Military Power and Policy in Asian States* (Boulder, Colorado: Westview Press, 1978).

provide incentives for countries to desist from building facilities that provide a weapons option, for example by establishing an international fuel insurance and supply system. The fourth avenue would stimulate consensus-building on basic nuclear issues so that countries learn to perceive common dangers and work together instead of against each other, particularly with regard to the commercial nuclear field. The fifth objective is to synchronize domestic U.S. nuclear policy decisions with international nuclear control efforts. The sixth concern is with measures that protect the motives of countries to encourage nonproliferation.[5]

The United States is to be commended for placing high priority on pointing out dangers inherent in the spread of nuclear weapons. It is necessary, despite criticism, that the world be continually exposed to the problem of misuse of technology, especially nuclear technology. The United States is the only nation that can fulfill such a role, being the one open superpower possessing multi-channeled communications with the largest number of countries in the world. One demurs, however, to its policy of lumping all near-nuclear countries in one group and adopting high-keyed tactics to enforce its will as well as to enunciate its principles. What would make more sense is that tactics be low-keyed, and, depending upon the attributes of the recalcitrant states, that they partake of tacit bargains where necessary and unavoidable, and impose sanctions only where these have a reasonable chance to take effect. That would require differentiation in the objectives of nonproliferation policy between one would-be proliferator and another, and indeed, in the style of negotiation itself.

It seems clear that since 1974 an emphasis on sanctions rather than bargaining has characterized U.S. nonproliferation policies toward India. Building upon incorrect charges that India had used U.S.-supplied materials to conduct its nuclear explosion, the new administration has withheld enriched uranium fuel for the Tarapur nuclear power station.[6] Within the ambit of deliberations of the London nuclear technology suppliers' group of states, the Soviet Union has been persuaded to withhold the transfer of heavy water coolants for the same nuclear

---

[5] Statement of Professor Joseph Nye, Deputy to the Undersecretary of State for Security Assistance, Science and Technology (U.S.), as reproduced in the *Harvard University Gazette*, November 10, 1977, p. 1.

[6] Under the provisions of the new Nuclear Nonproliferation Act, 1978, the U.S. Nuclear Regulatory Commission, in the first ruling of its kind on April 27, 1978, denied India's request for supplies of enriched fuel for the Tarapur nuclear power station. President Carter has overridden the NRC ruling, but the Act permits Congress to countermand the Presidential ruling within two months.

Whatever the sequence of immediate events, the major fact is that India would be a delinquent under the terms of the new Act within two years unless it accedes to full-scope safeguards.

power station. The demand on India is that it open all its nuclear installations and activities to international inspection in return for the enriched fuel and heavy water.

Whether India's intent be judged peaceful or military, it is unlikely that it would today accept a countrywide monitoring—or full-scope safeguards as they are termed—of its nuclear activities for the modest *quid pro quo* offered in return. Enriched uranium fuel and imported heavy water are required for only the Tarapur nuclear power station. The Tarapur station is not indispensable, although the Indian government's public stance may insinuate as much. While Tarapur's rated capacity was to be 480 megawatts on full steam with two generators, only one generator has actually functioned. As for the heavy water, India has five heavy water plants under construction whose completion over the next few years will obviate the need for any imports.

What would be India's options in response to U.S.-initiated sanctions against the Indian refusal to accept full-scope safeguards? The following responses would be possible:

1. Convert the Tarapur reactors to accept plutonium, which is produced locally, instead of enriched uranium. Indian nuclear engineering personnel have said that they could undertake such reactor modifications.

2. Substitute a thermal power station for the nuclear-based source of power. Within the terms of the original contract the United States is obligated to provide sufficient time to India in case such alternate arrangements are necessitated.

3. Seek a clarification ruling from the International Court of Justice on the unilateral changes made in the Tarapur agreement by the United States. Simultaneously, withhold further payments to the U.S. Export-Import Bank which provided the foreign exchange component of construction costs.

4. Acquire proprietary rights over the spent fuel accumulated at Tarapur—which, otherwise, would revert to the U.S. on demand and after a mutually-agreed financial reimbursal to India of the costs of the material.

Assent to full-scope safeguards would amount, in essence, to Indian acceptance of the Nonproliferation Treaty without formal signature. While keen to improve Indo-U.S. relations after the freeze of the Nixon years, India's new political leaders have nevertheless rejected, through a series of low-keyed pronouncements an imposition of discriminatory safeguards on Indian nuclear activities. Differing from the previous Indian leadership more in degree than kind on nuclear matters, the policy stance of Prime Minister Desai and Foreign Minister Vajpayee can be summarized as follows:

1. Further nuclear explosions are ruled out for the foreseeable future. If

necessary at all, the PNEs will be carried out after due notice is served to the world community and representatives are invited to attend the experiment.

2. India would not accept unequal obligations or sign the Nonproliferation Treaty unless mandatory for all states.

3. India would not accept mandatory one-way discriminatory safeguards on its indigenously-created nuclear facilities.

4. Safeguards and inspection of such nuclear facilities as were constructed through international arrangements would continue to be acceptable.

5. The effort at improving India's nuclear technology and sophistication in line with ongoing programs would continue; such as, work toward the development of indigenous breeder reactors based on thorium fuels.

Beyond the reality of India's enhanced national capabilities, desire for equality in the international system, and the volition of its political elites lies another barrier to Indian acceptance of exclusive nuclear arms control measures. A situation pertinent to the country's domestic politics is that the new government is on the defensive against opposition charges of substituting surrender (to Western influence) for self-reliance. In that context, any Indian leadership would provoke resentment and loss of electoral support, particularly among the articulate sectors of Indian society, if it were seen as scuttling a nuclear policy whose essentials have gone undisputed since the earliest years of independence.

The real problem with the Indian nuclear detonation is that its accompanying professions of peaceful intent are widely disbelieved. It is feared that other states will attempt what the Indians are really suspected of doing: embarking on a nuclear weapons program under the cover of peaceful applications of nuclear technology. This brings us to conflicting assessments of Indian intent, capability, and strategic interaction with other states.

My opinion is that the actual decision to go ahead with the nuclear test was taken during the events that led to the creation of Bangladesh. For a few months preceding the 1971 war, India found itself opposed by all three major military powers: the United States, the Soviet Union, and the People's Republic of China. There were indirect threats, conveyed by Henry Kissinger to Indian leaders, of Chinese intervention if India intervened in East Pakistan. Direct threats were presented through orders to U.S. Naval Task Force 74, led by the nuclear-armed USS *Enterprise*, to sail up the Bay of Bengal. According to other Indian analysts, the nuclear test decision was as much the consequence of scientific bureaucratic momentum within the country as of any hardheaded strategic calculations by its leaders.

It is difficult to choose between one motive and another or to ascribe weights to their respective importance within Indian intent governing the nuclear test decision. Let us assume, for purposes of argument, that there was some strategic input in the decision to proceed with the test. Given the circumstances of the period, I believe the Indian nuclear test decision was understandable. The fact is that since its military performance in the 1971 war and the nuclear test, India is treated differently by the great powers, although the latter may deny it. No one speaks any more of maintaining a military balance in the subcontinent. The nuclear test itself insinuates that India's demonstrated nuclear weapon potential can be converted into an operational capability, and that techniques once learned cannot be unlearned.

Despite imprecision of the motives for going nuclear, the fact remains that Indian policymakers cannot now ignore the strategic consequences of the action. The country has already, for instance, paid the price of being targeted by the nuclear forces of the superpowers. It will never be untargeted again no matter what safeguard documents it signs now. So, why should it sign? Second, Indian intelligence reports leaked to the news media foretell a definite Pakistani commitment to a nuclear explosion by the early 1980s. When, and if, that happens, the South Asian scene will be unalterably changed, and the entire set of rules and premises for interaction between India and Pakistan will have to be recast.[7]

It is wrong to assume, however, that Indian leaders could, in the interim, seriously conceive of their country as a nuclear weapon power with just one successful nuclear explosive device. A "bomb in the basement or on the shelf" philosophy for India is meaningless against militarily inferior Pakistan, and useless against militarily superior China. So an actual decision to proceed with the development of a nuclear strike force is minimally what would make India into a nuclear weapon power. No such decision appears to have been taken by the Indian government. Trigger lists of items and activities that lead toward the acquisition of a nuclear strike force are maintained by the great powers and any Indian effort in that respect would be quickly revealed.

It is probable that an indigenous long-range delivery system capability will become available to India by the mid-eighties. Indian space research establishments begun in 1967 had by 1974 successfully developed the following: inertial guidance systems, telemetry equipment, rate gyroscopes, heat shields, nose cones, electronic payload systems, on-board miniaturized computers, and a wide variety of high specific-impulse solid and liquid propellants. In the same year, the Chairman of the Indian Space Commission publicly stated that the country already possessed the ability to produce a missile with a 1,800—2,000-mile range using

---

[7] The problem is that, irrespective of what the Pakistanis actually do, the Indians—aware of others' doubts about their nuclear plans—cannot but assume adversary effort to the same end. As such, it is unlikely that the Indian "weapons option" could now be surrendered even though the weapons may not be made.

locally developed solid fuels and guidance systems. In 1975 an Indian-fabricated 300-kilogram satellite was launched under an arrangement with the Soviet Union using a Molniya rocket, and a second one was to go in early 1978. A project to develop a four-stage rocket with orbital launch capability is due to be completed by the early eighties. By the late 1980's, India plans to have more powerful space launch vehicles capable of lofting satelites weighing between 600 and 1,200 kilograms into geostationary earth orbit at 40,000 kilometers.

With the preceding goals, success to date, a current complement of approximately 10,000 space research personnel and larger numbers in training, Indian space activities are, next to China's, certainly the most ambitious in the Third World. But they will not provide long-range missile capability until 1985. Thus India can give its nuclear and space activities a strategic weapons shape only after the lapse of another eight to ten years. In the interim period, it would be foolhardy and presumptuous for any Indian policymaker to conceive of strategic doctrines, nuclear strike force purchase prices, or weapons-use scenarios.

The reality is that, even assuming the most negative interpretation of Indian objectives, arms control proponents have at least another decade to consider serious purpose and equitable measures before India could be viewed as possessing the operational capability to become a nuclear-weapon-and-delivery-system power. This intervening period is crucial for nuclear arms control efforts, but only if the Indian nuclear explosion is seen as the symptom and not the cause of the dangers of nuclear proliferation engulfing the world.

What is required is that the general nonproliferation debate move from its heavy emphasis on arms controls for others to a consideration of the issues as they concern all states of the international system. I believe the new U.S. administration is engaged sincerely in such an effort. Other states, particularly a few middle level powers of which India is one, will wait to see how such effort is translated into practice.

The current picture of intrasuperpower arms control attempts remains unclear. Reports about agreement on a comprehensive test ban are followed by information that the ban would be limited to three years and pertain only to peaceful nuclear explosions! Success in SALT II negotiations is compromised by disagreement over the development of cruise missiles and the neutron bomb.[8] A rekindled interest in the dangers of nuclear proliferation after the Indian explosion remains unconnected in the eyes of arms-supplier states, with the danger that results for bordering regions from the vast conventional arms supply

---

[8] In a lonely but courageous act, the U.S. President recently postponed production and deployment of neutron bombs despite the advice of a majority of his high-level national security advisers.

to the Persian Gulf and possibly, in the future, to China. It would be naive to expect that India would ignore the strategic impact on itself of the latter developments. Indian policymakers also suspect that nuclear weapon-making techniques and materials have secretly been supplied to South Africa and possibly Israel. The choices that are made in the mid-eighties by Indian leaders will, frankly, reflect their concern with the preceding type of imperfections in the arms control environment as they see it from New Delhi.

There is another, perhaps more realistic, view that assesses the current premises of nuclear arms control measures as merely reflecting of the inequality of states, and therefore meant to persuade the majority of states to accept such a reality. If that is the case, I do not see how India would accept formal status in the international system lower than that of China, Britain, or France. Indeed, a number of second order powers are likely to challenge, in the coming years, an international hierarchy frozen in the mold of the Second World War. In such a situation, a realistic view of the unequal international system must also take into account and prepare for the possibility of changes in the inequality of states.

A third view is that irrespective of the arms control measures worked out between the superpowers, a number of states will continue to seek nuclear weapons as long as arms control remains a symbol and fact of international power. Considering the worldwide, autonomous spread of technology, many states will inevitably acquire the means for making nuclear weapons. All that can be hoped for is a reduction in the speed with which nuclear weapon-making processes spread around the world.

In the current framework of international power, the Indian nuclear explosion was merely an inconvenience. While creating some confusion for arms controllers, it was no more than the forerunner of what is likely to happen in the future. If a certain measure of nuclear proliferation beyond the present five nuclear weapons powers is inevitable, the arms control debate needs to move from a consideration of stopping the process to managing its safe onset in the coming years. Though that was not its objective, the Indian nuclear test may have served a very useful purpose by bringing such matters to the surface of international concerns. Meanwhile, it should be noted that India has refused, despite blandishments, to release its sensitive nuclear techniques to other states in the Third World. Nor has it accepted the suggestion put forth by Yugoslavia that major nuclear technology recipient states join in a counter-cartel to oppose the sanctions being effected by the London nuclear technology supplier states group.

Science and Technology in India: Their Role in National Development

F. A. Long

I do not see any way out of our vicious cycle of poverty except by utilizing the new sources of power which science has placed at our disposal.

—Jawaharlal Nehru, 1958[1]

It is now widely agreed within developing nations that better application of science and technology is a major element in accelerated national development. As the above quotation indicates, political leadership in India reached this conclusion more than two decades ago. Indeed, soon after it attained independence India began to vigorously develop its capabilities in science and technology and new technologically based industries. This chapter examines the character of Indian developments in science and technology, their application to national development, and their increasing role in India's relations with its neighbors and the world.

In evaluating the potential of a nation's science and technology to contribute to national development, one must focus on the overall science and technology system. This structure is composed of policies, people, laboratories, and technology-based industries. In examining this system, there are a variety of aspects which might be the principal focus. In this chapter, major attention is on the role of scientific and technological research and development (R&D) in enhancing technology innovation in industry and agriculture in India. The approach will be to treat sequentially the following items, each of which is a major component of the system:

1. Planning activities for science and technology (S&T) with particular attention to application of science and technology to Indian development.
2. The availability of trained manpower, including trained scientists and engineers, technology managers, and skilled technicians.
3. The level, character, and productivity of the national programs of research and development (R&D). We shall be concerned here with (a) the R&D

[1] Jawaharlal Nehru, "The Tragic Paradox of our Age," *New York Times Magazine*, September 7, 1958.

infrastructure, that is, the laboratories and institutes that have responsibility for R&D, and (b) the nature and productivity of the programs that are in place.

4. The manner in which the R&D programs contribute to national development by enhancing the efforts of industry, agriculture, and related activities. This section will focus on technology innovation and the role of R&D programs in enhancing innovation.

5. Longer-range aspects of the application of R&D to development, including prospects for innovation in a few of the highest technologies. There also will be a short analysis of the role of R&D and technology innovation in agriculture and rural development.

Before proceeding with these analyses, it is useful to position the overall study by noting some of India's special characteristics, which influence its utilization of science and technology.

India is an immense nation: second largest in population; seventh largest in geographic size. It is a country of great contrasts and large regional differences. It is on the average a very poor country, but it has developed a large industrial base. Even though its per capita GNP in 1973 was only about $117,[2] its total GNP is the ninth largest in the world.

As a nation committed to a socialist pattern of society, India has given great stress to national planning. The country is now operating within its Fifth National Five Year Plan, and for the first time this general national plan is accompanied by a separately developed five-year plan (1974-79) for science and technology.[3] India's complicated mixture of public and private sector industry links directly to its national utilization of science and technology. Agriculture is wholly private; most heavy industry and such national services as rail and air transportation, electric power production, and communications are in the public domain; private enterprise plays a dominant role in many of the high-technology industries as well as in most of the small-scale and cottage industries.

India's prime application of technology to industry has focused on import substitution, with many Indian industries shielded from outside competition by substantial entry barriers to imports. Indian exports have been growing rapidly in recent years, although in total volume they are still only a small fraction of

[2] United Nations Committee on Trade and Development, *Handbook of International Trade and Development Statistics* (TD/STAT. 6), 1976.

[3] Government of India, Department of Science and Technology, National Committee on Science and Technology, *Science and Technology Plan, 1974–79* (1973).

national production.[4] Products of modern technology play only a small role in these exports; with the exception of engineering goods, all of the items in the "first ten" of exports are either based on natural resources (for example, sugar and iron ore), or represent comparatively older technologies (for example, textiles and leather goods).

Indian Planning for Science and Technology

Since India has given great stress to national planning almost from the first days of independence, it is not surprising that specific attention has been given to planning for science and technology. The surprise, rather, is that specific formal planning for S&T arrived so relatively late. The first Indian five-year plan for science and technology became available in 1973, and covers the period from 1974 to 1979. It is a document of the National Committee of the Department of Science and Technology, not of the Indian Planning Commission which produces the five-year plans and annual plans for the nation. A central argument for a plan is in the following quotation from the 1973 document: "Without a national plan for science and technology, we run the risk of fragmented effort by different agencies with possibilities of duplication and waste. At the same time, scientific and technological tasks crucial to the economy cannot be left unattended to for want of planning and coordination."[5]

The National Committee for Science and Technology (NCST) set up a major program to analyze twenty-four sectors of science and technology. Each sector committee was charged to study critically the status of its own sector and to evolve suitable programs of research, development, and design. The separate analyses then were combined by the NCST, which ultimately issued the final draft plan. This is a massive document, two volumes with roughly 600 pages. The brief first volume outlines the central elements of the plan and summarizes recommended financial outlays. The much more extensive second volume gives more complete details on the state of the various sectors, the recommended R&D, and proposed financial commitments for the 1974—79 period. Among the recommended new laboratories are an R&D Center to be established at the Indian Petro-Chemicals Corporation, an Institute for Energy Studies, and a Laboratory for Solar Energy. The plan recognizes the need for close coupling of R&D to industry and makes a number of recommendations designed to foster this.

The wide coverage of fields in science and technology and the many explicit

---

[4] Hannan Ezekiel, Chapter IX.

[5] Government of India, Department of Science and Technology, National Committee on Science and Technology, *Science and Technology Plan 1974—79*.

analyses and recommendations make the draft plan a thoroughly useful document. One gathers informally that it has had considerable influence on the Planning Commission's recent annual plans. The comments that follow should not, therefore, be viewed simply as criticisms of the S&T plan, but rather as observations on what seem to be missing elements which, if addressed, will make a later plan still more useful.

As an example of the kinds of problems addressed, the plan identifies as an area of national priority the need for a national information grid for scientific, technological, economic, and social information and recommends the establishment of a National Information System for Science and Technology that would report to the Department of Science and Technology. It recommends considerable expansion in R&D for several areas of modern technology, including electronics, and makes specific suggestions about the desirability of a number of new research laboratories for these fields.

The chief emphasis of the plan is on programs that are to be supported and performed by the central government. While it recognizes the significance of R&D by the private sector and assumes this effort should increase, it gives no explicit attention to the expected contributions from this sector in discussing R&D needs in the various fields. Thus the plan's recommendations for R&D in the important chemical industry deal only with programs to be carried out in the public sector, ignoring the fact that current R&D expenditures of the private portion of the chemical industry are substantially larger than those of the public sector. Therefore recognition of and encouragement for the private sector R&D probably ought to be a central element in a plan for this industry.

A good feature of the S&T plan is what it calls its "utilization-oriented approach." Very strong emphasis is on S&T for development of India. Given this emphasis, it is somewhat surprising that the plan gives almost no explicit attention to what one might call the "big picture," that is, where India is going, what its major social and economic problems are, what the overall state is of programs for generating and applying S&T and what kind of integration of S&T with other efforts will be needed to best address the problems of development. There is, for example, virtually no discussion of the major problem of expanded agricultural production. No assessment is given of India's projected energy needs and ways to meet them. There is no analysis of the state of India's educational system for scientists and engineers or of the need for new educational programs to supply the experts that the coming decades will demand. Finally, there is almost no discussion of the complex systems interaction that must come into play if R&D is to lead to successful technological innovation. If S&T is itself viewed as a system with inputs of men, money, and materials, and with outputs of knowledge, development, and innovation, then the question of the best linkages of this system to other elements of the national effort becomes central to reaching decisions on the level and character of the S&T system itself.[6]

It is probably asking too much to expect the first formal plan for S&T, which had as its principal goals to examine current and projected R&D programs and to make specific recommendations for 1974–79, also to look at these broad system and interaction problems. Perhaps the most reasonable expectation is that this sort of overall analysis might well be an early and high-priority objective for the Department of Science and Technology as an essential preliminary to its development of the second five-year plan for science and technology.

India's Scientific and Technical Manpower

The single most impressive statement about India's scientific and technical manpower is that India contains the world's third largest number of trained scientists and engineers, exceeded only by the USSR and the United States. Table 8.1 gives a breakdown of scientific and technical personnel into four broad categories of science, engineering, agriculture, and medicine, and shows the growth rate since 1950.[7,8] Over the twenty-one-year period of this table the average rate of growth was 9 percent annually. Even though this growth rate has not been maintained, there are now approximately 1.5 million Indians with graduate or postgraduate degrees in these four categories of science and technology, an impressive accomplishment by the universities of a new nation.

When India attained its independence, it already had a significant group of universities. As with the British universities of the time, strong emphasis was on what would now be called "arts and sciences," to the comparative neglect of the applied sciences and engineering. Since independence, the Indian university system has developed greatly both in numbers and in breadth of coverage. In

---

[6] A possible explanation for the near absence of discussion in the Plan on basic policy and strategy issues for science and technology is that these were the subjects of a preliminary document, "An Approach to the Science and Technology Plan," which the National Committee on Science Technology issued in early 1973. The analyses in this approach of such central issues as technology innovation, imbalances in R&D programs, and the linkage of policies for S&T to national plans are admirably cogent and hard-hitting. The difficulty is that a reader of the Plan cannot know whether these analyses and their implicit recommendations have been formally accepted and hence constitute an essential underpinning to the Plan itself.

[7] Government of India, Department of Science and Technology, National Committee on Science and Technology, *Research and Development Statistics, 1973–74.*

[8] Government of India, Department of Science and Technology, National Committee on Science and Technology, *Research and Development Statistics, 1974–75.*

Table 8.1   Growth in India's Scientific and Technical Personnel

(in thousands)

	1950	1960	1971
Engineering and Technology			
Degree	21.6	62.2	185.4
Diploma	31.5	75.0	244.4
Science			
Postgraduate	16.0	47.7	139.2
Graduate	60.0	165.6	420.0
Agriculture			
Postgraduate	1.0	3.7	13.5
Graduate	6.9	20.2	47.2
Medicine			
Degree	18.0	41.6	97.8
Licentiate	33.0	34.0	27.0
Total	188.0	450.0	1,174.5

Source: Government of India, Department of Science and Technology, National Committee on Science and Technology, *Research and Development Statistics, 1974–75*.

1953–54, there were 30 universities with a total enrollment of 238,000 students. In 1974–75, there were 111 institutions that were "deemed to be universities" with a total enrollment of 2.37 million.[9] This latter number was split between 0.35 million in the universities proper and 2.02 million in affiliated colleges.[10] Roughly 10 percent of the students are studying at the postgraduate level. Teaching staff in these institutions in 1974–75 was 27,839 in the universities and

[9] University Grants Commission, *Annual Report for 1974–75*.

[10] These are quasi-independent units with their own faculties and separate, often distant, facilities. Curricula and examinations are, however, set by the mother university.

133,950 in the affiliated colleges.[11] Even though the growth in the number of students in science has slowed down considerably in recent years, enrollment in the basic and applied sciences in 1974–75 was approximately 30 percent of the total, divided as follows: science, 19.6 percent; engineering/technology, 3.8 percent; medicine, 4.5 percent; agriculture and veterinary science, 1.5 percent. Serious efforts are underway to increase the availability of advanced education in the applied sciences and engineering. One-third of the twenty-four new universities that were established in the years 1970 through 1975 are in the applied sciences, principally agriculture.[12]

Most analysts of the current status of Indian universities argue that the level of support is seriously deficient in providing the desired quality of education. There is great variability in level of support. The central universities are generally best off, but even these lack many elements considered essential in the West. Among the inadequacies most commonly pointed to are: inadequate laboratory and library facilities; inadequate equipment; a shortage of foreign books and journals; inadequate funds for research. The majority of these complaints apply particularly to the requirements for teaching the basic and applied sciences.

The central University Grants Commission (UGC), which constitutes the principal support for research and special programs in universities, is expanding its support, but in total this support still remains small: only Rs 59 million, or $7 million, in 1973–74.[13] This is only about $60,000 per institution. To enhance university capabilities in graduate training and research, the UGC initiated in 1963 a program of Centers of Advanced Study and in 1972 a related program of Special Assistance to Select Departments. As a further step, UGC proposes during the Fifth Five Year Plan to develop six regional instrumentation centers at universities, which will make available sophisticated instruments and library services to the regions they serve. This plan is yet to go into effect. Although the UGC program for university Centers of Advanced Study is clearly desirable, its impact on R&D in science has not been large. As of 1974–75, there were only fourteen centers in science, with only two in physics and two in chemistry.

Demand for graduate engineers appears to be high in India. The situation is quite different for science graduates. A special census of 1961 showed that 40 percent of science graduates were in non-technical employment and 16 percent were unemployed; for postgraduates in science, the figures were 17 percent in

---

[11] Government of India, University Grants Commission, *Annual Report for 1974–75.*

[12] Ibid.

[13] Ibid.

non-technical employment and 7 percent unemployed.[14] The current situation is not greatly different. Perhaps not surprisingly in view of the extent of under-employment, salaries for scientists remain low, both relatively and absolutely. Data for 1970 indicate that salaries for Central Government Administration Services staff are roughly twice as high as those for Ph.D. scientists.[15] Table 8.2 shows the spread of salaries in early 1973.[16] Salary levels remain low in the major government agencies, which employ over three-fourths of scientists and engineers in R&D; salaries, particularly in the upper levels, are higher for scientific and technical personnel in the smaller private sector. Growth rates of numbers of university students in science were high through the 1960s but have recently dropped sharply. Some part of the explanation must be these discouraging employment and salary statistics.

In considering the application of science and technology to industry and to development generally, there are two other categories of trained people that are important: skilled technicians and trained technology managers. India has not gone far in explicit training programs for technicians in scientific and technical fields. The relatively substantial R&D programs under governmental auspices constitute a training area for such technicians, but there is concern about the inadequate number of such skilled technicians as instrument operators and repairmen.

Formal training in management, by contrast, has received considerable emphasis recently. There are three Indian Institutes of Management (at Calcutta, Ahmedabad, and Bangalore), all with new or recently expanded postgraduate programs. Postgraduate courses in business administration also are expanding and new degree courses in management have been approved for two universities.

Large numbers of Indian students, particularly in science and engineering, go abroad to complete their training. The exact number of such students is uncertain, since so many Indian students independently develop support for study abroad. One estimate is that there are currently more than 10,000 Indian students study-ing in the United States alone. The total number of students abroad is perhaps double this number, which would imply that 4,000 to 5,000 will complete their training each year. Roughly half of these return promptly to India and constitute,

[14] K. Ray, "Policy on Scientific and Technical Manpower," in *Science Policy Studies*, ed. A. Rahman and K. D. Sharma (Bombay: Sumaiya Publications, Ltd., 1974).

[15] A. Rahman *et al.*, *Science and Technology in India* (Delhi: Indian Council for Cultural Affairs, 1973), pp. 158–59.

[16] Government of India, Department of Science and Technology, National Committee on Science and Technology, *Research Statistics, 1973–74*, Table 11.

Table 8.2   Salary Structure of Scientific and Technical Personnel
in Research and Development Establishments, 1973

(Salaries in rupees per month)

	In Major Government R&D Agencies a/			In Private Sector		
Pay Categories	Number	Percent	Salary Range	Number	Percent
Below 425–700	27987	63	Up to 400	404	19
425–700	2725	6	400–599	496	24
550–900	4157	9	600–799	344	16
650–1200 & 700–1300	6044	14	800–999	225	12
			1000–1499	310	15
1100–1600	2733	6	1500–1999	127	6
1500–1800 & 2000 & up	1080	2	2000–2999	113	5
			3000 & above	59	3

Source: Government of India, Department of Science and Technology, National Committee
on Science and Technology, *Research and Development Statistics, 1974–75.*

a / The agencies are: DAE, DRDO, CSIR, ICAR, ICMR and ISRO (See Table 8.4).

therefore, a major source of scientists and engineers with modern training. These
foreign-trained scientists and engineers do well in India, commanding considerably
higher than average salaries [17] and experiencing higher than average employment
rates, factors that undoubtedly impel students to go abroad in the first place.

There is frequent concern about the "brain drain" implications of those
students who remain abroad after finishing their training. The cost to the nation
of this loss of trained manpower is surely large. However, given the high
unemployment that characterizes scientists in India and the strong ties between
emigrant Indians and their homeland, an optimistic view of these scientists abroad
is to think of them as a ready reserve available to India when the level of activity

[17] Rahman *et al., Science and Technology.*

in science and technology leads to higher demand (and higher salaries) for scientists and engineers.

Thus, numbers of scientists available to India seem ample for current and foreseeable needs. There are relatively shorter supplies of trained managers and engineers, but the university system is responding by expanded programs in these areas. As technical needs change, shortages may arise in particular fields, such as electronics engineering or solid-state chemistry, but with adequate support from the government the universities should be able to respond.

The quality of training of scientists and engineers, however, leaves room for serious concern. The inadequacies of Indian colleges and universities in such basic training elements as textbooks, libraries, laboratory equipment, and modern instruments cannot help but affect the quality of training students receive. These inadequacies are particularly serious for postgraduate training in the most advanced areas of science and engineering. Who will train the modern polymer chemists, the solid state physicists, and the advanced electronics engineers that India already needs and will need increasingly in the future? A partial but surely unsatisfactory answer is that many of these scientists and engineers are being trained by universities in the West. Given the problems of a brain drain, of inappropriate training, and of difficulties in integration, it would seem far wiser to increase greatly the capabilities of Indian universities to train students at the cutting edges of science and engineering. This would imply a greatly enlarged program of Centers of Advanced Study and a considerably expanded program of assistance to highly qualified graduate students and to university research programs that are coupled to graduate training. These programs would be costly, but probably less so than the loss of foreign exchange from supporting students abroad.

Research and Development:
The Indian Effort in Its Size and Nature

Support and Performance

India has greatly expanded its programs of scientific and technological research and development (R&D) during the past two decades. In 1958–59 the total public and private sector expenditure on R&D was Rs 229 million. An additional Rs 59 million was spent on "related S&T activities" for a total of Rs 288 million. By 1974–75 these expenditures had increased to Rs 2,859 million and Rs 585 million, respectively, for a grand total of Rs 3,444 million, or roughly $400 million.[18] Throughout this period, the largest share of support for R&D has come

---

[18] Government of India, Department of Science and Technology, National Committee on Science and Technology, *Research Statistics, 1974–75*, pp. 53–54.

from the central government of India. In 1958—59 the expenditures for R&D and related S&T activities came almost 97 percent from the government of India, with the remaining 3 percent coming from the separate states. In 1974—75 about 80 percent of the expenditure came from the government of India, 10 percent from the state governments, and 10 percent from the private sector.

Tables 8.3 and 8.4 summarize the expenditures by agencies of the government of India for R&D.[19] Table 8.3 gives data by major sector. Table 8.4 lists expenditures by six major scientific agencies and expenditures by ministries and departments. Research funding for these ministries and departments has risen even more sharply than for the major scientific agencies, and as of 1974—75 they accounted for roughly 20 percent of the total R&D expenditures by the central sector.

The utilization of R&D funds allotted to the agencies and ministries occurs almost entirely within the R&D facilities under their direct jurisdiction.[20] This amost complete congruence between provision of support for research and performance thereof contrasts sharply with the situation in most developed Western countries, where a very large fraction of research is performed by the private sector. Comparison of the situation in India with that in the United States and Japan is illuminating. In the United States, nongovernmental funds support about 45 percent of the R&D expenditures, with most of the rest coming from the federal government.[21] In the performance of R&D, however, the private sector in the United States is dominant, spending almost 70 percent of the total R&D funds. Expenditures for R&D performance by U.S. government agencies were only 18 percent of the total in 1975; R&D expenditures by universities constituted 9 percent of the total. Japan presents an even more striking comparison in that private industry financed 74 percent of Japan's R&D and

[19] Ibid.

[20] Table 4 would seem to imply that an important exception was the universities, given the funding that comes to them from the Ministry of Education, via the University Grants Commission. However, this covers a number of expenditures beyond research. For 1974—75 the Department of Science and Technology (DST) estimated a total research expenditure in the universities and technology institutes of India of Rs 80 million, which is about 3 percent of the total expenditures for R&D.

[21] Government of India, Department of Science and Technology, National Committee on Science and Technology, *Research Statistics, 1973—74;* Government of India, Department of Science and Technology, National Committee on Science and Technology, *Research Statistics, 1974—75;* U.S., National Science Foundation, *National Patterns of Research and Development Resources, 1953—75* (1975), pp. 75—307.

Table 8.3   Expenditure on Research and Development and Related Scientific
and Technological Activities

(Millions of rupees)

	1958—59	1969—70	1974—75
a) Expenditure on R&D			
Central Sector	217.8	915.9	2,209
State Sector	10.0	122.2	293
Private Sector	01.5	128.1	357
Totals	229.3	1,166.2	2,859
b) Expenditure on Related S&T Activities			
Central Sector	58.8	296.7	586
Totals (a) + (b)	288.1	1,462.9	3,445

Source: Government of India, Department of Science and Technology, National Committee
on Science and Technology, *Research and Development Statistics, 1974—75.*

performed 66 percent of it.[22] In contrast to Japan and the United States, about
90 percent of Indian R&D is supported by the government and is performed by
governmental laboratories and institutions. The role of the private sector is minor
as either support or performance.

Indian states spent about 10 percent of R&D funds for 1974—75 and employed
about 12 percent of the total R&D manpower. Agriculture, fisheries, livestock,
and irrigation together accounted for almost three-fourths of the state's R&D
expenditures, with much smaller amounts for public health and for industry. On
the average, state R&D facilities are small and apparently not very well supported.
In 1973—74 there were 135 state R&D establishments with 12,000 employees,
yet the total R&D budgets of the states was only Rs 129 million.[23]

[22] Japan, *Economic Yearbook* (Tokyo: 1976—77), pp. 61—63.

[23] Government of India, Department of Science and Technology, National Committee on
Science and Technology, *Research Statistics, 1973—74,* p. 21.

Table 8.4   Expenditure on Research and Development in the Central Sector

(millions of rupees)

Name of Organization	1958–59	1969–70	1974–75
A. Major Scientific Agencies			
1. Department of Atomic Energy (DAE)	77.6	207.2	307.2
2. Council of Scientific and Industrial Research (CSIR)	51.0	186.8	322.3
3. Defense Research and Development Organization (DRDO)	15.0	145.4	401.6
4. Indian Council of Agricultural Research (ICAR)	37.2	137.7	260.3
5. Indian Council of Medical Research (ICMR)	5.1	15.6	25.2
6. Indian Space Research Organization (ISRO)	. . .	. . .	429.9
7. Other	. . .	. . .	74.4
Total (A)	185.9	692.7	1820.9
B. Ministries/Departments			
1. Commerce	4.6	10.5	5.8
2. Communications	0.9	2.8	26.4
3. Defense	. . .	37.8	81.0
4. Universities	3.4	18.0	79.5
5. Heavy Industry	. . .	. . .	41.8
6. Irrigation & Power	4.2	20.4	24.8
7. Petroleum & Chemicals	0.2	28.3	69.9
8. Railways	4.1	26.6	44.5
9. Steel & Mines	. . .	19.0	27.3
10. Others*	14.7	59.7	50.5
Total (B)	32.1	223.1	451.5
Grand Total (A&B)	218.0	915.8	2272.4

Source: Government of India, Department of Science and Technology, National Committee on Science and Technology, *Research and Development Statistics, 1974–75.*

* Others include Ministries/Departments of: Education—IITs/IIsc, Health & Family Planning, Industrial Development, Information & Broadcasting, Science & Technology, Tourism & Civil Action, Works & Housing, Home Affairs, Shipping & Transport, Statistics and Supply.

Research expenditures by India's public sector industries are included in the tabulated R&D expenditures of the supervisory ministries. In 1974, of the 101 industrial enterprises in the public sector only 42 reported involvement in R&D activities. These 42 listed R&D expenditures as Rs 210 million, which was about 0.5 percent of their sales. R&D expenditures by public sector industries (including defense) constitute only 7 percent of the national total and 8 percent of government expenditures for R&D.

Expenditures for research and development by private sector industry in India in 1974–75 amounted to Rs 360 million, which is 12 percent of the national total. Some 273 private concerns reported having R&D establishments. As a fraction of sales the overall expenditure was 1.09 percent, but there were wide variations, ranging from 4.1 percent of sales for instrument manufacturing to 0.4 percent for the paper industries.[24]

Basic research apparently constitutes about 10 percent of Indian R&D, with expenditures of roughly Rs 300 million in 1974-75. Well over half of this expenditure was made by the major scientific government agencies. Although most research institutes emphasize applied research, a few give strong emphasis to basic research. The Tata Institute for Fundmental Research of Bombay, the Physical Research Laboratory, and the All-India Institute of Medical Sciences have first-class research facilities and enjoy excellent international reputations. Indian universities are large producers of basic research, but the estimated expenditures for university research in 1974–75 were only Rs 80 million (an average of about Rs 0.8 million, or $100,000, per institution).

India's level of expenditures for R&D and related S&T activities ranks tenth or twelfth among the nations of the world. When reckoned as a percentage of GNP, India's figure for 1974–75 of 0.5 percent for R&D gives it a somewhat lower ranking, but still one that places it among the leaders of the less developed nations. By this latter measure India ranks somewhat below Korea and Taiwan but above Nigeria, Pakistan, and most of the nations of Africa and South America. In terms of any of these comparisons, India's national investment in science and technology is a very substantial one.

Shortly, we shall be turning to the role of Indian R&D in technology innovation, but it is appropriate first to comment on India's R&D productivity as

[24] There is a tendency to suggest that most industrial R&D in India is primarily for quality control and technical service and to play down its significance to new developments. There is, however, evidence that some of this research is of top quality judged by international standards. The research director of a large multinational chemical concern, which has a joint venture in India employing roughly 60 R&D people and with sales of roughly $10 million, had this to say about the work "as absolutely equivalent to the one performed in our European laboratories. Otherwise, we could hardly have displaced important basic research over to there."

measured by output of new scientific and technical knowledge. A conventional way to make this measurement is to count numbers of scientific and technical publications. Some very recent studies of this sort have been made of the world scientific literature by counting publications for 1973 as listed in *Science Citation Index* of the U.S.-based Institute for Scientific Information. This index covers 2,300 journals and generally is considered to be the best available world analysis of mainstream science. For a number of reasons, the analysis is probably biased somewhat against developing nations like India. Even so, India ranks very high in the international production of scientific literature. It is eighth in the ranking of national production and is the only less developed country (LDC) that appears in the top ten. The next most productive LDC accounts for only about one-tenth as many publications as India.

An analysis of the national factors that correlate with output of research publications gives further evidence of India's special productivity. Study of the linkage of productivity with national income shows that scientific publication correlates reasonably well with total GNP of nations and also with per capita GNP. India ranks well above the correlation lines for these measures, whether they are combined or taken separately. In the words of the analyst, "The [correlation] equation predicts that a country with India's GNP and GNP per capita should produce 811 scientific publications in 1973. In point of fact, India produced 6,880 scientific publications." [25]

An earlier analysis by V. B. Rangarao considers specifically the numbers of scientific publications in India. [26] This analysis is based on Indian *Science Abstracts* and hence gives much more emphasis to local publications. Rangarao lists 9,804 publications for 1965, an impressive number which he nevertheless characterizes as "low" relative to the numbers of scientists engaged in R&D. About 40 percent of these research publications originated in universities, which is remarkable in view of the relatively small support that university R&D programs have received. [27]

[25] J. D. Frame, F. Narin, and N. P. Carpenter, "The Distribution of World Science," *Social Studies of Science*, Fall 1977.

[26] B.V. Rangarao, "Scientific Research in India," *Journal of Scientific and Industrial Research* 26 (1967), 4: 166; reprinted in *Science Policy Studies*, ed. Rahman and Sharma, (Bombay: Somaiya Publications, Ltd., 1974).

[27] The discussions of this section have focused on the broad development of science and technology in India, but, in fact, a few individuals have played a large role in directing these efforts along the paths that have been followed by others. The roles of two scientists of great influence in establishing the immediate post-independence trends of Indian science and technology, Homi Bhabha and Megnad Saha, have been treated in a recent book (R.S. Anderson,

India's Major Scientific Agencies

The six major scientific agencies of Table 8.4 have a dominant role in Indian R&D activity: in 1974—75 they accounted for almost two-thirds of the nation's R&D expenditures and for roughly 80 percent of those by the central sector.

The major thrust of the six agencies is toward comparatively high technology. Three high-technology agencies—Atomic Energy, Space, and Defense—account for well over half of the total expenditures of the central sector.[28] For a nation whose first industry is agriculture and whose exports are principally agricultural, R&D expenditures for agriculture are disproportionately small. Expenditures for medical research are almost an order of magnitude smaller still.

The six major agencies differ significantly in their approaches to R&D programs. Their major characteristics are summarized below:

1. Department of Atomic Energy (DAE) spent Rs 307 million on R&D in 1974—75, roughly 15 percent of the total expenditures by the central sector of government. It vies with the Indian Space Research Organization (ISRO) as the most integrated of the R&D agencies in India. A principal effort of DAE has been in the development of nuclear power for India. DAE devotes major funds to its R&D laboratories but it also sponsors industrial undertakings on uranium and other components of atomic power. A second major activity of DAE has been its work on nuclear explosives, which culminated in an underground nuclear explosion in the Rajasthan desert in 1974. Finally, DAE has responsibility for studies on applications of nuclear knowledge to other research fields, and is the nation's supplier of radioactive isotopes for research.

2. The Council of Scientific and Industrial Research (CSIR), which in 1974—75 accounted for 15 percent of R&D expenditures by the central sector, is the major civilian and industrial research organization of India. It was started before Indian independence, but its major expansion was in the fifties and sixties. Currently CSIR has responsibility for forty-four different laboratories and institutes with a wide variety of fields and char-

---

Building Scientific Institutions in India, Saha and Bhabha, [Montreal: McGill University Press, 1975]. Bhabha was primarily responsible for establishing the Tata Institute of Fundamental Research in Bombay, which rapidly became and has remained a scientific research establishment of the highest stature. He also played a central role in the establishment and growth of India's Atomic Energy Commission and the Department of Atomic Energy. Saha was less influential at the level of national policy but was of great significance in the development of Indian science.

[28] Government of India, Department of Science and Technology, National Committee on Science and Technology, *Research Statistics, 1974—75,* pp. 53—54.

acteristics. Following Morehouse,[29] the institutions under CSIR jurisdiction can be divided into six categories: (a) discipline-oriented laboratories like the National Chemical Laboratory; (b) commodity laboratories like the Central Leather Research Institute; (c) multipurpose laboratories; (d) museums; (e) information and documentation centers; and (f) cooperative research associations like the Textile Industry Research Association.

3. The Defense Research and Development Organization (DRDO) had been one of the faster growing of the major scientific agencies of India and is now one of the largest. By 1976 it had jurisdiction over thirty-two R&D establishments covering such fields as armaments, electronics, rockets and missiles, and radar technology. In contrast to the Department of Atomic Energy, DRDO appears not to be deeply involved in the production phases of military systems. These appear to be principally handled by the Department of Defense, which itself has a sizable R&D budget (see Table 12.4). For 1974–75 the sum of R&D expenditures by DRDO and the Defense Department was Rs 483 million and constituted about 17 percent of total public and private Indian expenditure on R&D.

4. The Indian Council on Agricultural Research (ICAR), in the words of the 1976 *Reference Annual* on India, "is the apex body to plan, undertake, promote, and coordinate agriculture and animal husbandry plans including research, education and field application."[30] The ICAR program is complex, involving a network of research laboratories, support for agricultural universities, and a series of coordination projects. Funding for ICAR was Rs 260 million in 1974–75.

5. The Indian Council of Medical Research (ICMR) is largely responsible for medical research in India. It has eight permanent research institutes which focus on specific medical problems, such as the Cholera Research Center, and works closely with two other institutions with broad research assignments: the All-India Institute of Medical Sciences and the Postgraduate Institute of Medical Education and Research. Given the large responsibility assigned to ICMR, its current budget, Rs 25 million in 1974–75, is surprisingly modest.

6. The Indian Space Research Organization (ISRO) is a 1971 spin-off of the Department of Atomic Energy and, like DAE, is characterized by considerable vertical integration. There are large R&D programs on space tech-

[29] Ward Morehouse, *Science in India* (Bombay: Popular Prakashan, 1971).

[30] Government of India, Ministry of Information and Broadcasting, Publications Division, *India, 1976: A Reference Annual.*

nology and substantial programs of management and manufacture. Included, for example, are a rocket propellant plant and a rocket fabrication
facility. The R&D budget for ISRO has grown rapidly, and for 1974–75
was Rs 430 million, which made it the largest of the scientific agencies.

The Linkage to National Development

A large fraction of India's R&D is oriented toward development. A perennial
world-wide question, and one which concerns India, is how to link R&D programs
in science and technology most effectively to the development process itself;
that is, to the desired improvements in health, standard of living, and quality of
life that the term development implies. Speaking broadly, the problem is to link
the products of the R&D establishments with the agencies, industries, and entrepreneurs directly involved in the processes of development.

Implicit in the earlier descriptions of Indian R&D agencies are four rather
different models for the linkage of R&D to development: (a) the "private enterprise model," which uses the spur of profits and internal company growth, (along
with other incentives if necessary) to encourage private industries to develop their
own R&D programs; (b) the "vertically integrated government department," for
example, the Indian Department of Atomic Energy, where all the activities between R&D and production are integrated with the same Ministry or Department;
(c) the "agricultural model," which combines government-operated R&D establishments and governmental information and extension services to carry the
information to the small enterprise (the farmer); (d) the "independent government R&D establishment," such as the many laboratories of CSIR. For each of
these models there are problems in coupling R&D programs to broad goals of
national development. Coupling between the R&D generator and user is probably
closest for a single industry that has its own R&D program, and this close coupling
has been a particular virtue of the private enterprise model to the Western world.
For a profit-oriented industry, the principal objective is not simply successful
R&D, but commercially successful technology innovation, which implies bringing
products or processes into actual, productive, market-oriented use. Western
analyses suggest that no more than half of the costs and time of technology innovation relate to R&D itself; the remainder is costs of engineering design, manufacturing design, and marketing development. It is obviously necessary that the
industrial enterprise be involved in these latter activities, and this in turn has led
to the conviction that technology innovation thrives when there is a close interactive effort between the R&D group and the production elements of the enterprise.

A strength of the "private enterprise model" is that the close coupling of R&D
with production and sales units makes it particularly effective in technology

innovation. From the standpoint of a national planner, the weakness of this model is that the innovations on which private enterprise works may not be those that command top priority for national development.

The "integrated government department model" offers an interesting way of coupling R&D to public sector industry. The existence of R&D and production groups within a single department fosters good communications, although in practice there may be frequent difficulties. Also, one can expect the goals of the department to be consonant with those of the national development plan. A weakness of this model is that the discipline of the marketplace is not available to guide the industry. This is perhaps least consequential with the so-called basic industries, for example, iron and steel. It is most serious in the production of consumer goods where the marketplace is an essential corrective. A second weakness is that interactive linkages of the R&D groups with the industrial production groups may be difficult to establish, especially if the groups are geographically separate and report to different divisions of the department.

The "agricultural model" of government-operated R&D establishments, with governmental information services to take the information to the farmers, represents an obvious response to the small size of the individual industries (the farms) and the need to take account of regional differences in climate and resources. The chief difficulties with the model are that (a) the R&D establishment may have poor coupling to the ultimate R&D users and hence may not be adequately responsive; and (b) this kind of R&D establishment is not well suited to developing the technology for modern industrial products which are increasingly utilized in agriculture: for example, fertilizers, pesticides, and agricultural machinery.

With the fourth model, the "independent government R&D establishment," it is relatively easy (at least in principle) to insure that R&D programs of laboratories are consistent with national development priorities. Establishing central laboratories is a rational response to two frequent characteristics of developing nations: (a) many industrial firms are so small that they find it difficult to operate their own research laboratories; (b) there are efficiencies to be gained in the use of expensive equipment, libraries, etc., by developing fewer but larger central laboratories. The weakness of this model is that coupling between R&D establishments and users may be particularly poor. A related model, which shares many of these characteristics but which may give better coupling between R&D and industry, is the cooperative industrial research association.

In the framework of these models, India has strongly opted for government-operated laboratories and integrated government departments. India has assigned a relatively minor role to the universities. For agriculture in India, the R&D system follows closely the model that characterizes most nations: government-operated laboratories and extension services are used to disseminate information, but there is considerable reliance on industry for R&D on fertilizers and pesticides. For the generation and coupling of R&D to industry, India utilizes all three of the other models, but gives principal stress to government-operated laboratories and integrated government departments. Most of the R&D done by the quasi-independent laboratories of CSIR is oriented toward civilian industry. This is also true of the R&D done by DAE, where integration between R&D and the industrial development of nuclear energy is close. Some fraction of the research done under the rubrics *Defense* and *Space* is probably directly applicable to civilian industry. However, the majority of the effort within DRDO and substantial fractions of that in DAE and ISRO is oriented toward defense.

The amount of research done directly by industry is small. The approximate figures for 1974–75 are Rs 210 million by public sector industries; Rs 360 million by industries in the private sector; approximately Rs 20 million by the states. The total is about 20 percent of national R&D expenditures for the year. Even this modest percentage may somewhat overstate industry's share, since it would appear that significant amounts of the R&D expenditures of both public and private sector industries might in other countries be labeled technical service or quality control, that is, they are probably oriented more toward current production and marketing than toward developing new or improved products and processes.

To summarize, India has developed a substantial R&D establishment, chiefly funded by the central government, with responsibility to work on all of the important areas of Indian industry and technological needs. Major emphasis goes to support of R&D in defense, space, and atomic energy. Measured by the objective international yardstick of numbers of research publications, the Indian R&D system is vigorous and productive. Research in universities is relatively poorly funded, to a degree that might reasonably lead Indian planners to worry about the quality of advanced technical training that will be available in India. The Indian R&D efforts are chiefly carried out in government-funded, government-operated laboratories; R&D programs within Indian industry are relatively small, particularly so for the public sector industries. The concern about this national structure for R&D is whether it adequately feeds into industry the needed R&D for rapidly improving the level of civilian technological activity and for reducing dependence on imported technology.

Technology Innovation in India

The term *technology innovation* encompasses the set of activities that brings a potential new element of technology from conceptualization into actual use. Technology innovation is a multistage process that typically starts with R&D. This is followed by a set of steps, often labeled commercialization, that include: engineering design and development, manufacturing development, and market development. One can also appropriately speak of innovation when a firm licenses and brings into use a new technology, whatever the source. Thus, a steel company is innovating when it licenses and installs the Austrian-developed oxygen process for steel making; a farmer is innovating when he puts into practice the miracle rice package of new seeds and new procedures.

Analysts in developing nations (LDCs) often discuss the progress of their industries toward self-reliance by comparing the level of innovation stemming from imported technology (usually considered bad) with the amount of technology innovation that arises from indigenous research and development (considered good). This kind of analysis misses some of the important points. Technology innovation does not begin or end with the acquisition of technology. Preceding or accompanying the acquisition of new technology is a basic decision to strive for innovation. If the technology is to be imported, there are questions of its appropriateness, the terms of license or royalty, and most important of all, the degree of adaptation needed for it to conform to the factor endowments of the country that has imported it. Following acquisition come the stages of adaptation, engineering, manufacturing design, and market development.

To the enterprise or agency that decides to follow this path, technology innovation is a risky business, and the attractions of imported technology are manifold. First, the technology is usually proven in the sense that it has been carried through engineering and manufacturing design stages to the point where the particular steps of processing, packaging and marketing are all well understood. Second, the product of the new technology will itself often be proven; that is, a good deal will be known about its market acceptance, even if this is for a different market. Third, the costs (even if high) will be definite. All these items help decrease the uncertainties that the industry faces. It is thus not surprising that an LDC enterprise wishing to minimize risk in innovation will give first thought to imported technology.

However, there are usually also important disadvantages to imported technology. Licenses can be costly and may carry various restrictions. The scale of the technology may be larger than desired by an LDC. The amount of adaptation required to fit the technology to a labor-surplus and capital-short economy may be very substantial. The illuminating phrase "technology assimilation" has been used by Ranis[31] to characterize the modifications and adjustments that may be needed. However, statistics show that there is extensive technology importation by all nations, developed and less developed. It also appears that most tech-

---

[31] Gustav Ranis, "Industrial Technology Choice and Employment: A Review of Developing Country Evidence," *Interciencia* 2 (1977), 1:11.

nologies can be successfully assimilated even by nations whose factor endowments differ considerably from those of the country that originated the technology. The small industries of developing nations turn out to be particularly successful in assimilating technologies stretching capital and increasing the use of labor.[32]

Governments of developing nations generally play an explicit role in programs of technology innovation and particularly of technology importation. Social pressures often spur national leaders to accelerate the pace of industrial development and, since local capabilities are often inadequate, this quickly leads to importation of developed technology. To counter and control this, governments are commonly led into support programs for indigenous R&D, training programs for scientific and technical manpower, licensing programs for technology importation, and, occasionally, incentive programs for encouraging R&D by private industry.

India has given considerable attention to all of these kinds of support programs. The next paragraphs consider the various paths to technology innovation and the character of support given to each of them by Indian industry and government.[33]

Technology Importation and Adaptation

Importation has been overwhelmingly the most important source of new technology for India.[34] The benefits to the nation from technology importation are evident. Numerous major undertakings are based on technology which initially was imported. For example, the heavy machinery industry has become a major one for India. The technologies involved have almost all been imported from Europe, particularly from Germany and England. The resulting industry has grown rapidly and now contributes substantially to exports as well as to machinery needed for internal development and national defense.

While granting these accomplishments, many Indian analysts stress the costs of technology importation, including specific costs of foreign exchange and general

---

[32] Ibid.

[33] Two recent book length analyses, which focus on Indian programs for application of technology, are those of Rahman and Behari. The first, A. Rahman, *Science, Technology and Economic Development* (Delhi: National Publishing House, 1974), considers several aspects of Indian science policy including problems of industrial growth. It includes specific analyses of two industries, pharmaceuticals and iron and steel. The second, B. Behari, *Economic Growth and Technological Change in India* (Delhi: Vikas Publications, 1974), treats technological change and economic development more broadly, giving consideration to both agriculture and industry.

[34] Rahman, *Science Technology and Economic Development*, p. 117.

costs from undue technology dependence. A recent analysis by Ray admits to the general need for international collaborations that lead to imported technology and know-how, but argues strongly against what he calls "indiscriminate foreign collaborations," which in his words "undermine a country's basic economy through unnecessary drain of foreign exchange, competition with indigenous undertakings, diversion of work parties outside the country, and demoralizing the local entrepreneurs and expertise."[35] Ray's concern is that the Indian enterprises involved are not adequately addressing the needs for technology adaptation and for development of indigenous R&D capabilities.

In keeping with concerns of this sort, the Indian government has long exercised tight controls over technology importation. It has greatly restricted the entrance of multinational corporations into the country, requiring among other things that all new foreign investments in Indian industry be by way of joint enterprises, with Indian majority interests the norm. Specific imports of foreign knowledge and equipment are controlled by a rigorous licensing procedure, with parallel controls on other aspects of the industrial system.[36]

Since industries in both the public and private sectors import technology, it is clear that the problem is a pervasive one. It is difficult to decide whether too much or too little technology has been imported and whether, in Ray's words, the importation has been too indiscriminate. A recent analysis of India's industrialization had this to say:

> It is impossible to judge whether India imported too much technology and of the wrong kind. . . . Indian industry, unlike Japanese, is not distinguished by its expenditure on R&D (research and development) and the record of repeated purchases of technology from abroad in a number of industries has been disappointing. It is difficult to see, however, what governmental policy could have achieved in this respect, by regulation. In some degree, the failure to innovate and imitate in technology is itself a symptom of the inefficient, totally sheltered-markets approach to industrial development in the country since the Second Plan. . . .[37]

Most enterprises that import technology apply to it substantial adaptation efforts, often to adjust the new technology to local factor endowments, sometimes to improve the efficiency or product quality resulting from the imported technology. One would expect local industrial R&D laboratories to play a large

[35] K. Ray, "Foreign Collaboration," in *Science Policy Studies*, ed. A. Rahman and K. D. Sharma (Bombay: Somaiya Publications, 1974), p. 389.

[36] Behari, *Economic Growth*, p. 31.

[37] Jagdish N. Bhagwati and Padma Desai, *India, Planning for Industrialization* (London: Oxford University Press, 1970), p. 226.

role in adapting technologies that their industrial facility acquires. From this viewpoint, the comparatively low level of industrial R&D in India is a matter of concern. Nevertheless, Indian industry has effectively adapted, or in a broader sense assimilated, much imported technology. The question of the proper role for government-financed R&D laboratories in technology adaptation will be discussed later, but it is noteworthy that senior CSIR officials have urged more effort by CSIR laboratories toward this problem of technology adaptation.

Many countries, notably several in Europe, have assigned a large role to industrial research associations for developing new or modified technology and especially for diffusing new developments in technology (and in such related matters as industrial standards, quality control, and industrial pollution) to the separate units of the industry. One might expect the use of industrial research associations to be large in developing nations, since the production units of many of the industries involved will be so small that they are unable to support individual R&D programs and might, therefore, prefer to rely on the coordinated R&D program of an industrial association.

India has a group of some fifteen industrial research associations, eleven with support from CSIR. However, even though they may have useful roles in coordination, information exchange, and maintainence of standards, the role of these associations in technology innovation and adaptation cannot be large. Their R&D expenditures are quite small, averaging in 1974-75 only about $300,000 per year for the nine associations for which data were available.[38] In the main, the existing associations are for industries that are characterized by mature technologies with small prospects for major innovation, such as the textile and cement industries.

It is entirely possible that an expanded role for industrial research associations would be very beneficial to India. There are numerous industrial areas where the efforts of a lively research association could lead to greatly improved research programs and could especially enhance programs of horizontal, that is, internal, transfer of technology. Indeed, this kind of collaboration could be particularly useful for a country as large and diverse as India where barriers to diffusion of knowledge may be particularly large.

Innovation From Indigenous Research and Development

An increased output of indigenous R&D that can be applied to technology innovation is essential if India is to reduce its dependence on foreign technology

---

[38] Government of India, Department of Science and Technology, National Committee on Science and Technology, *Research Statistics, 1974-75*, p. 55.

and yet continue to expand its agricultural and industrial development. There are two rather different local sources of the required innovations: R&D from industry and R&D from the laboratories of various government agencies.

Currently, Indian industry is characterized by heavy dependence on imported technology and a comparatively small in-house R&D effort ($70 million in 1974-75 for private and public sectors combined, or only 0.06 percent of sales). Actually, the overall role of industry in technology innovation is almost surely larger than this implies, since much technology adaptation necessarily occurs in industrial plants, yet frequently is not labeled R&D. In its 1974—75 report on R&D the Department of Science and Technology argues strongly on the need for more in-house R&D by industry and notes several measures that the government of India has taken to encourage R&D by private sector industries: provision for write-off income tax calculation on all capital and operating expenditures for R&D; an income tax deduction of 133 1/3 percent of expenditures for government-approved and sponsored research; liberalized policies for importing equipment and materials.[39]

R&D in the private industrial sector has in fact been growing rapidly, from Rs 160 million in 1970—71 to Rs 360 million in 1974—75.[40] Even so, one wonders whether still more vigorous measures for expanding private sector R&D might not be desirable; for example, a tax on industrial sales which would be remitted to enterprises with approved R&D programs, in the manner now employed by Peru.[41] The desirability of such a tax for India is briefly presented

[39] Ibid., p. 27.

[40] Ibid., Table 6.1, p. 64. These and similar figures must be viewed with some caution. Information on the R&D expenditures by industry have been seriously sought after only recently and there is a good possibility that some of the recent reported increases are due, in part, to better data collection.

[41] The Peruvian plan for support is an expanded program of industrial R&D by use of taxes on industry called the ITINTEC system where the acronym stands for what in English would be "Industrial Technology Institute." ITINTEC operates within the Peruvian Ministry of Industry and there are similar groups operating in the Ministries for Mining and Telecommunications. The broad charter for ITINTEC is to enhance and improve the industrial R&D activities in Peru, using funds that become available by a 2 percent tax on the net income of the enterprises of the industrial sector (with similar taxes on enterprises of the other sectors). ITINTEC encourages the industries that have been taxed to submit research plans of their own with the expectation that the collected tax monies from them will be remitted if their R&D programs are approved by ITINTEC. By this device, most of the expanded R&D effort will be done by the industries themselves. If an industry chooses not to submit an R&D program, ITINTEC will utilize the funds from the taxes to accomplish the R&D itself or to contract for R&D that it believes relates to the needs of the industry. (See F. R. Sagasti, "The ITINTEC System for Industrial Technology Policy in Peru," *World Development* 3 (1975): 867.

in "An Approach to the Science and Technology Plan," of 1973 and is alluded to in the Plan itself but seems not to have been further explored.[42]

What is truly surprising is the comparatively low level of R&D by India's public sector industries, where one might expect the pressures for further development of indigenous technology to lead planners and budget makers to support a particularly rapid acceleration of R&D activity. There has been recent growth in R&D by this sector, but the total remains small: Rs 210 million in 1974–75, of which almost 40 percent was for the defense industries. For the 42 public sector industries (out of 101 total) that reported having R&D programs in 1974–75, R&D as a percentage of sales was only 0.5 percent. If R&D for the defense industries is excluded, expenditures for the remaining 36 public sector industries that report doing research are only 0.3 percent of sales.[43] And most public sector industries report no R&D at all.

Given the large and continuing emphasis on expansion of public sector industry in India, the development of adequate in-house R&D programs focused on enhanced technology innovation for these industries should probably be a major national objective. A conceivable alternative strategy for public sector industries is to have the large scientific agencies, notably the CSIR, generate R&D. This, however, raises the difficult problem of adequate coupling mechanisms between R&D laboratories and industrial innovators.

CSIR is the government R&D agency that particularly has been looked to for civilian industry in India. Concern about inadequate coupling within CSIR of R&D to Indian industry has been a recurrent theme in Indian analyses of industrial development and continues unabated. As only one example, the 1965 analysis of CSIR by the U.S. Battelle Memorial Institute speaks repeatedly of the great difficulties in obtaining effective linkages between the laboratories and industry.[44] Part of the problem is that the research programs of the laboratories tend to be generated by internal decisions of scientific and technical personnel, and in the absence of good linkages to industry, these programs will only occasionally be closely relevant to industrial needs and priorities. Of equal importance is the necessity of close interactive collaboration between industry

---

[42] Government of India, Department of Science and Technology, National Committee on Science and Technology, *An Approach to the Science and Technology Plan* (1973), p. 35.

[43] Government of India, Department of Science and Technology, National Committee on Science and Technology, *Research Statistics, 1974–75*, pp. 24, 63.

[44] Battelle Memorial Institute, *Final Report on a Study of Selected Laboratories and Departments of CSIR* (Springfield, Va.: National Technical Information Service, 1965).

and laboratory if a promising development from R&D is to result in a successful industrial innovation.

The CSIR has recognized the need for linkages and has made a number of moves to develop them. Guidelines have been established that require the R&D of laboratories to be strongly focused on industrial problems. Provision has been made for CSIR scientists and engineers who have developed a commercially interesting product to take leave from CSIR and establish a business venture. In spite of these efforts, the difficulties inherent in the separation of R&D from other aspects of innovation remain and therefore make it difficult for CSIR laboratories to perform the functions of the closely coupled industrial laboratories which have characterized most of the West. A good recent statement of the problem was given by Y. Nayudamma, the long-time Director General of CSIR:

> In India, most of the production is based upon either imported or self-generated technology whether in the public sector companies or private enterprises, not to talk of the subsidiaries of foreign companies. The capability for research, design and development is mostly confined to the government-funded institutes or State-funded national enterprises. . . . [This] poses a technological hazard. On the one hand, a national research and development system which carries with it large numbers of the scientific, technological and engineering community remains unproductive because it does not get interlinked with the production system, on the other hand the production system remains dependent upon the sources of technology outside the country and becomes increasingly dependent upon outside sources for its technological inputs, sustenance and progress. Thus it is a doubly wasteful situation. . . . [45]

Indian industrialists tend to agree with this analysis, but not surprisingly also tend to put much of the blame on the laboratories themselves, as the following comments indicate: "there is a feeling that research institutions have not succeeded in throwing up worthwhile processes because they lack the incentive to go out in the field and seek possibilities even if they have the commitment to do so. . . . Moreover the gap between the laboratory and the factory remains unbridged because rarely, if ever, is the industry associated with the laboratory at the right stage."[46]

[45] Y. Nayudamma, "Technology Transfer," paper delivered at the Indian Institute of Electrical and Electronics Engineers, Inc., Bombay, February 19, 1976.

[46] S. Subramaniam, "Scientific Research for Import Substitution," *Journal of Industry and Trade* 25 (1975), 1:41.
In late 1977, the new Janata government proposed a major reorganization of CSIR, transferring most of the development oriented CSIR laboratories over to the relevant government ministries. The objectives were to minimize duplication and to obtain closer links between the laboratories and the public sector industries, which they might serve. The proposed restructuring has come under strong attack and it is now doubtful whether the changes will be made. The problem of effective linkages will, however, remain.

Clearly, a better bridging mechanism is needed between laboratory and factory. In principle, one exists in India. The National Research Development Corporation (NRDC) was established in 1954 specifically to develop indigenous technology and to help secure utilization by industry of the R&D results from governmental laboratories and other R&D establishments. For many years, however, the activities of NRDC were at so low a level that its contributions to Indian Industrialization were insignificant. Recently its growth has been rapid, although the program is still small. In 1973–74, the sum of royalties plus premiums paid into NRDC was Rs 3.1 million; in 1969–70 it was Rs 1.2 million. In 1973–74, 238 licensing agreements were signed; in 1968–69, only 67. Also in recent years, NRDC has moved from simple licensing to joint development projects with industry to which NRDC can contribute up to 50 percent of costs. A 1974 example is a Rs 12 million program of jointly sponsored pilot plants for petrochemical processes.[47]

The NRDC program is, however, still small relative to the nation's needs. Furthermore, as NRDC Managing Director C. V. S. Ratnam has pointed out, there remain serious problems in technology assimilation and horizontal transfer of technology which are beyond the charter of the NRDC.[48]

International Comparisons of Technology Innovation

In their programs for national development and technology innovation, the procedures used by countries with private enterprise and mixed economies exhibit many common features: governments typically play a large role in guiding development; governmental restrictions on imported technology are common; governments typically aid industrialization with such measures as tariffs on imports and subsidies for exports; a crucial transition point is a country's shift from use of new technology primarily for import substitution to an emphasis on development of exports; another important transition is the shift from virtually exclusive reliance on imported technology to increasing dependence on indigenous R&D for technology adaptation and innovation. To illustrate these points in more detail, we list below some features of the programs to two nations that have made remarkable progress in national development, Japan and South Korea.

Japan's industrialization was characterized by two major periods of very

---

[47] Government of India, National Research Development Corporation, *Annual Report, 1973–74.*

[48] C.V.S. Ratnam, "Problems of Transfer of Technology," *Commerce* 13 (November, 1975), 3364, special supplement: 15.

rapid development: the early Meiji period of 1870–85 and a post–World War II period, 1950–1965. The salient features of these are: [49]

(a) In the earliest days of development Japan depended extensively on foreign advisors.

(b) It rapidly increased its cadre of scientists and engineers, sending many of its early students abroad for modern training.

(c) Industrial development was almost exclusively in the hands of private enterprise, with strong governmental monitoring and assistance.

(d) In the 1950–65 period, technology innovation was achieved almost entirely by adaptation of imported technologies.

(e) There were tight governmental controls on the kinds of technology that could be imported, but controls have gradually been relaxed.

(f) Governmental incentives encouraged a rapid build-up of industrial capabilities for technology innovation.

(g) A shift in emphasis from import substitution to development of exports occurred soon after World War II.

(h) Industries were protected by strict restrictions on foreign imports and foreign investment.

South Korea's moves toward industrialization and national development share many features with Japan's. The compression in time for development by Korea is remarkable: as late as 1962 South Korea's GNP per capita was only $87; by 1974, it was over $500. Among the more significant elements in Korea's rapid development after 1962 were: [50]

(a) The existence of a large body of trained scientists and engineers.

(b) A phased plan of development which first emphasized import substitution and older technologies, such as textiles.

(c) In the second phase, 1967–71, emphasis was on developing the heavy and chemical industries with expansion of exports from the light industries.

(d) Strong reliance on private enterprise to effect technology importation and innovation.

(e) Explicit governmental monitoring and guidance including licensing controls over technology importation.

---

[49] T. Ozawa, *Japan's Technological Challenge to the West* (Cambridge, Massachusetts: MIT Press, 1974).

[50] Korea Advanced Institute of Science, "Science and Technology and the Development of Korea," (Seoul, Korea: 1973). H.S. Choi, "Science and Technology Development for Industrialization in Korea," *World Development*, 1977.

(f)   Rapid build-up of governmental aid for R&D and information transfer.

(g)   Governmental measures to encourage indigenous R&D and technology innovation by industry.

Several of the steps in the above two lists have also been employed by India. The major differences between India and these two countries have been the latters' more explicit reliance on private enterprise for technology innovation and the greater governmental encouragement of innovation in industry. Also significant are the decisions by Japan and Korea to give strong encouragement to developing industrial capabilities for the export trade. Many of India's endowments differ considerably from those of either Japan or Korea; for example, India has more natural resources on which to build industry and a much larger internal market to absorb industrial products. However, some of the critical transition points that Japan and Korea faced, including strong emphasis on exports and strong encouragement of technology innovation by industry, have not yet been reached in India.

The past two decades have seen very substantial progress in the introduction of new technology into Indian industry and agriculture. A number of industries have either been newly established or greatly expanded: for example, the heavy machinery industry. There has been large growth in a number of modern technology areas, including atomic power and chemicals. A wide variety of products that hitherto had been imported are now being manufactured in India, including such basic items as heavy machinery, electronic consumer goods, fertilizers, and pharmaceuticals. The growth rate in industrial production has been high.

These new industries were almost entirely based on imported technology. That dependence on imported technology remains high is a matter of considerable concern to many Indian analysts, particularly since the national effort in R&D has undergone manifold expansion. The difficulty is that Indian programs of technology innovation and adaptation have developed slowly. The amount of R&D done by Indian industry is small. This is true for both private and public sector industry. The situation is perhaps better for industries within the integrated Departments of Atomic Energy and Space, but these are not mainstream industries for the civilian population, as chemicals. electronics, light machinery, and durable goods are. A large component of the problem is establishing and maintaining interactive associations between industries and government-supported R&D laboratories, which are administratively and geographically separate. It will perhaps not be enough simply to urge greater communication and collaboration between governmental laboratories and industries. Some substantial structural changes are probably needed. One of the more obvious would be to insure that industries themselves develop substantially larger R&D programs than they now have. This would permit industries to produce more technology innovation on their own. It would also give industries the expertise to permit the development of closer and more interactive links with governmental laboratories.

Science and Technology for Agriculture and Rural Development

In view of agriculture's central importance to India, no discussion of science and technology for India would be complete without its consideration. About 80 percent of Indians live in rural districts. The majority of the Indian work force is involved in agriculture. About 40 percent of India's GNP results from agricultural production. Of the ten largest Indian exports in recent years, five stem from agricultural production: sugar, jute, tea, leather, oilcake.[51]

India's agricultural resources are immense. The Gangetic Plain of Northern India has been called the world's greatest single agricultural production area. Experts argue that India has the potential to become the major food exporter of the world. India's range of agricultural regions is unique, going from fully tropical regions to subtemperate regions of the Himalayan foothills.

The complexities of the agricultural production and distribution system are such that R&D designed to improve it virtually must take a systems approach. Furthermore, the wide spectrum of intellectual fields involved (plant genetics, land use planning, hydrology, photosynthesis, entomology, organic chemistry, to name only the obvious) requires that the approach also be multidisciplinary.

Responsibility for R&D on agricultural problems in India is shared principally by the central government and the states. The chief operating entities are agricultural universities, research institutes, and field stations. However, the industrial sector makes important contributions, particularly in the fields of agricultural machinery, fertilizers, and pesticides and herbicides. At the central government level, principal responsibility is in the hands of the Indian Council of Agricultural Research (ICAR). The Council, reorganized in 1964, predates independence. It has become one of the major scientific agencies of the central sector. Its R&D budget of Rs 260 million for 1974–75 is only slightly smaller than that of CSIR. ICAR supports and manages twenty-three agricultural institutes, of which three have been assigned national status.[52]

In addition to its own research programs, ICAR assists agricultural research stations of the states with a program of matching grants. It also gives significant support to agricultural universities. Finally, it has overall coordinating responsibilities for the entire Indian R&D effort in agriculture.

---

[51] Ezekiel, Chapter IX.

[52] Government of India, *Indian Council of Agricultural Research Handbook*, (Delhi: 1971).

Indian agricultural R&D appears to have come of age during the past decade. A principal spur seems to have been the advent of the short-stem, high yielding miracle grains. India has not merely adopted imported strains of rice and wheat, but has embarked on a vigorous program of plant genetics and field testing to produce modified strains designed for its own needs and climate. [53]

Since the new strains of rice and wheat require both fertilizer and application of pesticides and herbicides for maximum yields, there has been increased attention to R&D for both of these. Efforts in new formulation of pesticides and improved efficiencies in production are almost entirely within the hands of the chemical industry, but most field testing activities are accomplished by government-supported institutes. The level of indigenous R&D activity for agricultural chemicals does not seem very large, however, and a good case can be made for considerable expansion. A similar case can probably be made for an expanded program of R&D on agricultural machinery, where the problem again is to develop equipment that fits India's needs.

The problem of how to improve the lives of the 75 percent of Indians who live in rural villages goes far beyond improvement in agricultural practices. The areas of need include education, public health, water supply, electrification, energy supply, communication, transportation, rural industry, and of course agriculture. If significant improvement is to be obtained, there will need to be progress in all these areas, the implication being that a multifaceted approach is essential. Furthermore, the problem is so large that the direct intervention of the central government is almost mandatory. It thus becomes presumptuous to propose for science and technology anything more than a supporting and collaborative role. Nevertheless, technology is needed, and R&D on specific rural and village problems can contribute. The directions in which to go are clear enough. Technology for the dispersed village must be simple, inexpensive, and easy to maintain. Industries must emphasize high labor intensity and minimal capital requirements. Because of the problems of transportation and communication, the scale of industries will normally be small. Many of these desired characteristics are at variance with those typically considered appropriate for urban industries. In this sense, the R&D problem can be considered a problem of technology adaptation to fit the village situation.

An excellent illustration is the possible application of solar energy to village needs. In principle, this seems ideal. Solar energy is plentiful in India and small solar units are appropriate in themselves and suitable for small scale use. But if the needed characteristics of simplicity and inexpensiveness are to be obtained,

---

[53] Government of India, Indian Council of Agricultural Research, *Agricultural Research in India: Achievements and Outlook,* (Delhi: 1972).

R&D programs will be different from those for urban and developed nation applications. Ideally, new directions will be developed in a village context, with R&D people working directly with villagers and responding to their social as well as technical needs.

All of this is now well appreciated in India, and the Janata government is committed to giving major attention to agriculture and rural industries. A start already has been made on the need for new R&D; CSIR laboratories have been explicitly asked to work directly with villages, and at least one ongoing CSIR program involves "adoption" of a entire rural district.[54]

Improving the lot of the rural poor constitutes one of the world's greatest challenges. Indian scientists and engineers, brought up with personal knowledge of the problems and positioned so as to proceed with the required collaborative R&D, are in a unique position to help make major progress on what is a problem worldwide, not just in India.

Comments on Two High Technology Industries

This section gives brief comments on two potentially important high technology industries for India: electronics, because it has become a symbol of highest technology and a source of major exports for many developing nations; and alternative energy sources, because India, along with the rest of the world, will need to be thinking soon about energy sources other than coal, oil, and gas.

Recently, the field of electronics internationally has been one of the liveliest and fastest growing of the high technology areas. Within the field are such recent developments as: integrated circuits, high speed computers, microwave devices, and automated controls. Most of the R&D for these new developments has occurred in the western nations and Japan. However, assembly of instruments and devices based upon advanced electronic components has become important to such nations as South Korea and Taiwan, and assembled devices have become major elements of export. India has participated only slightly in this new industrial activity.

R&D in advanced electronics is a relatively new effort for India. Initially R&D in the field was to be found in a series of separate bodies: DRDO, DAE, Indian Telephone Industries, and so on. A planning, promoting, and coordination body, the Electronics Commission, was established in 1971, and parallel to it, a Department of Electronics.[55] By 1974—75, the budget of the latter had grown

[54] Y. Nayudamma and B.K. Nayar, "Gearing Science and Technology for Rural Uplift," *Invention Intelligence* 12 (1977), 1 and 2: 35—40.

[55] A. Rahman, *et al. Science and Technology in India.*

to Rs 40 million, which, however, leaves it ten times smaller than, for example, the Space Research Organization. The other principal governmental support of R&D in electronics comes from defense programs. Two of the thirty-seven laboratories supported by DRDO include the word electronics in their name, and one can also assume that some of the other DRDO laboratories make significant contributions to electronics. So, doubtless, do a few of the laboratories of DAE, CSIR and ISRO. Two public sector production enterprises do substantial research in electronics: Bharat Electronics, Ltd., which is operated by the Department of Defense and is presumably involved primarily in products for the military; and the Indian Telephone Industries. Together, these two enterprises spent Rs 45 million on R&D in 1974–75. The 1974–75 tabulation of R&D funding[56] shows a somewhat larger amount, Rs 65 million, for R&D by the private sector in the categories Electronics and Electrical Equipment. However, it is not unreasonable to assume that half or more of this total is for electrical equipment rather than for electronics in the modern sense of the term.

In view of the rapidly increasing role of advanced electronic devices in a wide spectrum of modern technology and in view of their importance to defense and space activities, it is surprising that the Indian R&D effort in this area has not grown more rapidly. In speculating on what measures for expansion might be useful and perhaps feasible, two or three come to mind. Relatively more R&D funds might be allotted to the public sector industries that are emphasizing electronics, particularly Bharat Electronics and Indian Telephone Industries. Furthermore, the charter to one or both of these companies might be broadened to include a larger assignment in selected areas of the most advanced technology, for example, integrated circuits and manufacturing from metal oxide semiconductors. India could also accelerate its electronics programs by encouraging joint industrial ventures in the private sector between Indian groups and technically advanced industries from the developed nations. This could bring India rapidly into production of advanced devices for internal use and export which, if in-house research were vigorously encouraged, could serve as a source of new indigenous technology.

Finally, India should probably upgrade its long-range research in electronics, possibly by coordination of the existing separate activities but probably by assembling a single high-level group. In view of the very large amount of activity in these fields throughout the world, the group should have the principal function of analyzing the implications of basic and applied research accomplished throughout the world in the relevant areas. It will be essential, however, that the group

---

[56] Government of India, Department of Science and Technology, National Committee on Science and Technology, *Research Statistics, 1974–75.*

itself be involved in R&D efforts. Otherwise its judgment in assessing outside R&D activities will rapidly deteriorate. Elements of the fields of electronics research also should be supported vigorously within Indian universities, which are both an appropriate place to perform basic research and a place to train future research and development people for the fields.

A strong case can be made for India to give considerable emphasis to R&D on alternative energy sources. India currently imports about three-quarters of its petroleum at a high price and at a serious cost of foreign exchange. Even if India discovers substantial oil and gas, the high value of petroleum in the export market and its utility for petro-chemicals will make a search for alternative energy sources important. Fortunately, India has substantial coal resources, but these probably cannot be counted on as a major energy source for more than a few decades.

There are other reasons why alternative energy sources might be particularly suitable for India. The nation is blessed with high levels of sunshine, making solar energy comparatively attractive. The dispersed character of Indian villages and the high costs of distributing electricity and gas also suggest that small-scale energy units, such as solar, geothermal or wind, might be particularly appropriate for India.

With the exception of nuclear energy, R&D on energy sources currently seems to be widely dispersed within the Indian science system, often operating at support levels which may well be subcritical. The "Science and Technology Plan, 1974–79" of the National Committee on Science and Technology has briefly addressed some of these problems in its write-up on fuel and power.[57] The plan recommends some new and expanded R&D programs in alternative sources, including a Laboratory on Solar Energy, but its recommended levels of expenditure fall considerably short of what would be required for a substantial program. The S&T plan also recommends a new Institute for Energy Studies/Planning, which appears, however, to be designed to focus more on national energy needs and applications than on new R&D efforts. On the other hand, such an institute could be an information-gathering unit and a national clearinghouse for the very large amount of R&D on new energy sources that will be going on worldwide and will thus become available for Indian consideration. Put another way, a moderate sized but high level Indian R&D effort on alternative energy sources could be useful in itself and as the center of an effort to link Indian R&D to that of the rest of the world.

The interesting challenge for India in tackling R&D on alternative energy sources will be to devise and implement an overall development process that simultaneously considers R&D activities, technology innovation, production, and use. The problem of new energy sources, although exceedingly important, is not immediately urgent. There is time to give careful thought to organizing the interactive R&D and production system that will bring the nation most rapidly into a situation where new energy sources (whether developed in India or elsewhere) are being tried in the field and entering into practical use.

There is an even more ambitious goal for R&D efforts in new energy sources to which India might reasonably aspire. Given its scientific and technical capabilities and its geographic location, India represents a natural site for a major worldwide center on the use of solar energy in the nations of the tropics. A well-planned Indian effort in this field might very well attract international support and rapidly assume the same significance to new energy sources as the International Agricultural Laboratories, such as India's own ICRISAT, have assumed in agricultural R&D.

Future Prospects for Indian Science and Technology

India's continued commitment to expanded programs of science and technology has given it a scientific and technological system whose international status is high by any of the following measures: numbers of scientists and engineers; expenditures on science and technology; production of scientific and technical knowledge; establishment of R&D programs oriented toward national development. The continued expansion recommended by the "Science and Technology Plan, 1974–1979" and this recommendation's apparently favorable reception by the National Planning Commission suggest that this strong national commitment to science and technology will continue.

The existence of these substantial scientific and technical capabilities offers India a number of interesting opportunities to employ several alternative or complementary strategies. India can continue to stress science and technology for internal development, emphasizing, for example, increased agricultural production and continued import substitution. Parallel with this, it can stress development of its natural resources and their conversion to products for the national economy. India also could orient its scientific and technical industries toward greatly increased exports, emphasizing products of modern technology. In doing so it would be following the paths already successfully traveled by Japan, Korea, and Taiwan. A somewhat different strategy available to India would involve working to become the scientific and technical leader for the underdeveloped tropical nations of the world. India has the potential, for example, to become a leader in R&D for tropical agriculture; for solar energy devices; for formulation of pesticides, fungicides and herbicides for tropical use; and for tropical marine biology and fisheries. Although these represent ambitious goals, any one of them seems feasible for the Indian S&T establishment to accomplish.

India may have considerably more difficulty making rapid progress in applying science and technology to its own development than in assuming an increased international role in S&T. The reason is that successful application of technology to industry and agriculture depends basically on the willingness and ability of production enterprises in these fields to commit themselves to a path of technology innovation. Even after they make this commitment, there must be continuing interactive linkages between the production systems and the science and technology system so that the latter can make effective contributions. So far India's record in promoting indigenous technology innovation and adaptation, and in building linkages between R&D establishments and industry has not been impressive. It is quite possible that some significant structural and organizational changes will be needed to permit more rapid progress.

There are a number of interesting new directions that India might appropriately investigate in considering more effective use of science and technology for development. Among them are:

1. Establishment of several high-quality centers of advanced training in universities and technical institutes that are equipped with modern laboratories and instrumentation as well as with the funds to award scholarships to superior students and support significant programs of modern research.
2. A scientific and technical information service that gives all scientists and engineers in universities and institutes up-to-date access to the world's scientific and technical literature.
3. Increased emphasis on R&D programs that emphasize a systems approach to the application of science and technology. Initial efforts might focus on improvements in agricultural production and in nutrition and health.
4. Major attention to development of R&D programs that improve the situation of the rural poor.
5. In-depth analyses of appropriate priorities and program balance for R&D in India. Among the items of particular interest might be expanded R&D for agriculture and the civilian economy; increased efforts on utilization of natural resources, including marine resources; specific programs dealing with advanced R&D in selected fields, such as electronics, pesticides, and solar energy.
6. Programs to expand substantially the R&D efforts in industry, both public and private. Principal focus would probably be on increased capabilities of technology innovation and technology adaptation.
7. Development of new or expanded collaborative international programs of R&D in technical areas where India's resources and R&D capabilities open the possibility for international leadership by India.
8. More consideration of the role of R&D and advanced technology in building up India's exports.

The bare delineation of this list of alternatives points to the need for careful analysis priorities for India's programs of science and technology and especially of the best ways of insuring that these programs contribute most effectively to national development. However, it is encouraging that India has the scientists and engineers, the research establishments, and the tradition of research productivity that make it possible to plan seriously for almost any of these alternatives. Given the very substantial capabilities that the Indian S&T system now has, the next decade should be a fruitful one for the application of science and technology in India.

Comment

Padma Desai

The significant conclusion of Dr. Long's paper is: the overall Indian science and technology program, while impressive compared to that of other poor countries, is inadequate and poorly organized in relation to the country's potential and requirements.

Approximately 25 percent of national R&D spending is directly used to promote innovation in industry and agriculture. The impact of these disbursements, as well as those of the overall program on development of products and processes being marketed or potentially marketable, must be assessed in relation to the institutional arrangements under which they are made. These arrangements are such that ninety percent of Indian R&D is completely funded and carried out by governmental agencies and laboratories. In contrast, as Dr. Long points out, private industry spends a dominant share of R&D outlays in the West.

Public sector R&D expenditures in India has been greatest in heavy industry and in such areas as atomic energy, space programs, and sophisticated defense equipment, areas where production capacities have overwhelmingly been imported rather than domestically manufactured. Import substitution of production capacities has been taking place mainly in private industry, which presumably is installing machines increasingly being produced in government heavy industry.

The Soviet Union has played a major role in providing equipment and associated technology to the Indian public sector's heavy industry, oil prospecting and refining, and defense production. Perhaps the most successful of the Soviet-supported projects are the Bhilai Steel Mill and the MIG Aircraft Factory. The most disastrous are the Mining and Allied Machinery Corporation and the Surgical Instruments Factory. The Heavy Machinery Corporation and the Bokaro Steel Mill are highly controversial.

The Soviets have provided design documentation along with equipment and technical assistance, thus enabling the Indian public sector to assimilate and innovate through learning by doing. To further build up indigenous know-how, India has adopted a policy of not accepting foreign industrial collaboration unless complete design documentation also is provided. The Soviets also have helped

India establish research, design, and engineering institutes that promote technological innovation and the adaptation of imported technologies to local conditions. The effects of Soviet assistance have been most notable in steelmaking, oil prospecting and refining, and fertilizer production.[1] Furthermore, the Soviet program of training Indian technicians to manage Soviet-collaborated plants has generally been meticulous and systematic.

The Soviets played a similar role in China and Cuba, as noted in the following observation by Genevieve Dean:

> Transfers of Soviet technical know-how were also important as a potential source of new technology in China. Soviet technical personnel seconded to Chinese projects, Chinese technicians and engineers trained in the Soviet Union, and the expansion of China's scientific research and experimental development facilities with Soviet assistance all contributed to the growth of an innovative capability in China, but again imposed a Soviet bias on China's technological development. The kinds of engineering design and development capabilities transferred from the Soviet Union to China were also mainly those associated with the capital-intensive, large-scale technologies of the heavy industrial sector. [2]

The question of whether India has received inferior technology for its heavy industry from the Soviet Union has to be assessed in relation to the alternatives available from the West. The West has sometimes been reluctant to participate in Indian heavy industry, especially in the public sector. For example, the proposal to give one billion dollars of aid to the Bokaro Steel Mill was vigorously championed by both President Kennedy and Ambassador Galbraith. But it was scuttled in the U.S. Congress, essentially on the ideological grounds that the United States should not commit massive funds to an Indian public sector project.

Incidentally, while the Soviets did not provide the advanced continuous-casting steel technology for the first stage of Bokaro, neither did the United States Steel Corporation propose it in its project report for the mill.[3]

---

[1] For details of these public sector research-design agencies, see John Roberts, "Engineering Consultancy, Industrialization and Development," *The Journal of Development Studies,* 9 (October 1972): 39–61.

[2] The emphasis on technological development in light industry and agriculture along with heavy industry began with the Great Leap Forward. For details, see Genevieve Dean, "Science, Technology and Development: China as a 'Case Study'," *The China Quarterly,* October 1971, pp. 528–529.

[3] For details of the technological aspects of the Bokaro Steel Mill and especially a blow-by-blow account of the removal of the Indian consulting agency of Dastur and Company from its potential role of designing and constructing some sections of the first stage of Bokaro, see Padma Desai, *The Bokaro Steel Plant* (Amsterdam: North-Holland Publishing Company, 1972).

In general, the arrangements with the Soviet Union and the socialist countries of Eastern Europe in the Indian public sector are without equity participation and provide equipment, consulting, and training for a specified project. In contrast, the arrangements with enterprises of developed market economy countries are generally with private Indian industry. They range from the supply of a patent to licensing and in some instances to a fully owned subsidiary. [4]

Most of the R&D in the high-technology areas (which include not only space research but also the activities in the National Physical and Chemical Laboratories) does not appear to have short-term developmental impact. But where it is not military oriented it could have long-term economic benefits.

Production, investment, and innovative activities in India are primarily carried out in a sheltered market, much as in the USSR and China. The major difference is that in India there remains a free flow of ideas. The industrial scene in India is rather like the sprawling, confounding Indian caste system. Most industries merely survive. A select few flourish by virtue of historical accident or privilege. There are only limited opportunities for the have-nots to dislodge the haves.

Finally, the Indian planning process has a multiplicity of goals. Some of them, such as the prevention of monopoly power, directly bear on the performance and potential innovation of private industry. Anti-big business objectives are being stressed with renewed vigor, and with important implications for private R&D.

These institutional arrangements suggest the following conclusions and questions:

1. Insofar as governmental R&D is oriented toward non-economic objectives, as it is in space and high technology, the capital-output ratio of such expenditures is likely to be very high, as Dr. Long observes. Because capital goods are imported there is little opportunity to learn current technology by production. Hence, R&D for innovation is likely to be rather frustrating and unproductive.

   Because of the high costs of R&D for innovation, one may ask whether import substitution in technology would not be as wasteful, from a strictly economic viewpoint, as import substitution in production. [5] Answering this

---

[4] For a discussion of whether these arrangements from both East and West result in the transfer of technology in developing countries in general, see Padma Desai, "The Transfer of Technology to Developing Countries in Framework of Tripartite Industrial Cooperation " (UNCTAD, Geneva: December 1975), no. TAD/SEM. 1/5-GE. 75-50407.

[5] On the latter, consult Jagdish N. Bhagwati and Padma Desai, *India: Planning for Industrialization* (London: Oxford University Press, 1970).

question is extremely difficult, for the production function relating R&D expenditures to innovation and output may often be a matter of speculation.

2. Next, the question arises as to whether Indian institutions are capable of transmitting industrial processes or products invented by governmental R&D for private commercial utilization. Some institutions, such as the Central Leather Institute and the Central Food Technology Research Institute, have impressive records. However, many others have had a negligible impact on the private sector.

China scholars have studied how the politicization of scientific activity and its organization in politically controlled institutions has affected the transmission of research findings to industry. In particular, their findings stress the adverse effects of the Maoist policy of "utilization, restriction and transformation" of Chinese scientists by requiring them to work on factory floors; of the adoption during the Great Leap Forward of the policy of "walking on the two legs" of foreign and domestic technologies; of the creation of the "counterestablishment" of "scientific" cadres trained in the factories and workshops.[6]

The shortcomings of Indian governmental R&D would seem to come from inability to relate product creation to market demands and design or from failure to provide for continuous debugging of new processes. The latter problem constitutes the core of Raymond Vernon's product-cycle hypothesis.[7] The need to sort out the problems accompanying introduction of new products and processes requires that manufacturing be located where the R&D laboratories are; that is, at home in the United States. However, manufacturing is often moved abroad to exploit lower wages, and so on, as soon as all the bugs have been taken out and the product-cum-process is more or less standardized.

3. Even R&D by private industry runs into difficulties under the closely regulated Indian economic regime. For example, suppose R&D leads to a new product. There is then no guarantee that it can be produced, given the

[6] For a well-documented and insightful discussion of the Chinese Communist Party's perceptions and attitudes toward science and its policies *vis-à-vis* the Chinese scientific community, see R.P. Suttmeier, "Party Views of Science: The Record from the First Decade," *The China Quarterly*, August 1974, pp. 146—168.

[7] For an early statement of the product cycle theory, see Raymond Vernon, "International Investment and International Trade in the Product Cycle," *Quarterly Journal of Economics* 80 (May 1966): 190—207.

constraints on product-diversification under the licensing system. Or the licensing authorities may not approve the large-scale enterprise required for a reasonable rate of return on a new process or product.

Misguided economic doctrines and policies also may cripple R&D by private industry: some influential economists used to argue that the output of consumer goods should be controlled to avoid luxury consumption. They ignored the possibility that consumer goods can be exported. The strict licensing of investment and production in these industries resulting from such views undoubtedly deterred R&D.

4. R&D is, of course, predominantly carried on by larger concerns which often pool their technical resources in international mergers. This creates concern about concentration of economic power, which may inhibit R&D expenditures. However, other ways of handling problems relating to the concentration of economic power have been suggested by many economists who are not of a *laissez faire* or conservative persuasion.

5. Do sheltered markets also affect the incentive to innovate? Does involvement in export markets promote innovation? These interesting questions were addressed by Professors Bhagwati and Srinivasan in their recent volume on India's foreign trade regime. They found no conclusive evidence that exports encourage technical innovation. On the other hand, product and design do seem to be adversely affected by the lack of competition and discipline in sheltered markets.[8]

6. Finally, let me turn to R&D for agriculture, a matter of the utmost importance to India. In doing so, I am finally succumbing to the temptation to compare the Indian performance with the Chinese. This can now be done with some plausibility, because more detailed information on both countries is now available.[9] An American delegation recently found that, except in rice farming, development of new higher-yielding and disease-resistant varieties of crops by Chinese institutes lagged significantly behind the Indian. Among the reasons cited[10] were the Maoist emphasis on the three-

[8] Cf. Jagdish N. Bhagwati and T.N. Srinivasan, *India* (New York: National Bureau of Economic Research, 1976).

[9] Elsewhere I have expressed some reservations about similar comparisons. For details, see Padma Desai, "Comparative Economic Performance of India and China: A Comment," *American Economic Review* 65 (May 1975), 2:365–67.

[10] For details, see Dwight Perkins, "A Conference on Agriculture," *The China Quarterly* (September 1976), pp. 596–690.

in-one principle of the scientist, technician, and peasant working together on the farm. This program certainly improved the efficiency of China's agricultural extension service but it did so at the expense of high-level research. Moreover, the American delegation argued that:

> China's emphasis on self-reliance, for example, not only seems to have cut off or limited China's contact with the work of agricultural scientists elsewhere in the world, but there also appears to be relatively little contact between plant scientists in different regions within China. . . Thus most of the experimental fields and laboratories that the delegation visited seemed rather inactive. What field research was going on was largely straightforward variety testing, not sophisticated field research, and some of the work observed may have been done earlier. Also, there was the question of whether the Chinese were training sufficient numbers of highly qualified younger plant scientists. Some members of the delegation, at least, had the impression that the Chinese still appear to be dependent on an aging body of plant scientists trained in the West and the Soviet Union.[11]

On the other hand, the Chinese appear to be far ahead of the Indian peasantry in efficient application of existing technology. The explanation lies not only in the commune form of rural organization with the commune production team as the accounting unit, but also in efficient water management. This includes, among other things, land developing, massive construction of reservoirs, and the extensive lining of irrigation canals with locally available materials.

I would conclude on a slightly despairing note by quoting one member of the American delegation, who said: "If you could hybridize the Indian and Chinese agricultural research and extension systems, you would have a very good system."[12]

[11] Ibid., pp. 603–04.

[12] Ibid., p. 603.

IX

India's Trade Prospects and Potentials

Hannan Ezekiel

By the mid-1970s, India had improved its export situation significantly. It is now exporting a greater variety of goods, and depends less upon any single region or country than at independence.

The opportunities for the future are good, and will be enhanced if India follows a new development strategy. If this new strategy is accompanied by liberalization of the import policies of the industrialized countries, then India may make a breakthrough in its development effort. This chapter presents estimates of exports under three sets of circumstances: continuation of the past development strategy; under a new strategy with trade liberalization in the West; and a new strategy without trade liberalization.

Patterns of Exports

India has remarkably widened and balanced the geographical distribution of its exports since it became independent in 1947. Four of the seven regions listed in Table 9.1 take about 20 percent of India's exports, while North America absorbs about 13 percent. India's top five export partners accounted for a smaller share of total exports in 1974–75 than in 1960–61, while the share of the most important trading partner decreased from 29 percent to 13 percent (Table 9.2). Twenty-five countries each absorbed more than 1 percent of India's exports in 1974–75.

With such a balanced distribution of its exports, India is no longer at the mercy of conditions in any single region. Annual fluctuations in demand and supply in any particular region can be met to some extent by adjusting exports to other regions. This is not true, of course, for commodities which go mainly to a particular country; such as iron ore, which goes to Japan.

Geographically balanced distribution also means that the growth of exports can be expected to be stable in the middle term because obstacles to expansion in any one region will have only a small effect on overall growth.

India's exports increased almost two and one-third times from 1950–51 to 1974–75 and there were sharp changes among commodities (Table 9.3). The

Table 9.1 Regional Distribution of India's Exports, 1974—75

Economic and Social Commission For Asia and the Pacific	21
European Economic Community	21
Eastern Europe	21
West Asia (including Iran, Egypt and Sudan)	19
North America	13
Africa (excluding Egypt and Sudan)	4
Rest of the World	3

Source: Appendix VI, "India's Foreign Trade by Countries and Economic Regions," *Export and Production Perspectives, 1980—81,* (New Delhi, Federation of Indian Chambers of Commerce and Industry), 1976.

Table 9.2 Five Main Countries Importing India's Products

1960—61		1965—66		1970—71		1974—75	
Country	Percentage	Country	Percentage	Country	Percentage	Country	Percentage
UK	29	USA	18	USSR	14	USSR	13
USA	16	UK	18	USA	14	USA	11
Japan	5	USSR	12	Japan	13	UK	9
USSR	4	Japan	7	UK	11	Japan	9
Australia	3	UAR	3	UAR	4	Iran	6
Total	57	Total	58	Total	56	Total	48

Source: Reserve Bank of India, *RBI Bulletin,* June 1976, Current Statistics Table 50.

Table 9.3   Leading items in India's exports in 1950—51 and 1974—75

(Millions of current U.S. dollars)

Category	1950—51		1974—75		Increase (%)
	Amount	Share (%)	Amount	Share (%)	
Cotton Textiles (excluding garments and other manufactures)	248	20	200	5	−19
Jute Manufactures	239	19	371	9	55
Tea	169	13	286	7	69
Leather and Leather Manufactures	55	4	189	5	244
Spices	53	4	77	2	45
Vegetable Oils	53	4	42	1	−21
Tobacco	30	2	101	2	237
Essential Oils	27	2	12	...	−56
Coir Manufactures	23	2	23	1	...
Mica	21	2	29	1	38
Others	345	27	2,851	68	726
Total of First Three Items	656	52	857	21	31
Total of First Ten Items	918	72	1,330	33	45
Total of All Items Excluding First Three	607	47	3,324	80	449
Grand Totals	1,263		4,181		231

Source: Government of India Department of Commercial Intelligence and Statistics, *Monthly Statistics of the Foreign Trade of India.*

dollar volume of cotton textiles, the leading category in 1950—51, dropped nearly a fifth, and exports of essential oils and vegetable oils also decreased substantially. The share of the three leading categories in 1950—51—cotton textiles, jute manufactures, and tea—dropped from 52 percent to 21 percent. Exports of other goods increased four and a half times, with leather manufactures and unmanufactured tobacco expanding most rapidly. In the leather group, finished leather and manufactures largely replaced raw and semifinished products.

By 1975—76, sugar, which was not even among the top ten exports in 1950—51, had replaced cotton textiles in first place. Other new items were engineering goods, iron ore, silver, garments, and oilcakes (Table 9.4). Only jute manufactures, tea, and cotton textiles still ranked among the first ten.

Economic Policy and Export Behavior

India's exports grew slowly from independence until the early 1970s primarily because development strategy emphasized heavy industry at the expense of both light industry and agriculture. This strategy was based on import substitution rather than export expansion and was influenced by a self-fulfilling pessimism about export prospects. The results of investment, production, and trade policies helped to confirm this pessimism.

During this period, a faith in controls and regulations as instruments of policy helped produce a self-perpetuating bureaucratic apparatus that was reluctant to give up its power. Industrial licensing was motivated largely by a fear of concentration of power in private hands. This fear often resulted in a scale of enterprise even smaller than the small size of the domestic market would have made necessary. It encouraged inefficient producers who were also protected by import restrictions.

In contrast, producers who were efficient and otherwise competitive faced severe problems. Domestic inputs were unavailable, expensive, or of poor quality, while imported inputs often could be purchased only after long delays. As a result, large stocks either had to be maintained at high cost, or were not available at all. Similar difficulties also were faced in obtaining essential components of machinery and equipment.

Exchange rate policy was also unsatisfactory because India's currency was generally overvalued. Even the major devaluation of 1966 did not really help exports: because of changes in taxes and incentives, effective devaluation for most export products was negligible.

Thus, a high-cost, inward-looking economy was created which did not have the efficiency, the flexibility, or the motivation to build export markets on a sustained basis.

Table 9.4 Projections of India's Exports to 1980—81 and 1985—86

(Millions of constant 1975—76 U.S. dollars)

	1975—76		1980—81		1985—86	
	Amount	Rank	Amount	Rank	Amount	Rank
Sugar	546	1	400	4	400	5
Engineering	472	2	780	1	1,650	1
Jute	287	3	292	7	316	12
Tea	274	4	305	6	325	10
Leather and Leather Manufactures	254	5	368	5	600	4
Textiles (excluding garments)	248	6	290	8	335	9
Iron Ore	247	7	405	3	620	3
Silver	198	8	205	13	250	14
Garments	168	9	240	11	375	6
Oilcakes	160	10	180	14	200	16
Marine Products	146	11	250	10	340	8
Iron and Steel	144	12	500	2	625	2
Gems and Jewelry	142	13	255	9	350	7
Carpets and Other Handicrafts	117	14	220	12	320	11
Chemicals	116	15	179	15	315	13
Cashews	111	16	150	16	208	15
Tobacco	107	17	100	18	110	18
Spices	82	18	90	19	90	19
Coffee	77	19	108	17	187	17
Major Items	3,896		5,317		7,616	
Others	659		1,020		1,681	
Total	4,555		6,337		9,297	

Source: For 1975—76, Government of India, Department of Commercial Intelligence and Statistics, *Monthly Statistics of the Foreign Trade of India;* for 1980—81 and 1985—86, projections by the author.

Nevertheless, certain pragmatic measures did favor export expansion. These measures resulted from the acute foreign exchange shortages accompanied by periodic exchange crises into which the basic development strategy drove the economy. A variety of measures ranging from industrial licensing concession to export incentives offset, to varying degrees, the adverse effects the basic policies had on the country's export prospects.

The relatively rapid growth in exports after 1970–71 is the result of a combination of factors. Successful control of inflation in India, while world inflation continued at a rapid pace, gave India a price advantage. The accompanying recession in domestic demand, particularly for engineering products, made Indian producers turn actively to external markets. In addition, the steel industry increased utilization and expanded capacity, including new capacity for production of certain types of special steel. This made raw materials more available to the engineering industry, and increased India's ability to export iron and steel. Moreover, conditions affecting world demand for India's main exports were particularly favorable. Demand for engineering products in West Asia surged upward after the sharp rise in oil prices in 1974.[1] At the same time, extremely high prices for sugar raised India's export earnings without any increase in quantities exported. Simultaneously, as a result of changing conditions in the world market, silver exports from stocks became a major exchange earner, contributing to the sharp spurt in the value of total exports.

India's exchange rate policy was extremely favorable to exports during most of this period. From August 1971 to September 1975, the rupee was tied to sterling, a floating currency. Being weak, sterling drifted steadily downward in relation to most of the other major currencies, and the rupee followed it. Between 1971 and 1975, the combined devaluation of the rupee against the dollar, deutsche mark, yen, and pound sterling, calculated on a trade-weighted basis, amounted to over 25 percent.[2]

The oil crisis severely jolted the Indian economy. As a result, the need to promote exports became widely recognized. Even those who continued to press for a development strategy basically oriented to heavy industry and import substitution conceded that promotion of exports was necessary. By this time, a section of the bureaucracy strongly entrenched in the system had acquired a vested in-

---

[1] See for example, "Exporting Engineering Goods and Skills to the Gulf Countries," *Business Environment*, October 1, 1977. The term "gulf countries" as used in this article covers the region described in this paper as West Asia.

[2] Based on calculations made by the author using exchange rate data from *International Financial Statistics* (Washington: International Monetary Fund) and trade data from the various sources on which the tables used in this paper are based.

terest in export promotion. It pushed vigorously but pragmatically for increased exports. These efforts succeeded because other conditions also strongly favored export expansion.

The Present Development Strategy and Exports

The likely value of India's exports in each of 19 major categories of goods has been projected to 1980–81 and 1985–86. The author has judged the likelihood of success of efforts being made or envisaged to promote increased supplies or exports of each category. These judgments are based on past trends and future prospects of various factors influencing exports.

Two broad assumptions were made. The first is that the basic development strategy that has governed the country's economic and social policies since the beginning of the second plan will remain fundamentally unchanged. The fifth plan adheres more closely to the strategy than the third and fourth. However, the new government seems likely to move away from this strategy. The possible effects of such a change are taken into account in alternative projections of exports reported in a later section of this chapter.

The present development strategy is based on the approach suggested by P. C. Mahalanobis when the second plan was being prepared and has underlaid all the five year plans since.[3] (See Mellor, Chapter 4.) It is sometimes suggested that the Mahalanobis strategy was not fully reflected in the various plans and that, in any case, the plans are not fully reflected in actual economic developments. The harsh impact that a rigorous implementation of the strategy would have produced was mitigated by pragmatic adjustments of policies. These adjustments resulted in investment in industries and sectors that would have had little or no priority under the basic development strategy.

However, the evidence is strong that the economy has been pushed quite powerfully in the direction indicated by the strategy. The strategy's impact is best seen in the fact that the value added in the capital and intermediate goods sector of industry increased from 29 to 30 percent of total value added by industry in the early 1950s to around 55 percent in the late sixties.[4] This proportion remained around this level for some years as a result of various pressures, particularly those from the balance of payments. However, the fifth plan called for an increase to 65 percent by 1985. If there is no change in strategy, this objective may well be achieved, perhaps with a delay of about five years.

[3] See Mellor, Chapter 4, pp. 5–10.

[4] See Narottam Shar, "Industrial Development in India Since 1947: A Survey" in Vadilal Dagil, ed., *A Profile of Indian Industry* (Bombay, 1970).

This development strategy favors import substitution over export expansion and carries with it the adverse effects such a policy can produce. However, the import substitution has been quite selective. For example, investment in the fertilizer industry is preferred to investment in agriculture even though the value of the food imports saved or food exports generated by agricultural investment would be many times the value of fertilizer imports (net of imports of fertilizer raw materials) that would be saved by the same volume of investment in the fertilizer industry.

The second assumption is that further pragmatic adjustments in trade and investment policies to promote exports will be made, even though they are sometimes in conflict with the strategy. Pragmatic policies on investment, production, and trade have been mainly responsible for the significant expansion in exports so far and will contribute greatly to a likely increase in the next decade. The results of such policies, however, differ from those of a change in basic development strategy.

The projections in Table 9.4 show iron and steel exports increasing four times; engineering products, three times; carpets and other handcrafts, chemicals, iron ore, gems and jewelry, coffee, leather and leather manufactures, marine products, and garments, more than twice; and cashews, by half. These categories, which accounted for about 44 percent of exports in 1975—76, will make up about 54 percent in 1980—81 and more than 60 percent in 1985—86.

The table also shows that the share for stagnant or slow-growing products—sugar, jute, tea, textiles (excluding garments), silver, oilcakes, tobacco, and spices—which was 42 percent of exports in 1975—76, will decline to 29 percent in 1980—81, and to 22 percent in 1985—86.

India's total exports are projected to increase more than 39 percent from 1975—76 to more than $6 billion in 1980—81; and to more than $9 billion in 1985—86. This would mean growth rates of about 7 percent annually for the next five-year period, and of about 9 percent for the second. However, these growth rates compare unfavorably both with those of the immediate past, and with those projected by the government for the fifth plan period.

The favorable condition that boosted growth rates of exports in the last few years cannot be expected to continue. Inflationary pressures in India are beginning to build up again. Domestic demand has begun to strengthen as measures are being taken to deal with the recession. This will reduce the strong incentive to export. Growth in industrial production will make increasing demand on domestic steel production, so that exports of iron and steel by 1980—81 are likely to be below the high levels expected for 1977—78 and 1978—79, although still much higher than in the past. The world price of sugar will fall to more reasonable levels, and India is likely to have less for export. Silver is unlikely to contribute as dynamically to export growth as it did during the recent past. And the exchange rate of the rupee is no longer helping exports as it did during the last few years.

In spite of all this, the export growth rate projected for the medium-term future is not very far below that of the immediate past and is therefore quite high by historical standards. This relatively good growth is due primarily to several factors. First, the adoption of the Generalized System of Preferences by the United States and other countries of the Organization for Economic Cooperation and Development (OECD) though subject to many limitations, favors expansion of exports of certain products. Second, West Asian demand for steel, engineering goods, and a wide variety of other products is likely to continue to rise rapidly, and India will continue to benefit from this. Third, the sharp jump in capacity utilization in existing steel plants and increased new capacity has created a steel surplus, which may be maintained over the decade ahead.[5] Also, the assumed continuation of pragmatic policies and programs would be likely to improve supplies of various products for which markets exist abroad, such as iron ore and garments.

Because of India's investment policy, it is not surprising that the export growth rate was relatively low ar first. Over time, however, India's strategy could lead to a surge in exports from industries favored by the strategy. It could be argued that this is exactly what has happened in the recent past and that exports will rise even more sharply in the near future. To put these developments into their proper perspective, two points need to be made.

First, in spite of the emphasis on heavy industry and import substitution, heavy-industry products account for only a relatively small proportion of export growth since 1971—72. Comparatively little growth is projected for the next decade as well. About 84 percent of the increase in exports between 1971—72 and 1975—76 and about 73 percent of the increase projected to 1985—86 come from sectors other than those toward which the development strategy is oriented. (This assumes that iron and steel, all engineering goods other than consumer durables, 75 percent of the exports of chemicals, and 10 percent of other exports, are products of heavy industry.)

Second, growth in heavy-industry exports is obtained at an extremely high investment cost. Justification for the investment strategy chosen by India was supposed to be the rise in the domestic investment ratio that would result from an increased supply of capital goods in the economy.[6]

---

[5] Production of finished steel in the integrated steel plants rose sharply from 4.9 million tonnes in 1974—75 to 6.9 million tonnes in 1976—77. Tata Services, Ltd., *Statistical Outline of India, 1978* (Bombay, Tata Services, Ltd. 1978), Table 60.

[6] P.C. Mahalanobis, "Some Observations on the Process of Growth of National Income," *Sankhya* 12 (September 1953).

In adopting their development strategy, the Indian authorities gave particular attention to import quotas and other restrictions that some of the countries that could be major markets for India's goods had imposed or were likely to impose. Their projections gave a pessimistic view which, when extended to exports in general, justified a development strategy based on import substitution. Attention does need to be paid to constraints on the markets for India's exports in framing the country's policies, but experience has shown that undue attention to these constraints results in the adoption of a development strategy that makes exports, even to the countries imposing such constraints, much smaller than they could have been otherwise. Inadequate attention has been devoted to increasing exports in non-traditional markets.

The internal constraints arising from unsatisfactory domestic policies are largely responsible for past stagnation of exports. Nowhere is this better illustrated than in the case of cotton textiles. Fearful of the effects of market constraints, India has suffered a steady fall in its share of textile markets. In contrast, Japan and such developing economies as Hong Kong, Taiwan, and South Korea have expanded their exports of these products tremendously over the same period.[7]

Market constraints also result from market forces, such as competition from other products or slow-growing foreign aggregate demand. Even here, however, the domestic policies of exporting countries can play a very important role. Quality improvements, cost reductions, greater regularity in supplies, and more R&D aimed at finding new uses for products can help expand exports at a steady pace, even in what appear to be stagnant or shrinking markets.

India's major exports can be classified into those for which market constraints are most important, those for which supply constraints are the critical factor, and those for which both seem equally important.

The market is the critical constraint for exports of jute, tea, tobacco, spices, and silver. Deliberate restrictions imposed by importing countries are important only for tobacco. European Economic Community (EEC) countries restrict tobacco imports from India, mainly for the benefit of some of their associate countries which are India's competitors. Projections for tobacco show extremely slow growth in export earnings, but there are still opportunities to increase earnings at a somewhat faster rate by improving quality, changing the product mix, and processing the tobacco further. Efforts in this direction are, as yet, inadequate.

----

[7] This has been extensively documented. A recent analysis is presented in John W. Mellor, *The New Economics of Growth: A Strategy for India and the Developing World* (Ithaca, N.Y.: Cornell University Press, 1976), pp. 209–214, particularly Table VIII-4.

For jute, the slow growth of the market has been mainly due to competition from such substitutes as paper, polyethylene and other film, and bulk packaging. However, growth also has been restrained by unsatisfactory quality, uncertain supplies, and high, wildly fluctuating prices. Demand shot up sharply when jute began to be extensively used for carpet backing, but even this market is being lost to flexible films. Yet little work is being done to find other uses for jute.

Silver is a special case because sales are made from stocks but exports depend ultimately on world demand. For spices and tea, constraints arise from development of competitive sources of supply and slow growth in consumption. Market constraints and domestic supply are equally important for exports of leather and leather manufactures, textiles, garments, and carpets and other handicrafts. Market constraints for each arise from restrictions imposed by industrial countries to protect domestic industries. However, Iran's progressive withdrawal as a supplier of carpets and the growth of the market in West Asia (including Iran) has made the problem, at least for the next few years, mainly one of increasing supplies.

For the first three groups of products, unfortunately, import restrictions in industrial countries are extremely important. As a result of past policy failures, India's exports are low, particularly for textiles and garments. There is great scope for changes in domestic policies to improve India's competitive position not only in the industrialized countries but also in West Asia, where markets are expanding rapidly.

Supply is the major constraint for sugar, engineering products, iron ore, oil-cakes, marine products, iron and steel, gems and jewelery, chemicals, cashews, and coffee. Markets for these products are established and growing. The domestic problems that face them differ widely, but detailed studies show that for many policy improvements and additional investment could make a vital difference to export earnings.

The items in the "other" category are mostly products of agriculture and allied activities. Among them are foodgrains, processed foods, woolen and silk fabrics and garments, and forest products. Markets exist in Europe and North America, though some products will have to overcome import barriers. For many, demand in West Asia is strong and will increase sharply over the next decade as per capita incomes rise. India is particularly well situated geographically to take advantage of this increased demand by making appropriate adjustments in investment, production, trade, and tax policies.

The "other" products also include cement, coal, and a variety of other minerals. Markets exist for these products in Pakistan, Bangladesh, West Asia, and elsewhere. The main problems are production, transport, and other domestic factors.

Generally, the main constraints on the expansion of the "other" category of exports come from domestic factors rather than markets. Yet the present development strategy neglects these products, as it neglects many of those in the major categories, on the specious argument that the markets for India's products are not likely to be adequate.

Pragmatic Indian policies can make important changes in the level and geographic pattern of Indian exports. A good opportunity is offered by Africa which is close by and where India has good political relations with most countries. Economic development in most of these countries is increasing incomes. Particular opportunities may be presented by Libya, Algeria, and Nigeria—all increasingly prosperous oil exporters—and by Portugal's former colonies, especially after they achieve political stability and begin economic development. India could export to African countries a variety of goods ranging from machinery and equipment for their development programs to consumer goods. Yet India's efforts have been inadequate and its exports small.

Any change in the situation in southern Africa will strongly affect India's exports. Rhodesia's economy is roughly comparable in size to that of Kenya, which took almost $20 million worth of exports in 1974–75 and was second only to Nigeria among India's African export partners. Should the anticipated political changes come about, Indian exports to Rhodesia could become significant. In addition, if basic political changes occur in South Africa and India ends its ban on trade with that country, the potential market for Indian goods would be substantial. South Africa is affluent, has a large population, and is close to India.

Latin America's share of India's export trade has remained insignificant since independence. A serious study of Latin American market conditions and requirements, followed by the setting up of institutional arrangements and proper shipping services, could pay rich dividends.

India's exports to North America are also low in relation to that region's share of world output. The national income of the European Economic Community as a whole is approximately equal to that of the United States, but the former has a far greater share of India's exports. The USSR, with a national income and a share of world trade both far smaller than those of the United States, is India's top export partner. Surely there is an opportunity for expanded export to the U.S. market.

Within South Asia trade with Pakistan also has been limited by political factors. Geographical contiguity and increasingly complementary economies suggest that the potential for trade between the two countries is substantial. Since Bangladesh has emerged as an independent country and has developed independent trade relations with other countries, it has become an important trading partner, accounting for well over one percent of India's exports in 1974–75.[8] India's exports to Pakistan could easily account for as much, though the pattern would be different. India's relations with Pakistan have improved somewhat and trade between the two countries has commenced. If this improvement continues, India's exports to Pakistan are likely to be large by 1980–81 and increase through at least 1985–86.

Although its relations with China have been bad, India has refused to establish normal relations with Taiwan. However, India may be able to improve relations with China without ending trade with Taiwan as the United Kingdom, the United States, Japan and other countries have done.

India has traded with the USSR and with other eastern European countries to the economic benefit of both. Negotiations may become more difficult if India moves further away from the Soviet Union. This will not necessarily reduce trade with the Soviet bloc, though the bloc's relative share would fall if India increases exports to other markets.

An Alternative Strategy and Export Prospects

Within the framework of this limited study, it is not possible to determine in detail the effects on export prospects of a shift in investment in favor of export expansion, light industries, and agriculture and its allied activities.[9] However, the significance of such a change can be shown by noting that investment requirements for modernization of the Indian cotton textile industry are probably less than the cost of a single integrated steel plant.[10] Similarly, if the cost of a basic petrochemical plant were used instead to expand downstream petrochemical in-

---

[8] India's exports to Bangladesh in 1975 amounted to $60.6 million out of India's total exports in that year of $4,299.3 million. International Monetary Fund, *Direction of Trade Annual* (Washington: International Monetary Fund, 1976), p. 137.

[9] For the justification for adopting such a policy, see Hannan Ezekiel, *The Pattern of Investment and Economic Development* (Bombay: University of Bombay, 1967) and John W. Mellor, *The New Economics of Growth*. For the long-term implications of adopting such a policy see Hannan Ezekiel, *Second India Studies: Industry* (New Delhi: Macmillan Co., 1976) and Hannan Ezekiel, *Second India Studies: An Overview* (New Delhi: Macmillan Co., 1978).

[10] The Modernization plan drawn up for (but not included in) the Fifth Plan by the Task Force on Textile Industries had an estimated total cost of Rs 532 crores, Special Supplement on Cotton Textile Industry, *The Economic Scene*, March 1977, p. 319. A more thorough-going programme could cost 50% more, say Rs 800 crores. In contrast, an official paper estimated that a medium-sized 3 million tonne integrated steel plant with infrastructural facilities would cost Rs 1800 crores, *The Economic Scene*, July 1977, p. 499.

dustries, the subsequent increase in output would more than offset the cost of the imports it would replace.[11]

A wide range of exports should benefit significantly from an investment strategy that favors agriculture and allied activities. For example, during 1975–76, natural rubber production exceeded consumption by over 12,000 tons. Relatively large stocks had accumulated and the government permitted 15,000 tons to be exported. The domestic price of top quality rubber was Rs 5200 per ton, much lower than the world price.[12] Valuing exports at a conservative price of Rs 7000 per ton, these exports earned over Rs 100 million, or nearly $12 million. Raising production from existing trees and planting new imported ones, should make it possible to increase exports to a hundred thousand tons. At the above price this would yield about $80–85 million in constant dollars by 1985–86.

The main reason for the slow growth of exports of Indian alcoholic beverages—rum, beer, gin, and whiskey—is domestic constraints. India has a large production base for such exports in its huge sugar industry and in the hops now being produced in such places as Himachal Pradesh and Kashmir. Unfortunately, the short-sighted attitude of state governments regarding the so-called loss of revenue from exports has so far prevented such exports from becoming significant. If these difficulties are overcome, it should be possible to raise export earnings from alcoholic beverages at least to $120–150 million in constant dollars by 1985–86.

Increased production of foodgrains is more likely to result in reduced imports than increased exports, though trade opportunities might result from special attention to basmati rice and other varieties of foodgrains for which there are large markets in West Asia and elsewhere. However, it is possible that the rise in employment resulting from the new investment strategy could raise demand for foodgrains faster than the supply increases, resulting in significant foodgrain imports.

Prospects for increasing exports of many other products are also promising. The total for exports of the "other" group could be very large. By 1985–86, many of the items in this group may be classified separately, perhaps being replaced by other products as new markets open up.

More investments should be made in the production of final products or components of final products for which capital-output and capital-employment ratios are generally low. Imports of the necessary raw materials and intermediate goods—for which these ratios, economics of scale, and rates of technological change are

[11] The Investment costs of a petrochemical complex at Uran near Bombay have been estimated at Rs 1200 to Rs 1500 crores, *The Economic Scene*, April 1976, p. 254.

[12] See "Rubber: Good Export Prospects," *Business Environment*, July 30, 1977.

generally extremely high—should be allowed easy entry. These are the same principles that justify a shift to foodgrains based on imported fertilizer. On this basis, increased exports of garments may have to be accompanied by some increases in imports of cotton, synthetic fibers, and possibly fabrics. Similarly, increased exports of light engineering products could reduce exports and increase imports of iron and steel.

These principles can also be extended to the chemical industry, especially petrochemicals. Development of the plastics industry on the basis of imported petrochemical products could well make Indian exports of plastic products among the most dynamic of India's exports in the next decade.

If the suggested strategy is adopted, imports of foodgrains, oil seeds, vegetable oils, and fertilizer raw materials will fall. Imports of fertilizer, iron and steel, synthetic fibers, fabrics, chemicals, and machinery (including spare parts and components) will rise. The total for both imports and exports is likely to be much higher than under the existing strategy. The dominant position of foodgrains (the imports of which will fall) implies, however, that the rise in the levels of both will be less than might otherwise be anticipated.

Income and employment under the new strategy will grow much more rapidly.[13] Thus, it seems likely that the ratio of India's exports to its national income will rise less, while the ratio to world exports will rise more under the new strategy than under the present one.

If the new strategy is adopted immediately, many of these changes could become evident by 1980–81 while others will take more time to be implemented and to significantly affect imports and exports. By 1985–86, however, the export-import picture should be significantly different.

If India adopts the new development strategy,[14] the availability of markets will become of great importance, as illustrated by the need to expand the export of textiles, fabrics, and leather products both to industrialized countries and to markets outside these countries. More restrictions by industrialized countries on imports of textiles, garments, and leather products would create difficulties for India's new strategy. Moreover, such restrictions contradict the overall policies of industrial countries aimed at encouraging the rapid economic development of less developed countries. It is self-defeating to provide economic aid to less developed countries and at the same time restrict exports from those countries that best fit their resource endowments.

---

[13] The more rapid growth in income and employment under the new strategy is the main justification for its adoption. See John Mellor, *The New Economics of Growth* and Hannan Ezekiel, *Second India Studies, An Overview.*

[14] See also Chapter 4, p. 27.

Industrialized countries also should recognize that such import restrictions are ultimately not in their own interests. The domestic industries protected by such policies generally need to be replaced by industries that offer more productive employment. Protection only slows this process. Of course, a sharp increase in imports of the products of such industries over a relatively short period creates severe problems of adjustment. Therefore it is necessary to assist labor and capital to shift to other industries as smoothly as possible.

If the OECD countries were to adopt such policies, they would make a powerful contribution to the more rapid development of the LDCs. However, the strong protectionist sentiment in most of them is strengthened by their existing economic difficulties. Strong leadership will be required to overcome this, and to provide effective programs of adjustment assistance.

The industrialized countries may fail to liberalize their policies in spite of strong arguments in favor of doing so. But India may be able to expand its exports of textiles, fabrics, and leather products significantly in markets outside the industrialized countries: Eastern Europe, non-European Economic Community countries, West Asia, Economic & Social Commission for Asia and the Pacific (ESCAP) countries, Africa, and South America. Also, industrialized countries do not restrict imports of all the products that India could easily produce in larger quantities under the new strategy. Thus, India could benefit tremendously from the adoption of the new development strategy even if there were no general liberalizing of imports of textiles, garments, and leather products by the United States and other OECD members.

The prospects for India's exports, with or without a change in its development strategy, must be considered in relation to the changes in West Asia as a result of the sharp rise in oil prices. In fact, the main markets for many of India's products in the next decade are likely to be countries in West Asia that have benefited from the oil price increase, where import restrictions to protect domestic industries are unlikely to arise.

Total exports of Iran, Iraq, and Saudi Arabia—with a combined population in 1975 estimated at over 53 million—rose from $5,604 million in 1970 to $55,414 million in 1975, an increase of 889 percent.[15] In 1975, their total exports were one-third greater than those of the United Kingdom, somewhat greater than those of Japan and France, approximately equal to those of Belgium and Holland combined, and a little over half of those of the United States.

---

[15] Mid-year population estimates for 1975 (in millions) are: Iran—33.01, Iraq—11.12, and Saudi Arabia—8.97; Total 53:10. Country pages, *International Financial Statistics* (Washington: International Monetary Fund).

Imports of the three countries amounted to only $25,814 million in 1975. Although high in absolute terms, imports were low in relation to exports and are therefore bound to rise rapidly.[16] Several factors should assist this rise. Massive investments are being made from oil revenues, mainly in infrastructure and in heavy industry (steel plants, oil refineries, etc.). These investments will rapidly increase income and consumption. But these increases will not be accompanied by a corresponding increase in domestic production of consumer goods.[17] Moreover, the value of exports will continue to mount, supplemented by earnings from the huge amounts invested abroad or added to reserves in the last few years. These earnings will increasingly affect the payments of interest and profits, and the purchase of services abroad by these countries. They are bound to reverse the direction of net flows on these accounts. Because of all this, imports in constant dollars should at least double their 1975 level by 1980–81 and will probably triple it by 1985–86. This would mean increases of more than $25 billion in five years and more than $50 billion in ten years.

The imports of these countries during the last few years consisted, to a much larger extent than normally would have been the case, of capital and intermediate goods of all kinds. This composition of imports reflected the nature of their investment programs. In the future, a large proportion of the substantial increase in imports is likely to consist of consumer goods, including a wide variety of food products. With a change in its strategy of development, India should be in a strong position to take advantage of this situation.

Even with the adoption of the alternative strategy, the actual composition of India's production and exports will depend upon the investments and policies of the next few years. The projections of possible exports under both present and new strategies take into consideration the conditions affecting the investment, production, and marketability of the different products. Nevertheless, the results must be understood as being at best only general indications of the future composition of India's exports. The analysis also has assumed that India will: make a serious attempt to achieve and maintain a high share of the rapidly expanding imports of West Asia; make a deliberate effort to expand its exports to Latin

---

[16] Imports in 1975 were: Iran $7,032 million, Iraq $4,423 million and Saudi Arabia $14,359 million; Total $25,814 million. *International Financial Statistics* (Washington: International Monetary Fund.

[17] This has been extensively documented. See for example section on "Adjustment in the Petroleum Exporting Countries" in U.N. *Supplement to World Economic Survey, 1975: Fluctuations and Developments in the World Economy*, New York, 1977 (E/5873/Rev. 1; ST/ESA/59).

America, non-EEC Europe, and Africa from current low levels; attempt to expand its exports to North America; and re-establish trade on an open basis with both Pakistan and China. The results are shown in Table 9.5.

A change in the pattern of investment and policies favoring production and export of light-industry products is likely to significantly increase exports of leather and leather manufactures, sugar, garments, gems and jewelry   marine products, carpets and other manufactures, cashews, oilcakes, coffee, spices, and other items. Total exports of engineering products are likely to be higher. Within the engineering group, exports of consumer durables and other light engineering products are likely to be much greater. Exports of heavy engineering products will remain unaffected over the next decade because of the large unutilized capacity in these industries and because a certain amount of investment would continue in these industries even under a new strategy.

A shift in the strategy toward the garment industry is likely to increase garment exports significantly. But substantial investment in the textile industry may not result in a rise in exports of textiles unless the major industrialized countries liberalize their import policies.

The position for chemicals is much more complicated. An extensive program of investment in heavy chemicals, particularly petrochemicals, is underway. It may prove difficult to slow this growth significantly within the period under consideration. Investment in the production of intermediate and final goods is likely to absorb some of the basic chemical products that would otherwise have been exported. At the same time more of these goods are likely to be consumed within the country as income and employment rise more rapidly. Thus, after taking these factors into account it has been assumed that under the new strategy exports of chemicals will be only slightly higher in 1985—86, though they might start to rise sharply thereafter.

With increased exports of light engineering products and a greater domestic consumption of these products as a result of the higher incomes generated by the new strategy, less steel is likely to be available for exports. Exports of steel are, therefore, likely to be significantly lower under the new strategy.

Exports of iron ore, tea, jute, silver, and tobacco are likely to remain unaffected by the new strategy.

Trade restrictions primarily affect textiles, garments, leather and leather manufactures, carpets, and a variety of products in the "other" category. Restrictions also are in effect for certain types of engineering products, mainly those in which investment is likely to be increased if India adopts the new development strategy. If the OECD countries liberalize import policies, India's exports of each of these groups of products will likely be higher than projected. In this case increased exports of engineering goods will tend to reduce the available surpluses of steel and to cut steel exports still further.

Table 9.5   Alternative Projections of Exports, 1985—86

(Millions of constant U.S. dollars)

| Item | Present Strategy | | New Strategy | | | |
| | | | Without Trade Liberalization | | With Trade Liberalization | |
	Amount	Rank	Amount	Rank	Amount	Rank
Engineering	1,650	1	2,000	1	2,500	1
Iron and Steel	625	2	375	9	150	18
Iron Ore	620	3	620	6	620	7
Leather and Leather Manufactures	600	4	1,000	2	1,400	2
Sugar	400	5	...	...	600	8
Garments	375	6	800	3	1,200	3
Gems and Jewelery	350	7	650	5	650	5
Marine Products	340	8	700	4	1,000	4
Textiles (exluding garments)	335	9	340	11	500	9
Tea	325	10	325	13	325	12
Carpets and Other Handicrafts	320	11	500	8	650	6
Jute	316	12	316	14	316	13
Chemicals	315	13	350	10	350	10
Silver	250	14	250	17	250	16
Cashews	208	15	260	16	260	15
Oilcakes	200	16	300	15	300	14
Coffee	187	17	335	12	335	11
Tobacco	110	18	110	19	110	19
Spices	90	19	160	18	160	17
Major Items	7,616		9,991		11,676	
Other Items	1,681		2,500		3,500	
Total	9,297		12,491		15,176	

Source: Projections made by the author.

India's total exports in 1985—86 under the new strategy, even without trade liberalization by the industrialized countries, would be about a third greater than under the present strategy. With trade liberalization they would be almost two-thirds higher. These projections should not be considered excessively high. Sharp increases in output in the relevant sectors can be brought about by relatively small shifts of resources from heavy industry. Also, India's national income will be correspondingly higher under the new strategy, but not as much as the higher exports would suggest.

Under the present strategy, the regional distribution of India's exports will change as Table 9.6 shows. The shares of West Asia and North America by 1985—86 and perhaps also of the "rest of the world " will grow. Exports to the EEC will increase substantially, but their share of the total may fall slightly. The shares of ESCAP (excluding Iran), Eastern Europe, and Africa may fall, even though total exports will rise.

Even without trade liberalization, large portions of the additional exports—particularly for products other than textiles, garments, and leather products—will go to North America, the EEC, and Japan. West Asia, however, will provide the natural market for a host of products for which India will have large exportable surpluses. The ESCAP region (except Japan) and the rest of the world will absorb the rest.

As a result, West Asia will dominate the regional distribution of India's exports. The shares of North America, EEC, ESCAP and Eastern Europe may remain more or less unchanged, though they will definitely be lower than that of West Asia. The share of both Africa and the rest of the world may be higher than under the present strategy.

If a shift in India's development strategy were accompanied by a liberalization of trade by the industrialized countries, the resulting additional exports—textiles, garments, leather and leather manufactures, carpets and other handicrafts, and certain types of engineering products—would go mainly to the industrialized countries. The shares of EEC and North America (as well as of ESCAP) would become higher, while those of West Asia and the other two regions would become lower.

A Note on Indian Imports

It can be assumed that over the next decade India will continue to be a net recipient of capital flows and that it will receive increasing amounts of foreign exchange in the form of remittances from Indian residents abroad. Since the balance of payments over the longer run is an important constraint on the country's growth rate, India is likely to follow policies that will take advantage of this situation to ensure that imports grow at an equal pace with exports. Imports are likely to continue to exceed exports at least over the next decade. The size of the

Table 9.6   Projected Distribution of India's Exports by Region

	1974–75	1985–86 Present Strategy	1985–86 New Strategy Without Trade Liberalization	1985–86 New Strategy With Trade Liberalization
			(percent)	
Economic and Social Commission for Asia and the Pacific	21	18	15	16
European Economic Community	21	19	16	20
Eastern Europe	21	17	15	13
West Asia	19	20	30	24
North America	13	18	16	20
Africa	4	3	4	3
Rest of the World	3	6	6	5

Source: For 1974–75, Table 9.1 above; for 1985–86, projections made by the author.

excess is determined by time lags in adjusting trade and development policies to the changing balance of payments situation, possibly by fluctuations in trade, and by development strategies and trade policies of industrialized countries. The composition of imports also is likely to change under different conditions.

Table 9.7 shows the structure of India's imports in 1975–76. Mineral oils and foodgrains accounted for almost 50 percent of the total. Imports of each exceeded the country's total trade deficit. Together with crude and manufactured fertilizers and iron and steel, these items accounted for nearly two-thirds of total imports. Machinery, including spare parts and components, was the largest item among other imports. Imports of iron and steel, an important item until recently, have fallen as steel production has expanded rapidly and as certain types of special steel have begun to be produced.

Most other imports consist of raw materials and intermediate goods required to

Table 9.7   India's Imports

(Millions of U.S. dollars)[a]

	1974—75		1975—76	
	Amount	Percent	Amount	Percent
Crude Oil and Petroleum Products	1,451	26	1,416	24
Foodgrains	958	17	1,547	26
Fertilizers, Crude and Manufactured	610	11	536	9
Iron and Steel	531	9	353	6
Subtotal	3,550	63	3,852	65
Food and Live Animals (excluding foodgrains)	112	2	99	2
Tobacco and Beverages	1	. . .	1	. . .
Crude Materials (excluding crude fertilizers)	214	4	209	4
Mineral Oils (excluding crude oil and petroleum products)	. . .	. . .	. . .	. . .
Animal and Vegetable Oils and Fats	44	1	21	. . .
Chemicals (excluding manufactured fertilizers)	370	7	331	6
Manufactured Goods (excluding iron and steel)	436	8	346	6
Machinery	872	15	1,019	17
Miscellaneous Manufactured Articles	59	1	61	1
Unclassified Imports	6	. . .	21	. . .
Subtotal	2,114	38	2,108	36
Total	5,664		5,960	

Source: "Changing Pattern of India's Imports," *Business Environment,* March 12, 1977.

a/ Converted from data in rupees at $1=Rs 7.9755 for 1974—75 and $1=Rs 8.65325 for 1975—76.

meet the needs of manufacturing industry. These include basic and intermediate chemicals for the chemical industry, cashews for the cashew-processing industry, and diamonds and other precious and semiprecious stones for the gems and jewelry industry.

Under the present development strategy, exports in 1985—86 are projected at about $9.3 billion. It would be safe to project imports in that year under the present strategy at between $10.5 and $11.0 billion in constant dollars. In 1975—76 exports were $4.5 billion; imports, about $6 billion. The projections for 1985—86 assume that India continues to receive as much foreign assistance as now, and that remittances from Indians abroad increase a little. Of course, if foreign assistance were increased, imports could be larger.

Oil imports by 1985—86 will depend on flows of oil from the recent oil discoveries in India and on increases in domestic demand as the economy expands. The most reasonable assumption is that oil imports are likely to rise slowly but steadily in value (even in constant dollars). However, any major new oil discoveries in India could reduce oil imports sharply.

Under the present development strategy, India's imports of foodgrains are likely to remain large over the medium term. They may rise if proposed programs to insure minimum foodgrains supplies to all are implemented. They will, of course, fluctuate from year to year, given the continued dependence of the harvest on the monsoon.

India has substantial programs for increasing production of chemical fertilizers through large, integrated fertilizer plants. Except for short periods, however, production has always lagged behind domestic demand.[18] Fertilizer imports are thus likely to remain large. Imports of fertilizer raw materials are likely to rise steadily as domestic fertilizer production increases.

Export projections for 1985—86, even under the present strategy, assume that pragmatic policies in favor of the textile and garment industries will be followed in the next few years. With insufficient attention being paid to agriculture, cotton production is unlikely to grow enough to meet the cotton textile industry's needs. India is likely to import more cotton more regularly than in the past.

India is also likely to become a fairly large importer of synthetic fibers, despite the large investment in its synthetic-fiber industry.[19] Imports of raw materials

---

[18] Production of nitrogenous fertilizers in thousand tonnes of nutrient relative to consumption (shown in brackets) was 98 (212) in 1960—61, 233 (575) in 1965—66, 830 (1479) in 1970—71 and 1535 (2031) in 1975—76. Tata Services Ltd., *Statistical Outline of India 1978*, Table 46.

[19] In view of the extremely high capital requirements of the synthetic fibre industry, the growth of supplies is not likely to match demand. The variety of fibres and yarns available

may increase slightly even though capacity is being set up to produce some of these materials. Although it has been suggested that India should permit large-scale imports of fabrics for its garment industry, India seems unlikely to do so with the present strategy.

With no change in the present strategy, imports of diamonds and other precious and semiprecious stones, raw cashew kernels, and wool will rise as exports increase.

Continued expansion of the domestic chemical industry and the projected expansion of chemical exports will call for some expansion in imports of chemicals other than fertilizers. The planned investment in the petrochemical industries, a great deal of which has already taken place, means that imports of petrochemicals will be much smaller than would otherwise have been the case.

An increase in India's foreign exchange resources by 1985—86 is likely to be used largely for the import of machinery, including spare parts and components. The government has already announced a relaxation of its import policies for capital goods.[20] Although this came too late to have a significant impact on imports in 1976—77, it will be reflected in imports in subsequent years.

While India now has a large and, in some respects, sophisticated machinery manufacturing industry, the demand will cover many areas for which no domestic manufacturing capacity exists. The domestic industry also may not be able to meet machinery demand for industries with rapid growth, or for industries which combine growth with large-scale replacement or modernization, as is likely in the textile industry.

Large-scale imports are likely in power-generating and transmission equipment. At present India is a major manufacturer and exporter of such equipment, but it may not be able to meet all of the demand created by some of the large power stations proposed for the next decade. If events force authorities to revise their power plans upward, as seems very likely, imports of power equipment may get a further boost. Imports could include types of equipment that the domestic industry can produce, but for which it cannot offer acceptable delivery dates.

India is likely to import ships and planes during the next few years. The government has announced plans for substantial investment in shipping. These plans involve purchases of ships from abroad as domestic shipbuilding capacity is small and limited to relatively small ships. Growth of India's domestic and international

---

abroad is also likely to be much greater than within the much smaller domestic industry. For polyester fibre, as in 1976—77, imports may occur to cover the shortfall in the supply of long-staple cotton for which it is an ideal substitute.

[20] "Booming Foreign Exchange Reserves and Liberalization in Imports," *Business Environment* (August 28, 1977).

air services will require imports of large, modern planes.

If domestic policies insure rapid growth in demand for engineering goods and if the projected expansion in engineering exports is realized, there will also be a substantial rise in imports of spare parts and components.

Significant changes in total trade are likewise projected if India adopts the new strategy. India's total exports in 1985–86 are projected at around $12.5 billion under the new strategy without any further relaxation of import restrictions by the OECD countries. Under these conditions imports are likely to total approximately $14 billion, $3.0 billion more than projected under the existing strategy.

If adoption of the new strategy is accompanied by liberalization of trade policies in the OECD countries, India's total exports are projected at more than $15 billion. Imports are then likely to be $16.5 to $17.0 billion, $6.0 to $6.5 billion more than with the present strategy.

Most of the individual changes are likely to be greater if there is trade liberalization. Oil imports are likely to be slightly higher under the new strategy than under the present one, mainly because of the more rapid growth of the economy.

Agricultural production should increase rapidly during the decade, as a result of its special place in the new investment program. Imports of foodgrains are likely to be virtually eliminated, unless the employment policy increases demand more than anticipated. Also, if the OECD countries liberalize trade, income and employment will grow at a faster rate, which may stimulate imports of food and agricultural raw materials.

The emphasis on agricultural production is likely to spur demand for fertilizers. Lower investment in the fertilizer industry is likely to result in much larger imports of chemical fertilizers, even after allowing for growth in production of organic fertilizers from biogas plants and town refuse treatment units, which will receive priority under the new strategy.

Even with the new role given to the textile industry, cotton imports may not be necessary because of the anticipated increases in cotton production under the new strategy. However, significant quantities of synthetic fibers for the textile industry and a variety of fabrics for the garment industry are certain to be imported as part of a program to strengthen the capacities of these industries to promote exports and economic growth.

Larger quantities of precious and semiprecious stones also will be imported, but imports of raw cashews and of wool should be lower because of greater domestic production.

Imports of basic and intermediate chemicals will be higher, and petrochemicals will be imported to provide the basis for a variety of downstream plastic and other industries.

Trade with the United States

India's trade with the United States has four main features. First, the balance of trade between the two countries has invariably shown a surplus for the United States.[21] Second, the United States has for many years had a large share of India's exports and imports. Third, in contrast, India has an insignificant share of U.S. imports and exports. Fourth, India's share in U.S. trade diminished substantially from 1966 to 1976, falling from 1.2 percent of U.S. imports to 0.6 percent, and from 3.5 percent of U.S. exports to 0.9 percent.[22]

Clothing, cotton piecegoods, leather, and footwear tend to compete strongly with U.S. domestic production. They account for $150 million, or a quarter of India's total exports to the United States (Table 9.8). The U.S. market absorbs slightly more than half of India's total exports of clothing, but India provides only 3 percent of U.S. imports (Table 9.9). India's share of the U.S. market is also small for cotton piecegoods and footwear.

India provides almost 16 percent of U.S. imports of leather. The United States may find it increasingly worthwhile to export raw hides and skins and import finished leather because the process of leather manufacturing is so laborious and polluting. At the same time, India is moving toward the export of finished leather rather than of rawhides and skins or of semiprocessed leather. There should therefore be little conflict of interest between the two countries.

The position of footwear is much different because of strong protectionist sentiment in the United States. Liberalization of imports will require a special effort along lines discussed earlier.

India of course wants the United States to liberalize imports of all these products, but it could also gain significantly if it is permitted simply to absorb a larger percentage of the natural growth of the market than its present share. For example, a 3.5 percent increase in U.S. clothing imports equals India's total exports of clothing to the United States in 1975–76. If India were to get, say, 25 percent of this growth, its clothing exports to the United States would rise by about the same annual percentage. This would be equivalent to an annual increase of approximately 10 percent in India's total clothing exports.

Based on the likely regional distribution of India's exports (Table 9.6), and assuming that the United States accounts for 90 percent of North American im-

---

[21] Reserve Bank of India, "Direction of India's Foreign Trade," *RBI Bulletin,* June 1976, Current Statistics Table 50, based on data from Government of India, Department of Commercial Intelligence and Statistics, *Monthly Statistics of the Foreign Trade of India.*

[22] "Expansion in Indo-U.S. Trade Relations," *Business Environment,* August 13, 1977.

Table 9.8   Commodity Composition of India's Exports to United States, 1975—76

(Millions of U.S. dollars)

	India's Exports to United States		India's World Exports	
	Amount	Share of Total (%)	Amount	U.S. Share (%)
Clothing	88	15	168	52
Jute Manufactures	88	15	287	31
Sugar	83	14	546	15
Cashews	46	8	111	41
Pearls	40	7	142	28
Fish and Fish Prep.	37	6	146	25
Cotton Piecegoods	32	6	248	13
Crude Animal and Vegetable Materials	25	4	250	10
Leather and Footwear	30	5	254	12
Coffee	19	3	77	24
Floor Covering and Tapestries	11	2	117	10
Metal Manufactures	11	2	472	2
Spices	9	2	82	11
Others	71	12	1,655	4
Total	590	100	4,555	12

Source: "Expansion in Indo-U.S. Trade Relations," *Business Environment*, August 13, 1977.
Data in rupees converted at Rs 8.65 per U.S. $.

Table 9.9   India's Share of Certain U.S. Imports, 1975—76

(Millions of U.S. dollars)

	Indian Exports to United States	U.S. Imports	Percentage Share of India
Cotton Piecegoods	32	1,234	3
Cothing	88	2,536	3
Leather	21	132	16
Footwear	9	1,301	1

Source: For India's exports to U.S.A., Table 9.8; for U.S. imports (for 1975), United Nations, *Yearbook of International Trade Statistics, 1976.* (ST/ESA/STAT/SER. G/25).

ports from India, India's exports to the United States in constant dollars in 1985—86 are projected to rise to around:
1. $1.50 billion under the present strategy.
2. $1.75 billion under the new strategy, without any liberalization of import policy by the OECD countries.
3. $2.70 billion under the new strategy with a liberalization of import policy by those countries.

The increase of almost $1 billion from trade liberalization shows its importance to India: only massive amounts of foreign assistance could equal it.

In 1975, the total imports of the United States amounted to almost $97 billion. If these imports increase at a rate of just over 4 percent annually, in constant dollars they will amount to $150 billion in 1985—86. India's share will then amount to 1 percent under the present strategy, a little over 1 percent under the new strategy without trade liberalization, and almost 2 percent under the new strategy with trade liberalization. This last projection does not take into account the higher level that total U.S. imports would reach if the United States liberalized import policy.

These figures imply that India's share in U.S. imports will rise somewhat above recent levels over the next decade. But they are by no means excessively large, particularly when considered in relation to increased export capabilities through adoption of the new strategy.

The rise in U.S. imports from India postulated above will be accompanied by corresponding increases in U.S. exports to India. The levels and nature of India's imports in 1985–86 under various conditions have been discussed in an earlier section.

The United States is a major supplier of most of the products India will import under the new strategy, particularly of the more sophisticated ones. It should, therefore, have no difficulty in expanding its exports to India as its imports from India rise.

Comment

Lawrence Veit

We are indebted to Hannan Ezekiel for a wide-reaching survey of India's export potential and for his analysis of how a shift of government priorities to agriculture and light industry at the expense of heavy industry could improve export earnings. Ezekiel's paper, like any extensive study, is bound to raise minor disagreements over fact, but the more significant comment falls into the category of putting his analysis of foreign trade into the perspective of India's larger political economy and the still larger context of the world economic environment. Accordingly, this comment is structured to deal first with a series of fundamental issues and later to question a few of the specific analyses and conclusions in Ezekiel's paper.

The most sophisticated methods of economic research have yet to provide a comprehensive means for measuring the psychological, transportation, quality, marketing, and numerous other factors that affect a country's competitive position for various products in world markets. Even so, one can question whether too much is assumed about how the shift to an agriculture and light industry strategy would affect India's foreign trade. It would help to know more about where India's comparative advantage lies, for generalizations about relative wages in poor and rich countries and how they dictate that poor countries should undertake tasks with high labor value-added are already well understood. In particular, which product lines within the category of high value-added by labor offer India the best opportunities, not just vis-à-vis the developed economies, but also relative to other developing countries? Land devoted to cashew cultivation, for example, might be withdrawn from some other use. But which one? Conceivably, it could preempt land from sugar, in which case even a stepped-up program of increasing productivity in sugar cultivation might not permit the supply of sugar for export to reach the targeted amount.

From a geographic viewpoint, shifting production patterns abroad raises important questions. Australia, for example, has altered its development policies since changing governments. It is now more inclined to expand its exploitation of minerals, including iron ore, a development that will narrow the scope for Indian exports of this commodity. As Ezekiel notes, the East Africans are becoming more aggressive in the processing of cashews. What about cultivation? Could India, given its costs of production based on market priced factors of production, compete with an expanded East African cashew nut industry? Is it not inevitable that the East Africans will gradually increase their share of value-added in cashew production and marketing, leaving less scope for a large Indian improvement in this area?

Answers to such questions may be clear in some instances but, as illustrated by the phenomenon of rapidly changing anchovy availability in Peru's waters or by the emergence of South Korea as the world's leading exporter of plywood, a large element of uncertainty is bound to exist. Perhaps nothing more can be added to the analysis of Indian export potential than a further emphasis on product and geographic diversification. But, unearthing more evidence of where India's comparative advantage lies would help pinpoint the somewhat unbalanced development strategy that would permit India to concentrate its efforts and, by achieving economies of scale in production and marketing, gain real success in particular export markets.

The success of India's export effort will depend critically on economic conditions in importing nations or, more generally, on the state of the world economy. Ezekiel is well justified in noting the Middle East as a market where India has done especially well recently and as a potential source of new exports. But are his assumptions about the rest of the world too sanguine? The problem is: as long as the internal political and economic elements of instability, which currently exist in many oil-consuming countries, are exacerbated by high oil prices—more through the adverse balance of payments effect than through income transfer or inflation—the world economy will remain unhealthy.[1]

Slow growth rates, the paradox of high unemployment coinciding with a new private investment preference for labor-saving technology, and underutilized industrial capacity may be features of this future world. If so, international trade is likely to rise only slowly as countries resort to various policies to stimulate domestic demand at the expense of imports. In this environment, any argument against protectionism, however logical and/or sympathetic to the poor, may not have much influence over public policy. Moreover, countries and companies can be expected to improve their prospects, sometimes through concerted action, by becoming more aggressive in world markets. Their competitive behavior will reduce the profitability of export activities and, in some cases, displace Indian exports.

These three features—depressed GNP growth in the major consuming nations,

[1] For a comprehensive statement of this view, see my article "Troubled World Economy," *Foreign Affairs*, January 1977, pp. 263–279.

protectionism, and heightened international competition—suggest that the next several years may not be an ideal time for seeking to expand export markets. And, ironically, the precise development that would permit the oil-consuming nations to accelerate their development and imports—less reliance on OPEC energy—implies that Middle East countries would have less foreign exchange purchasing power as a result of lower oil sales volumes (and possibly also lower price), thereby causing a retrenchment in India's new export markets in this area.

Among the market imperfections that bedevil theoretical economic investigation is the multinational company and the oligopolistic (sometimes even monopolistic) control it holds over particular technologies, markets, and so forth. To say that India should explore more fully the advantages it might derive from accelerated foreign investment in Indian manufacturing is to invite a variety of criticisms, some directly related to the behavior of multinationals, some related more generally to an Indian aversion to bigness and private enterprise. Be that as it may, the multinationals have played a leading role in some of the more successful developing countries. Thus, it may be less than revolutionary to suggest that India further pursue the issue of how international companies can be used to develop new exports. A further advantage of foreign investment, of course, lies in potential import substitution, to say nothing of the technological transfer, capital inflow, and domestic employment impact it may engender.

India's trade relations with Eastern Europe are fundamentally tied to its aid and political relations with that area, and not subject to the same analysis as relations with other nations. It is not inconceivable that India could combine better political relations with Washington and a major expansion of its trade with the Soviet Union. Several decades of experience provide ample evidence of Moscow's desire to gradually increase its economic ties with India. Although the two countries have increasingly found difficulties in maintaining a serious, nondefense-oriented aid relationship, bilateral trade has grown apace. In fact, the mutual needs have fit so well that the Soviets have even proposed partial integration of the two countries' five-year plans. Concerns to the contrary, neither India nor the USSR has shown an inclination to cool relations since Mrs. Gandhi's defeat. The aid relationship would probably be less significant if India were to change its development strategy away from the past emphasis on heavy industry. Even so, assuming India can supply goods that the Soviets need, and that Moscow is willing to part with commodities that India would otherwise have to acquire with foreign exchange, bilateral trade with Eastern Europe may be a significant source of growth.

It is surely true that India's past failure to increase it exports faster has been at least partly because of its decision to give priority to heavy industry instead of to agriculture and light industry. But to reverse those priorities would be merely a necessary, not a sufficient, condition for accelerated exports. The domestic forces arrayed against exports, which can be roughly classified as either institutional or more purely economic, must be considered before reaching the conclusion that a change of priorities would spur exports.

The institutional barriers to exporting and other forms of economic activity in India are well known.[2] The gap in Professor Mahalanobis' understanding of economics (especially his lack of appreciation of the flexibility foreign trade can impart to economic progress), cited by Ezekiel, is only one of the relevant factors. Equally important were the disincentives and inefficiencies introduced by the decision to involve the bureaucracy in almost every aspect of India's economic activity; the prejudice against private enterprise, especially the large domestic industrial houses and multinationals; and the government's efforts to skim off as much revenue as possible from export activity, which led, for example, to the export tax on jute and the loss of an important market to competing jute-producing countries, as well as to synthetics. Although it is inconceivable—and no doubt undesirable—that any Indian government in the foreseeable future will renounce planning and government intervention in the economy, the way in which official policy is formulated and implemented can have an extraordinary impact on the efficacy of the export effort.

It would be useful to go beyond these generalizations and to explore who can be expected to bear the future burden of producing for export and marketing abroad (government, multinationals, the large domestic houses, or other bodies); what incentives there will be to boost sales abroad; and how the Delhi and state bureaucracies will relate to the effort. Not least of the issues raised by the prospect of a higher level of exports is financial: what institutions will provide the needed domestic and external credit, at what price, and for what maturities?

Analyzing the impact of India's domestic micro- and macroeconomic policies on development and exports is difficult but has received enough attention to merit comment.[3] Ezekiel notes that India's recent success in exporting has been aided by the decline of the foreign exchange value of the rupee, due in part to the historical linkage of the rupee to sterling and the rapid depreciation of Britain's currency. The rupee's foreign exchange rate is now set according to the exchange rates of India's major trading partners, a system in which sterling can still have an important effect. But what of the future, when sterling is likely to be bolstered by the onrush of oil from the North Sea and possibly by other favorable develop-

---

[2] Lawrence A. Veit, *India's Second Revolution: The Dimensions of Development* (New York: McGraw-Hill Book Co., 1976).

[3] Jagdish N. Bhagwati and T.N. Srinivasan, *Foreign Trade Regimes and Economic Development: India* (New York: National Bureau of Economic Research, 1975).

ments? Will Indian authorities seek to prop up the exchange rate of the rupee to maintain the relationship with the British pound, or will they permit fundamental forces affecting competitive position to depress the foreign exchange rate? It is far from clear how India will resolve conflicts between its domestic objectives such as curbing inflation (implying the need for a strong rupee) and its international goals such as exporting (implying depreciation).

Looked at from a different angle, one would like to have a better feel for the relationship between India's domestic GNP growth rate and its exports, expecially under the proposed new strategy favoring agriculture and light industry. Historically, the first major stimulus to export growth came in the 1969–71 period when industrialists went looking for foreign markets because of the softness of domestic sales. To the extent that the large size and profitability of the home market limits the incentive for companies to sell abroad, India is akin to the United States. Is the Indian economy to become export led? Or are there constraints such that higher exports, by depriving Indian industry of needed inputs, could actually become a depressant on the home economy? Intuitively it is clear that higher exports would permit more imports, and that India should gain from the exchange as the laws of comparative advantage come into play. In fact, however, the proliferation of market imperfections, transport costs, and other barriers to international exchange suggest the need for more detailed analysis of this issue.

It is ironic that thirty years after independence the three most significant import items (food, fuel, and fertilizer) could all be replaced by domestic production if the government of India were to give this a higher priority. Countless studies have shown that water, hybrid seeds, pesticides, and fertilizer can be used to vastly increase food output.[4] Reserves of a variety of fuels (notably coal, oil, uranium and other atomic minerals) are available, although fairly costly to exploit. Furthermore, the pressing need for fertilizer and the unreliability of international supplies suggest the need for a multifold increase of domestic fertilizer production, even though this would require large capital investments.

India has already taken steps to reduce its imports of these three items, but if the issue of changing priorities is raised, then it would seem desirable to explore the relative merits of trying still harder to produce import substitutes. Not only might the cost be less than developing new export markets, the attendant risks might also be smaller. Thus, one must dare to raise the subject of import substitution on a selective basis, even though the debate will bring out some very undesirable autarkic sentiments.

The geographic and country analysis in Ezekiel's paper appears generally correct. One wonders, nonetheless, whether sales to Africa and Latin America could

---

[4] John W. Mellor, *The New Economics of Growth: A Strategy for India and the Developing World* (Ithaca, N.Y.: Cornell University Press, 1976).

really be increased without a very large effort on India's part. It is far from clear that India should concentrate more attention on these countries given (1) the limited size of population and low per capita incomes in most of them; (2) the import restraints dictated by shortages of foreign exchange; and (3) the frequent use by competing nations of supplier credits to finance exports. In contrast, India's exports to North America seem small relative to the potential size of this market. The United States, while hardly free of protectionist policies, is likely to be more liberal toward Indian exports than many other OECD nations. With notable exceptions, it eschews import quotas and it has no large former colonial constituency to which it offers preferences. Finally, it does not seem prudent to suggest that India's trade with China might by 1985–86 be as large as its trade with Iran or Japan. Even if China should make a sharp departure from its long-standing autarkic policies, it is unlikely to generate sufficient exports of its own production to afford to become a significant importer from India.

With respect to particular commodities, more than average uncertainty applies to exports of iron ore, iron and steel, and agricultural products. Australia and other countries are likely to be bringing new supplies of iron ore into the international marketplace at a time when depressed global demand is adversely affecting some of the largest users of iron ore and steel products. The iron and steel industries of most countries are now operating well below capacity, and world competition in this area is fierce. Moreover, technical factors such as the gradual substitution of lighter materials for steel in automobiles are reducing the growth of final demand. Comparably, because agriculture is one of the most heavily regulated economic sectors in most producing and consuming countries, one must ask whether India's markets for sugar, coffee, cashews, and other products will be growing very fast. In addition, will competition from other producers for these traditionally slow-growing markets leave Indian exports of these commodities with much growth potential? As a last point, while I sympathize with Ezekiel in his assumption that the "other" category of exports may grow rapidly, I think his assumption that it will increase fifty percent faster than the items he has looked at more specifically seems unjustifiably optimistic.

The central question to which these comments lead is whether India, in seeking to redress its longstanding underemphasis of exports, runs a danger of overshooting its objective, or of trying to get results within an unreasonably short period. True, the shift in priorities from heavy industry to agriculture and light industry—justifiable on purely domestic grounds—would tend to raise exports. But market development abroad and the domestic process of investment, labor training, quality control, and so forth take time. Thus, given the period of troubled world economies that appears to lie ahead, it may be more prudent for India to avoid a development strategy which depends too heavily on its making important break-throughs in export markets.

X

Reviving American Aid to India: Motivation, Scale, Uses, Constraints

John P. Lewis

The hypothesis of this chapter and the one following is that the United States, for reasons that do not primarily turn upon its concern for or linkage to India as a nation, may find cause rather soon to radically increase the flow of economic assistance to that country. This chapter first sketches the rationale for such a move and speculates about its scale, then considers whether it would be economically useful and examines the political constraints with which such a venture would have to contend. Chapter 11 tries to bring the issues into more concrete focus by laying out, for argument's sake, a particular pattern of aid revival that might be both constructive and politically feasible.

Rationale and Scale

India is not the favorite country of many Americans, including foreign policy makers and influencers, and including many who are well disposed toward developing countries in general. For a variety of good and bad reasons, soured perceptions of India were widespread in Washington and elsewhere in the United States before the Indira Gandhi government began a major encroachment on human rights in the "emergency" declared in June 1975.

The process of resounding yet orderly constitutional repair that India accomplished in 1977—the surprising way in which the regime chose at the beginning of that year to resubmit itself to comparatively open and fair vetting by the electorate and then the still more surprising outcome of that election—has been viewed with enthusiasm by many Americans. Yet this has only put the country-to-country relationship back to where it was some time before the emergency. The diplomatic branches of both governments wish to further rehabilitate relations. As for foreign aid, however, the diplomatic establishments of both countries are against going back to the "big aid" days of the sixties. The U.S. side does not see a strong geopolitical case for a heavy commitment of resources to South Asia; the Indian side wishes to avoid American intrusions. Both diplomatic establishments recognize that aid relationships, especially bilateral ones, have an underlying tendency (even though, with care, it can be curbed) to become conflicted and contentious. Thus, when they are thinking in essentially political and diplomatic terms, the aid resumption of which both governments now speak would be very limited. The accent of an aid program would be on mutuality, reciprocity, and civility. One would build modestly on the Joint Commission experiment begun by the two governments in October 1974.

The hypothesis of Chapters 10 and 11 is that something very much more ambitious (although not entailing, in any literal way, a return to the pattern of the sixties) may be in the wings—not because India is India, but because it accounts for three-fifths of the population of the whole Fourth World, that is, the poorest countries of the developing world.[1] A major shift in the American posture toward poor countries in general is under consideration in Washington. Strong voices in the administration, the Congress, and throughout the country are arguing that the United States must alter its grudging, largely defensive reaction to the demands for a new international economic order that have been reverberating through the developing world since 1973; that there are reasons of national interest, long and broadly conceived, as well as of conscience and global responsibility, for a more positive response from the world's most affluent great power; and that the response must be focused on the problems and needs of the planet's poorest people—who are disproportionately concentrated in the poorest countries. There is no way remotely consistent with the basic rationale of such a policy shift to bypass the country that will account for 60 percent of the new policy's main target group.

The further assumption in chapters 10 and 11 is that the policy dimension in which a major U.S. move on the North-South front will be easiest (not easy) in the next few years will be that of concessional transfers. Other items on the New International Economic Order (NIEO) agenda, notably those involving trade liberalization, especially with regard to processed commodities and manufactures, have great and, from a global perspective, constructive potential. But they are murderously difficult politically just now. Although such reforms deserve spirited pushing, one senses that many Organization for Economic Cooperation and Development (OECD) regimes may do well to avoid a net retreat on trade policy in the near term while their reemployment efforts continue to be impeded by inflation.

Foreign aid, despite its image of unpopularity and, indeed, the near certainty that it will experience few surges of spontaneous grass-roots support in the foreseeable future, does not engage congressional constituency politics to anything like the same degree as trade. To be sure, as committee and subcommittee chair-

---

[1] Enumerations of the Fourth World typically leave out China, less because of its prosperity than of its differentness.

men and ranking members, particular legislators do become specialized, expert, and determined in their opposition to foreign aid. Yet it is probably still true that no American congressman ever lost his seat for supporting aid; it is too low-salience a subject. Consequently, contrary to the familiar diagnosis (common in the United States since the early sixties) that the public ties the Congress's hands and the Congress the president's, expanded aid is one of those things where an American president stands a particularly good chance of getting an approximation of what he wants—if he is prepared to spend some of his scarce political capital in its behalf. This is all the more the case if a substantial part of the increased assistance sought can take the form of augmented food aid—where there is a reasonable probability that constituency politics will become engaged in *support* of the effort.

None of this is to say that aid expansion is easy, in the United States or in most other OECD countries. It could be argued that, until now, no American president since Eisenhower has been prepared to pay such high political opportunity costs for aid as these chapters contemplate. Yet my assumption is that if the Carter administration is genuinely serious about shifting the North-South posture of the United States and finds reason to concentrate its early effort on concessional transfers it may indeed—considering on the one hand the UN target of 0.7 percent of the gross national product (GNP) for rich countries' Overseas Development Assistance (ODA), and on the other the rather miserable 0.25 percent or so to which U.S. ODA lately has eroded—decide to move the fraction toward the 0.5 percent level by fiscal year 1982. Further, I assume that the president and his allies in the Congress could achieve most of this objective, raising the ODA fraction, say, to 0.45 percent of GNP, and that in a federal budget of $500 billion, ways could be found to keep the resulting extra $4 billion or so of U.S. transfers fiscally manageable.

For present purposes, the question then becomes how much of an expanded annual U.S. ODA total of, say, $8½ billion in 1977 dollars could be expected to go to India. In the middle sixties (1965 through 1967) the annual flow of net U.S.-originating ODA to India (bilateral grants, loans, and food aid plus the U.S. contribution to IDA loans, all net of repayments of principal and interest) was about $1.5 billion in 1977 prices, or about 20 percent of all U.S. ODA. Total U.S. ODA equaled about 0.5 percent of the gross national product. In Indian fiscal year 1976–77 U.S.-originating ODA, now consisting mainly of the U.S.-financed share of India's net receipts from IDA together with some PL 480 netted against India's servicing of past U.S. loans, had been reduced to about $200 million. This amounted to about 5 percent of U.S. ODA worldwide, which itself, as a fraction of the gross national product, had shrunk to half its value in the earlier period.

Under the general scenario of aid expansion being hypothesized, there are three reasons why India's share of the total could be expected to rise radically. First, it would be a principle of the scenario to concentrate concessional transfers on the poorest countries, with accommodations for the middle-income developing countries taking the form of better, more reliable access to private and institutional capital at less concessional rates, as well as such improved access to OECD goods markets as can be eked out politically.

Second, India's aid share in the past has always been a victim of the large-country problem. In arriving at their aid allocations all donors, including the United States, have tended to count flags rather than noses. The poor-*people*-oriented rationale of the kind of aid expansion being projected should lean against this tendency: Indians' per capita aid share should be penalized less than before by the fact that so many Indians are gathered under one flag.

Third, even if not replaced by a particular sense of closeness, the special prejudice against India that characterized official American attitudes following the 1971–72 troubles between the two countries presumably would be wiped away in the new era of North-South policy we are contemplating.

It would be consistent with these considerations for India, which accounts for 60 percent of the poorest countries' population, to account for at least 50 percent of the expanded U.S.-originating ODA. Yet a twenty-fold expansion of anything in a short period, let alone a ten-fold expansion of a country's relative share both of which would be implied—has a kind of *per se* implausibility. So let us scale down radically—by half—to a five-fold expansion of the relative share from 5 percent to 25 percent, and a ten-fold increase in dollar volume from $200 million to $2 billion. The present contention is that nothing less than this for India would be consistent with the theory of the general aid expansion being assumed.

Obviously, the arithmetic is rough. But the message is clear: any way one cuts it, a serious U.S. response to NIEO demands for transfers would mean a whacking rise in U.S. aid to India. To repeat, my working hypothesis is that within a few years (discussion below indicates that the increase would be spread over at least four years, not crowded into one or two) the level of concessional U.S.-originating transfers flowing to India through both bilateral and multilateral channels should, net of India's counterflowing debt service, rise about $1.8 billion in 1977 dollars. Given this order-of-magnitude premise, the questions we address are (1) whether such an aid expansion could be economically useful, (2) whether it would be politically and administratively feasible, given the conditions that (drawing on past experience and current perceptions) donor and recipient each would seek to inject into the transfers regime, and (3) what characteristics and composition would be most likely to render a rejuvenated Indo-U.S. aid program workable as well as constructive. This third matter is discussed in chapter 11.

The Economic Usefulness of Enlarged Transfers

There is no mystery about the answer to the question of usefulness. If greatly expanded transfers to India were phased in constructively and designed properly, and if internal policies were accommodating, these transfers could be enormously helpful. But the case for economic need warrants careful statement because (1) in India and elsewhere there has been so much recent emphasis on the virtues of self-reliance and (2) India at the moment gives the strange appearance, not only of doing better economically but, by her own past standards, of being chock-a-block with reserves of both food and foreign exchange.

It is true that India's recent economic performance has been better than usual. Agriculture had a record year in 1975—76 and, despite poorer weather, did not slip badly in 1976—77. Farm inputs are in reasonably good supply. Industrial efficiency has improved; operating rates, especially in the large public sector plants, are up sharply. Controls have been liberalized. Exports, especially such nontraditional types as iron ore and engineering services, have been gaining buoyantly. Smuggling and black market transactions have been sharply reduced, helping above-the-table remittances from Indians abroad to surge—a surge that is being sustained by the flow of Indian workers to the Middle East. Income tax enforcement has improved (although it still has a long way to go). Inflation, stopped in its tracks in 1975, revived in 1976, but in much more limited fashion. In the two years ending March 1977, one with good, the other with indifferent, weather, annual growth of real gross national product was more than 5 percent; it had averaged a scant 3.5 percent during the quarter-century beginning in 1950. Moreover, the two most conspicuous constraints on past growth are visibly relaxed. Foodgrains stocks held by the government exceed 20 million tons. (Ten years ago distinguished Indian agricultural economists were doubting India could assemble a buffer of as much as 7 million tons in the foreseeable future.) And the foreign exchange reserve, which was only $625 million as recently as March 1974, three years later had soared to $3.6 billion and is now approximately $5 billion, or ten months worth of imports at the current rate. But both of these stocks—of food and of foreign exchange—may be pleasant aberrations. The food position, although reflecting an underlying improvement in agriculture, is the work of good monsoons, a substantial inflow of earlier-arranged food imports, and effective maintenance of (incentive) support prices for farmers in the face of bumper crops. A couple of bad monsoons could wipe out the buffer; and there is no proof yet that the trend of agricultural output is outpacing trend expansion in the effective demand for food.

The surge in foreign exchange reserves is a particular surprise, given the dire forecasts everyone shared in 1974 after the oil price explosion. The expected jump in the import bill for oil, fertilizer, and food did indeed occur: it increased five-fold from fiscal year 1972—73 to fiscal year 1974—75. But a combination of exports gains, import restraints, increased aid funding, accommodations by the International Monetary Fund (IMF), and improvements in invisibles (mainly remittances) was sufficiently robust to convert an expected $350 million decline in reserves into a moderate gain in 1974—75, to add nearly $800 million in 1975—76, and to keep reserves rising to the levels just indicated.

It can be hoped that much of the recent export gain is projectable. However, the stimuli to exports provided by the slack in domestic markets during this period and by the downward float of the rupee while it remained tied to sterling presumably will not continue; some particular surges, for example, the surge in sugar in 1974—75, cannot be sustained; and the rate of grain from the break-through of engineering and other exports into Middle Eastern markets may taper. On the imports side, the dampening of oil imports that has been achieved by stern conservation measures probably can, without inhibiting growth, be extended thanks to the country's good luck with offshore oil exploration and now, at long last, the vigor with which that production is being brought in. But the sluggish importation of raw materials, components, and spare parts and of capital goods must be stepped up to facilitate industrial growth. Major portions of India's recent receipts of financial capital, including oil credits from Iran and Iraq and, in 1974—75 and 1975—76, $660 million from the IMF, were designed to cushion the first oil-price shock. Not only are they unlikely to be repeated; they have added to the nation's debt service burden (which in 1976—77 already was estimated at $860 million). Finally, it is unlikely that the remittances performance is fully sustainable. Some of it has probably been a transfer of stock, not of current income; the gains in, maybe even the level of, the flow from Indians working in the Middle East may soon fade.

In short, the likelihood is that with a normal mixture of luck, both the food and the foreign exchange reserves will be run down, especially if the country presses its expansion effort as it should. The need for such pressing is unabated: per capita, the country is still one of the world's poorest. The condition of its underemployed low-end poor still is abysmal. And if one looks beyond the cushioning temporarily afforded by good stocks, dimension after dimension of the development program that the country needs, and seemingly wants, faces a resources constraint.

The resources problem can be illustrated in three vital and linked policy areas: antipoverty proemployment programs, food policy, and food production promotion. Consider first, for baseline purposes, the pre-March 1977 stance of the Gandhi government on each of these policy areas: then the position, post-election, toward which the Janata government seems to have been moving in these areas.

The resources constraint on India's attack on low-end poverty and under-employment stood out starkly in the Fifth Five Year Plan document that the Indira Gandhi government's planning commission finally issued in September 1976 (halfway through the plan period, after pondering the international oil-, food-, and fertilizer-price shocks that had assaulted India during the start of the period). This was the same planning commission that in 1972 and 1973 had coined the concept of "minimum needs" in India and contributed to the international rhetoric attacking "trickle down" and demanding direct attacks on mass poverty and unemployment. The September 1976 document was almost totally silent on these subjects. This was not necessarily because the regime was not serious about its pro-poor purposes: at the same time state bureaucracies were being pressed from Delhi to redistribute land, distribute house sites to the landless, contrive nonelitist institutional substitutes for traditional money lending, promote minimum agricultural wages, and otherwise shore up the weaker classes. The blocking factor, rather, was resources. Once planners and financial authorities had made realistic (not optimistically understated) provision for the expansion of the economy's productive core, including agriculture—they aimed for 5 percent overall growth—they could not, in their projections, find enough resources domestic or foreign, to provide very much for the antipoverty "periphery."

In particular, the central planners made no move to generalize a supplementary employment scheme that, inverting the national priorities, the state of Maharashtra had commenced a year or two earlier. Under this arrangement Maharashtra has been allocating nearly $60 million off the top of its annual development budget to provide useful construction jobs on what are meant to be reasonably well-prepared and managed rural projects for all who are ready to do hard work under austere conditions at comparatively low wages. Applied nationwide, such a program could generate something equivalent to an extra income and employment to many more than that, because most workers would be part-timers. But it also would cost in the neighborhood of $1 billion a year, more than 10 percent of the total projected plan outlay.

The resource constraints on the antipoverty program were real as well as financial: whereas Maharashtra could count on drawing food from elsewhere in the country, there was no confidence that in a normal agricultural year India as a whole could meet the added food demand that would be generated by a massive employment scheme without extra imports. The same constraint inhibited the previous regime's food policy decisions. For decades India has been trying to manage food supply, distribution, and pricing with a shifting patchwork of *ad hoc* controls, "food zones," government attempts to procure from farmers at below-market prices, government retail ration shops, and occasional nationalizations of whole categories of wholesale food trade. Increasingly ministers and senior officials have been recognizing that this system is not only inefficient; by failing to stabilize consumer supplies and prices as domestic output fluctuates with the monsoons, it exacts two grievous costs: it subjects the whole development effort to disruptive, stop-go demand management; and because it is the poor who get crowded out of the market when prices surge, the impact of instability is grossly inequitable.

Moreover, there is some agreement about the shape of needed reforms. The country already has in operation two of the appropriate pieces for a market-stabilizing regime: a system of support prices for protecting producer incentive in bumper years and a central government foodgrains-trading corporation that by now has acquired some of the staff, expertise, warehousing, and other logistics required for conducting effective public stocking and trading. The reform program that appeals to many would have two parts. For the poorest classes of food buyers, rural as well as urban, there would be some (more effective) form of subsidized distribution. But, perhaps more important, the (rather well-articulated) private market on which general consumers would depend would be buffered by sufficient governmental buying, stocking, and selling to smooth consumer supplies and prices.

Successful implementation of such a rationalized food policy could be singularly constructive. But the politics are very difficult; for example, whereas the reform almost surely would require letting the private market work nationwide, India's history of recurrent droughts and famines has embedded a psychology of local protectionism vis-à-vis food. The would-be reformers, therefore, need a fail-safe resources position, and this is what the previous regime felt it lacked. First, there was no assurance that India will not for some time continue to run average food deficits (the World Bank projects 5–6 million tons annually). Second, the market-stabilizing model requires heavy average investment in buffers, and if the new food system were not established before the present stocks eroded, this would add to the system's net requirements. Third, more food subsidization for the poor would raise effective demand further. On all three counts, reformed food policy promised beyond the short run to require food imports that India could ill afford on nonconcessional terms.

A third example of an activity bottlenecked by resources has been food production itself. This is now and, indeed, was during most of the Gandhi regime the centerpiece of the Indians' own planning for core production areas. Yet resources remain an endemic constraint. Agricultural research is still underfunded. Many aspects of the development and management of that most pivotal of all subcontinental farming inputs—water—have been constrained by scant budgets: speedier completion of large and medium irrigation projects and development of distribution in their common areas, extension of minor irrigation schemes, the surveying of the country's copious groundwater resources and improvement of drainage in the plains, the promotion of coherent small-watershed management in nonirrigated areas.

More generally, if impressionistically, with regard to the linked set (especially water, fertilizer, and energy) of "new agriculture" inputs, there appears to be an array of large, potentially rewarding project possibilities that have not yet been properly evaluated, let alone taken up. Some of these (e.g., redeployments of the whole "eastern waters" system) would be inherently large undertakings with large indivisibilities. Others (e.g., rural biogas and solar energy possibilities) would, to be consequential, be large aggregations of highly decentralized ventures. The government of India can be faulted for not having done sufficient homework to know which of these hypothetical schemes make solid cost-effective sense. But the government has been inhibited, surely, by the feeling that however promising a proper benefit-cost analysis might reveal them to be, their absolute cost would exceed whatever spare room might remain in the financial frame once provision had been made for existing commitments. Yet if the gap between present Indian farming performance and potential is going to be narrowed with any speed, it seems almost certain that some of these lumpier investments must be undertaken.

As a newly formed amalgam, the Janata government is still defining its economic program. Its rhetoric is more explicitly aligned than that of its predecessors with what many of us in the past half-dozen years have come to call "the new development strategy": greater emphasis on agriculture, labor-intensive technology, small-scale industry, comparative-advantage exports, decentralization, and direct redressal of poverty. In each of the three policy areas just noted the new government shows positive inclinations. Given its political composition, there may be reason for skepticism about the depth of its net commitment to the kind of from-the-bottom-up rural reform the rhetoric espouses; all the same, the government is now projecting the early launching of a Maharashtra-type local works program nationwide on a 500 (out of 5,000) development-blocks scale. In the food policy area the government has decided, first in the case of wheat, then more significantly and bravely in the case of rice, to go to a "single zone," that is, to let the private market work nationwide. And the priority for agriculture—the scale, for example, of mooted investments in irrigation and drainage—is very high.

At the same time, during its first nine months the new government ran scared on the resources side. Its first (June 1977) budget was longer on continuity than change. The regime had to weather a temporarily renewed surge of inflation. And its fiscal instincts, lodging in those two seasoned and redoubtable Gujaratis atop the decision structure—the prime minister, Morarji Desai, and the finance minister, H. M. Patel—were distinctly conservative. It is argued below that whether or not India seizes its present growth-cum-equity opportunities, and whether, therefore, a major need for aid will emerge two or three years from now will depend heavily on the boldness with which the leadership commits the country's own assets to its alleged priorities. But first we ought to review the stakes at issue.

Elsewhere I have argued that India faces, instead of a continuous spectrum of macro policy options, more nearly binary alternatives.[2] Characteristically, post-independence India's average growth has been a sluggish, low-metabolism business. Spurts of acceleration never have succeeded in galvanizing the sprawling, almost multinational diversity of the Indian system into sustained commitment to a higher growth path. Repeatedly Indian planners have targeted (a judicious, middle-of-the-road kind of) 5 percent growth—and then have had to settle for a 3—3.5 percent performance that has raised average per capita income a scant percentage point annually and has left the low-end poor languishing in unrelieved poverty. For the period ahead one branch of the binary choice is more of the same. The other is to shoot for very much higher growth (say, on the order of 7 percent, implying 4.5 percent annual growth in per capita incomes) with the understanding that this would entail a fundamentally different quality of policy and scale of risk taking.

In a poor country a high-growth strategy has an inherent appeal—if it can be brought off. But what needs underscoring is the symbiosis between output gains and equity gains that could and should characterize a high-growth strategy in India at this juncture. First, what most requires filling out is the missing supplemental employment and antipoverty periphery of the development design. To fill out the periphery, of course, would directly attack the equity problem—although it cannot solve that problem unless and until it leads to or is accompanied by some redistributions of economic assets and political power. Second, filling out the present Indian program by employing underemployed labor in the labor-intensive production of additional productive assets would, just as obviously, increase current output directly, and raise further productive capacity. Third, an expanded employment program also would place a useful demand pull on the economy's current capacities for producing manufactured wage goods and thereby on industrial investment, especially private investment, decisions. For so poor a country, one of the odd things about India during virtually the whole of the past dozen years has been the sluggishness of internal demand. The condition persists even

[2]J.P. Lewis, "Growth and Equity in Two of the Poorest Countries: India and Bangladesh," in *Southern Asia: the Politics of Poverty and Peace,* ed. Donald C. Hellmann, *Critical Choices for Americans,* vol. 13 (Lexington, MA: D.C. Heath and Co., Lexington Books, 1976), pp. 79—138.

under the recently improved economic conditions. Explanations are complex and have varied over time, but what does seem clear is that private investment is being deterred by sluggish demand. A sizable and, especially, a reliable increase in demand could spur private investment—and this function could be played perfectly well by a rise in demand at the low end of the income distribution, where it also would have the greatest equity benefit.

The country's ability to pursue this course in an acceptably noninflationary fashion would be enhanced by—indeed, in the longer run, would largely depend upon—its ability to raise more domestic resources to public account. Yet it also seems obvious that the high-growth option could be made more feasible by a substantial increase in transfers. But is there reason to think that this apparent usefulness might be illusory—that extra inputs from outside might serve only to forestall extra internal effort?

Self-reliance is a healthy objective for any group or political jurisdiction. Yet absolute self-reliance is inconsistent with the principle of the progressive income tax as it is applied between rich and poor people in a particular area, or between subregions (e.g., California and Mississippi) of a national jurisdiction, or (weakly across national boundaries in a program of concessional transfers from rich to poor countries. The goal is to minimize the contraproductive impact of transfers while reaping as much benefit as possible from them.

That the issue is serious is a matter of record in India—particularly in the area of food aid. The criticism of the crutch effect that PL 480 food had in the late fifties and early sixties frequently has been overdone. It is not clear that if the government of India been under greater stress to promote domestic food production, the needed technology would have become available; or that the panic of worse food crises would have generated an environment for more effective indigenous agricultural research; or that a total absence of food aid would not have occasioned such traumatic food shortages and price inflation as to have collapsed the political system. Yet, given the lack of safeguards against disincentive effects, it does seem plain that the quantity of U.S. food aid, itself motivated by a fire-sale psychology, overshot the optimum target prior to 1965. It held off the day when Indian leadership had to devote enough of its own nervous energy to the problem of agricultural production.

However, policy lessons are, after all, sometimes learned from experience, and this one—that food aid must not again be allowed to deter indigenous productive effort—is one with which not only all students of development have been seized; so have donor agencies and governments, beginning with the U.S. government from 1965 onward; and, most importantly so has the government of India. The significantly higher priority that agricultural promotion has been accorded in Indian budgets, in institutional credit allocations, in assignments of officials, and in allotments of "high command" attention from 1965 onward; the way this priority has lately been sustained in a period of temporary (and relative) food abundance; the centrality that agriculture has come to play in the assessment of most Indian development analysts; and the greater voice that farmers have acquired in the political process—all these together afford reasonable assurance that the crutch syndrome will not be allowed to reappear. Furthermore, as will be noted in the next chapter, policy guidelines that could safeguard future food transfers against antiproductive impact are now rather widely understood.

The same kind of case can be made for concessional transfers in general—that, properly framed, conveyed, and received, they need not significantly displace indigenous effort. Furthermore, the argument can be turned upside down: not only is it unnecessary for there to be negative linkages between external resources and internal effort; in the Indian case presently two kinds of positive linkages are possible.

The first relationship is, in the present circumstances, a double-edged one. On the one hand, the prospect of more aid can help embolden the Indians' deployment of their own resources. The fiscal conservatism of the present leadership is not unusual. From the early fifties onward Indian macroeconomic policy has had a deep, usually abiding strain of financial prudence. One result is that, by developing country standards, India has had a comparatively good antiinflationary record over the past twenty-five years. But it also on average has not gotten as much expansion mileage from its resource availabilities as it might have done. In the late sixties, for example, in the first flush of the green revolution agricultural success while development loans from the aid-India consortium and U.S. food aid were still flowing abundantly, the Indian government supplemented its foreign exchange reserves rather then push expansion. One motive, surely (as will be emphasized below) was to cushion itself against the kind of performance conditioning of aid it had just been experiencing from the United States and the World Bank. But the choice also suited the government's dominant financial mores. Similarly, from mid-1974 to late 1975 the government of India (albeit with the help of a good monsoon and emergency powers over labor) stopped the 1972–74 price surge with a financial-policy vigor it seldom has equaled in behalf of expansion. Thereafter, in its last year and a half, the Gandhi regime cautiously held back from committing its unprecedented and mounting stocks of food and foreign exchange to a more ambitious growth-cum-equity program. And after the March 1977 election, even as both of these stocks kept edging upward, the expenditure decisions of the new leadership confirmed the expectation that it would be still more fiscally conservative than its predecessor.

In terms of psychology, therefore, there is a good case that the Indian government, knowing that its present accumulated resources may prove ephemeral, and being a habituated risk averter, is unlikely to launch itself toward the high-growth branch of its binary choice without the assurance of substantial further and reliable external underwriting. But this does not really suggest a workable scenario for success in the coming years. The circumstances also have an opposite edge. Even psychologically—if one now considers the psychology of donors—the proposition that the triggering of a bolder Indian effort must come from abroad, that the government of India must be coaxed into greater boldness, is implausible. It is unlikely to persuade external legislatures, including the U.S. Congress. Furthermore, there is also a compelling mechanical point: India quite literally is stocked *up* right now with the things—food and foreign exchange—that big aid can provide. Until the Indians themselves start drawing down their stocks by stepping up their public investment (thereby, via the generation of greater demand, their private investment) and their antipoverty efforts they will have neither room nor need for notably increased concessional transfers.

The double-edged relationship could become one of mutual deterrence: the Indians stay cautious and the United States, refraining from forward commitments, continues for some time to see no clear and present need. But the synergism could also run positively: recognizing the massiveness of their growth and antipoverty needs, the Indians commit themselves (as, at this writing, there are some signs they are beginning to do) to rates of response that they can presently afford but that probably are not sustainable for long without major increases in external inputs. The United States, having given sufficient assurances of the support it means to provide over the medium term, if adequate Indian effort leads the way, then moves as needed into the breach—not forever, but long enough for the international community to give India a fair shot (if indeed its own efforts remain effective and its access to foreign markets improves) to entrench fast growth, score major inroads on low-end poverty, and become substantially self-supporting.

Within India the positive scenario would be self-reinforcing. Once the economy were committed to the high-growth, proequity option, the inherent dynamism of the high-growth path would tend to strengthen agro-industrial linkages, generate growth-center externalities, induce private investment, require strengthening of infrastructure, build confidence in the export competitiveness of labor-intensive manufactures, and generally strengthen the hand of venturers and risk takers in the policymaking set.

Moreover, if the Indians have the courage to use rather than hoard their present assets, the existence of these assets can make our whole speculation about a radical expansion in U.S.-originating aid to India much less fanciful. If, from the Indian perspective, there were urgent need for a ten-fold expansion in

U.S.-originating transfers by fiscal year 1980, there would be almost no way operationally that this could be achieved. Further, it would be a traumatic undertaking in U.S. political terms. But if the Indians are prepared, on reasonable and conditional understandings, to stake most of the early incremental external costs of a high-option choice themselves, one is talking about a nonexplosive, albeit rapid, aid expansion. While this is not the place for a proper calculation of the phasing, it seems clear that the advance could be spread over at least four years. And this on all counts is more realistic.

The other possible affirmative linkage between increased transfers and domestic effort is conceptually simple; how politically feasible it is remains to be discovered. Perhaps the worst resources bottleneck impeding Indian development—especially rural development, particularly with respect to the provision of public employment and services to the poor—is the inability of the Indian government to gather resources to public account in the countryside itself. Agriculture's share of overall taxation is light, and of direct taxation almost trivial. (The central government collects no direct taxes from farmers, and most states collect very little.) The Indian tax effort outside agriculture, although capable of augmentation, is already quite substantial. Thus if there is to be domestic financing of a substantially enlarged, poor-oriented program of rural development, almost surely a good part of this financing will have to come from better-off farmers. The further probability is that this will be possible only if the locals in the countryside are given more say over the deployment of such resources. Decentralization and taxation, local self-government and local self-help may go hand in hand.

During the past fifteen years the theory of decentralization has gathered adherents: the practice has spread selectively, notably in Maharashtra and Gujarat; and, although many of the particulars have not yet been unveiled, decentralization is a dominant theme of the Janata Party. But meanwhile there has been precious little progress in the realm of local rural taxation.

One device—matching grants—for levering local fiscal effort is obvious enough, but it has not been significantly used. (In the case of local projects whose benefits flow to private recipients, the companion device of user charges for recouping the project costs from the beneficiaries *is* increasingly being employed in various guises.) If augmented transfers from abroad were now to provide a partial substitute for the missing internal funding of Indian development's antipoverty periphery, one possibility for a positive linkage between transfers and internal effort becomes apparent: perhaps some of the transfers should be reserved exclusively for lower-level jurisdictions, with their availability conditional upon the achievement of some additive resource raising by the local public authorities. This possibility will be explored in the next chapter.

Given a determined Indian lead, there is great scope for expanded aid to relax India's underlying resource constraints and help the government seize a high-growth option that would make good its populist purposes in a manner that, instead of deterring indigenous effort, catalyzes expansionist decisionmaking and perhaps induces greater assembly of resources at the rural grassroots.

This is our first set of conclusions. In a sense, such a case for giving Indian development a stronger external push has been there right along. Yet the time is also exceptionally propitious. On the whole, with the serious exception of population policy, the current array of Indian economic policies, carried over from the previous regime but modified and accented by the present one—the emphasis on agriculture; readiness to use the market as an adjustment mechanism; the promotion of exports, decentralization, and efficient labor-intensive modes of production; the focus on employment and the poor—never has been more promising. The country has its well-known cadres of scientific, technical, and professional personnel. Its stockpile of ready-to-go investment schemes is deficient, but the technique of competent project analysis is being seriously propagated. Relatively, not just absolutely, India's capacity to constructively absorb additional resources—first from its own reserves, then from others— probably outclasses that of any of the other poorest countries. The new government, for all its fiscal caution and erstwhile fragmentation, is under challenge to begin the achievement of sustained growth-cum-equity advances.

The Politics of Resumed Indo-U.S. Aid

In principle, government-to-government development assistance is a strange business—unless one is content to rely on the imperialism paradigm for interpreting any and all such transactions. Otherwise, I know of only three general conceptual models of the bilateral aid relationship; and of these, two are implausible, while the third has problems.

At one extreme, aid can be viewed as charity. But the resulting self-image for both parties is not only psychologically wearing, it quickly loses credibility. Governments are not *supposed* to be charitable. They are understood to serve the interests of their own, not other, constituents. In times of natural or man-made disasters abroad, they may, acting for their constituents, provide relief out of simple humanitarian motives. But to justify a continuing transfer relationship as sheer philanthropy would soon raise questions of legitimacy in the minds of both the donor government and its constituents. Similarly, it is hard for a recipient government to sustain the role of supplicant in the eyes of *its* constituents—or to keep its constituents persuaded that the external benefactor is giving its gifts selflessly.

At the other extreme is the model of a transnational progressive income tax. Here the discretionary aspect disappears, and compulsory levies gathered from the populations of rich countries (ideally without even the mediation of their governments) would flow to poor countries as a matter of right and routine. This is what the poor countries now are groping for in some of their new-international-economic-order demands; and it is probably the transfers mode that, once entrenched, (just as is now the case between California and Mississippi or the Punjab and Bihar), would be the least psychologically and politically corrosive in donor countries as well as recipient. Nor are some piecemeal approximations of it—the Special Drawing Rights (SDR)-link, before it was over-taken by liquidity events; or a world seabeds authority channeling royalties to member countries on the basis of need—unthinkable in the near and medium term. Yet a real world still dominated by nation states is not generally ready for the transnational tax model, whose feasibility depends on the existence of a supranational authority capable of imposing equitable assessments on unwilling member states and unwilling constituents.

This leaves as still the only viable format for most government-to-government concessional transfers the middle ground of a bargaining model, wherein bilateral aid is seen as a *quid pro quo* transaction between two juridical peers. This is the self-image that the bureaucracies on the two sides find most natural. But it must come to terms with an anomaly. Whereas the *quid* is plain enough in an aid relationship, the *quo* is less obvious and is subject to misinterpretation. Where aid has a naked political motivation, the consideration—use of an airfield, supportive rhetoric in the UN General Assembly—is straightforward. But in the case of "genuine" development assistance the *quo* becomes elusive. The general position is that (for whatever combination of reasons the donor finds persuasive) the donor has a selfish interest in the recipient's development. But this then translates into bargaining over the particular strategies, policies, and projects that the recipient government agrees to adopt for its own country's betterment. Such negotiation becomes inherently intrusive, carrying the implication that the donor's agents are better than the recipient's at identifying the recipient's own needs.

Thus it is that the politics of development assistance has a built-in fragility. With the best of intent and effort on both sides, they do not wear well; the capacity to deliver bilateral aid constructively tends to be a wasting asset.

Two partial exceptions to this rule come to mind. In the first place, it may lend credibility to aid-bargaining if the donor, acting out of larger or longer-term interests, in effect hires the recipient to adopt programs with externalities that spill beyond the recipient government's geographic boundaries and/or time frame. For example, a recipient regime, because of its short life expectancy, may be under pressure to concentrate on programs with quick returns, and may not be offended by an external donor's backing (via aid to education or otherwise) the interests of the next generation. Alternatively, the donor may use aid to persuade the recipient to undertake programs in ecological maintenance and/or repair whose benefits extend beyond the confines of the country that executes them.

In the second place—and, unlike the first, this one has a substantial history in the case of U.S.-to-India transfers—the intrusion can be cushioned by transferring resources through multilateral rather than bilateral channels. In theory the position of a multilateral intermediary like the World Bank is quite different from that of a bilateral donor. The World Bank is less likely to be suspected of political motives. It is not a juridical peer; on the contrary, it is partly "owned" and governed by the recipient. And, established by the international community as a repository of technocratic expertise, it can seek within its particular zone of competence to prescribe policy to the recipient with some of the same political impunity with which a medical doctor prescribes to his patient.

Yet, while it is not without validity, this theory of the World Bank or of the United National Development Program as a sanitized, nonoffensive intruder is rarified. The burden of the earlier argument stands: aid giving and receiving is an inherently conflicted, difficult relationship.[3]

The donor is biased toward intervening: first, because any parliament or bureaucracy that becomes committed to the promotion of development in a recipient country finds it hard to suppress the opinions it develops about needed courses of action; second, for entirely respectable accountability reasons (the donor organization is expending its constitutents' resources, and needs to be able to demonstrate good stewardship); third, because donors tend to build self-serving side conditions into their transfers.

Transfers that are source tied carry the assurance of a by-product benefit for donor exports; donors tie transfers also ("additionality") to domestic products that fail to penetrate the recipient's market commercially, so the by-product advantage is heightened while the benefit to the recipient is diminished. Aid may be tied to projects or other uses to serve the donor's sense of development priorities and/or accountability interests; but also source tying aid creates a degree of monopoly power for a limited set of donor-country suppliers (say, of heavy electrical machinery or fertilizer equipment). Likewise, side conditions (e.g., commodity tying) may reduce the real costs of a given dollar volume of transfers. Such tying certainly has characterized U.S. food aid in the past.

---

[3] Theodore Geiger may have been the first to apply the term, in his book, *The Conflicted Relationship: The West and the Transformation of Asia, Africa, and Latin America* (New York: McGraw-Hill Book Co., 1967).

A government receiving aid has just as strong a set of opposite biases toward transfers in the most flexible and fungible form. It would prefer resources that can be spent anywhere for any purpose: free foreign exchange without strings. With goodwill on both sides, it is not uncommon for the donor and recipient aid bureaucracies to surmount these counterpulls to converge on objectives, for the donor to defer to the recipient on most specifics in exchange for reciprocal accommodation on matters of particular concern to the donor, and for cooperating elements in the recipient government to use the donor to strengthen their hand in internal debates. But the fact is that neither government, typically, is a monolith; and in each polity forces further removed from the aid transaction tend to inject friction into the relationship.

A few points about the particular heritage that the aid relationship between the American and Indian governments has accumulated during the past quarter-century can be made with some confidence.

First, as the first and largest of the European colonies to win independence after World War II, and as a state that from the beginning of its independence has aspired to great power status, India has always been especially jealous of its autonomy. It was not accidental, for example, that throughout the fifties, when the field offices of the U.S. bilateral foreign aid agency was being called U.S. Operating Missions or USOMs in many other Asian countries, the government of India required the equivalent unit in India to retain the more limited and inter-active title of Technical Cooperation Mission. Nor was it accidental that the Indian Planning Commission and Finance Ministry never really accepted a team of resident foreign advisors.

India's characteristic inclination toward managerial, technical, and policy self-reliance was fortified by the high quality of some of its bureaucrats, scientists, technologists, and enterprise managers—and, in a way that often is not remarked, by her size. Across a broad spectrum of the disciplines and skills needed for development there appeared to be, even prior to independence, a fair number of Indians who were not only gifted but highly qualified by training and experience. But it was not so much that there were *relatively* more such talented and qualified persons in India than in other developing countries; in a manpower pool of such scale, their absolute numbers were large enough for a widely diversified set of professional elites quickly to reach that critical-mass status where they could begin effectively to multiply themselves. Moreover, for all its diverse and fractionalized character, from the beginning the new nation state had reasonably effective techniques (for example, via civil-service recruitment) for drawing the best from the breadth of its national talent pool into senior positions. (The geographic and regional breadth of the draw was good even if recruitment did not tap very far *down*, in a class sense, into the populations' stock of potential talent.) Thus, from independence onward it was not uncommon for a great variety of Indian subsystems—central and private state government departments, larger private and public enterprises, cooperative networks, universities, research institutions—to be run by very competent people. And new institutions had a fair shot at such leadership.

The existence of this thin but broad spread of high-quality expertise has colored the attitude that the government of India, from the fifties onward, has taken toward foreign private investment, welcoming such investment only where it brings distinctive inputs of needed technology and capital not otherwise available. Foreign investors have been pressed to share their equity and to Indianize their technical staffing as well as their management.

Moreover, the country's early layer of professional sophistication had a series of consequences for that aspect of foreign aid that usually has been called technical assistance. From the beginning India was, in its requests for such assistance, fairly exacting (to the extent it could control quality) as to the credentials of the foreign specialists supplied, and disinclined to let external advisors gravitate into *de facto* direction of indigenous activities. Aid-funded university teams and other external actors often played a lighter, less pivotal role than in other countries (although their catalytic function as well as the connected overseas training was often critical). Moreover, a number of institutions—agricultural universities, IITs, IIMs, applied research institutes—got built with considerable speed and a quite reasonable incidence of success. By the same token, India's professional head start meant that the classic institution-building phase of technical assistance, especially under bilateral auspices, was *appropriately* over the hump and phasing down by the end of the sixties.

Finally, looking to the future, the same pattern of early professional self-reliance may actually make India somewhat more receptive now to a new, more reciprocal pattern of technical cooperation than other countries whose scientific and institutional development is less advanced. Across a range of disciplines, the best Indian professionals, as their penetration of the international market attests, have no further reason to be insecure or defensive. At the same time, they are mindful of the severe resource constraints under which most Indian education and technology-adapting and innovating institutions generally labor; constraints that appropriate kinds of transfers could relax.

The essence of this first feature of the Indo-American relationship is that no developing country has given Americans, indeed all donors, better reason to be sensitized to the recipient's appetite for independence. Yet India's commitment to autonomy may now have matured sufficiently to be more easily reconciled with useful forms of resource supplementation.

A second long-standing feature of the relationship has been the noncongruence of Indian and American foreign policy. Early in the relationship—by the mid-fifties—there was an evident inconsistency between Nehru nonalignment and Dullesian cold warring. The concept of nonalignment has embraced the maintenance of constructive rapport with the USSR: many Indians have seen the USSR as a relevant developmental, although not political, model; it is a country with which a number of them had a good deal of generalized (socialism versus capitalism) ideological sympathy; once the United States (in the early sixties) decided not to supply substantial arms, the USSR became India's principal external defense supplier; Indo-Soviet links strengthened as the two countries' relations with China worsened; and although far less important than India's economic dependence on the West, Indo-Soviet trade-aid relations for twenty years have been a critical dimension of Indian development design.

At times the traces of generalized anti-Americanism creeping into official Indian discourse have been quite strident. Yet the official Indian commentary on Vietnam—certainly, in retrospect, the most vulnerable and anti-American of India's comments—would have to be judged comparatively restrained overall. And in North-South dialogues in the UN and elsewhere—since the OPEC price explosion as well as earlier—India has tended to play a moderating role within the Third World camp.

Thus the government of India usually has not fallen into knee jerk anti-Americanism even though two issues have caused it great distress: arms to Pakistan (reaching a climax in 1971—72, of which more below) and the sense that the United States has seldom taken India as seriously as a nation numbering one-seventh of mankind and aspiring to at least regional and Third-World greatness deserves. (Since 1972 the latter irritation has been aggravated by the deference that the United States has lavished on China.) But generally India has, even when deviating from them, remained sensitive to the political values it shares with the Western democracies, has sought constructive relations with the United States, and (even after 1971) has taken pains to avoid any simple identification with the socialist bloc.

Probably this moderation has owed much to a third feature of the aid relationship that began in 1952, namely, that over the course of two decades the Indians found that American aid tended in its basic characteristics to be surprisingly neutral politically. Whenever it would help sell the program to the U.S. Congress, or for that matter to the U.S. Secretary of State, American aid to India was peddled as a cold war exercise. But the fact was, as the program built up to massive proportions in the fifties and continued through the sixties it had no easy consistency with a Dullesian, alliance-oriented foreign policy. Rather, the aid program was a testimonial (1) to the fact that the American government is seldom monolithic, either in its purposes or its programs; (2) to the dedication that an alliance of American bureaucrats, legislators, scholars, and opinion leaders came to have to poor-country uplift in general and to Indian development in particular; and (3) to the profound inertia that attaches to almost any U.S. government program once it is well launched.

None of this is to say that the Indo-U.S. program in the fifties and sixties was exempt from political baggage. The transfers became source-tied; eventually they bore the burden of "additionality"; terms were tightened; food was pushed when it was in surplus; there was a tendency (albeit one partially neutralized within the U.S. government itself) to press the Indian government to favor the private over the public sector; and the program became an outlet for the energies of more American technicians than the Indians were sure they needed. Yet few crude (e.g., pro-Vietnam) political strings ever actually were tied to the aid; in its organizing and early browbeating of the India-aid consortium as well as in its launching of such innovations as nonproject loans, the United States was the mobilizer of the whole phenomenon of OECD assistance to India; and for all of the effort's flaws, inadequacies, and baggage, its motivating rationale quite evidently was development promotion.

In combination, the three characteristics just discussed determined the texture of the relationship in the middle sixties. But then two series of events first wore the relationship severely, and then almost demolished it.

In the first place, during the middle and later sixties the U.S. government, working in tandem with the World Bank, subjected the government of India to a strenuous and sustained dose of performance conditioning. The exercise had the basic characteristics that were identified previously with the bargaining model of "genuine" development assistance. The principal vehicles used for levering Indian policies were nonproject (or program) development loans—although, thanks to the flamboyance of President Johnson's "short-tethering" of food aid during the drought years of 1965—67, it was widely believed in the United States and even by many in India that PL 480 was the main vehicle for pressuring Indian reform. (The trouble with food, especially drought-relief food, is that it lacks credibility as a leverage tool: it is hard for the recipient to believe that the donor really is going to let people starve for lack of policy performance—although Johnson managed to sustain the suspicion that he just might.)

The policy targets were, in the minds of the donors at the time (and in my mind, still) thoroughly virtuous—heightened agricultural priority and a new agricultural strategy, liberalization and the thinning out of what had become an incredibly inefficient maze of internal controls, correction of an overvalued exchange rate. The targets were shared by a powerful and dedicated set of Indian government ministers and officials, whose hands were strengthened by the performance conditioning. And the reforms were in large part adopted—in some measure lastingly. Indeed, although programs have fluctuated since then (in part because of the U.S.-led collapse of new transfers in the early seventies), the turn toward the proagricultural and promarket strands of present policy came at this time. Thus it would be wrong to suggest that, measured by its intended objectives, the exercise was a substantive failure.

But the adverse reaction to the phenomenon of performance conditioning itself became deep and bitter. To some extent this was a response to the heavy-handedness of President Johnson's personal imprint on the proceedings. More important, it reflected the inherent corrosiveness of the practice. But in addition, by the late sixties the Indians felt they had been cheated. In 1966 they had undertaken the most politically hazardous brace of reforms (devaluation coupled with import liberalization) with the support of a substantial rise in the level of consortium nonproject loans. The moves probably cost the Congress Party rather severely in the 1967 parliamentary elections. But worse, in the emotional reaction it provoked, was the fact that the aid increment evaporated after a single year, when the government had thought it had a clear understanding that the new nonproject aid level would be sustained in support of liberalization for several years. Senior officials felt they had bargained away a corner of their birthright for a bad promissory note.

The curtailment of assistance and then its further decline in the early seventies diminished the country's capacity not only for liberalization but also for other development reform. Yet, as we have seen, the Indian response was to throttle back on expansion even farther than the diminished aid availability required, thereby building the country's foreign exchange cushion. A decision appears to have been taken never again to let India become so exposed to donors' pressures.

Finally, after this period of erosion, such political goodwill as remained in the Indo-U.S. aid relationship was fractured by the 1971 Nixon-Kissinger tilt toward Pakistan. There will be no attempt here to rehearse the events of that period, but two points must be borne in mind. In the first place, there had been keen and prolonged Indian discontent with the standing American policy of heavy arms aid to its treaty ally, Pakistan. If the government of India was prepared most of the time to be fairly philosophic about the noncongruence of its world view with that of the United States, it had no such forbearance about intrusions that attempted to forestall what India saw as its inevitable regional dominance in the subcontinent. Thus the events of 1971 poured salt on a raw wound of long standing.

Second, it is well to remember just how explosively hostile was the Indian reaction to the events of 1971. Indians' indignation was enthusiastically self-righteous. They saw the American failure to protest the trampling of human rights and lives in East Bengal as reprehensible, and their own role in housing and supporting refugees as burdensome, forbearing, and efficient. They were incensed by the continuing leakage of American arms to Pakistan and what they saw as U.S. deception on that subject. They were dismayed by the vehemence of the U.S. tilt when the latter finally became overt. And they were infuriated by the apparent effort of the United States to intimidate India by steering an aircraft carrier into the Bay of Bengal.

The anger was encompassing. Scarcely an Indian voice was raised in defense of American behavior. All Indian Americophiles felt betrayed, and most took pains to say so. The rancor was not preoccupying for long; it was quickly upstaged by euphoria over India's military success in the east and the establishment of Bangladesh. But in the process a bitter view of the U.S. government had been seared into Indian minds; and while the distrust was concentrated on the administration in power in Washington, its effects linger.

The old animus has receded, of course, and especially with the new Janata regime, there is eagerness to attribute a markedly new set of attitudes and intentions to the Carter administration. Yet in trying to judge the political context in which a major resumption of U.S. aid to India would have to operate, it would be foolhardy not to recognize that the history of the past twenty-five, and especially the past fifteen, years has created some major inhibitions.

Given the history, a veteran of the Indo-U.S. relationship might be forgiven the whimsical suggestion that, if we now want to revive aid to India in a big way, the best thing really might be to send cash in a plain brown wrapper. But not only is this an altogether fanciful idea for all of the old reasons, including the need for public accountability within the United States as to uses of taxpayers' monies; there is a strong disposition now to condition augmented transfers in a new way, namely, to target them on the low-end poor.

As noted in the second section of this chapter, the call for revamped development strategies that no longer rely on trickle-down but directly address the income and employment needs of the low-end poor within the poor countries has been in ascendency worldwide since the early seventies. Sentiments of precisely this sort animated the "new aid strategy" initiated in the Congress and adopted for the U.S. economic assistance program in 1973. Especially during the past eighteen months, there have been rising voices in this country and elsewhere linking the poor-targeting concept to suggested augmentations of aid.

One knows that several senior officials of the new administration have come to office with considerable sympathy for this approach. What gives it even greater authority is a widely held perception of the requirements of domestic U.S. politics. If there is any chance, it is argued, of getting the American public to accept expanded aid, it will only be if such constituencies as organized labor and blacks can be assured that the increment will be going to the genuinely needy, and will not involve taking away from poor Americans to give to rich Indians.

What about the probable Indian response to a new (antipoverty) phase of performance conditioning? Plainly, most of the influential members of the government of India would prefer to do poor targeting of their own style at their own pace without pressure from outside. At the same time, if the analysis in the second section of this chapter is right, present Indian development policy is *substantively* compatible with such a thrust. Logically, the government's program should welcome external reinforcement of its antipoverty periphery. And there may be some senior Indians who are sufficiently impatient with the internal rate of attack on low-end poverty problems to welcome external leverage in this instance, however much they may deplore it in principle.

Thus there is no *a priori* basis for judging a future American effort to steer resources toward the Indian poor a nonstarter. If attempted and in some measure implemented, it would, for the reasons earlier adduced, be likely to wear out Indian receptivity in due course. But this is not to say, any more than was the case with the agricultural and liberalization reforms of the late sixties, that the effort would therefore be denied lasting impact.

At the Indian end the political feasibility of experimenting with new levels and kinds of antipoverty aid probably would depend on a variety of specific and practical issues: What particular forms would the new transfers take? What would be the mix of the increment—all poor targeted or only partly? What would be the bilateral-multilateral division of labor? How far down into the country's decision-making hierarchy would the aid program's propoor leverage seek to penetrate? And how actively, frequently, and directly would the United States seek to participate in the decisions it was trying to affect?

These are among the questions to which I turn in the next chapter. But in doing so it is essential to understand that any renewed effort to do Indian leaders' thinking for them will be asking for trouble; that it will tend to make an inherently conflicted relationship more difficult; and that it would have a chance of even medium-term success only if done with great sensitivity and self-restraint.

XI

Revived Aid: A Possible Scenario

John P. Lewis

There may be a persuasive North-South case for raising the annual flow of U.S.-originating overseas development assistance to India by as much as $1.8 billion in 1977 dollars over the next four years. If the Indians themselves take the needed initiatives, such augmented transfers could help them adopt a high-growth, high-equity strategy in a way that would energize efforts at the local level. But the aid program would have to pick its way through politically treacherous terrain.

In the first section of this chapter, we present a series of guidelines that the U.S. government might impose on its policy design in the Indian case. In the second section we suggest a policy design. The guidelines and the policy design are based on the assumptions and diagnoses made in chapter 10.

Design Principles

We can assume U.S. aid resumption would be coupled with new emphasis on channeling assistance to the poor. If, operationally, one flinches from this conclusion, substantively one welcomes it; later in this chapter we speculate at some length about the forms that segments of a resumed program might take. But the *nonexclusivity* of poor targeting, or of aid focused directly on basic human needs, would have to be a basic principle of the revived effort. To promote equity in India one must also promote growth, and there is no good way that all the external support that should be brought to bear on the growth objective can be imparted exclusively through poor-targeted channels. For the reasons next noted, the peculiarities of the U.S. position might allow it to concentrate its bilateral effort on the antipoverty side. But it would be a great pity if, for example, the United States were to successfully press a similar narrowing of objectives on the World Bank.

As to the balance between the poor-targeted part and the rest of the Indian program, there is no particular reason for making the principle more precise than that the composite program should have room for the serious accommodation of both. It can be assumed that those demanding that U.S. aid have an antipoverty thrust will not be satisfied with tokenism; moreover, other donors, including the World Bank, will be aiming some of their transfers in similar fashion. On the other hand, the need will remain for sizable volumes of transfers that do not flow directly or exclusively to the low-end poor. Not only must the United States, as a revived leader of aid to India, be concerned that these other aspects be adequately represented in other donors' contributions; it should include some of these aspects (e.g., debt relief and gap-filling food aid) in its own bilateral effort.

In any large and serious multidonor development assistance effort, one donor, usually the largest, tends to acquire the role of residual donor; in this role, after duly exhorting its colleagues, it tries to pick up loose ends, fill critical gaps, and make the whole design work. In India that role was already shifting from the U.S. bilateral program to the World Bank Group by the end of the 1960s, and it shifted decisively, of course, after 1971–72.

In the scenario we are contemplating, U.S.-originating aid would rapidly increase to a higher level than the recent Bank Group level. This, of course, does not automatically mean that the Indo-U.S. bilateral program would outpace World Bank/International Development Association aid deliveries to India, the aid mix would depend on how much multilateral aid rose as the result of general expansion in the IDA program and also on how much of the U.S.-originating increase was channeled via the Bank Group and other multilaterals. In the hypothetical program sketched below, U.S. bilateral aid and assistance from the Bank Group would wind up about equal. But no matter how this quantitative comparison came out, the United States would *not* resume the role of residual donor. It would, to be sure, dramatically resume the role of a consortium leader and pattern setter; for example, it might encourage such colleagues as Germany and Japan to adopt more forthcoming postures. But it would aim most of its own bilateral assistance toward antipoverty uses.

As an accident of the way things have gone in India and in the rest of the donor consortium since 1972 while the United States has been sitting on its hands, the United States now has the option of reentering the game—even reentering in a big way—as predominantly an antipoverty and food aid specialist. The present status of Indian development design (which makes a much more substantial provision for the production-function core than it does for the antipoverty periphery) makes it appropriate for the United States to go a long way toward taking up this option. Despite the scale of its projected reentry, it can responsibly leave the residual problems—the loose ends, necessary gap filling, and the monitoring of general economic policy—to the World Bank.

The World Bank now has abundant expertise, and with an augmented U.S. contribution it will have adequate resources, for looking after these things as much as they need to be looked after from outside. To the Indians the World Bank is somewhat more acceptable in this capacity than a revived U.S. bilateral program would be. Moreover, there is reason to believe that the government of India is more capable than it was a decade ago of covering the residuals and keeping the picture pieced together itself.

Such a division of labor between the United States and the World Bank would have attractive implications for the scale and responsibilities of the American field mission in India. But it would require support for the more diversified and complex role of the Bank.

I now turn to a series of design principles (as many as seven) each of which might warrant separate billing. But together they constitute a collective answer to an underlying question: How far should one expect the U.S. executive branch to go in supporting those modes of transfers that would be most helpful to Indian development? Generally, as the preceding chapter suggested, there has been conflict between aid modes, forms, and procedures that would maximize benefit to the client and, on the other hand, those self-serving side conditions and constraints that donor-country interest groups have sought to attach to transfers. A premise of the present analysis is that if the new administration opts for a major revival of aid to India at all, it will do so for reasons that make it anxious to maximize the effectiveness of aid.

Hence a general assumption of the hypothetical program below is that the administration will try to do the job right: it will lean hard in favor of arrangements that increase the usefulness and effectiveness of the program for the recipient. But it will not tilt at windmills; not only will it insist that the program retain reasonable accountability, it will accept certain self-serving biases or constraints as unassailable for the moment. My own estimate of what this posture might mean to the specific choice of aid modes is spelled out in the following seven points. The first four and the last one tend to represent choices tilted in favor of the recipient; the fifth and the sixth, accommodations to U.S. political realities. Every one of the points is arguable; different analysts might come up with different profiles of the procedural limits toward which a program seeking maximum effectiveness would be pressed. But the principle is that the executive-branch would intend to press such limits.

Multilateral Versus Bilateral

India has a distinct (not overwhelming) interest in seeing American resources move through multilateral rather than bilateral channels. The World Bank Group represents an extraordinary and, by now, internationally quasi-homogenized concentration of expertise in development analysis and administration; in particular, it has a comparative advantage for handling the increment of capital projects funding that may be in order in India. As just noted, it also would suit U.S. strategy for the Bank to remain the lead monitor of and dialoguer about

Indian development policy.

Thus I would expect the administration to press for expanded multilateral allocations. Recently there has been concern that the Congress has been abrogating its right to judge the worthiness of recipients, especially on human rights grounds, by transferring resources to the multilaterals. Nevertheless the feasibility of winning enlarged multilateral aid from the Congress is probably greater than it was five or ten years ago—in part because of disenchantment with the difficulties and repercussions of bilateral operations. In particular, the strongest self-interested source of discontent with multilateral allocation, namely, that they cannot easily be source tied, appears to be quiescent—and perhaps can be kept so, especially if enlarged contribution to IDA and other multilaterals are paralleled by an expanded bilateral program that is indeed source tied.

At the same time, it would be unreasonable to expect the United States to route all of a greatly enlarged volume of aid to India through multilateral channels. Given the procedures and the professionalism that help make the World Bank an attractive intermediary, its capacity almost surely would be overtaxed if it tried to handle the whole surge in American transfers to India herein contemplated. Such an attempt, moreover, could create intercountry and interregional allocative problems with the Bank: the United States would be repairing a deep hole in its intercountry aid profile, but the Bank has had no such hole. Thus a move by the Bank to encompass the whole of a return of Indo-American aid to reasonable levels might trigger protests by World Bank directors.

Furthermore, having chosen to specialize in antipoverty assistance to India, the United States, partly for American political reasons and partly because of the bureaucracy's involvement with the subject and its desire to experiment creatively, would be reluctant to commit the central components of the effort to homogenized World Bank treatment. Finally, as the overwhelmingly dominant potential supplier of food aid, it is quite unreasonable—simply on dog versus tail grounds—to expect the United States to multilateralize most of that assistance category.

These estimates suggest expansion on both the multilateral and bilateral fronts, with different categories of aid handled by each.

Continuity

For decades developing countries have been asking for assurances of multiyear aid funding (in order to facilitate their multiyear planning) and for decades they have been told that for donors governed by parliaments who favor one-year money bills this tends to be impossible. Until now, that has been the right message. Indeed, one of the things that caused development assistance in the Kennedy administration to get off the mark slowly was the time initially spent chasing the "continuity" will-o'-the-wisp. But if one is speculating about a general remodeling of development assistance, it may finally be time to do something on this count.

For one thing, if more transfers are now to be multilateralized, in principle the multilaterals have some capacity for stocking resources and, against such cushions, entering into reliable multiyear commitments. The trouble has been that commitments have tended to go out the front doors of these institutions as fast as or faster than donor-country contributions have come in the back; and this typically has not been because the intermediaries have committed imprudently vis-à-vis reasonable expectations about contributions it has been because some donors have been slow. Thus one blow the Carter administration can strike for the continuity cause will be to persuade the Congress not merely to raise contributions to the multilaterals, but to raise them (especially, in the India case, U.S. contributions to IDA) in more forehanded fashion.

Beyond this, the present suggestions contemplate some procontinuity experimentation with the U.S. bilateral program itself. What might be considered is a kind of stock-replenishment approach. In the past the efficiency of aid delivery systems often has been judged by the speed with which they move resources to the client. Long pipelines have been a sign of failure—and justly so when delayed disbursement reflects transfers so encumbered with strings, constraints, or hard terms that recipients are reluctant to use them. But in the present Indian case, at least regarding things that may be emerging as appropriate components for a U.S. bilateral program, the need may be less for a maximum annual flow of specified resources than it is for an assured availability of such resources. This is most obviously the case with food aid that is intended to close gaps or rebuild buffer stocks. But the U.S. government may also wish to condition its provision of transfers, whether of food or of dollars, to antipoverty uses on certain kinds of indigenous performance (one possibility we shall be discussing further is some kind of matching assembly of local resources). Yet, for reasons of history, one of the last things U.S. aid should try to reintroduce into India is detailed, old-styled performance conditioning. An alternative might be to make available a stock or fund of resources whose purposes had been negotiated with some care, which without further external pressure of intervention would be released to the intended uses if and as triggering criteria were met. Under the stock replenishment formula the donor's undertaking would be to keep returning a particular resources stock to a particular level for an agreed term of years. The recipient would provide an accounting *ex post*, but would be able to withdraw freely (up to a certain annual maximum) as it judged disbursement criteria were satisfied.

It seems unlikely that such arrangements would inject an unacceptable degree of added uncertainty into U.S. budgeting. Needed rates of annual replenishment would vary, but would have an upper boundary and often could be forecast. On the U.S. side, it might well be possible to get multiyear authorizations, if not appropriations, for a limited number of such arrangements. On the Indian side, multiyear arrangements could encourage the government of India to overcome excessive financial caution and start getting more mileage out of its resources.

Consortium Versus Nonconsortium

In the general debate over new-international-economic-order issues the socialist countries have been enjoying the role of a nonplaying cheering section. The Third and Fourth Worlds as well as the Organization for Economic Cooperation and Development (OECD) countries should try harder to pull them into the game. But a resumption of major American aid to India is not the right context in which to convert such purposes into sticking points. East European aid to India, although spasmodic and often not particularly successful, is substantial. The aid is repayable in Indian exports, and while that certainly does not make it burdenless, it does make repayment easier in Indian eyes. And for the three years ending with 1975-76, the ratio of debt service on East European aid to Indian exports to rupee-payment areas was less than 15 percent; the comparable ratio was about 20 percent for consortium aid.

If, as recommended below, the Indian aid consortium were to make a major move toward debt relief, certainly it would be desirable for this to be paralleled by a similar concession by the CMEA countries—with India taking its chances on sustaining its volume of exports to Eastern Europe. The Indians should be encouraged to seek such relief. But it would be difficult for the United States, after the lapse in its own program, to attempt to stipulate conditions concerning concessions to be obtained from the socialist donors—or, for that matter, from the Organization of Petroleum Exporting Countries (OPEC), whose recent transfers to India have been quite generous.

For the members of the consortium, as the bulk suppliers of aid to India, to hinge their actions on the performance of other donors would reflect a casualness of commitment that would dampen the energies of the principal actor in Indian development policy, the Government of India itself.

Grants Versus Loans

Of all these principles the following may be the most shocking, because of our convention of avoiding the obvious on this subject. If the administration in Washington undertakes a major recasting of North-South policy, it should be to make explicit something we have known for a long time: as vehicles for concessional transfers to the poorest countries, development loans have always been a rather bad second-best choice. They should have been grants all along. There never was a persuasive reason to expect that an economy like India's would grow so buoyantly and yet with such a restrained response to its own internal poverty that, within the time frame of even the longest-term development loans, an aggregate net surplus would become available for transfer to foreigners.

The alternative of continuing to give the recipient new concessional loans with which to pay off old loans makes little sense. The alternative of forcing it into the international commercial loan market faster than it is ready to go makes even less sense, and is likely to undermine quickly such limited credit worthiness as the country is building in that market. Finally, the notion that concessional loans somehow force the recipient to be more businesslike or efficient than grants do is a canard: concessional loan terms already are too soft to serve as proper internal allocative guides; in any event, a host-country government, if it is at all rational, has a keen incentive to optimize its use of scarce foreign capital, whatever the terms on which that capital comes—and donors have the same opportunity to encourage such optimization.

My hunch is that the Congress may be ready for such candor on the part of the new administration. If so, the United States should not only convert its own new bilateral transfers to India essentially to grant terms, it should carry over the same philosophy to the issue of debt relief; and it should urge the philosophy on other members of the consortium. [1]

Bilateral Tying

A judgement that a venturesome administration now should press for radical reform on the loans versus grants issue but should probably pull in its horns and settle for source-tied bilateral aid is based partly on fallible political intuitions. Although the loans-versus-grants question will arouse generalized hostility to aid give-aways, source tying is of interest to particular constituencies that stand to

---

[1] In principle the same argument can be made for a conversion of IDA terms from their present (very soft loan) condition to outright grants. This, obviously, could not be confined to India, and the change could not extend to the World Bank's own loans, whose sources are the financial markets. But with IDA wholly funded by grants from donor governments and confined to poorest-country beneficiaries, the advantage of being able to recirculate such capital to further beneficiaries on a fity-year cycle probably is outweighed by the advantage of, meanwhile, being able to deliver larger benefits to the presently neediest countries. However, the grant element in IDA financing is already very high, and there is a limit to how much even a bold scenario should try to take on. Hence I have deleted the point from the present design.

benefit from tied-aid exports. It is part of my political speculation that these constituencies, particularly in the face of a determined presidential push, will prove more formidable than those who oppose grants.

In part, however, the trade-off I propose between boldness on loans versus grants and cautiousness on source tying reflects an assessment of their comparative importance. The loans-versus-grants issue is the more traumatic of the two issues in terms of the generalized debate it will generate. Once achieved, its beneficial ramifications for the poorest countries can be great; and if there is a chance of getting it in the first flush of a push for major North-South reform in the United States, if should be gotten while the getting is good. On the other hand, aid tying, although it faces pockets of dug-in opposition, is a less flamboyant issue; it already has some history of relaxation (early in the Nixon administration); and it can be gotten incrementally. Moreover, if as here proposed, the additional project-funding resulting from the expansion of U.S.-originating transfers were mainly done through the World Bank, the worst form of tying (i.e., "double tying," to sources *and* uses) would be largely avoided. Thus bilateral source tying is one of the nonideal compromises that I would leave in the India aid revival package.

The Role of Food Aid

The other compromise would be willingness to have a substantial part of the augmented U.S. transfers take the form of U.S. bilateral food aid (which, by definition, of course, would be source tied). The requirement that it accept a sizable fraction of its transfers in the form of U.S. food (assuming the right terms, of which more is said below) would be a low-cost compromise for India. In all probability there will be an average need in some years for food imports to close a demand-supply gap (thereby permitting the rebuilding of buffer stocks after bad crop years). Extra food imports will also be needed for meeting the extra demand generated by new public works and other redistributive programs. And if food must be imported, to be "constrained" by aid to import it from the international market's overwhelmingly dominant supplier is small constraint indeed.

The rationale for positing a major role for food aid in the present scenario is essentially a U.S. domestic political one. The costs of American food aid—budgetary costs, opportunity costs in terms of commercial exports foregone, and pressure on American living costs—will be higher in the period ahead than during the present era of surpluses. The extent of these costs can be substantially affected by the manner and skill with which food aid is put into the system at the U.S. end. My assumption is that if this is done with some skill, food aid will continue to have sufficiently favorable farmer and agriculture-committee constituencies to make it, on average, somewhat easier to get from the Congress than equal amounts of dollar transfers.

Further substantive discussion of Indian uses of food and needed U.S. policy adjustments is reserved for the appropriate points in our catalogue of hypothetical aid components.

Accountability and Transfer Procedures

The final principle for policy designers has been telegraphed in good part in the earlier discussion of the stock-replenishment concept. If revived American assistance, especially if it tries to deliver something as inherently intrusive as aid targeted at the low-end poor, is to avoid generating unacceptable frictions quickly, the administration will have to devise a peculiarly light yet serviceable set of reins for managing the program—reins that provide reasonable accountability and yet are responsive to the delicacy of the situation.

Part of the answer will be to multilateralize a good part of the program while staunchly resisting disruptive demands for American auditing and other forays into the multilateral institutions of types that would not be allowed to other contributing governments. As to much of the bilateral program, the formula deserving emphasis would contain four elements: first, careful bilateral negotiation of a particular program's objectives and operating criteria; second, bilateral negotiations of a program's key operating procedures; third, strictly unilateral—that is, Indian—operations, in accordance with the Indians' interpretation of the agreed substantive and procedural ground rules; fourth, periodic Indian reporting of implementation, which, in the case of stock-replenishment schemes, would automatically trigger replenishment as uses of stocks were reported—until the multiyear periods of agreements had run their course, when the whole program would be subject to donor reconsideration and renegotiation.

Program Elements

Within the framework provided by the analysis in chapter 10 and, more particularly, the principles just recited, it seems to me that a massive Indo-U.S. aid resumption package might consist mainly of (1) debt relief, (2) an expansion of IDA-type project funding via the World Bank, (3) a principal assault on the low-end poverty target via the additive employment route using something I will call an antipoverty fund that would be externally supported by inputs of bilateral program grants and food, and (4) some additional food for buffer-stock renewal. Furthermore, a hypothetical policy design might make overlapping provision for the support of ecological gains, and it should address the subjects of technical cooperation and program management. These elements and aspects are considered in the following paragraphs.

Debt Relief

In India the "debt problem" is not one of imminent default. Nor, even in the context of longer-run flows and capacities, is it a matter of the burdensomeness of official debt per se—the country's aggregate official debt service averaged only 17 percent of its merchandise exports in the three years ending in 1976–77. The problem, rather, concerns the role of debt service as a diminisher of, or of debt relief as a vehicle for, net transfers. The thrust of the present discussion is that India's growth and equity performance can be accelerated by a substantial increase in development assistance. Debt relief is a particular form of aid. What part should it play in the total aid package?

The answer to which the United States should help lead its consortium colleagues is dictated by two considerations. The first is the matter of principle already discussed: as concessional transfer vehicles, loans have been a poor second best all along, and as opportunity affords, the situation should be corrected retrospectively as well as prospectively. The second consideration is the flexibility—that is from the recipient's viewpoint, the quality—of aid. Straight-forward forgiveness of convertible-currency debt payments has the quality of free foreign exchange. In view both of the improved efficiency with which the government of India seems ready to use external resources and of the U.S. government's apparent inclination to channel much of its own increased contribution into restricted antipoverty uses, it will behoove the United States to favor the inclusion of a sizable component of this most flexible form of assistance in both its own and others' aid offers.

India's servicing of consortium debt was estimated at $682 million in 1976–77. Of this, payments due on the World Bank's own loans (estimated at $91 million for 1976–77) cannot readily be postponed or canceled, and IDA debt servicing was $32 million. But aside, perhaps, from bits and pieces of bilateral lending that are alleged to present payment problems similar to those presented by World Bank loans, the rest is eligible for debt adjustment.

As a negotiating target for the United States within the consortium one can put forth the proposition that all bilateral concessional debt payments, including interest, should be forgiven as they fall due. Such a program of debt relief that matches debt service dollar for dollar would compare with a ratio of debt relief to debt service that, in 1975–76, for example, ranged from highs of 67 cents on the dollar provided by Austria and 56 cents by Belgium and the Netherlands down through figures in the 40 to 50 cent range for Denmark, West Germany, Japan, and the United Kingdom, to zero for Canada, Norway, and the United States.

Each donor, under this approach, would dispose of India's obligations to that particular donor as a component of an annual volume of fresh aid at least as large as the debt service coming due. The only inequity in this arrangement would be that, to the extent debt relief is a more self-sacrificing form of aid for its lack of tying and strings, donors with large fractions of scheduled debt receipts to fresh aid would be providing relatively more sacrifical aid mixes. But there would actually be a kind of rough justice: donors with high debt-relief/fresh-aid fractions would tend to be either those whose past terms had been hard or those whose current effort had slacked off.

For the United States under the massive aid revival herein hypothesized, a program of full continuing relief of accruing debt payments would be relatively modest. Total U.S.-originating transfers to India would rise rapidly from about $200 million in 1976–77 to some $2 billion. U.S. debt receipts from India in 1976–77 were about $150 million. Should that figure rise toward $200 million by the time the expanded aid level were reached, debt relief would account for about 10 percent of U.S.-originating assistance or about 15 percent of U.S. bilateral aid. If the Congress and interested groups of the American public could be persuaded of the greater efficiency that a good measure of foreign-exchange flexibility could mean to an economy at India's development stage, then it should also be possible to persuade them of the merit of providing up to $200 million of American resources in this untied form, partly as a means of levering an additional $400-500 million of such resources out of the rest of the consortium.

The foregoing, to repeat, is suggested as a negotiating target. The United States should not let debt relief be blocked by a few small consortium members; but it would be appropriate to insist on mutuality from such large and financially competent donors as Japan, Germany, and perhaps France. The end result might be less ambitious than the position outlined. But the cause should not be pressed lightly. Where it does not distort the aggregate overseas development aid allocations among the poorest countries, debt relief for those countries makes excellent economic sense. And in the Indian case it would be a nice foil to bilateral poor targeting.

There are two final points. First, the present suggestion would not amount to "debt cancellation"; what would be canceled would not be whole debts, but only annual principal-cum-interest payments in a manner that creditors could review and modify through time. Second, those advocating that service on official debt be forgiven should directly confront loose talk to the effect that such action would demolish India's credit worthiness in international financial markets. It should do exactly the reverse. It would increase the foreign exchange available for backing selected commercial borrowing by Indian enterprises and institutions.

Multilateral Project Funding

In connection with the current replenishment of IDA, there has been some sentiment in Congress for directing the administration to bargain with the World Bank for a reduction in the share of IDA funds going to India. Such an effort, of course, would be at odds with the orientation of these chapters. If the administration finds there is good (North-South) reason to persuade Congress to raise India's share of all U.S.-originating transfers from 5 percent to 25 percent, it would make little sense to simultaneously try to pull down India's share of IDA lending from its present 40 percent. Keeping India's present share where it is would be one way of facilitating the hypothesized multifold expansion in total U.S. concessional flows to India. If that 40-percent share were maintained, then perhaps something like $200 million would go automatically as the U.S. contribution to the increased funds that will be going to India as the result of the enlargement in IDA's global program. As to the present scenario, the question is whether *more* of the $1.8 billion increment should go through World Bank channels.

Here there is the general case, already made, for multilateralizing as much of the increment as feasible. But there is also an efficiency case: some of the additional resources should go into major projects; the World Bank is the most competent of all institutions in the conduct of external project funding; it may also have an advantage in projects that cut across national boundaries; it would be redundant for the U.S. bilateral program to resume extensive capital-projects business in India.

As noted in Chapter 10, the Indians may be sitting on some very large, high-return capital project possibilities on which (partly because of the apparent unavailability of needed finance) they have not yet completed the preliminary homework. Some possibilities, for example, rural biogas and solar energy installations, would involve many small, decentralized units. A number of others imply integrated, only partly divisible, large projects. Some of the most interesting—Indo-Nepalese hydroelectric development of tributaries of the Ganges, possibly coupled with linked supplies of Indian fertilizer to Nepal; the management of the Ganges and Brahmaputra "Eastern Waters;" the supply of natural-gas-based Bangladesh fertilizer production to eastern India—cut across national boundaries and therefore are doubly difficult to analyze.

The water subgroup is especially intriguing, costly, and very possibly rewarding. Some of its items are glamorous: deep pumping inland from the northern banks of the Ganges to "wring out" the southern fringes of the world's greatest groundwater reservoir, increasing the flow past the Farakka Barrage into Bangladesh in the dry season and raising the ground's retention capacity in the next monsoon; digging a more northerly link between the Brahmaputra and the

Ganges and backflowing some of the Brahmaputra's exuberance into groundwater storage along its course; pumping surplus river and groundwater from the Gangetic plain uphill into the water grid of (usually) dry streambeds that nature has provided on the Deccan plateau. Some possibilities, especially the systematic drainage systems that irrigation authorities have been neglecting in South Asia for centuries despite the insistent needs posed by the flatness of the Indo-Gangetic plain, are dull but vital.

One result of a buoyant expansion in American aid to India should be to relieve the external-resource constraints on serious pursuit of such potentially vital projects, but in a way that encourages, and does not seek to substitute for, the necessary South Asian effort. The best external agent for such an undertaking would be the World Bank. The Bank has a better chance than a bilateral donor, in the case of the transnational projects, of helping the Indians, Bangladeshis, and Nepalis into mutually beneficial accords. Moreover, it has the habit of imposing upon host governments the requirements for rigorous project preparation and justification that should apply in these cases. It shares (as does, now, the Indian government) the same biases toward the priority of agriculture and of agricultural inputs that would animate the U.S. government in providing the project funds. The World Bank is more alert than it used to be to the need for project designers to select appropriate technologies. Likewise, it is now strongly biased toward building into such projects the strongest feasible direct and indirect benefits to the low-end poor.

Taking account of all this, the present scenario by the end of the hypothesized buildup would route an extra $400 million of project money through the World Bank, making the total increased funds channeled via the World Bank Group $600 million, or one-third of the overall annual U.S.-originating increment. IDA cannot accept funds earmarked for a particular recipient, but the World Bank can accept special earmarked contributions from a donor and administer them on IDA terms, an arrangement that presumably would forestall or dampen complaints from other developing (or donor) countries that the World Bank/IDA portfolio was being skewed toward India.

In view of the extensive analysis and preparation that remain to be done on the kinds of projects suggested, and of the careful manner in which the World Bank would and should proceed, the rate of special project funding would build up to the targeted level gradually over a period of years. But the Indians would know sooner that extra funding of this scope was available for such purposes if the homework were well done and if it identified investments with high social returns.

Antipoverty Bilateral Assistance

The most distinctive component of a resumed Indo-American aid program might well take the form of an antipoverty fund designed to promote the employment and welfare of the low-end poor. Such an undertaking would require careful advance exploration by both governments and then extensive negotiation of purposes and ground rules. In this initial speculation I would not entirely rule out direct contributions to any of a variety of minimum needs; for example, nutritional supplementation for particularly vulnerable target groups, literacy programs, selected improvements in rural health services, protected village drinking water supplies. However, in an economy where there is such urgent need to engage idle or low-productivity labor, the labor-intensive creation of productive assets directly attacks the poverty problem through the additive employment route. Therefore the case seems compelling for concentrating most U.S. antipoverty funding on labor-intensive construction and certain other wage-intensive public-service projects.

Within the construction field it may be that some of the new funding would properly go for labor-intensive projects (e.g., portions of state highways, large irrigation works) too large to fit within the confines of small local jurisdictions. Rural works organized along special, nonlocalized (e.g., "land army") lines might be eligible. There would certainly need to be some provision for projects employing the urban poor, but the case would be strong for using the bulk of the new resources to fund localized supplementary works and construction in rural areas.

One shorthand formula for such an approach might be to extend Maharashtra's employment guarantee scheme (described briefly in Chapter 10) nationwide. However, one can imagine specific features that might be changed. Nationally the program might be headed by an agency in which the leadership at the Centre would sustain a keen interest and that would set policies and monitor and report performance. This group at the Centre might disburse resources to a set, let us say, or state-by-state antipoverty boards. The initial distribution to each would be proportional to population, perhaps inversely weighted by average income per capita. But if a state fund, as the result of generating qualified projects at a faster than average rate, were drawn down faster than average, it would probably be replenished more quickly.

It might be appropriate, if the government of India concurred, to use the program to strengthen local self-government and promote administrative decentralization within the states. In this event, on the one hand, state boards would need a degree of autonomy from the state secretariats and should include nonofficial as well as official members; on the other hand, project proposals would be expected to originate at local levels. Typically they would come from one layer or another of the *panchayati raj* (local self-government) structure, with lower-level proposals passing up the line for clearance; but there might also be provision for assistance to schemes proposed by voluntary agencies, cooperatives, and other nonofficial bodies other than private enterprises.

Such a program could have a broad and enduring impact on Indian rural development if it could serve to lever more local fiscal self-help. At least some categories of grants from state boards might be available to local bodies only if and as the latter demonstrated increased assembly and commitment of their own resources. Along with local taxes or the equivalent for projects yielding collective benefits, local bodies would need to show a program of user charges for recouping costs from the private beneficiaries of projects; and when they made subsequent proposals, they would be expected to report their cost-recovery record on earlier projects.

If the program adopted a matching-grant philosophy, the matching, particularly early on, would not need to be rupee for rupee; and state boards, guided by policies from the Centre, would probably scale matching requirements between better- and worse-off areas and/or project clienteles. But it would be important to begin building the local self-help pattern; and, to the extent the program incorporated this feature, it would diminish worry about local bodies choosing wasteful or low-priority projects and not implementing them effectively. Local people know their own needs, and if they are choosing among alternative projects whose direct effects do not spill significantly beyond the local jurisdiction itself, their sense of priorities and their demands for effective management are likely to be quite as sound as those issuing from on high, *especially* if they are betting some of their own resources.

In screening proposals, state boards would not be wholly passive on the matter of local projects' substantive purposes and characteristics. They would need to screen out local proposals that would substantially spill (especially negative) externalities on areas beyond the proposing jurisdiction—for example, water management or other farm-related schemes that would treat only part of a small watershed to the disadvantage of the rest or that would have adverse effects downstream—and reserve these for jurisdictions large enough to internalize most of the externalities. Moreover, state boards would, one hopes, be guided by some spatial strategy for rural development that would favor infrastructure projects helping the emergence of a network of rural growth centers. Nor would it be unreasonable for particular state boards at particular times, while leaving scope for local preferences, to reflect certain sectoral or functional biases—for example, toward irrigation or drainage or village-to-growth-center roads or schoolhouses—in their approvals of local proposals. But at the Centre and at the state levels the main disciplining of the program would be through the enforcement of a number of process norms, of which the following is an illustrative list:

1. All projects would have to meet minimum labor-intensity standards. At least a certain percentage (perhaps 50 percent) of their budgets would need to be wages for unskilled labor.

2. Wage rates, preferably of a piece-rate type, would be closely related to the local market rates for local landless labor.

3. Use of labor subcontractors would be discouraged, and if accepted, the rates at which contractors could skim workers' wages would be bounded.

4. Projects would be asked to show their potential for employing the educated unemployed.

5. Project authorities would need to demonstrate their continuing access to the necessary relevant professional and paraprofessional (e.g., engineering) expertise.

6. Local bodies would have to demonstrate a modicum of management capacity. Project authorities would have to demonstrate a rudimentary understanding of cost effectiveness, keep adequate books, and (both to encourage participatory decisionmaking and discourage corruption) prove a continuing openness of information locally about project purposes, operations, and finance.

7. In their proposals local bodies would need to show reliable plans for postconstruction operation of facilities, including, as necessary, agreements by governmental departments to operate and maintain them. The maintenance record of a local authority's past projects would become an important part of its case for new ones.

It is clear that many rural local bodies in India would not be able instantly to begin satisfying a very exacting set of process criteria of this sort. However, the scope of the indigenous potential for responding to such standards can easily be underestimated. Also, if both the central and most state governments were committed to making the antipoverty-fund approach work (the U.S. government would be foolish to enter into the arrangement unless it were strongly persuaded such was the case) a great deal could be done by state governments across the country to speed the pace at which local bodies could propose and execute competent projects. Governments could, for example, establish dispersed small technical staffs available to clusters of local authorities, set up training programs, provide manuals and materials, and supply services from departmental staffs, nonresident consultants, university students and local college faculties.[2]

----

[2] While the preceding sketch is fairly extensive, it skims over a great deal that is discussed at greater length in J.P. Lewis, "Designing the Public-Works Mode of Antipoverty Policy," in *Income Distribution and Growth in the Less Developed Countries,* ed. C.R. Frank and R.C. Webb, (Washington: Brookings Institution, 1977). In particular, in that longer treatment I deal with the political dynamics of such decentralized reform, which while overtly seeking income and employment benefits for the low-end poor, delegates decisionmaking to local political-social-economic elites, who may subvert the egalitarian purpose of the program. This possibility and the resulting need, therefore, for a reformist regime to worry about a parallel

The donor's procedural relationship to an antipoverty fund has been substantially indicated already. The donor's goal would be one of conditioning without pressure: it would provide a fund of resources whose disbursement would be triggered by the approval and progress of projects that satisfied criteria consistent with the negotiated purposes of the program. Implementation would be wholly by the government of India (and its subordinate jurisdictions), which would provide a running account of performance. Periodically, the whole arrangement would be subject to joint review, renegotiation, and possible renewal. But except for this, there would be no donor pressure on the recipient to draw down resources for the earmarked purposes and under the stiplulated conditions faster than the Indians involved collectively wished.

With this deliberately passive style, such dynamism as the United States imparted to Indian antipoverty policy would be directly related to the quantum of conditioned resources it supplied. For all of the talk about rural public works in the past, in most countries at most times the investment in such schemes—judged by aggregate antipoverty and employment needs—has been trivial. In the present case, as already suggested, something on the order of a nationwide spread of the present Maharashtra guaranteed-employment scheme—or perhaps a bit less—would represent commitment on a scale that could begin to make a genuine difference. This might create the equivalent of 4 million full-time jobs (hence giving part-time employment to several times 4 million workers) and cost the equivalent of $1 billion annually.

Scaling down slightly, let's take a target number of $900 million. I would hope that the incentive provided by the external assistance would induce Indian self-help (preferably, as indicated, additional resources raised locally) of, say, a third of the total. This suggests that the annual *availability* of resources that the United States should offer to generate an antipoverty, employment-creating investment program of major proportions might be on the order of $600 million. (As noted, not all of this would be used in the first years, but the money should be available.)

It has been suggested that there may be a U.S. political argument for providing a portion of such bilateral transfers in the form of food aid. The demand pull that added employment would place on food from the Indian side would converge with whatever supply push might exist on the American side. A rough calculation indicates that a $900 million employment program could generate extra food

strengthening of the political muscle of the poorer and weaker classes would be likely to be matters of lively interest to those on the U.S. side who would help to design an anti-poverty fund scheme. But these are sensitive questions; as has been indicated, the Indian regime seems to be more than nominally inclined toward greater political as well as economic equity; and U.S. representatives probably would do well not to introduce domestic Indian political issues into their anti-poverty negotiations more explicitly than the sketch in the text suggests.

demand of about $500 million.[3] However, although concessional food will be politically cheaper than dollars for the U.S. government, food's advantage will decline as the quantity of required food aid rises. Moreover, the government of India, when in doubt, would prefer dollars to food, retaining the option if necessary to use free foreign exchange to buy food commercially. Therefore I would suggest the following breakdown of a $600 million annual ceiling on U.S. contributions to the antipoverty fund: for food aid, $300-400 million; for dollar program grants, $200-300 million. The latter item is the main component of the overall package (aside from the food itself) that, it was suggested earlier, one could expect to be source tied.

This is not the place for a detailed discussion of how food aid dedicated to the support of poverty-reducing employment would be factored into the Indian economy. But it must be emphasized that the present scheme implies no commitment to the payment of wages in kind, which probably should be avoided as an inefficient mode of food distribution. Instead, it would not be difficult to devise an arrangement whereby, probably through the Food Corporation of India, American food contributed to the antipoverty fund would be sold in regional markets at places and times conforming to the pattern of project activity, with the proceeds accruing to state antipoverty boards (which might need a revolving bank credit to piece the sequence together).

As noted earlier, there is an unused rationale for American aid to India that might make good sense in the late 1970s and beyond. As a government that at times can afford to cast itself as a kind of surrogate for planetary interests, the United States might offer to partially compensate India and/or particular sub-jurisdictions within India for undertaking environmental maintenance and repair work whose benefits would spill outward to present and especially future inhabitants of the globe generally.

The Himalaya is a particularly fragile ecological system. As its population increases, wood scavenging, overgrazing, and the spread of field crops to terrain where they do not belong are scarring the majesty of the range and washing much of its topsoil forever downhill. Forests are gone or retreating in many parts of India; the Deccan plateau is eroding seriously, and as the holding power of uphill slopes diminishes and reservoirs silt up, seasonal flooding worsens on the Indo-Gangetic plain, waterlogging many areas and increasing the loss of soil to the sea.

---

[3] My assumptions are that the labor content of the programs would be 50 percent; that general income multipliers of 2 would apply to the expenditure and (negatively) to the added indigenous-taxation aspects of the program; and that the income elasticities of food demand for project laborers, for those receiving the non-labor-cost half of program expenditures, for the mainly better-off rural classes from which self-help taxes would be raised, and for the generality of consumers who receive multiplier income are, respectively, .7, .3, .5, and .4.

Most of the direct impacts of this ecological deterioration, to be sure, are sustained within the borders of the Indian Union, and the Indian government has forestry, soil conservation, and water management programs aimed at checking the losses. But the government's margins are narrow and other priorities urgent. In particular, it has not yet found sufficient resources for restructuring the economies and lifestyle of hill peoples into patterns that have optimal downstream effects. Given the world's interest in the preservation of Indian agriculture as well as the natural features of the subcontinent, the cause of Indian conservation is an obvious one for external support.

In the present sketch of a radically expanded U.S. transfer program I would put this cause not as an added possibility, but as one that cross-hatches the two preceding subsections. Those have mooted $600 million of additional World Bank-Bank-IDA funding and a bilateral contribution of up to $600 million annually to an antipoverty fund. Both of these loose numbers contain a good bit of room for an ecological priority. Indeed, a number of the capital project possibilities mentioned—biogas, solar energy, drainage—would have important environmental dimensions; the World Bank would do well to favor other conservation schemes. Similarly, most such work is conspicuously labor-intensive and therefore could readily be incorporated within the activity that the antipoverty fund would support. It should be noted, however, that the characteristics of self-help and local initiative emphasized in the earlier discussion would *not* fit many of the ecological works cases, where the object, often, is to engage locals in work without major local returns or to dissuade them from activity (e.g., goat husbandry in the hills) that is privately and/or locally attractive.

Hence, if the antipoverty fund were to have a serious environmental thrust, there would need to be a separate segment of the program, not operated on a matching-grant principle, in which the initiative would run not from the grassroots upward, but from the programmers downward. Local groups would be hired to do the state's or the nation's or the world's work. The inclusion of this procedurally inverted side might in fact increase the speed with which the total antipoverty effort could begin to register major employment and income effects. Without compromising the time-consuming leverage of decentralized project formation and local resource raising, there could be a widespread launching of ecological projects under the auspices of existing departmental organizations.

Additional Food Aid

In addition to the $300-400 million of American food aid (say 2 to 2.5 million tons) hypothesized above as partial support for additive employment programs, the Indian economy for some years yet is likely to have an average need for food imports to supply demand at existing prices.

The evidence is strong that the United States does not need to hang back from filling part of this need for fear the Indians will slack off on their agricultural promotion effort. Instead, an easier and especially a more secure food-supply position could yield powerful benefits in the realm of both growth and equity.

Thus the case for an additional slab of food aid is strong. The real question is how much, and here I would tend to be conservative. First, although the World Bank guesses that the average gap may be 5-6 million tons for several years, the Indians' own more ambitious domestic production targets deserve to be taken seriously. Second, despite the U.S. domination of the international food market, there is no reason why part of the Indian concessional need should not be met by such donors as Canada and the EEC. Third, and most important, what India needs from the United States even more than a large-scale food commitment is reliability, and at the U.S. end there will be a trade-off between the two.

For a country as large as India, whose domestic food shortfalls often are synchronized with shortages elsewhere and, in any event, have their own thudding impact on the international market, there is no good way of holding secure food reserves in the form of foreign exchange. The only base upon which such a country, especially with so cautious a government, is likely to build a market-stabilizing food regime is that of an ample in-country buffer. Left to the vagaries of domestic production, the present high buffer will tend to erode. A modest but assured annual supply from abroad that can slow that erosion (and that even in very good years can be squeezed in against the next bad monsoon) can therefore make a disproportionate contribution to—although it cannot by itself assure—food security.

For this purpose I would propose about 2.5 million tons of concessional American grain annually. Together with the grain available for the antipoverty fund, this would make a total of 4.5 to 5 million tons. More difficult than the quantity would be the new terms and priorities implied at the American end. For India and for other poorest countries a new kind of "Title I" PL 480 food aid not only should go as outright grants, it should have a priority, not a residual, claim on the U.S. national foodgrains budget. It is gratifying that such an upgrading of the development food assistance priority is not being contemplated within the Carter administration as an integral part of a new U.S. North-South posture. If confined to transfers to the poorest countries of the comparatively modest proportions I have suggested for India, it may be acceptable. There might be a one-time incidence of upward pressures on Soviet, European, and American food prices as a new fixed but limited set of aid claims was incorporated into the top of the national food budget. But even this upward pressure may be avoided if we make the change in a period, such as the present, of U.S. abundance, and if, thereafter, the U.S. economy is buffered from the claims of a steady outflow of concessional development food assistance by a stock the government has reserved for that use.

One further political thorn should be included in the food aid scenario: some of the old PL 480 restrictions on the recipient (e.g., restrictions on the recipient's right to export agricultural commodities) are developmentally pernicious and should be scrapped. Even so modified, food, up to a point, may be easier to get than loan/grant dollars for an administration intent upon expanding concessional transfers.

Technical Cooperation

By now, notional estimates (shown in table 11.1) have been ventured of the annual pattern in 1977 dollars to which U.S.-originating aid to India might build up over a period, say, of four years. Since we have already allocated the whole of the hypothetical program expansion I set out to discuss, it might appear that the scenario leaves no room for expanded technical cooperation. But this does not really follow, for the comparative financial scales are too disparate: the items above are all very large, round numbers, whereas at its peak in the 1960s, the annual cost of the U.S. bilateral technical assistance program never much exceeded $10 million. A technical cooperation budget several times the previous level could be fitted into the cracks and crevices of the global numbers cited in

Table 11.1   Estimated Pattern of Annual U.S.-Originating Aid to India
(Millions of U.S. dollars)

Fund	Estimate
Debt Relief	200 million
World Bank	600 million
IDA (200 million) Special Projects (400 million)	
Antipoverty Fund	600 million
Dollars (250 million) Food (350 million)	
Food (buffer reinforcement)	400 million
Total	1,800 million

table 11.1. Thus, under the revived aid hypothesis, money would be no reason for stinting on technical cooperation.

In one sense, nevertheless, the scenario would play down this area. As discussed in chapter 10, India, chiefly because of its considerable success in exploiting the underlying advantages offered by the scale of its manpower pool, is farther along than most poor countries—certainly than most of the poorest—in building technical and institutional capacity. It has very many universities, institutes, and all manner of applied research centers in the physical and social sciences, some of which, although cramped for resources and, in the case of teaching institutions, overburdened with students, do very good work. The time is largely past for bilateral technical assistance in the classic didactic pattern, which involved teams of resident Western advisers and technicians who aided the establishment and structuring of new institutions and, in certain instances, counseled official agencies.

One sees little room for a renewal of such assistance in the three sectors that dominated the U.S. technical assistance program in the past. In agriculture, enough of the new state-level agricultural universities are sufficiently rooted to help bring along some of the others. The crop research system is manned and is becoming structured nationwide. Under World Bank auspices Israeli specialist David Benor has in fact injected some evidently potent new methods into Indian agricultural extension very recently, although this is probably the exception—most further institutional and technical innovation and adaptation (for which there is a continuing need) will be indigenously led. In the population field, as noted briefly earlier, Indian policies and programs face an urgent need to regroup in the aftermath of the March 1977 election; but almost surely, in this newly complicated, still sensitive field, a reentry of U.S. technical assistance (which played a useful attention-raising role earlier) would be counterproductive. Indian education and literacy needs are critical and difficult, but at the primary and other mass-education levels of that have been most undernourished there is little evidence that Western specialists have much to offer.

However, as Chapter 10 also anticipated, there is a second side to the picture. India's head start technically has readied it for a new, interactive phase of technical cooperation, which external resources can assist. For one thing, there is scope for strengthening the World Bank's growing practice of building technical support and training components into its project funding by drawing on, among others, Indian institutions, consultants, and expertise. Beyond this, many of the pivotal (regional as well as national) Indian institutions need better facilities for interacting with scientific and other counterpart communities abroad. For example, as in one development-related discipline after another the best Indian universities move into an "import substitution" phase of Ph.D. training, they will need selected foreign Ph.D. fellowships to fill subject-matter gaps in local faculties; a sprinkling of visiting professors to fill out and reinforce those faculties; an abundance of postdoctoral fellowships to broaden fresh top-rank doctoral graduates who previously would have received their degree training abroad; and a variety of opportunities for senior staff to interact with colleagues abroad. As the recent *World Food and Nutrition Study* nicely spells out for its fields of concern (without specific reference to India), indigenous research institutions could benefit from marginal inputs of foreign exchange, better connections with international research centers, and two-way interchanges, including mutually interesting collaborations, with counterpart institutions in the United States and elsewhere.

All of this, together with an appropriate increase in the U.S. contribution to India's share of United Nations technical cooperation budgets—and together with institutional inputs to the requirements for proper program monitoring noted below—could well claim (still within the "cracks and crevices" of the big numbers above) some multiple of U.S. AID's technical assistance budget of the 1960s. Yet I would not see the U.S. field mission back in the business of mediating and managing technical cooperation in the old, heavily staffed fashion. The proper technical cooperation policy would be complex and pluralistic; it would depend considerably on how receptive the government of India is to the promotion of nonofficial, people-to-people and institution-to-institution interchange; and it lies beyond the scope of this discussion. However, although the new technical cooperation needs are important and warrant substantial support, it is imperative that responses to them should not be allowed to slip back into the technical assistance forms, let alone the concepts, of the past.

The administrative theme of this scenario is that a most useful, remarkably enlarged Indo-U.S. aid program could be effectively run on the U.S. government side with only a small presence in India. I have just dealt with technical assistance, which typically has accounted for the bulk of AID missions' staffing. Capital projects, together with the often prickly residual donor's functions would be left to the World Bank. Buffer-reinforcing food aid would be a macro operation (although, by passing over it, I do not necessarily mean to vote against some volume of the PL 480 Title II-type distribution of food to target groups by voluntary agencies). And pains would be taken to lodge the implementation of the most innovative, intrusive, and institutionally complex piece of the "big aid" program—the antipoverty fund—unilaterally with the Indians.

Plainly, such a program could be managed in the field by a quite small, very good staff. One of the two functions that would require a high quality of staff work is obvious: careful negotiation of pivotal working agreements, especially those concerning the antipoverty fund. The other essential function would be monitoring, and its importance can scarcely be exaggerated. The U.S. economic aid agency, in Delhi and in Washington, would be presiding over a massive set of U.S. taxpayers' investments in Indian development, of which a most careful reckoning would be owed. Along with its continuing cross-examination of program performance data flowing from the Indian government, a perceptive and informed staff would need regularly to convey to the executive branch, the Congress, and interested constituencies of the American public reliable political and economic interpretations of India's growth and redistributive achievements, prospects, and intentions.

Half of the needed external analytical infrastructure on which such interpretations would draw—the Indian half, represented by the emergence of competent, in some cases distinguished, applied development research institutes at the national level and in most regions of India—is in place and probably would be accessible to Ameican monitors via consulting contracts. The other needed half—competence of American universities in South Asia-focused development studies—was never very strong and is in a state of disrepair. Therefore an important, whether or not obvious, analogue to the kind of policy venture we have been examining would be a relatively small but decisive investment in the building of such expertise.

Conclusion

Of the many missed subjects in my two chapters, perhaps two deserve a word. Some readers will wonder at the neglect of multinational companies and foreign private investment. This, surely, is a significant dimension of the Indo-U.S. relationship. But the tendency of much American commentary is to grossly exaggerate the potential of multinationals for either good or evil, at least in the Indian context. Foreign companies are not about to mastermind, subvert, or (in any big way) bilk the Indian system; nor is there a prospect of their supplying large parts of the answers to India's problems. For many reasons—but, most important, as a matter of sheer scale—foreign private investment is not a serious alternative to the kinds of transfers we have been examining.

To bypass the subject of human rights may be an even more glaring ommission. It could not, of course, have been sidestepped in a discussion of this kind drafted before the end of Indira Gandhi's emergency. Then, I would have argued as I argue now, that the economic rights of the world's poor should be at least as basic a concern of American policy as their political rights; that, of the two, their economic rights can be more directly, albeit marginally, addressed by aid policies; that it is the number of poor people in India together with the country's capacity for self-help and redistributive reform, not the condition of political rights, that *primarily* motivates economic assistance to that country; and that whereas it is entirely appropriate for the United States to take a critical view of encroachments on human political rights whenever they occur, it should be slow to allow such encroachments to prevent it from assisting promising attacks on poverty.

Now, of course, the Indians themselves have gone such assessments one better. They have recommitted their development problems to constitutional processes and have reconnected the causes of human needs and human rights. In so doing they have raised the stakes for development, for whereas they have proven that a poor country can shake off repression, it can probably remain free only with broadening benefits for the poor.

It is the extra edge to the game that one hopes may reverse the negative imagery about India with which the previous chapter began. The case for aid resumption we have examined has been a cold-blooded one: logically, there is no way that three-fifths of the Fourth World, whatever its name, can be left out of a serious North-South demarche. But the constitutional-democratic process by which India is trying to effect its reforms, we always tell ourselves, and the Carter administration now tells us again, is one to which Americans have deep ideological ties.

Comment

Uma Lele

Lewis's paper deals with an impressive range of issues related to U.S. assistance to India and is written with a high degree of sensitivity on the questions he addresses. Lewis's experience in administering U.S. assistance to India at a crucial time in the relations between the two countries gives him a particular advantage in writing comprehensively and thoughtfully on this subject.

I agree with much of the diagnosis in the Lewis paper, including his analysis of factors that have soured Indo-U.S. aid relations, and of the preconditions necessary for making future U.S. aid to India a mutually beneficial and agreeable experience. Perhaps it is because of these large areas of agreement with his paper that I find it difficult to be convinced of the basic thrust of his argument about resuming aid to India.

It is not so much the aid amounts, which are after all meant to be indicative of the overall magnitudes, that I find bothersome. Rather, it is Lewis's optimism about raising U.S. assistance to India in a relatively short period of three to four years—especially on the basis of "mutuality, reciprocity, and civility"—that I do not share.

My major difficulty lies in the very arguments Lewis makes in support of increasing assistance to India. His foremost argument rests on humanitarian considerations, since a majority of the world's poor live in India. However, when applied to giving long-term assistance—as distinct from short-term disaster relief—the humanitarian justification does not seem to be conducive to promoting the relationship of mutuality, reciprocity, and civility, as is evident from the experience Lewis cites. Humanitarian assistance has increasingly been viewed, both by American and Indian policymakers, as a sophisticated version of the "begging bowl" concept, which is antithetical to achieving equality in the relationship. Given the starving millions that India contains, America wonders how India can expect to be treated as its equal, particularly on matters related to foreign policy, on which more is said later. Indians, on the other hand, find it difficult even to accept—let alone request—assistance on any basis other than equality. They, therefore, convey an impression of being ungrateful and lacking in graciousness.

Lewis's other argument, that India is likely to reach a higher rate of growth through U.S. assistance than it would otherwise, implies that savings are a greater constraint to India's development than the factors discussed later in these comments. Finally, in making a case for India's readiness for a push, Lewis interprets it to mean readiness in policy and in an institutional sense, as well as in a willingness to base future economic planning on large sums of U.S. bilateral assistance. However, the past experience, particularly with U.S. bilateral assistance points to the risks involved in such dependence.

If aid to India were to be resumed truly on the basis of mutuality, there would need to be a greater emphasis in the justification of U.S. assistance on the more positive considerations that seem to be special to India. The fact that even someone as sympathetic to India as Lewis did not bring these positive factors to bear in his paper indicates the difficulty of realizing the objective of equality. First, India is the largest democracy and has earnestly returned to the principle of human rights to which the United States—particularly under the Carter administration—has said it attaches high weight. If American aid were to be allocated on the criterion of human rights, no country would qualify more for U.S. assistance than India, particularly if present levels are viewed in per capita terms. Second, India has a substantial absorptive capacity relative to a number of other developing countries that already receive greater per capita U.S. assistance than even the levels proposed by Lewis for India. Due to greater institutional and manpower development, India has the capacity to make use of large amounts of foreign assistance in a more effective and efficient manner than most other developing countries. Third, India has groped for the ideal of meeting basic human needs longer than most other developing countries, with a few exceptions such as China and Vietnam which have achieved such objectives by revolutionary means. After all, the concept of intermediate technology as a way of increasing employment and incomes of the poor received attention in India as early as the 1950s; that is, during the First Five Year Plan, although our understanding of the issues involved in the use of intermediate technology is certainly greater now than it was then. Also, the concept of minimum needs was first operationalized formally in India's Fifth Five Year Plan (on which more is said later). The United States has most consistently and overtly opposed systems that achieve such objectives by revolutionary means. Fourth, India is an already large and potentially large market for U.S. exports similar to the market offered by China. U.S. business interests should therefore be expected to figure more strongly in promoting U.S. assistance than they seem to have thus far. Because of its size, India has been one of the developing countries' major importers of heavy capital equipment and food grains from the United States on a commercial basis. If prospects for India's development are as good as Lewis argues them to be, there should be far greater scope for expanding U.S. exports to India in the future than there has been in the past.

In the past these positive factors have not received much weight in the justification of U.S. assistance to India. On the positive side, humanitarian considerations have been the most important factor prompting American aid to India. The other factor has been the containment of China. Considerations based on U.S. self-interest have, however, been frequently outweighed by apprehension about India's policy of nonalignment, lack of support to the United States on certain critical foreign policy issues, explosion of the nuclear device, and interest in purchasing enriched uranium and heavy water for nuclear power plants. India's position on the North-South issues, including opening of U.S. markets for manufactured goods to developing countries and the law of the sea issues, have not helped in improving its popularity in the U.S. Congress. Particularly given the seeming inability of India to ensure food for its millions of poor, many in the U.S. Congress have resented India's foreign policy positions on these various matters. The Lewis paper does not provide an adequate justification as to why, in the future, the U.S. apprehension about these matters should not outweigh U.S. concerns about human rights and U.S. commercial interest as indeed they have done in the past.

Even if aid were available on the basis that Lewis outlines, how realistic is his assumption of India's willingness to base its future stepped-up economic planning on the basis of continued U.S. assistance? As is so well documented in the Lewis chapter and in several other chapters in this book, the U.S. role in performance conditioning has led to much ill will in official circles in both countries. Although top levels of administration change in both countries, the civil servants and economists who advise on these issues do not turn over rapidly, particularly in India. These problems and tensions are, therefore, not forgotten as quickly as Lewis assumes in his paper. Besides, the so-called Congressional mandate to reach the poor in developing countries does not make U.S. aid less interventionist, it only changes the basis of performance conditioning from overvalued exchange rates to poor targeting, a subject that the Lewis paper discusses at considerable length. (Incidentally, for a number of reasons, I find the phrase "poor targeting" unfortunate.) However, the reality of designing programs that would reach the poor—as seen by policymakers in India—needs greater exploration and understanding than Lewis has provided, particularly in view of the sensitivity with which outsiders must treat these issues if communications between donor and recipient are not to break down.

In developing such an understanding, the point made earlier needs reiteration; namely that India's leadership has shown a substantial commitment to dealing with the poverty problem, albeit within its present institutional framework, that is, without radical restructuring of Indian society. The realization of the minimum needs objective of its Fifth Five Year Plan has, however, been bogged down

by a number of political and economic realities. First, experience shows that en-
suring basic needs is largely academic without providing the poor with a solid productive base. In the case of landless and marginal farmers, who constitute the
majority of the poor in India, productivity and incomes will probably not be improved without redistribution of land. Public works are a way of generating employment, but are only marginally effective when viewed in comparison with
the magnitude of the poverty problem. When asset distribution is unequal, even
public works such as road building or land leveling ultimately largely benefit
those who have productive assets, although short-term employment benefits may
accrue to the landless. A democratic government that has been brought into
power largely by the alliance of middle-level peasantry and the trading classes in
rural areas is finding it difficult to deal with the problem of land distribution
frontally, a point that Lewis has not emphasized adequately. And any interference
from outside agencies, particularly from the bilaterals, in dealing with this fundamental problem is likely to create more ill will and misunderstanding than the
continuation of a large aid program could sustain.

The role of asset distribution in determining who benefits from poor targeting
is even greater than it appears on the surface, because of the close interaction of
control of economic resources with political power and social status. The greater
the asset disparities at the local level, the greater the difficulty in planning effective employment programs for the poor through a participatory decentralized
approach, which has had much appeal in donor circles recently. Also, the greater
the likelihood of programs being controlled by the local political elite for their
own benefit, the greater the need for outside scrutiny, whether it be from the
central government or from a foreign donor. Effective agrarian reform can, therefore, frequently reduce the need for external interference.

The situation with regard to asset distribution, political power and hence the
potential for decentralized planning varies immensely among parts of India.
However, in areas where the need for employment generation is the greatest, as
in parts of Bihar and Eastern Uttar Pradesh, the need for institutional reform is
also greater than Lewis has stressed. It is not clear from Lewis's paper, for instance, how the issue of institutional reform would be dealt with under increased
U.S. assistance for poor targeting in light of Indian sensitivity to outside interference, and particularly in the context of India's present democratic framework.

Meeting the basic needs objective also means committing large recurrent budgetary resources on salaries, wages, and operating costs of personnel and facilities
involved in implementation of programs. Once expansion of such activities takes
place, the newly created expectations make it difficult to retract them without
political costs. Unless the country's domestic tax base is raised substantially to
sustain such activities—not an easy task in a democratic system—the basic needs

objective must be met either by reallocation of recurrent resources from what appear to policymakers to be expenditures of equal priority, such as development of (capital-intensive) physical infrastructure and heavy industry, or alternatively through continual external assistance. The former implies sacrificing the broader objectives of nation building and overall economic growth, which may often be perceived in the military power context by outsiders. The latter involves dependence on external sources. The risks in the latter approach are perceived to be high, particularly as aid-giving countries have not developed ways of committing their assistance on a long-term basis. If anything, the recent trend in the U.S. Congress has been to link assistance closely to its periodic review of the country's performance. Lewis very correctly emphasizes the importance of long-term aid commitments, continuity, and program loans rather than close external scrutiny, project aid, and short-term commitments. Continuity of commitments would be just as crucial in the long-term infrastructure projects that Lewis has outlined, given the lumpiness of those investments. Again, I find it difficult to believe either that the domestic economic effort would be redirected at the cost of India's overall economic and political objectives or that long-term U.S. aid commitments could be achieved without what to India may seem to be unacceptable interference in domestic political affairs, given the political realities within which foreign assistance is provided by the United States.

There is a third dimension of political and economic reality of a broad-based development strategy that Lewis has not stressed fully. Increased expenditure of recurrent budgetary resources, which would benefit the poor, tends to be inflationary in that it raises effective demand for essential goods such as food and clothing among the low and the middle income classes. This leads to a push for higher urban industrial wages. The Janata Government, which has given a relatively free reign to the labor unions, seems apprehensive about the possible inflationary implications of a more expansionary economic policy—despite the 20 million tons of grain stocks, over U.S. $5 billion in the form of foreign exchange reserves, and a great deal of prodding by international financial agencies to follow more expansionary economic policies. The government's unwillingness to do so even under these favorable circumstances perhaps best reflects the intensity with which it wishes to minimize the political risks of losing elections domestically and depending on assistance externally, particularly if there should be one or two bad crops that could wipe out both the grain and the foreign exchange reserves. On the other hand, by now it is generally recognized that India would not be able to achieve the annual growth rates of 5 to 7 percent that Lewis refers to without, among other things, inflating internal effective demand. This indicates that the problems related to India's development, and certainly those involving the poor, are integrally related to her political system and her strong desire to be self-reliant.

They require some difficult policy decisions by the government that have not been forthcoming.

If guaranteed to be available over a long term on the scale that Lewis envisages, outside assistance would certainly affect the basic decisions of India's policy-makers, provided of course that the assistance is not seen to be a patronizing or interventionist handout, but is based on a genuine understanding of the political realities within which a democratic government must operate. The spirit with which assistance is given and received would thus be of the utmost importance. In the present state of relationships between the two countries, however, it is doubtful if the necessary mutual trust and understanding exists to work out aid arrangements on the basis of mutuality, reciprocity, and civility.

XII

Conclusion

John W. Mellor

What will be the pace and pattern of India's political and economic development over the next few decades? What are the options? Does India's development matter to the United States? Does U.S. policy matter to India? How should U.S. policy toward India fit into the broader framework of U.S. foreign policy?

The papers in this volume contribute to answering these questions, although the answers raise substantial points of disagreement among the authors and commentators. They differ most emphatically on whether the U.S. should resume substantial bilateral assistance to India, and also disagree on whether such assistance would in practice facilitate development and significantly advance U.S. interests. Opponents and proponents of such assistance have very different assumptions about its objectives, however, and much of the debate stems from different expectations about the context and substance of resumed bilateral aid.

Although they disagree on many issues, the authors consistently and strongly challenge the standard public stereotype of India as a nation incapable of initiating its own development. On the contrary, as the chapters by Weiner, Mellor, Quester, Long, and Ezekiel make clear, India has made substantial, perhaps even extraordinary, progress. India left its colonial era poorly equipped to preserve its national integrity and freedom of action in a difficult and hostile world environment. Since then, India has built a domestic base of political, economic, technological, and trade capabilities consistent with a large and growing international role. The first 30 years of independence saw India lay the foundation for its goal of growth to major power status. The second 30 are likely to see that aspiration realized.

Weiner describes India's evolution into a pluralistic, democratic society with a broadening base of political support. He notes the many difficulties encountered and the substantial tensions that remain. Progress has been uneven, and the political system retrogressed into a centralized, authoritarian regime for several years under Indira Gandhi. But the authoritarian episode occurred during a period of great economic stress associated with sharp decline in foreign assistance, and the Indian political system is now much less vulnerable to direct outside attack or influence than it was at independence. Nevertheless, given the instability of so many political systems in rich countries as well as poor, it seems unlikely that India's system is fully coalesced, that there are no longer ideological alternatives, or that external forces do not matter.

India's economic development as described by Mellor significantly parallels its political development—it began weak and narrow based, but broadened over time, and its rate and direction fluctuated considerably. The substantial foundation India has built over the first 30 years of independence offers scope for greatly accelerated growth in the future, and the strategy India selects will determine how soon accelerated development will occur, how great it will be, who will benefit, how autarkical it will be, and which major powers India will have close economic relations with. India has already made key choices affecting the structure of its economy—for example, the change during the 1950s towards a heavy-industry strategy, and the apparent shift in the late 1960s and the 1970s towards more emphasis on agriculture and small to medium scale industry. Future choices will depend substantially on internal political and economic forces, particularly as these forces determine the capacity of various socioeconomic classes to provide resources for public and private sector purposes. Choices concerning the resources available through trade and capital flows and military and political security will affect India's relations with other nations.

India already has a substantial scientific and technical capacity, although there is need for considerable improvement in quality. This development of scientific expertise is broadly described in Franklin Long's paper, reinforced by George Quester's more specialized treatment, and further confirmed by Onkar S. Marwah's statement of military capability. A commitment to scientific and technological advance was made by Prime Minister Nehru in 1958 and by physicist Homi Bhabba, who even before independence foresaw a major place for India in nuclear energy development.

Questions of economic and political development are closely linked with India's scientific capacity. Decisions about the deployment of scientific capacity and the eventual attainment of technological leadership interact with the choice of an economic growth strategy and India's international role. For example, the long debate over whether India should turn its nuclear capability to explosive applications illustrates how external forces affect India's strategy.

The growth of the Indian economy and its scientific and technological capability have created numerous trade options. Hannan Ezekiel documents the extent to which India has already diversified its trading partners. He points to the rapid exploitation of the enormous new export potentials in the Middle East and suggests nascent potentials in other Third World regions. For the future, India has the option of continuing the old, relatively autarkic patterns of growth with little commercial interaction with the rest of the world or of adopting a much more expansionary course: for example, selling more to the industrial nations and buying capital-intensive goods in return; or trading capital goods to Third World countries for raw materials or convertible currencies that they have obtained from raw material exports to the West. Ezekiel illustrates the strong link between choice of sectoral emphasis in domestic investment and growth in the size and composition of trade. Further, it is clear that while autarkic growth in the Second and Third Five Year Plan periods resulted in short-run losses in both domestic growth and trade, it has provided a base for growth of exports and for a more interdependent strategy of development.

India's emergence as a middle power is the product of political, economic, and technological policies dictated largely by its global aspirations. Baldev Raj Nayar's paper contrasts India's development and aspirations with the American stereotype of India, which departs so far from reality that it creates confusion and tension.

U.S. policy is a product of this stereotype portraying India as poverty-stricken and helpless, which has changed little in 30 years. The stereotype emanates in part from, and is reinforced by, the American foreign policy establishment, which is notably conservative, has long been oriented towards Europe, and relegates responsibility for relations with Asia and Africa to its less ambitious and aggressive members. The State Department includes India in its Near East and South Asia component, which is under an assistant secretary of state who is almost totally occupied with Israel-related issues. Relations with India are handled primarily by a deputy assistant secretary four levels removed from the secretary of state! A more effective U.S. policy toward India would be based not on an obsolete stereotype, but on India's rate of growth, on the weight given the global questions of ideology, population, and natural resources in which the Third World already figures strongly, and on Soviet-American relations.

While India has followed a generally nonconfrontational approach to foreign policy, Nayar's paper makes it clear that longer-term options, including the nuclear, contain an increasing potential for conflict. The faster India grows and the more important its ideological, commercial, and political relationships become, the more likely it will be that its global aspirations will conflict with American positions.

Here the United States faces a dilemma. Given the constancy of Indian objectives and the extent of their achievement, it seems likely that India will continue to follow an independent foreign policy. The choice facing the United States is whether to facilitate the rise of an independent position for India and in the process influence, at least marginally, the form that it might take; or to follow policies that do not support and may even discourage Indian growth in power, but that may turn India against broader U.S. interests. The second of these choices may be characterized as "benign neglect," the first as "development support." Development support is surely the more prudent for the long run, but it requires maturity in attitude and subtlety of policy for which there is little precedent. U.S. opposition to India's growth is likely to be indirect rather than overt because of strong domestic support for humanitarian and population control measures. For example, in the past a policy of benign neglect has been rationalized by emphasizing India's substantial reserve of foreign exchange and food, its intransigent position on nuclear inspection, its support for Arab aspirations, and its tendency to moralize.

Whatever course is followed, tension between the two countries is inevitable. India finds it less necessary than formerly to accept United States hegemony in South Asia. This will gradually become the case in adjacent regions as well. Good relations will require somewhat more adjustment by the United States than India, perhaps further increasing U.S. impatience. The fact that U.S. public opinion has hardly begun to adjust to the rising importance of Third World powers exacerbates the difficulty. The United States will face similar problems with other Third World nations as relative power relationships change.

A policy of benign neglect implies that India's development is of little consequence to major international issues facing the United States, or that Indian policy cannot be influenced in any case. The latter assumption recognizes India's dedication to an independent position but fails to recognize the extent to which its domestic and foreign policy decisions are indirectly influenced by the global environment, which is dominated by the United States.

A policy of development support would assume that the speed and direction of India's growth could be made favorable to U.S. interests; in other words, that India's development does matter to the United States and that U.S. policy can influence it. To be effective, such a policy should support an appropriate development strategy and reinforce complementary policies, but it cannot be expected to reconcile all conflicts.

Trade and aid are the crucial elements of U.S. economic policy towards India. The costs and benefits of technology transfer and commodity policy are more difficult to judge but are also important. In each area, the United States has significant policy options.

In the long run, expanding trade is, of course, much more important to India's development than aid, because trade not only provides foreign exchange for key capital-intensive and high-technology imports, it offers effective demand for domestic industry in a context highly favorable to high rates of saving and investment.

Hannan Ezekiel's chapter makes three major points concerning U.S. trade policy with India. First, India's capacity to export has increased dramatically in the last few decades and could grow even more in the future. Second, India's range of actual and potential trading partners has broadened greatly. Third, not only would imports increase greatly as a result of a trade related strategy, the imports could be highly complementary to United States production.

In 1976, trade between India and the United States was roughly in balance at about $0.8 billion. In the mid-1950s, when relations were most favorable, 38 percent of India's imports came from the United States; the figure dropped to 13 percent in 1972–73 when relations were at their nadir, but rose to 25 percent in 1976. Based on Ezekiel's projections of total trade in 1985, and the maximum 38 percent proportions of the past, the United States could have a $12 billion export market in India. Even half that amount, a minimal expectation, would mean that the U.S. was developing a stake in a rapidly growing, potentially massive market.

Strained relations and U.S. reticence to expand trade would encourage India to return to more autarkic development policies and to increase trade with Third World countries. India's emphasis on capital-goods production relative to consumer goods would reduce interdependencies not only between India and the United States, but between industrial and developing nations generally.

U.S. support of India's development would emphasize international agreements favorable to the classes of commodities exported by India. Moreover, it would convey an attitude of sympathy and concern for Indian exports that would encourage substantial sales of Indian goods on U.S. markets. An expansionary trade policy would facilitate growth of U.S. imports of labor-intensive products, including clothing, textiles, light consumer goods, processed agricultural commodities, and labor-intensive capital goods. Such imports would be opposed by the domestic industries affected. However, India's exports to the United States are only a small proportion of U.S. imports of such commodities so that trade policies toward India are likely to be affected more by international relations than by domestic political factors.

Imports are strongly influenced by discretionary administrative decisions concerning classification of commodities for tariff and quota application and by discretionary negotiations on quotas. An expansionary trade policy would mean decisions conducive to taking the risks inherent in entering new markets. The spectacular performance of Taiwan and South Korea in U.S. markets is related not only to their strong political position in the United States but also to favorable administrative decisions that created an environment attractive to potential exporters.

U.S. exports to India under a development support policy would be facilitated by major expansions of credits from the Export-Import Bank, whose predilection for capital goods and sophisticated technology would encourage such a policy.

In addition, India's impeccable record of debt repayment, its strong reserve position, and its accelerated growth create a favorable economic context for such action.

Even though trade may be preferable to aid in meeting long-run objectives of both India and the United States, the potential importance of aid should not be underrated, particularly in the short run. Modest levels of per capita assistance can make large differences in the investment rate of countries with low per capita income. India's per capita foreign aid is less than half the $7 level typical of low-income Third World countries. That $7 figure is less than Indonesia receives at present, and less than half of the levels of Tanzania and Chile only a few years ago. If aid to India were raised to the $7 average, it would total over $4 billion a year, more than twice the 1978 level, which is already substantially higher than that of the immediately preceding years. Aid at such a level would increase the amount of foreign exchange available to India by more than one third and would allow it to expand total investment by more than a tenth. More resources for investment to the public sector would help break the power and transportation bottlenecks that restrain profitability and expansion of private investment. Most important, such assistance could profoundly affect the pace and pattern of India's development, and hence a wide range of political forces.

Somewhat over half of India's foreign assistance from Western countries now comes through the International Development Association (IDA), the World Bank subsidiary that makes highly concessional loans. In the longer run, the World Bank's more commercially priced loans, the large commercial banks, and the International Monetary Fund may be important sources of financial flows to India. The United States is a powerful influence in each.

A policy of benign neglect would, in the short run, concentrate on reducing India's share of IDA disbursements. There was a concerted effort, led by the Treasury Department, to do this in the early months of the Carter administration. India had been receiving about 40 percent of total IDA funds, a level that represented a compromise between the share commensurate with India's population, particularly in low-income categories, and the desire for a broad national representation in IDA disbursements. India has 55 percent of the total population of the countries that received IDA loans in 1975–76 and 1976–77, and 60 percent of the low-income population of countries eligible for IDA loans. India's 40 percent share of IDA funds is probably a reasonable compromise, since its highly developed institutions and large numbers of trained personnel give it a greater capacity than other low-income countries, even on a per capita basis, to productively use assistance. The effort by the United States to reduce that share (at one point to as low as 25 percent) was, of course, an overt attempt to politicize the World Bank in the interests of a single donor. Although that effort failed, in no small part due to Senator Humphrey's intervention with the U.S. Administration, a sustained effort in the future might well succeed.

There are several ways in which the United States could implement a policy of development support to India. First, it could support increases in India's share and in the total size of IDA disbursements. Second, the United States could support an increase in the volume of the World Bank's more commercial loans in response to the increasing rate of private credit to India through the Eurocurrency market and loans by the large private banks. India's excellent record of repayment, its substantial foreign exchange reserves, and its long history of conservative fiscal policy suggest a potentially large role for private lending to India if bilateral relations are favorable.

U.S. policy towards future evolution of the International Monetary Fund will be of particular importance to India. The IMF has begun to develop policies more relevant to the needs of developing countries. Clearly, what is needed is for the IMF to facilitate transitions of developing countries from relatively tightly controlled, autarkic systems of growth to strategies that place more emphasis on rapid increase of foreign trade, employment, agriculture, and complementary industry. When Taiwan and South Korea made such a transition in the late 1950s and early 1960s the critical guarantees of foreign exchange came largely from the United States. Under present circumstances, and particularly for a large country like India, risk bearing would have to be provided by the IMF. The IMF has been encouraging more expansionary policies in India, encouragement which has merit given India's substantial reserves of foreign exchange and grain. However, for such encouragement to be responsible, the Fund must stand ready to finance two or three years of substantial deficits if expansionary policies overshoot the mark, natural calamity strikes, or external economic pressures mount. India's trade and foreign exchange represent only a small proportion of its gross national product (GNP), so small errors in tuning the economy, or bad weather, can easily cause changes of one or two billion dollars a year in the balance of payments. Indian perceptions of how the Western community will respond to such a situation will have an important influence on how expansionary its policy will be.

In its bilateral program, the United States has already gone about as far toward benign neglect as possible. Gross aid flows to India from the United States by the mid-1970s had dropped to a level roughly equivalent to India's $150—$200 million annual repayments to the United States for past aid, and by the late 1970s considerably below that level.

Bilateral assistance under a policy of development support would most likely be near the levels delineated by John Lewis. Lewis derives his proposal from two considerations: first, the relation of India to the total amount of U.S. foreign assistance; and second, the relation of India to the global objectives of foreign aid.

In the mid-1970s, the ratio of U.S. official development assistance to U.S. national product was less than two-thirds the average for the other industrial nations. If the U.S. share were raised to match that of the other industrial nations, the absolute increase in aid would be large—perhaps too large for most low-income countries which are so deficient in institutional development and trained personnel that they could not effectively utilize large increases in assistance. However, India is much better prepared to do so. Therefore a large increase in assistance to low-income nations would require major participation by India. Conversely, if participation by India is ruled out, utilization of assistance would be at low levels, with a correspondingly limited aggregate impact on global poverty.

To attain the global objectives of mitigating poverty and reducing population growth rates, assistance to India must be significant on a per capita basis and therefore large in total. But the amount of per capita assistance proposed by John Lewis is small compared to that received by Taiwan and South Korea, which are dramatic examples of successful foreign assistance. It is not even large compared to U.S. bilateral assistance to India in the late 1950s or early 1960s.

The United States has a special role to play in technical assistance because of its technological dominance in both agriculture and industry. Though the financial requirements of technical assistance are modest, its impact on development is large because of its contribution to the training of personnel and the growth of institutions that enable a developing nation to utilize capital assistance.

Because technical assistance is based on cross-cultural exchanges of people, it has a high political impact, particularly when relations are tense. John Lewis's proposals for technical assistance are meant to appear modest. However, he suggests a considerably higher level of technical assistance to India than the United States has provided before. Long points out that in the past, American technical assistance was largely organized and administered by the U.S. government. He proposes that India administer future technical assistance because Indian personnel and institutions have reached a level of development that permits utilization of substantial numbers of technical people at the operating level.

Franklin Long's paper also clearly indicates a major capacity to utilize such assistance. Long stresses the need for centers of excellence in India, perhaps at the best agricultural universities and institutes of technology. The United States has made a major contribution to such efforts in the past. It could do so again. On the other hand, a justification for benign neglect would emphasize that India already has many trained people, does not request technical assistance, and will not accept it in the forms in which it is offered.

A development support approach would carefully suit technical assistance to the needs of India and the resources of the donors. It would recognize the special advantage of technical assistance to both donor and recipient, particularly in aligning institutions in a manner conducive to comfortable interaction between countries.

The most important gains to the United States and other industrial nations from a development support program would be progress towards humanitarian objectives, reducing population growth rates, fostering democratic institutions, expanding human rights, and favoring evolutionary rather than revolutionary change in a major Third World country. This argument assumes that these objectives would be facilitated by faster growth and by reducing financial and other risks that accompany it.

There is much evidence to support the argument that the tensions that resulted in despotic government under Indira Gandhi were aggravated by deteriorating economic conditions associated with the decline in aid from 1965 to 1975. Expanding foreign aid offers the prospect of reduced national political tensions by allowing the interests of more groups to be met at lesser domestic cost. There is the very clear danger, of course, that satisfying some of these interests in the short run merely postpones difficult choices and results in higher longer-run cost. To avoid postponing choices requires a high level of sophistication of donor and recipient alike. One might hope, however, that the time is now right for getting India into a period of genuine independence from concessionary bilateral assistance, as is implied in the Mellor and the Lewis papers.

It should be noted in passing that U.S. assistance to India was largely eliminated during a period of democratic government. There was thus little scope for further reduction when Mrs. Gandhi established an authoritarian regime in June 1975. Trade flows also had declined. The U.S. potential to influence assistance from the multilateral agencies was reduced by the very heavy pressure from the United States to increase loans to the increasingly totalitarian regimes of Chile, South Korea, and the Philippines.

In addition to fostering the development of democratic institutions, increased assistance may contribute to friendly relations, which would facilitate useful interchange between the United States and India on global issues. This would help to formulate more workable American policies which India could support. Nayar and others make it clear that India cannot be expected to sacrifice significant interests for foreign assistance, particularly when that assistance is small relative to the nation's total resources. Nevertheless, the United States and India have many common interests, which friendly working relationships would foster. Incidentally, even during the Kissinger period of tense relations, the United States often turned to India for help in reaching compromise positions with the Third World. India has maintained a relatively stable, conservative position on global issues and has a well-trained experienced diplomatic staff. This makes it easier for U.S. diplomats to get down to the facts of a situation and determine where self-interests lie. Improving that relationship or preventing its erosion is valuable to the United States and other industrial nations.

The United States has expressed special concern on the population issue. As John Mellor reports, the Desai government has clearly opted for the rural development, high-employment strategy most likely to create an environment conducive to rapid decline in population growth rates. A return of the economic pressures of the Indira Gandhi authoritarian period might well push India into such a political situation again and result in adoption of a strategy of growth that would further delay decline of birth rates. It is, of course, unlikely that future totalitarian regimes would choose the forced family planning that played such a key role in Mrs. Gandhi's demise.

Finally, an enlarged bilateral assistance program would facilitate increased trade and private investment flows. These would arise directly from tying aid to U.S. exports and from faster growth, and indirectly from more favorable trade rules.

The benefits to the United States and other Western, industrial nations from development assistance to India may be great. But they tend to be long term, intangible, and difficult to attribute directly to foreign assistance policy. In contrast, the costs tend to be more immediate and tangible, even though the financial elements are not large in relation to total government expenditures. The financial costs of John Lewis's proposal for aid to India represent about 20 percent of the Carter administration's proposed expanded foreign assistance budget, which is less than half of one percent of U.S. GNP. Assistance to India would represent less than one-tenth of one percent of GNP and less than four-tenths of one percent of the total federal budget.

John Lewis's program for India would require numerous changes of policies and practices from those the United States adopts toward other developing nations. These changes include more emphasis on choice of broad programs rather than specific projects and greater autonomy of choice, particularly in technical assistance. Such changes would set new precedents for other countries which would involve additional political costs if they were not followed. However, George Quester's chapter, which deals primarily with nuclear proliferation, discusses the reasons why India should be dealt with differently than smaller countries on a wide range of issues other than nuclear policy.

Of primary importance is the effect of U.S.-Soviet relations on U.S. policy concerning India. Facilitating India's development into a broadly participatory democracy would serve the long-run interests of the United States, but in the short run it may seem advantageous to view India as more of an ally of the Soviet Union and a competitor with China. Placating China by adopting a benign neglect policy toward India may appear to be a way to strengthen the U.S. position vis-à-vis the Soviet Union. Such trade-offs between long- and short-term interests have weighed heavily on U.S.-Indo relations. For instance, during periods of large-scale U.S. assistance to India, there was emphasis in congressional testimony on the containment of China. More recently, relations with India have deteriorated as those with China have improved.

The short-run, domestic political costs of substantial support to India are likely to be high. At the very least, it will take a few years of active political leadership to reduce them. A trade policy supportive of Indian exports, even though the proportion of U.S. trade affected was very small, would be opposed by the low-wage sectors of the U.S. economy. Experience shows that even small disadvantaged domestic producers are more powerful than consumer or export interests.

Of more concern are India's poor image in the United States and the unreadiness of the U.S. electorate to comprehend the implications of the rising power and autonomy of the large Third World countries. It will be particularly difficult for the U.S. electorate to understand a sophisticated U.S. policy of development support, which cannot be expected to divert India from its own long-term interests of maintaining policy options and will strengthen India's position against the United States when interests clash. Differences on nuclear issues are a striking example. If the United States perceives its support to India entirely in humanitarian terms, it is not surprising that it resents lack of support on a big power issue that it believes to be of no concern to India. An effective development support policy that forwards U.S. interests can be implemented only if the public views those interests in a long-run context.

Reflecting the electorate's perceptions of India, many legislators have taken positions contrary to effective development support for India. An administration policy of development support will have rough political sailing until these positions can be reversed. Similarly, several key appointees in the Carter administration in practice oppose policies favorable to Indian development. These too would take time to turn around.

Public, legislative, and bureaucratic positions have been shifting the last few years, as has the establishment press. The number of news and human interest stories favorable to India has been much greater than at any time in the last decade, while the number of unfavorable mentions has been declining.

What can we conclude about future U.S.-Indo relations? Perhaps the only certainty is that what happens in India will be of increasing importance to the United States. Whether U.S. policy can influence events and policies favorably is much less certain. It is equally uncertain how much priority the United States will attach to influencing India.

Geopolitical forces, especially those relating to China and the Soviet Union, favor the policy of benign neglect of India. What is uncertain is whether such neglect will result in mounting internal and external pressures on the Indian economy that will turn India to totalitarianism of the right or left. The foreign policy trade-off is one of short-term *realpolitik* gains against long-term ideological and economic losses.

In the final analysis, U.S. relations with India will depend on recognition of the long-run importance of ideological affinity, the subtle relationship between economic development and ideological orientation, and the inappropriateness of simple "good guy-bad guy" distinctions in international affairs. The U.S. role is much more difficult than India's because the United States must make most of the adjustment in its thinking and policies. Until such adjustment occurs, Uma Lele's somewhat pessimistic views seem all too realistic. One is inclined to add that American study of the Bhagavad Gita and its sophisticated exposition of life in a world lacking simple moral absolutes would facilitate this adjustment.

The old power structure must eventually adapt to the growing ability of the Third World, especially of the rising middle powers such as India, to influence world events. India has taken a conciliatory and evolutionary approach to its foreign relations in the last few years. One may hope that the increase in congressional initiatives in Third World diplomatic issues will lead eventually to an enlightened pursuit of U.S. long-term interests in a world of more broadly shared power.

Authors and Commentators

William J. Barnds is a Senior Research Fellow at the Council on Foreign Relations in New York. He has specialized in Asian affairs and United States foreign policy toward Asia for more than twenty years, and is the author of *India, Pakistan and the Great Powers* and other books dealing with United States-Asian relations.

Padma Desai is a Research Associate at the Harvard Russian Research Center and Visiting Professor of Economics at Boston University. She has served as a consultant with many international agencies, including the United Nations Economic Commission for Asia and the Far East, the Organization for Economic Cooperation and Development, the United Nations Conference on Trade and Development, and the United Nations, and is "Reviews" editor for the *Journal of Development Economics.* Her major publications include three books on Indian trade and industrialization and a fourth on Soviet aid to the Bokaro steel plant.

Hannan Ezekiel is an Economic Consultant in Toronto and Visiting Associate Professor at Glendon College, York University. He was Chief of the Financial Studies Division of the International Monetary Fund and Chief Economic Consultant of Tata Economic Consultancy Services in Bombay. He is the author of four books, including *The Pattern of Investment and Economic Development* and *Second India Studies: An Overview.*

Uma Lele is Senior Economist in the World Bank's Eastern Africa Projects Department. She served as a Visiting Professor and Senior Research Fellow at the Center for International Studies at Cornell University and authored or co-authored three books and numerous other publications dealing with various aspects of rural development in Africa and India. Her most recent book is *Design of Rural Development: Lessons for Africa.*

John P. Lewis is a Professor of Economics and International Affairs at Princeton University. He was a Senior Fellow at the Brookings Institution, a member of the President's Council of Economic Advisors, Dean of the Woodrow Wilson School of Public and International Affairs at Princeton University and Minister Director of the United States Agency for International Development Mission to India. He is author of *Quiet Crisis in India: Economic Development and American Policy.*

F. A. Long is a Henry Luce Professor of Science and Society at Cornell University and is currently Co-Chairman for the United States of the Joint Indo-U.S. Sub-commission on Education and Culture.

Onkar Marwah is a Research Fellow with Harvard University's Program for Science and International Affairs. He has held appointments with the Indian government as a member of the Indian Administrative Service. Dr. Marwah has written extensively on strategic and security issues of the Third World and was recently awarded a Rockefeller Foundation grant for research on nuclear proliferation problems.

John W. Mellor is Director of the International Food Policy Research Institute. He was previously Chief Economist of the United States Agency for International Development and prior to that was on the faculty of Cornell University, where he specialized in agricultural economics, economics, and Asian studies. He is the author of *The New Economics of Growth: A Strategy for India and the Developing World; Developing Rural India: Plan and Practice;* and *The Economics of Agricultural Development.*

Baldev Raj Nayar is a Professor of Political Science at McGill University in Montreal. He is the author of *Minority Politics in the Punjab,* which won the Watumull Prize, and *American Geopolitics and India.* He also contributed to *Foreign Policy* and *Comparative Politics.*

Philip Oldenburg is an Assistant Professor of Political Science at Columbia University. He has written on municipal government in India and on United States foreign policy during the 1971 Bangladesh crisis.

George H. Quester is a Professor of Government at Cornell University, where he teaches courses in international relations and arms control. He is the author of *The Politics of Nuclear Proliferation* and of a number of journal articles on the subject of nuclear proliferation.

Lloyd I. Rudolph is a Professor of Political Science at the University of Chicago. He is co-author of *The Coordination of Complexity in South Asia,* a report for the Commission on the Organization of the Conduct of Foreign Policy. He is completing a book with Susanne Hoeber Rudolph on the political economy of India and its neighbors for the Council on Foreign Relations 1980s Project.

T.N. Srinivasan is currently Special Adviser to the Development Research Center of the World Bank while on a leave of absence as a Research Professor at the Indian Statistical Institute in New Delhi. He is co-author with Jagdish Bhagwati of *Foreign Trade Regimes and Economic Development: India,* co-editor with

P.K. Bardhan of *Poverty and Income Distribution in India,* and has contributed to several professional journals.

Phillips Talbot is President of The Asia Society. He was a *Chicago Daily News* correspondent in Asia, Executive Director of the American Universities Field Staff, Assistant Secretary of State for Near Eastern and South Asian Affairs, and United States Ambassador to Greece.

Lawrence Veit is International Economist and Deputy Manager of Brown Brothers Harriman and Co. in New York. He served as United States Treasury Representative for India and Nepal in New Delhi and Research Fellow at the Council on Foreign Relations. He is the author of *India's Second Revolution: The Dimensions of Development* and numerous articles and books on the international economy.

Myron Weiner is a Professor of Political Science at the Massachusetts Institute of Technology and Senior Associate of its Center for International Studies. He served as a consultant to the United States Department of State and Agency for International Development, and the National Security Council. He has written extensively on politics of South Asia. His most recent books are *Sons of the Soil: Migration and Ethnic Conflict in India* and *Elections in India: The Parliamentary Elections of 1977.*

Conference Participants

Perspectives on India: The Economic and Political Context for Policy

Seven Springs Forum, Mount Kisco, New York
September 22—September 24, 1977

Mr. William Barnds
Council on Foreign Relations

Dr. Padma Desai
Russian Research Center
Harvard University

Mr. Davis Dillon
Program Director,
India Activities
The Asia Society

Mr. Thomas Dine
Director, National Security,
Committee on the Budget
U.S. Senate

Dr. William Blanpied
Director, Ethics and Value in
Science and Technology Program
The National Science Foundation

Mr. Michael Dwyre
Officer in Charge, India Desk,
Bureau for Asia
Agency for International Development

Dr. Hannan Ezekiel
Economic Consultant

Mr. Eric Griffel
Office of Programs and
Policy Coordination
Agency for International Development

Mr. Selig Harrison
Carnegie Endowment for
International Peace

Dr. Uma Lele
Eastern African Projects Department
The World Bank

Dr. John P. Lewis
Professor of Economics and
International Affairs
Princeton University

Dr. Franklin A. Long
Henry Luce Professor of
Science and Society
Cornell University

Dr. Onkar S. Marwah
Program in Science and
International Affairs
Harvard University

Dr. John Mellor
Director, International Food
Policy Research Institute

Dr. B. S. Minhas
Development Research Center
The World Bank

Dr. Baldev Raj Nayar
Professor of Political Science
McGill University

Dr. Philip Oldenburg
  Assistant Professor of Political
    Science
  Columbia University

Dr. George H. Quester
  Professor of Government
  Cornell University

Dr. Lloyd I. Rudolph
  Professor of Political Science
  University of Chicago

Dr. T. N. Srinivasan
  Development Research Center
  The World Bank

Mr. John Sullivan
  Assistant Administrator for Asia
  Agency for International Development

Ambassador Phillips Talbot
  President, The Asia Society

Mr. Thomas Thornton
  National Security Council

Dr. Lawrence Veit
  Brown Brothers Harriman and Co.

Dr. Bevan Waide
  Chief Economist,
    South Asia Region
  The World Bank

Dr. Myron Weiner
  Professor of Political Science
  Massachusetts Institute of Technology